The Book
of
RULERSHIPS
Keywords from
Classical Astrology

J. Lee Lehman, Ph.D.

A division of Schiffer Publishing, Ltd.
1469 Morstein Road
West Chester, Pennsylvania 19380 USA

The Book of Rulerships: Keywords from Classical Astrology

J. Lee Lehman, Ph.D.

Library of Congress Number: 92-060607
International Standard Book Number (ISBN): 0-924608-13-7

Manufactured in the United States of America

Published by Whitford Press,
A division of
Schiffer Publishing, Ltd.
1469 Morstein Road
West Chester, Pennsylvania 19380
Please write for a free catalog.
This book may be purchased from the publisher.
Please include $2.95 for postage.
Try your bookstore first.

Contents

Introduction: The Basis for Rulerships   5

Key to Abbreviations   25

Alphabetical Listing of Rulerships   27

Planetary Rulerships   237

Sign Rulerships   307

House Rulerships   331

Glossary of Medical Terms   345

References   349

Introduction:
The Basis for Rulerships

In picking up this reference book, the reader will quickly see the resemblance to two other books: Rex Bills' *The Rulership Book*, and Anne Ungar and Lillian Huber's *The Horary Reference Book*. Superficially, this is true, and I owe Bills (since he came first) a debt for designing the organization which is used here.

There are, however, some deep philosophical differences which divide this book from the others, as well as their cousins in the cosmobiological world, Reinhold Ebertin's classic *Combination of Stellar Influences,* and Michael Munkasey's more recent *Unleashing the Power of Midpoints* and *The Concept Dictionary.*

If you examine the books by any of these authors, you will not find any source for the rulerships they give. Who says Venus rules potatoes? Or that Saturn rules querulousness? Or that Uranus rules adultery (with the help of Venus and Neptune)? These are all entries in Bills. This breeds the first problem, because without sources it is really impossible to evaluate the rulerships given. Does everyone agree? Trying to get different astrologers to agree on anything is rather like herding cats. We need to know if one individual is completely anomalous, are we looking at different philosophies between different schools, or worse, are the authors using the same word with different meanings?

For example, although Ungar and Huber's book owes a deep debt to Bills as source material there are differences: Ungar and Huber added more medical terminology and utilized the concept of derived houses more consistently. Consider relationships. Bills gives them to the Air signs while Ungar and Huber take the horary approach, giving contractual or "romantic, with commitment" to the seventh House, and "romantic, without commitment" to the fifth House. Here the difference is natal versus horary. Bills is equating "social signs" with relationships; Ungar and Huber are asking, where would you place the horary question? This is a case of "same word, different meaning." But the differences continue even when both sources treat the same concept. Bills gives abscesses to Jupiter and the Moon (and notes: "see part of body involved") while Ungar and Huber state Mars, with Pluto co-ruling. Now, who is right, especially given that neither source invented the planetary rulership of abscesses? Within the existing astrological literature, there is no easy way to evaluate this question. In this book, if you turn to abscesses, you will see that Dariot, Lilly and Partridge gave Mars as a ruler of abscesses, probably because of the reddish inflammation often accompanying them. Dariot, Lilly and Saunders gave the Moon, probably from the pus or liquid found in an abscess. Saunders alone mentioned Taurus and Jupiter, and Dariot also gave Leo. We see that Bills grabbed part of the tradition, while Ungar and Huber favored a different part. In this case, Bills also maintained an anomalous rulership, Jupiter. This book enables the reader to return to the original source to decide which rulership is appropriate to the work at hand.

Many readers may be mumbling, so who was Dariot anyway? The sources used in this book were selected for their historical significance in the development of astrology. The Cast of Characters is:

- Ptolemy, the "Greek" that was the most quoted Medieval source, through his work *Tetrabiblios*. He was a polymath who worked out (or published) the geometry subsequently used in planetary position calculations. Ironically, he may not even have been an astrologer, but merely a compiler of the practices of his day.
- al-Biruni represents Arabic astrology from the Medieval Period.
- Claude Dariot was a French physician of the sixteenth century, whose book on horary in its English translation was a strong influence on - not to mention direct source for - William Lilly. The edition here is not pure Dariot. It is the second English edition, which was considerably enlarged by Nathaniel Spark. While less interesting as a historical source, its rulership lists are more detailed.
- William Lilly was the master *par excellence* of horary technique, whose work *Christian Astrology* has certainly been the most influential book on horary ever written. This work also covered natal astrology. He was a successful almanac writer, and was distinguished by his contemporaries for having predicted the Great Fire of London.
- Nicholas Culpeper made his reputation by translating medical remedies into English and publicizing them; his *English Physician* was a best-seller of the day. His herbal has not been out of print since that time. It has been the nucleus for many more modern herbals as well.
- John Gadbury was a former student of Lilly, who broke out of the pattern of presenting horary and natal equally, emphasizing natal astrology.
- Richard Saunders was hailed by Lilly and others as the cream of the crop of medical astrologers in the seventeenth century.
- William Ramesey's *Astrologia Restaurata* remains the definitive work on electional astrology from the seventeenth century.
- John Partridge was the first of the now famous seventeenth century British

astrologers to use the Placidus House System (it was controversial in the Protestant England of Partridge's day because Placidus was a Catholic monk). He was hailed by Raphael I (R. C. Smith) in the nineteenth century as the greatest of all British astrologers. This praise resulted in the publication of an abridged edition of Lilly by Zadkiel (R. C. Morrison), a rival of Raphael.

The second, probably more important, difference represented by my book concerns the definition of the concept of rulership. As I showed in my earlier book, *Essential Dignities*, astrologers since Raphael I in the nineteenth century invented the idea of equating Sign rulership with similarity: how much like Pluto is Scorpio compared to, for instance, Gemini. The ancient approach, however, was completely different. In the ancient system, the question asked was: how strong is this Planet in a sign?

This subtle difference, never explicitly discussed by the astrologers of the nineteenth century, resulted in a further skewing of the meaning of a planet in dignity. This is best illustrated by example. There is a rule that goes back at least as early as Bonatus (actually Guido Bonatti, thirteenth century) to the effect that a malefic (read Saturn or Mars) is less malefic if it is dignified (Aphorism 41). Henry Coley translated it as: "If an Infortune, being Significator, be in his own House or Exaltation, or in his own Terms or Triplicity, or in Angles or Succedent Houses; for by all these means he is fortified, and shall be counted strong as a Fortune." In a horary question, this means that in interpretation some of the problems of angular Saturn may not apply when Saturn is in Libra, Capricorn or Aquarius. (Examples of these problems: Saturn in the seventh House may mean that the Astrologer may err; Saturn in the tenth House, the Astrologer will gain no credit by answering the question; Saturn in the first House, the Querent is lying.)

This book is being written while Saturn is in Aquarius. The experience of a number of classical horary astrologers during the transit of Saturn through Capricorn and Aquarius had confirmed this aphorism: angular Saturn has been *less* malefic, but not something to be ignored! Consider what most astrologers have said about Pluto in Scorpio, also the placement at the time of this production. With the AIDS crisis, issues of rape and abortion invading every aspect of political life, not to mention slumping economies, few if any astrologers are trumpeting how wonderful Pluto is right now! Yet using Bonatus' rule, since Pluto is treated as a malefic even if it isn't called one, it should be on its best behavior! Clearly any attempt to mix the "new" Outer Planet rulerships with the older "Ptolemaic" rulerships produces a hybrid which contains significant logical flaws!

The other problem with the modern rulerships is that they completely ignore a substantial component of the ancient rulership system, namely *five* essential dignities, not just Sign and Exaltation. No one has seriously tried to integrate modern rulerships into the other three dignities. A half-hearted, and totally obscure attempt was made by Johndro, circa 1934. But it would be a monumental endeavor to successfully integrate the modern planets into the remaining three dignities (Triplicity, Term and Face) because of the amount of ancient symbolism embedded in these three. They were considered to be in part derivative of the main rulerships (Sign and House), and in part derivative of the properties of the planets themselves. For a full discussion of this topic, please see *Essential Dignities*, Chapter Five.

Because of the modern practice of equating planet, house and sign, many astrologers have lost the ability to distinguish between them. It is not uncommon for a modern astrologer to equate Gemini Rising with Mercury or the third House as if there were no difference whatsoever in these concepts. This is even codified by Dobyns as the twelve letter system; in our example, Gemini Rising is one of the manifestations of the Letter Three.

At first glance, the equation of planet with sign and house (Mars = Aries = 1st House) has certain virtues especially for teaching. But the only evidence that this was used in ancient times, was found in assigning parts of the body to houses from Sign rulerships. The twelfth House had rulership of feet as did Pisces. But Jupiter did not. (Remember, there is no Neptune here, so Jupiter is sole ruler of Pisces.) However, a closer look at the modern method of equivalency reveals questions.

The eighth House rules death, sex, wills, and the spouse's money, but are all of these that similar to Mars or Pluto? Pluto is generally used for a serious windfall financially. Not all (or even most) inheritances are large enough in size to qualify for Pluto, and certainly Mars doesn't look anything like it. Is all sex plutonic? Have we gotten to the stage where rape is the metaphor for sexuality? I hope not. As for death, doesn't the image of Saturn as Father Time and the Grim Reaper come more often to mind?

If we equate planet with sign, there are further problems. How does Uranus - sudden change - correlate with Aquarius' fixed air? What about the Aquarian stubborn side?

The Reader may justifiably ask: If the classical approach is "right," then how is it that the so-called Modern Rulerships became established in the first place? If the equation of planet, sign and house is violated so frequently, then how did its theory become so pervasive? One answer to this question, I believe, is given by the triumph of Natal Astrology almost to the exclusion of Horary Astrology. In particular, there has been a radical shift in the focus of Astrology from *predictive* (whether Horary, Mundane, Natal, Medical, Weather or Electional) to *descriptive*. The particular brand of descriptive astrology practiced today has been almost completely colored by psychological considerations. Thus, to many practitioners,

Astrology has become nothing but a symbol set, rich in metaphor. In a therapeutic setting, the mythology of the planets and signs becomes a way to describe situations at enough of a distance to be meaningful to the client. The problem with this approach is that, as symbols, there is little way to "prove" or "disprove" anything. The layers of meaning represented by Jupiter or Mars necessitate that the astrologer and client alike will tend to focus on only those pieces of the myth that most apply to the situation at hand, forgetting that they have thrown out major portions of the complete picture of the planet or sign in question.

A related issue has plagued many psychological theories and experiments. It is known as self-attribution. Self-attribution is the tendency to believe what a person in authority (the therapist or astrologer) says about oneself. Because of this tendency to believe an authority figure, it is almost impossible to test a theory based on client feedback. The *only* test to Astrology in the past was prediction, and that is *still* the best one now. It has also been seldom used of late. Thus, much moss has grown.

I should state clearly that I do not for one moment believe that the Twelve Letter Zodiac System is in any way stupid, or even completely wrong. At its best - and its best is what has attracted so many astrologers - it represents a method for picking out significant themes in a person's life. Unfortunately, the way that it is used by many astrologers who give lip service to the differences between planet, sign, and house, blurs the meanings of these three distinct concepts.

I would further observe that the Twelve Letter Zodiac is attractive because it helps the astrologer to synthesize a reading out of a series of disparate components. Why is a new method necessary for this? How did the Astrologers Royal in centuries past manage literally to keep their heads without this method? The answer is that earlier astrology was practiced with methods developed for prediction. There have been so many simplifications and omissions of technique in the shift from predictive to descriptive astrology that a new synthesis *was* necessary. How critical the Twelve Letter Zodiac is to a particular astrologer may reflect that astrologer's view of her or his function. Is this function to act as therapist or to tell the client what may happen next week?

Curiously, the planet = sign = house equation is not the only, nor even the most dominant theory of the planets. The other major modern theory of the trans-Saturnian Planets is that they represent higher octaves of inner planets: Uranus is the higher octave of Mercury, Neptune of Venus, and Pluto of Mars. If this is so, then we should see a shift of natural rulerships from the three Inner Planets to the three Outer Planets when natural rulerships have been reassigned. Table One on page 10 is from my discussion in *Essential Dignities*, in which I compared rulerships assigned by Bills to those given by al-Biruni. The Table shows only those cases where Bills had given rulerships to the Outer Planets. Naturally al-Biruni, who did not know of the Outer Planets, had given these same concepts to the Ptolemaic Planets. This Table accordingly shows the "transfer" of rulerships to Outer Planets. If the "higher octave" theory is true, then there should be a preponderance of Mercury shifts to Uranus, Venus shifts to Neptune, and Mars shifts to Pluto. We do not observe this. What we do observe in the case of Neptune and Pluto is a noticeable shift from Saturn; hence the old Great Malefic is being seen to share duties with two or three New Malefics. (See *Essential Dignities* for the full listing on pages 102-107.) Some examples, though, to give the flavor: al-Biruni gave adulterers to Venus, Bills, as mentioned previously, to Uranus; al-Biruni gave confusion, narcotics and fraud to Saturn, Bills to Neptune; al-Biruni gave poisons to Saturn, Bills to Neptune, Mars and Pluto.

Table 1. Attributions in al-Biruni
(for the Lights and Mercury through Saturn)
which are ruled by Uranus, Neptune, or Pluto in Bills.

Planet	Uranus	Neptune	Pluto
Sun	4	1	1
Moon	0	5	1
Mercury	1	2	1
Venus	1	4	4
Mars	4	0	5
Jupiter	2	0	2
Saturn	2	7	6

This Table raises perhaps more questions in addition to providing evidence against the higher octave hypothesis. The shift in words from the Moon and Venus to Neptune is intuitively gratifying. However, in modern rulership tables Neptune has replaced Jupiter as the ruler of Pisces. If there were any evidence that the classical astrologers supported the Planet = Sign = House hypothesis, we would expect a switch in words from Jupiter to Neptune. There is none. In the same vein, there is a much lower transference from Saturn to Uranus than either Saturn to Neptune or Saturn to Pluto. The only place where somewhat of a case may be made is a switch from Mars to Pluto, though the amount of interchange from both Saturn and Venus to Pluto is equally interesting. Clearly, the patterns here do not support the Planet = Sign = House hypothesis either.

What this little exercise shows, by contrasting what people say (Uranus is the higher octave of Mercury) compared to what they do (Bills' list), is that most modern astrologers treat the trans-Saturnian planets as three more malefics. And these same people complain about how awful classical astrology is when classical has only three malefics (Saturn, Mars and the South Node), while modern astrology has six! No wonder there has been such a concerted effort to eliminate the very word *malefic* as if it represents an archaic idea!

Because of these problems raised by modern interpretations of the planets, both inner and outer, I decided it was time to go back to classical sources to explore this concept of rulership more extensively. This approach also meets another need: a systematic source for determining the classical rulership for something. This reference is an adjunct for anyone practicing classical style horary, or wishing to add classical methods to their natal work.

It was my profound interest in classical methods which led to the one hard decision about this book: completely excluding the trans-Saturnian planets from consideration. This was an unfortunate necessity: many modern books are so biased by the Planet = Sign = House equation that the description of the planet often barely rings through. There are good modern works on the Outer Planets. Two that come to mind are Ginger Chalford's on Pluto and Stan Barker's on Neptune. Unfortunately, even these authors are, from the standpoint of rulerships, somewhat hazy. An author who is unclear on the concept can scarcely be expected to apply that concept well.

For application of natural rulership, we must await publications by authors of a classical bent who explore those Outer Planets from a post-modernist perspective.

In the meantime, all is not lost for the user of this book who wants a rulership for something that didn't exist in the seventeenth century or earlier when the sources given here were written. The modern classical approach, which is basically the same as it was in days past, takes the object of interest and asks, What is it like? An automobile in the 20th century serves much the same purpose as a horse or carriage in the 17th century. Olivia Barclay has noted that the parts of an airplane may be considered to be analogous to those of a ship, though she gives rulership of aircraft to Uranus.

Of course we have the Outer Planets, and most Neo-classical types would use them for natural rulerships, such as Uranus for electrical devices, Neptune for addiction or forgetfulness, Pluto for rape or power politics.

I shall close this introductory section by returning to a topic I began in *Essential Dignities*: rulerships of plants. As I indicated then, this topic may seem somewhat obscure, but it is an excellent model for how the rulerships work. For the nonbotanical types, I have minimized the use of botanical nomenclature and discussed rulerships in general with plants as the example.

There are, as usual, people to thank. Margaret M. Meister has fought me tooth and nail on every word, and this was beneficial! My father, Dr. Alan D. Lehman, is still superb at wielding the red pen. I have had stimulating discussions with Olivia Barclay about rulerships within the context of the Qualifying Horary Diploma Course, of which she is Founder and Principal. Donald Weiser provided me with many helpful out-of-print resources. The San Francisco Horary Group - Janet Carter, Nicki Michaels, and Jacalyn Thompson - keeps me on my toes whenever I visit. Betty Lundsted provided helpful editorial assistance. Part of this Introduction was presented at the 1991 History Day sponsored by the Astrological Lodge of London: I thank Annabella Kitson for the opportunity to present it.

Botanical Interlude Revisited: Plant - Planet Rulerships
The concept of rulerships, as we have inherited it, has actually included two discrete elements:

- Sign rulerships, including the five essential dignities of Rulership, Exaltation, Triplicity, Term and Face, as well as mutual reception.
- Natural rulerships, the attribution of a thing to rulership by a sign, planet, or house.

From a classical standpoint, there is little controversy about Sign rulerships, except for some variation in Triplicity rulership, and two discrete sets of terms (the so-called Chaldean and Egyptian terms). Many modern astrologers (i.e., from the 19th century onward) have attempted - with varying degrees of success - to add the three trans-Saturnian Planets into the Sign and Exaltation rulerships while ignoring the existence of the other three dignities.

Contemporary astrologers, whether classical or modern in style, are almost in universal agreement that the trans-Saturnian Planets can be natural rulers. The controversy (which is not necessarily a split between classical versus modern) is over which logic to use when assigning these natural rulerships.

The modern assumption - backed by a certain amount of classical philosophy if not evidence - has been that rulerships should be assigned based on the Doctrine of Affinities, or as Paracelsus put it, the Doctrine of Signatures. The natural ruler of an object should be that planet, sign, or house most *like* that object. (This is the philosophical justification for the modern Mars = Aries = First House concept. It is believed that Mars is the planet most *like* Aries, and Mars is the planet most *like* the First House. However, this Doctrine was not evoked classically to support this simplified equation. Furthermore, this equation violated the house cosignificators. For example, Mercury was Cosignificator of the first House.)

Unfortunately, astrological works dating from the seventeenth century and earlier lack explanations or discussions of the methods of assigning rulerships.

We do know, however, that rulerships were assigned, and continue to be assigned, right up to the present moment, as new concepts/things are invented/ discovered. The purpose of this section is to examine how this process was really practiced in the classical period to give us insights into how to proceed. To accomplish this I have selected a specific subject area: plants. Plants are an ideal subject for study. They have a long and well documented place in astrological history through the frequent publication of herbals - very popular books listing plants, their medical uses, and of course, their astrological affinities. We should remember that up to the seventeenth century it would have been almost unthinkable for a medical diagnosis to be given without adequate astrological training. Even the great fourteenth century critic of astrology, Nicole Oresme, granted the efficacy of medical and meteorological uses of astrology.

I have already treated the specifics of one particular herbal, namely Culpeper's, at length in my previous book. What I would like to do here is to compare Culpeper's rulerships with rulerships given by five other sources: al-Biruni, Claude Dariot, William Lilly, John Gadbury, and William Ramesey.

I should mention that I was limited in the available possibilities for seventeenth century sources by the number of plants listed by any one author: for example, John Partridge's *Vade Mecum* only discussed a few plants, scarcely enough for consideration.

The number of plants taken from each source is shown in Table 2 . Naturally, given the fact that Culpeper's was the only herbal in the group (the others were general purpose astrology texts), Culpeper listed more plants.

Table 2 . Number of plants mentioned in different sources.

Source	Number of plants
al-Biruni	58
Dariot	130
Lilly	162
Ramesey	204
Gadbury	283
Culpeper	394

Unfortunately, among the sources there was not as much overlap as I would have liked. There were two groups of writers who strongly agreed: Dariot-Lilly-Ramesey and Culpeper-Gadbury. Although the total number of agreements between Gadbury and Culpeper is higher than between each pair of Dariot, Lilly, and Ramesey, two factors make Dariot-Lilly-Ramesey the winner in agreements.

These factors were: (1) Gadbury listed more total plants than Ramesey, Lilly or Dariot, so the proportion of hits to total plants is actually lower for Culpeper-Gadbury; and (2) Gadbury disagreed with Culpeper a greater percentage of the time than Ramesey and Lilly did with Dariot. Lilly's agreement with Dariot is not surprising since Lilly quoted Dariot extensively throughout *Christian Astrology*. Given the fact that Nathaniel Sparks was a contemporary of Lilly, it seems likely that he leaned on Lilly as a source. In Ramesey's case it is unclear whether he was following Dariot or Lilly or both since both Dariot and Lilly's works were available to Ramesey prior to the publication of *Astrologia Restaurata*. (Lilly had serialized a number of items from *Christian Astrology* in his almanacs.) I have summarized those cases of overlap for all author combinations in an appendix to the introduction beginning on page 21, which shows whether the different sources agreed or disagreed with the rulerships for a given plant.

The functioning of this table may seem a bit mysterious so let's sort it out by some examples. Dariot and Lilly both assigned rulership of the daisy to Jupiter. Culpeper and Gadbury assigned the daisy to Venus. This would result in the following tallies:

> Dariot - Lilly: agreement
> Dariot - Gadbury: disagreement
> Dariot - Culpeper: disagreement
> Lilly - Gadbury: disagreement
> Lilly - Culpeper: disagreement
> Culpeper - Gadbury: agreement

In this case, four authors result in six combinations. Please note that the only way to score a disagreement is on a pair basis.

While it is only practical to list disagreement on a pair by pair basis, agreement can be shown on a larger scale. For example, Dariot, Culpeper, Lilly and Ramesey all gave the shepherd's purse (*Capsella bursa-pastoris*) to Saturn: in the preceding Table, this would be shown as agreement by Culpeper-Dariot-Lilly-Ramesey.

The problem with this mode of presentation is that it tends to make the disagreements more prominent. However, the translation of the true agreement is shown by summing any combination line which contains the two authors, plus the pair grouping. For example, the al-Biruni - Culpeper pairings come from al-Biruni-Culpeper alone (3), plus al-Biruni - Culpeper - Gadbury (1), plus al-Biruni - Culpeper - Dariot - Gadbury - Lilly - Ramesey (5). The sum is 9. This is worked out fully in Table 3 on page 15.

Table 3. Agreement between Sources,
showing only pair-by-pair combinations.

Authors	Agreement	Disagreement
al-Biruni - Culpeper	9	11
al-Biruni - Dariot	15	10
al-Biruni - Gadbury	9	9
al-Biruni - Lilly	18	15
al-Biruni - Ramesey	18	12
Culpeper - Dariot	33	30
Culpeper - Gadbury	142	14
Culpeper - Lilly	49	40
Culpeper - Ramesey	37	31
Dariot - Gadbury	41	23
Dariot - Lilly	139	4
Dariot - Ramesey	103	2
Gadbury - Lilly	44	30
Gadbury - Ramesey	36	32
Lilly - Ramesey	134	2

This table shows clearly that there was more agreement than disagreement in all cases of pairings between any of the sources except al-Biruni and Culpeper. However, now the level of agreement between Dariot-Lilly-Ramesey, and Culpeper and Gadbury, is all the more striking. Can there be any doubt that Dariot was Lilly's primary source for rulerships (97% agreement when the same plant is listed), just as Culpeper was Gadbury's (90% agreement when both list the same plant)?

What does this then say about plant rulerships? To begin to sort out this intriguing question, let us examine the cases of strong agreement. These are shown in Table 4 on page 16.

Many of the plants given in these sources are not ones which are especially familiar to us, but most of the plants in the Table are immediately recognizable, being primarily food plants, spices or poisons. These plants have rulerships assigned which are part of readily identifiable properties: sharp taste in the case of Mars, for example. (Carduus benedictus, a thistle, which may not be immediately familiar, follows the descriptive nature of Mars: spiny leaves!)

Table 4. Examples of Agreement between Sources.

Plant	Ruler	Sources
Apple	♀	al-Biruni - Dariot - Gadbury - Lilly - Ramesey
Ash	☉	Culpeper - Dariot - Gadbury - Lilly - Ramesey
Carduus	♂	Culpeper - Dariot - Gadbury - Lilly - Ramesey
Eyebright	☉	Culpeper - Dariot - Gadbury - Lilly - Ramesey
Fumitory	♄	Culpeper - Dariot - Gadbury - Lilly - Ramesey
Garlic	♂	al-Biruni -Culpeper - Dariot - Gadbury - Lilly - Ramesey
Hemlock	♄	Culpeper - Dariot - Gadbury - Lilly - Ramesey
	♂	Dariot - Lilly - Ramesey
Hemp	♄	Culpeper - Dariot - Gadbury - Lilly - Ramesey
Henbane	♄	Culpeper - Dariot - Gadbury - Lilly - Ramesey
Mustard	♂	al-Biruni -Culpeper - Dariot - Gadbury - Lilly - Ramesey
Nettle	♂	Culpeper - Dariot - Gadbury - Lilly - Ramesey
Nightshade	♄	Culpeper - Dariot - Gadbury - Lilly - Ramesey
Onions	♂	al-Biruni - Culpeper - Dariot - Gadbury - Lilly - Ramesey
Poppy	☽	Culpeper - Dariot - Gadbury - Lilly - Ramesey
	♄	Dariot - Lilly - Ramesey
Radish	♂	al-Biruni - Culpeper - Dariot - Gadbury - Lilly - Ramesey
Rose	♀	Culpeper - Dariot - Gadbury - Lilly - Ramesey
	♂	al-Biruni
Rosemary	☉	Culpeper - Dariot - Gadbury - Lilly - Ramesey
Vines	☉	al-Biruni -Culpeper - Dariot - Gadbury - Lilly - Ramesey

You may notice in examining the Table that there are *no* Mercury-ruled plants listed. All the authors assigned plants to Mercury, but multiple authors did not agree on Mercury rulership for the same plants. This is especially interesting because all authors stated that Mercury takes on the coloration of other planets with which it associates. "Mixed" and "complex" were frequently used words to describe Mercury. It thus appears that quicksilver alludes even the astrologers! One may also note, that a rose, by any other name may smell as sweet, but if, like al-Biruni, you are concerned with thorns, then it is Mars-ruled!

There is a strong correlation in Culpeper between the medicinal use of the plant and the rulership he assigned. (Three quarters of the Jupiter-ruled plants had medicinal properties thought to be useful in treating Jupiter-ruled diseases.) The other authors require different explanations.

The flora present in al-Biruni's location was certainly different from that of England and France. There are several floral groups in between Northern Europe and Asia Minor. Thus, although al-Biruni's plants may be translated as the same name as our sixteenth and seventeenth century sources, the likelihood that he was referring to the same genus and species is fairly remote, except for cultivated plants. Clearly, the discrepancies between al-Biruni and the other four are quite understandable.

Of course Dariot, Lilly and Ramesey were part of the same tradition. However, they were all primarily classical astrologers, and thus, more influenced by the Doctrine of Affinities than Culpeper, who was primarily a pragmatic apothecary. His major claim to fame, after all, was to produce his herbal using the English names instead of Latin ones, and to emphasize English plants rather than foreign ones - foreign, that is, to him! We may speculate that Gadbury, originally Lilly's pupil, then later a rival almanac writer, may have chosen deliberately to strike out on a different path.

We may conclude that there were therefore two acceptable models for rulership: a medical one, and a non-medical one based instead on the popular philosophical doctrine of affinity. This latter concept permeated the Medieval worldview in many areas beyond Astrology: it is the essence of the Macrocosm-Microcosm dictate: As Above, So below.

What evidence do we have for the idea that astrologers of a non-medical bent used physical appearance as a basis for rulership ascription? The texts themselves! Table 5 on page 18 gives statements these authors made about the kinds of plants which are ruled by the various planets. With few exceptions, these descriptions fit well with our concepts for the general meaning of the planets.

In *Essential Dignities* I showed that there was little relationship between the physical appearance of the plant and the natural rulership given in Culpeper's work. The lists by Dariot-Lilly-Ramesey show much greater adherence to the Doctrine of Affinities. We are thus confronted with an interesting paradox: we can accept Culpeper/Gadbury's rulerships - and consider medicinal uses primary - or we can accept Dariot/Lilly/Ramesey's lists - and consider physical appearance as primary. Since this began as a case study of rulerships, with plants as the example, we may note that the medical option may be something intrinsic to plants only, and not a general consideration. Perhaps we could state that medical rulerships may be the special case here regarding plants, with the Doctrine of Affinities the general case for things other than plants. We may also accept Culpeper/Gadbury's rulerships for a medical situation, and the Dariot/Lilly/Ramesey rulerships for a general one.

Table 5. Physical Descriptions of Rulerships.

Description	Ruler	Reference
"Bitter taste"	♂	Lilly, page 54
"Bitter trees"	♂	al-Biruni, page 244
"Colored herbs"	♀	al-Biruni, page 244
"Complex flavors"	☿	al-Biruni, page 244
"Fruits with rough skins"	♂	al-Biruni, page 244
"Prickly trees"	♂	Dariot, page 21
"Pungent trees"	♂	al-Biruni, page 244
"Pungent/evil-smelling trees"	☿	al-Biruni, page 244
"Red"	♂	Ramesey, page 54
"Savoury Herbs"	♀	al-Biruni, page 244
"Shade trees"	☽	Lilly, page 82
"Sharp-pointed leaves"	♂	Ramesey, page 54
"Smooth-leaved plants"	♀	Lilly, page 75
"Sweet-smelling flowers"	♀	al-Biruni, page 244
"Thick, juicy leaves"	☽	Dariot, page 27
"Thorny or Prickly"	♂	Ramesey, page 54
"Used for divination"	☿	Dariot, page 26

It certainly is clear that there may be more than one classical method when it comes to natural rulerships.

This still leaves one question unanswered: what do we do with the trans-Saturnian planets? To be sure, one part of the answer has already been provided: assign natural rulerships based on the Doctrine of Affinities. This, however, leaves two problems. The first is that the understanding of these three planets has become so intertwined with the Planet = Sign = House equation that many astrologers are unable to give coherent definitions of these three bodies *apart* from that alleged equation. (One seldom sees serious discussion about how the suddenness associated with Uranus is supposed to correlate with the fixed nature of Aquarius, or the revolutionary aspect of Pluto is supposed to mate with equally fixed Scorpio.) The second problem is really a question: should natural rulerships already assigned to the Chaldean Planets be reassigned to Uranus, Neptune and Pluto?

We cannot stress too much the importance of understanding the rationale behind the rulership assignations of any author so that the astrologer is not led to an incorrect delineation. It is also crucial that we understand the origin of natural rulerships and that we not become slaves to any listing which may be at hand.

Guide to the Perplexed: How to Use this Book
I have observed that many contemporary astrologers have avoided becoming too involved in classical methods and classical books because they are hesitant to deal with two impediments. The first is style: "*s*"'s that look like "*f*"'s in the printing font of the period, and archaic spelling. The second impediment is the suspicion that our lives today are simply so different that the old stuff just isn't relevant. On the other hand, classical fans respond by minimizing the differences in language and life-style. I propose that both sides are partially wrong. It is true that it is possible to adjust to typefaces and spellings. As some astrologers have trouble reading another astrologer's chart wheels, we cannot dismiss the visual as merely trivial. I have, however, largely solved this problem within this book by presenting both modern spelling and typeface, though the archaic spellings are often indicated if not immediately obvious.

The differences in language are not what one would suppose. The English of the seventeenth century is similar to modern English, but not identical. It is interesting in this regard that we Americans seem to have less trouble than the British. It seems that our standard American dialect is closer than modern British to seventeenth century English. However, I urge two things on the budding classical astrologer: French is very useful because many of the English words which have French cognates are used in the seventeenth century with the modern French meaning. For example, the word "judgment." Modern English speakers would tend to see this word as the noun form of "judge," as to weigh the evidence in a trial. But in fact it is the same as the French "jugement," which has maintained somewhat better its original technical meaning: *prediction*!

To help, I would recommend an edition of Shakespeare that has a glossary, such as the *London Shakespeare* (Simon & Schuster) to those readers who wish to study the classical material further. Seventeenth century English is intermediate between Modern and Shakespearian English. Such a glossary would be especially helpful to anyone who wishes to study some of the more confusing cases of multiple rulerships, whether in classical context or in modern sources. Several examples:

> *bladder* can be the organ or a pustule
> *book* can specifically be the *Bible* or learning in general
> *burn* can mean to infect with a venereal disease
> *clerk* may refer to a scholar.

Shakespearian scholars have not solved all of our astrological language problems, though. There are some conventions of language which are really technical terms. The dividing animal between large and small animals (sixth House and twelfth House) is the sheep. I hope to discuss these conventions in a future publication.

In recognition of some of these difficulties of language, I have attempted to translate archaic into modern terminology where possible, while still retaining the original for those studying the classical texts directly. This has been especially necessary in two areas: Latinized city names, and medical terminology. In the latter case, there is an Appendix to help ease the pain of adapting the medicine of Galen to that of today. Even so, I have not been successful in all cases. Words I have not been able to trace are marked with an asterisk (*). They may represent archaic usage, archaic spelling, or even typographical errors.

As for the alleged life-style differences: people fell in and out of love, lied to and cheated on each other. They worked, changed jobs, traveled, got sick and died. These considerations are certainly not any different today. The major differences - technological innovation, emancipation (partial though it may be) of social and gender classes, increased leisure time - are obvious enough for the intelligent reader to consider in the interpretation of older writings. And while seventeenth century authors were often coy about their references to genitals and sex, they were much less squeamish in asking about death. Whether natal or horary, the astrologer routinely treated the Native/Querent's death, or the death of those around him or her. Now we tiptoe around the "ethics" of discussing death as surely as our past colleagues tiptoed around sex. Have we really evolved so far? *Plus ça change, plus c'est la même chose!*

Finally, I view this book as serving two major purposes: as a reference when you need to know what rules apply (or whatever), and as a guide to the classical texts themselves. First and foremost, this is a reference book on rulerships; second, this is a classical concordance. It is out of a sense of respect for the classical material that I have maintained the contradictions and disagreements. The reader may evaluate and decide who is right, who is wrong, or whether the difference was indeed a result of either the usage of the word (different meanings), or, like our botanical example, different usages of the concept (appearance versus medical use).

When the reader examines this text, there will be times when virtually all the sources agree, and times when virtually all the sources disagree. Both are instructive. When all the sources agree, the reader can safely conclude that there is one tradition, and one meaning to the word. When there is substantial disagreement, the reader needs to sort out the differing rationales to discover the correct rulership to use in the present moment. While this may seem a warts-and-all presentation, it avoids the danger of obtaining the meaning from an arbitrary simplication or deriving the meaning from a belief in what the rulership *should* be. Disagreement suggests cultural diversity, or a change in meaning through time. Gadbury said that the natal chart represented the birth of the body, while the horary showed the birth of the mind. Here we call for the exercise of the mind to go beyond the birth - to the meaning of the rulership.

Today we are living in an exciting time for the study of classical astrology because more classical texts are available to the astrologer who wants them than at any time since Partridge. One thing I guarantee: if you take the time to study the methods, and stalk the classical rulership, it will change your astrology! Happy hunting!

Appendix. Agreement between Sources.

Authors	Agreement	Disagreement
al-Biruni - Culpeper	2	11
al-Biruni - Dariot	0	10
al-Biruni - Gadbury	0	9
al-Biruni - Ramesey	1	12
al-Biruni - Lilly	3	15
Culpeper - Dariot	0	30
Culpeper - Gadbury	113	14
Culpeper - Lilly	9	40
Culpeper - Ramesey	4	31
Dariot - Gadbury	3	23
Dariot - Lilly	26	4
Dariot - Ramesey	4	2
Gadbury - Lilly	3	30
Gadbury - Ramesey	1	32
Lilly - Ramesey	21	2
al-Biruni Culpeper Gadbury }	1	n/a
al-Biruni Culpeper Ramesey }	1	n/a

Authors	Agreement	Disagreement
al-Biruni Dariot Lilly	1	n/a
al-Biruni Dariot Ramesey	1	n/a
al-Biruni Lilly Ramesey	1	n/a
Culpeper Dariot Gadbury	1	n/a
Culpeper Dariot Lilly	10	n/a
Culpeper Gadbury Lilly	3	n/a
Culpeper Gadbury Ramesey	3	n/a
Culpeper Lilly Ramesey	2	n/a
Dariot Gadbury Lilly	8	n/a

Authors	Agreement	Disagreement
Dariot Lilly Ramesey	58	n/a
al-Biruni Culpeper Lilly Ramesey	1	n/a
al-Biruni Dariot Gadbury Lilly	1	n/a
al-Biruni Dariot Gadbury Ramesey	1	n/a
al-Biruni Dariot Lilly Ramesey	6	n/a
Culpeper Dariot Gadbury Lilly	1	n/a
Culpeper Dariot Gadbury Ramesey	1	n/a
Culpeper Dariot Lilly Ramesey	5	n/a

Authors	Agreement	Disagreement
Culpeper Gadbury Lilly Ramesey	3	n/a
Dariot Gadbury Lilly Ramesey	9	n/a
al-Biruni Dariot Gadbury Lilly Ramesey	1	n/a
Culpeper Dariot Gadbury Lilly Ramesey	12	n/a
al-Biruni Culpeper Dariot Gadbury Lilly Ramesey	5	n/a

Key to Abbreviations

Unless noted, page numbers are from the cited edition.

AB = al-Biruni.

CU = Culpeper. Page numbers are not given because of the number of editions in print.

GA = Gadbury.

LI = Lilly.

PA = Partridge.

PT = Ptolemy.

RA = Ramesey.

RS = Saunders, first part.

S2 = Saunders, second part. After page 208 in the 1677 edition, the pages were reset to 1 with no cover page. Following the convention of the day, the first word of the subsequent page is printed in the bottom of the preceding page: that word on page 208 is "General," which is in fact the first word on the next page "1," here rendered as S2-01.

* means that the meaning (or spelling) of the word is unclear.

Note: Genus and species are given when known for many of the plants. Botanical nomenclature consists of two names, the genus and the species. If you see two names together that are strange, and somewhat latinesque, it's probably a plant.

Alphabetical Listing
of Rulerships

* Indicates that the meaning of a word is unknown

-- A --

Abandoned Business 9th House AB276
Abasing ♃ LI063
Abdomen, Inferior Parts ♎ DA010
Abdomen 6th House PA044
Abhorrer of Vices ♀ in 9th House GA059
Abraham's Balm (Agnus-Castus) ☽ RA063
Abscess (Apostem[ation]s, [A/Im]posthumes) 4th House RS100
Abscess (Apostem[ation]s, [A/Im]posthumes) ♎ RS017
Abscess (Apostem[ation]s, [A/Im]posthumes) ☽ DA026, LI082, RS021
Abscess (Apostem[ation]s, [A/Im]posthumes) ♃ RS019
Abscess (Apostem[ation]s, [A/Im]posthumes) ♂ DA020, LI246, PA013,
   RS020
Abscess (Apostem[ation]s, [A/Im]posthumes) ♌ DA008
Abscess (Apostem[ation]s, [A/Im]posthumes) ♉ DA006, RS016
Abscess, Opening of 3rd House AB276
Absent 7th House AB276
Absent Party, Dead or Alive 1st House DA090, GA242, LI151
Absent Sibling Status 3rd House GA254, LI189, PA063
Abundance ♀ PT185
Abundance ♃ PT183
Abundance of Spittle ☿ DA025, LI079
Abyssinia ♄ AB242
Acacia ☿ LI272
Acacia ♄ LI272
Accidents 1st House LI130
Accidents of Feet & Toes 7th House RS100
Accidents of the Bowels 10th House RS100
Accidents of the Kidneys 10th House RS100
Accidents of the Limbs 7th House RS100
Accountants ☿ GA071, LI078, PA110, RA061
Accounting ☽ AB254

Accumulates Fortune by Work ☿ in 4th House GA050
Acer ♃ CU
Acer pseudoplatanus ♀ CU
Achaia (Hill Near Carystus) ♍ DA009, PA074
Achates (Agate) ☿ DA025, LI079
Aches ♊ PA005
Aches ♓ PA010
Aches in the Joints ♄ RA051
Achillea ageratum ♃ GA068
Achillea millefolium ♀ CU, GA070
Acne ♈ PA004
Aconite ♄ CU
Aconitum anthora ♄ CU
Actaea spicata ♄ CU
Active ♂ PT353
Active Person ♌ PA006
Acute in Business ☿ in 4th House GA050
Adamant ♂ RA055
Adamant (Stone) ♂ DA020, LI068
Adamant (Stone) ☉ LI072
Adamine ☉ DA022
Adaptable ☽ AB250
Adder ☿ RA062
Adder ♄ LI060, RA051
Adder's Tongue ♋ CU
Adder's Tongue ☽ CU, GA072
Adder's Tongue ☿ DA025, LI079, RA062
Adherents of Prevailing Religion ☽ AB253
Adiantum capillus veneris ☿ CU, GA071
Adiantum capillus veneris ♀ LI075, RA060
Administering Justice ♃ AB250
Administrations (of the Dead) 8th House GA056
Administrations Given by Prince ☉ in 3rd House GA049
Adornments ♀ LI556, PT337
Adult Life ♎ AB231
Adult Life ♏ AB231
Adult Life ♐ AB231
Adulterers ♀ LI074
Adulterers and their Children ♀ AB252
Advancement in Rank 1st House AB276
Advantageous Things 11th House AB276

Adversaries Great & Powerful ☉ in 12th House GA063
Adversary in Lawsuit 7th House LI372
Adversary's Second (Duel) 8th House PA045
Adverse Fortune in Negotiation ♄ in 5th House GA051
Adversity 12th House AB275
Advice 3rd House LI194
Advice Good or Evil? 3rd House GA256, LI192
Advised ♄ LI539
Advocates ☿ GA071, LI078, PA016, RA061
Advocates ♂ LI556
Advocates ♃ LI555, PA108
Aegopodium podograria ♀ GA070
Aegopodium podagraria ♄ CU
Aemilia ♌ DA008
Aereal ♊ PA005
Aestival, Restful ♋ AB230
Aestival, Restful ♌ AB230
Aestival, Restful ♍ AB230
Aetites (Stone in Eagles' Nests) ☉ DA022, RA057
Aetites (Stone in Eagles' Nests) ♀ RA060
Affability ☿ AB250
Affability ♀ LI556
Affability ♃ AB250
Affable ☉ GA069, LI070
Affable ♒ LI538
Affable Conversation ♃ LI062
Affairs ☿ RA062
Affairs of Eunuchs 6th House AB276
Affairs of Women 6th House AB276
Affairs, the Beginnings of 11th House AB276
Affectionate ♀ PT357
Affectionate ♃ PT347
Affliction 12th House LI056, PA047
Affliction ♄ AB252
Africa ♋ PA074
Africa ♍ LI096
Agaric ☿ in ♌ CU
Agaricus ☿ in ♌ CU
Agaricus campestris ☽ RA063
Agaricus campestris ☿ in ♈ CU
Agate ☿ LI079, RA062

Age of Life Best for Querent 1st House LI134
Age Spots & Pimples (Face) ♎ PA007
Agencies ☽ AB254
Agents 5th House PA043
Agility ☿ LI541
Agnes ♀ LI341
Agnus-Castus (Vitex) ☽ RA063
Agrimonia eupatoria ♃ CU, GA068
Agrimonia eupatoria ♋ CU
Agrimony ♃ CU, GA068
Agrimony ♋ CU
Agrimony (Water) ♃ CU
Agrimony (Water) ♋ CU
Agrippina [=Cologne, Germany] ♐ DA011, PA075
Ague ♂ RS020
Aiming at High Things ☉ PA014
Aiming at Honorable Matters ♃ GA067
Aiming at Lofty Matters ♃ GA067
Air ♃ AB247
Air in the Heart ♃ AB245
Air Which Causes Tree Growth ♎ AB230
Ajuga chamaepitys ☿ GA071
Ajuga chamaepitys ♂ CU
Ajuga reptans ♀ CU, GA070
Alabaster ♀ DA023, LI075, RA060
Albania ♑ DA012, LI098, PA076
Alchemilla vulgaris ♀ CU, GA070, LI075
Alchemists ♂ DA021, GA068, LI067, RA054
Alchemy ♂ LI556
Alchstade (Place)* ♏ DA011
Alder ♀ CU, GA070
Alder (Black) ♀ CU
Alder (Black) ♋ CU
Alder (Common) ♀ CU
Alder (Common) ♓ CU
Alder Tree ☿ DA025
Ale-Houses 5th House LI053
Alehoof ♀ CU
Alewives ☽ LI081
Alexander (Herb) ♃ CU, GA068
Alexandria, Egypt ♓ DA014, LI099, PA076

Algiers ♋ LI095
Algiers ♏ DA011, PA075
Alice ☉ LI341
Alkakenge ☿ LI272
Alkakenge ♄ LI272
Alkanet ♀ CU
Alkanna tinctoria ♀ CU
Allheal (Valeriana) ♃ RA052
Allheal (Valeriana) ♄ GA067
Alliances with Leaders ♀ PT185
Alliaria petiolata ☿ CU
Alliaria petiolata ♃ GA068
Allies & Support of Kingdom 2nd House PA042
Allies of a Country 2nd House LI052
Allium cepa ☽ LI082
Allium cepa ☉ LI273
Allium cepa ♂ AB244, CU, GA068, LI068, RA054
Allium sativum ☉ LI273
Allium sativum ♂ AB244, CU, GA068, LI068, RA054
Allium schoenoprasum ♂ CU
Allum ☿ LI272
Allum ♄ LI272
Almonds ♀ DA024, RA060
Almonds ♃ LI064, RA053
Almonds, Bitter ♂ AB243
Alnus glutinosa ♀ CU
Alnus glutinosa ♓ CU
Alnus nigra ♀ CU, GA070
Alnus nigra ♋ CU
Aloes ☉ LI071, RA057
Alopecia 1st House RS100
Alps ♌ DA008, LI096, PA074
Alsace ♎ DA010, LI097, PA075
Altars of Churches ♃ LI064
Althaea officinalis ♀ CU
Althaea rosea ♀ CU
Altica (Attica?), Greece ♐ DA011
Amaranthus ♄ CU
Amaranthus hybridus ♄ CU
Amaryllis, African (Clivia) ♑ PA076
Amassing Treasure ♄ PT341

Amazedness ♃ DA019
Amazonia ♒ DA013, PA076
Ambassadors 5th House GA051, LI053, PA043
Ambassadors 9th House AB276
Ambassadors ☽ PA110
Ambassadors ☿ LI078, PA016, RA061
Amber ☿ AB243
Amber (Plant) ☉ DA022, LI071, RA057
Amber (Plant) ♀ DA024, LI075
Ambergrise ♀ RA060
Ambitions ☉ LI556
Ambitious ☉ DA022, PA109
Ambitious ☿ LI077
Amethyst ♃ DA019, LI064, RA053
Amethyst (Multi-Colored) ♂ LI068
Amethyst, Multi-Colored ♂ RA055
Amiable ♀ LI556
Ammunition 11th House PA046
Ammunition of a Country 2nd House LI052
Ammunition of Besieged Town 5th House PA043
Ammunition of Kingdom 2nd House PA042
Ammunition of Town Besieged 5th House LI053
Amputation ♐ DA011
Amsterdam ♋ LI095
Anacyclus pyrethrum ☿ CU
Anal Canal, Middle (Pecten) ☿ RS182
Ancient Dwellings 4th House LI052
Ancona (Italian Fowl) ♈ DA006, PA073
Andrew ☉ LI341
Anemia (=Green Sickness) ☽ PA018, RS021
Anemone ♂ CU
Anemone nemorosa ♂ CU
Anethum graveolens ☿ CU, GA071
Angelica ☉ GA069
Angelica ☉ in ♌ CU
Angelica ♄ DA018, LI059, RA050
Angelica archangelica ♄ RA050
Anger ♂ LI067
Anger, Proneness to ♂ RS020
Anguish 8th House LI054
Angusta ♑ PA076

Animal, Large Missing Where? 12th House DA125
Animals Living in Holes ♄ AB246
Animals, Aquatic, Small ☿ AB246
Animals, Beautifully Colored ♃ AB246
Animals, Cloven Hooves ♃ AB246
Animals, Domestic ♃ AB246
Animals, Edible ♃ AB246
Animals, Large 12th House GA062, PA047
Animals, Nocturnal ☉ AB246
Animals, Small (smaller than sheep) ♀ LI075
Animals, Small (smaller than sheep) 6th House GA053, LI053, PA044
Animals, Small Unfortunate ♂ in 6th House GA053
Animals, Small Querent Benefit? 6th House GA272
Animals, Speaking ♃ AB246
Animals, Speckled ♃ AB246
Animals, Terrestrial, Small ☿ AB246
Animals, Trained ♃ AB246
Animals, Wild, White Hooved ☉ AB246
Anise-Seeds ☿ DA025, LI079
Ankles ♒ DA013, LI098
Ankles ♓ LI246, RS015
Ankles 11th House GA061, LI056
Ankles 12th House RS015
Anne ☉ LI341
Anorexia ♄ RS019
Anthemis cotula ♀ CU
Anthony ♂ LI341
Antimony ♀ AB243
Antimony ♂ DA020, LI068, RA055
Antiquities ♄ RA050
Ants (=Pissmire) ☿ LI079, RA062
Antwerp ♎ DA010, PA075
Anus ♄ AB248
Anus ♏ LI246
Anus 8th House LI245
Anus 9th House LI055
Anxieties 12th House AB275
Anxious ♄ AB250
Apes ☿ LI079, RA062
Aphrodisiac, Orchid (Satyrion) ♀ DA024
Apium graveolens ☿ CU, GA071

Apoplexy ☽ LI081, RA064, RS021
Apoplexy ♃ DA019, LI063, PA012, PT429, RA053, RS019
Apoplexy ♄ LI059
Apoplexy ♈ DA005, LI093, PA004, RS016
Apostem see Abscess
Apostemations see Abscess
Aposthumes see Abscess
Apothecaries ♂ GA068, RA054
Appearance, Well Composed ♍ PA006
Appetite ☽ RS015
Appetite Loss ♀ RS021
Apple ♀ AB244, LI075
Apple ♃ AB243
Apple Tree ♀ GA070, RA060
Apples, Sweet ♀ DA024
Apprehension ♂ PA013
Apprehensive ☿ GA071
Apricot Trees ♃ AB244
Apricots ♀ DA024, LI075, RA060
Apt ☿ PA094
Apt for Arts & Sciences ☿ in 4th House GA050
Apulia, Italy [=Puglia] ♌ DA008, LI096, PA074
Aquilegia vulgaris ☽ GA072
Aquilegia vulgaris ♀ CU
Aquilegia, Italy [=Aquileia] ♏ DA011
Aquileia, Italy [=Aquileia] ♏ DA011, PA075
Arabia ♒ LI099
Arabia ♃ PT145
Arabia ♎ PT157
Arabia ♄ AB242
Arabia ♐ DA011, PT145
Arabia ♀ AB242, DA024, LI076, PT157, RA060
Arabia foelix ♐ PA075
Arabian Desert ♒ DA013, PA076
Archangel ♀ CU, GA070
Arctium lappa ♄ RA050
Arctium lappa ♀ CU, GA070
Aretium, Etruria ♍ DA009
Arezzo, Italy [=Aretium] ♍ DA009
Argentina ♎ DA010, PA075
Ariana, Persia ♑ DA012

Arithmeticians ☿ DA025
Arles ♎ LI097, PA075
Arm Diseases ♊ LI094, RS017
Arm-pits, Botches ♌ RS208
Arm-pits, Sores ♌ RS208
Armenia ☉ AB242
Armenia ☿ PT147
Armenia ♊ DA007, LI094, PA073, PT147
Armies 12th House AB275
Armoracia rusticana ♂ CU, GA068
Armorers ♂ GA068, LI067, RA054
Arms 3rd House AB277, GA048, LI052, PA042, RS015
Arms ♊ DA007, LI245, RS015
Arms Long ☿ GA071, PA016
Arms Long ♊ DA007
Arms, Diseases of ♊ PA005
Army Commanders ♂ PA109
Aromaticus* ☉ RA057
Arrach (Garden) ☽ CU
Arrach, Stinking ♀ GA070
Arrogant ☉ LI070
Arrogant ♂ PA093
Arrogant ♏ LI538
Arsenic ☿ AB243
Arsenic ♂ DA020, LI068, RA055
Arsenic Monosulphide ☉ AB243
Arsenic, Yellow ☉ AB243
Arsenick see Arsesmart
Arsesmart (Arsenick) ☉ DA023, LI071, LI071
Arsesmart (Arsenick) ♂ CU, GA068, LI068, RA054
Arsesmart (Arsenick) ♃ DA020, LI064
Arsesmart (Arsenick) ♄ CU
Arson ♂ PT185
Artemisia abrotanum ☿ CU, GA071
Artemisia absinthium ♂ CU, GA068
Artemisia campestris ☿ CU
Artemisia dracunculus ♂ CU
Artemisia maritma ♂ CU
Artemisia pontica ♂ CU
Artemisia vulgaris ♀ CU, GA070, LI075
Arteries ☿ AB247

Arteries ☉ PA014
Arteries ♃ AB247, DA019, LI246, PA128, PT319, RS014
Arthesia ♍ PA074
Arthritis ☽ RS021
Arthritis ♃ RS019
Artificiers ☿ PA016
Artist (Astrologer) 7th House LI054
Artonicum (Arsenick) ☉ DA023, LI071
Arts (E.G., Astrology, Medicin ☿ PA110
Arum maculatum ♀ RA060
Arum maculatum ♂ CU, GA068
Asarabacca ♂ CU, GA068
Asarum (Ginger) ♂ LI068
Asarum europaeum ♂ CU, GA068
Asclepias syriaga ♃ CU
Ash Tree ☉ CU, DA023, GA069, LI071, RA057
Ash Tree ♀ RA060
Ash Tree ♃ LI064, RA053
Ash, Wild ♀ LI075
Ash-Color ☽ DA026
Ash-Color ♃ DA019, LI063, RA052
Ash-Color ♄ DA017
Asia Minor Sea Towns ♉ DA006, PA073
Asking Horary Questions 1st House AB276
Asparagus ♃ CU, CU, GA068
Asperula cynanchica ♃ CU, DA019, LI063
Asperula cynanchica ♉ DA006
Aspiring ♃ LI062
Asplenium ♄ GA067
Asplenium ruta muriana ☿ GA071
Ass ☿ AB246, LI541
Ass (Anatomical) ♏ DA010, LI246
Ass (Anatomical) 8th House LI245
Ass (Animal) ♄ LI060, RA051
Ass (as in Hole) ☿ LI078
Ass, Wild ☉ AB246
Ass, Wild ♂ LI068
Assarum ♂ DA021
Assaults ☿ PT187
Assaults ♂ PT185
Assistance from Friends ☉ in 11th House GA061

Assistance in Counsel 11th House LI056
Assistance of Princes 11th House PA046
Assistants 2nd House AB275
Assyria ☿ PT141
Assyria ♍ DA009, PA074, PT141
Asthma ☿ PA017
Asthma ♀ RS020
Asthma ♃ PA012
Astragalus gummifer ♂ CU
Astringent ♄ AB240
Astrologer ☿ AB254, GA071, LI078, PA016, PT335, RA061
Astrologer ♊ LI451
Astrologer ♏ PT391
Astrologer ♍ LI451, PT391
Astrologer 7th House PA044
Astrological Propensity ☽ in 9th House GA059
Astrology ☿ in 9th House GA059
Astronomer ♊ LI451
Atheist ♀ GA070, LI074
Atheist ♂ in 9th House GA058
Atheist ♃ GA067, PA012
Atheist ☊ in 9th House GA059
Athenian Territory ♍ LI096
Athens ♍ DA009
Atriplex hortensis ☽ CU
Atriplex hortensis ♀ GA070
Atriplex patula ♀ CU
Atropa belladonna ♄ GA067, RA050
Attainment of Knowledge (Divination) 9th House AB275
Attainment of Knowledge (Stars) 9th House AB275
Attica, Greece? (=Altica) ♐ DA011
Attorneys ☿ GA071, LI078, PA016, RA061
Attraction ♀ S2-45
Attraction ♂ PA128, S2-45
Augsburg, Germany ♑ DA012
Augusta ♈ DA006, LI094
Augusta Vindelicorum [Augsburg] ♑ DA012
Aunts 6th House GA053, LI053, PA044
Aunts, Maternal ☽ AB249
Austere ♄ LI058, PT341
Austerity ♄ LI539

Austria ♀ DA024, LI076, RA060
Austria ♎ DA010, PA075
Austria, Higher ♎ LI097
Author of Strife and Contentions ☿ GA071
Authorities, Petty ☉ PA014
Authority ☉ in 1st House GA046
Authority ☉ in 10th House GA060
Authority ♃ PA108
Authority Figures ☉ LI556
Authority, Absolute 10th House AB275
Autumnal ♎ AB231
Autumnal ♏ AB231
Autumnal ♐ AB231
Avaricious ☿ PT361
Avaricious ♄ PT341
Avenion ♐ PA075
Avens ♃ GA068
Avignon ♐ DA011
Awkward Figure ♄ AB249
Azarbaijan ☽ AB242
Azure ♄ RA051
Azure Color ♃ PA011

-- B --

Baboon ☽ RA064
Baboon ☉ RA058
Babylonia ☿ PT141
Babylonia ♀ AB242
Babylonia ♃ AB242, DA020, LI065, RA053
Babylonia ♍ DA009, PA074, PT141
Back ♂ RA054
Back ♌ DA008
Back ♄ AB248
Back 5th House GA051, LI053, PA043
Back 10th House RS097
Back Between Shoulder & Precordiac ♌ RS015
Back Between Shoulder & Precordiac 5th House RS015
Back Diseases ♀ LI075
Back Pain 10th House RS100
Back Pain ♃ DA019, RA053, RS019

Back Pain ♌ LI095, RS017
Back Pain ♎ DA010
Back Pain, Small of the ♀ RS020
Back, Great Heats ♎ LI246
Back, Hips 7th House AB277
Back, Lower ♐ RS015
Back, Lower 9th House RS015
Back, Small of the ♀ DA023, PA015
Back, Small of the ♂ LI246
Back, Small of the ♎ DA010, RS015
Back, Small of the 6th House LI245
Back, Small of the 7th House RS015
Back, Weakness ♎ LI096, RS017
Backbiting ♄ LI539, PA092
Backbone ♌ LI246
Backbone 8th House LI245
Backbone Pain ♃ LI063
Backbone Pain ♎ DA010
Bactriana, Persian Asia ♎ DA010, PA075
Bad Companion ♂ AB250
Bail 12th House AB275
Bailiffs ♂ GA068, LI067, PA013, RA054
Bakers ♂ GA068, LI067, PA013, RA054
Bakers ♐ LI451
Balding by Forty ♐ DA012
Baldness ☉ DA022
Baldness ♈ DA005, LI093, RS016
Baldness (Alopecia) 1st House RS100
Ballad-Singers ♀ LI074
Ballota nigra ☿ CU
Balm ☉ DA022, GA069, LI071, RA057
Balm ♃ CU, RA052
Balm ♋ CU
Balsam ♃ DA020, LI064
Balsamita major ♃ CU, GA068
Bamberg ♊ DA007, LI094, PA074
Banished People 7th House LI054
Banishment 12th House GA062
Bankers ☿ AB252, PT335
Banking ♃ AB254
Banquets 5th House GA051, LI053, PA043

Banquetting ♀ in 5th House GA052
Barbados ♊ PA073
Barbary Coast ♏ LI097
Barbel (Fish) ♂ LI068, RA055
Barber, Profession of ☿ AB254
Barberry ♂ CU, GA068
Barbers ☿ AB254
Barbers ♂ GA068, LI067, PA013, RA054
Barfly ♀ GA070
Bargains ☿ PA110
Barin (= Bairn = Barn) ☉ DA022
Barley ☉ DA023, LI071, RA057
Barley ☽ AB243
Barley ♃ AB243
Barley ♄ CU, GA067
Barley Stacks (like Hay Stack) ♍ LI096
Barns (Barin = Child) ☉ DA022
Barns ♊ DA007, LI094
Barns, Straggling ♎ LI096
Barons ☉ GA069, LI071
Barren ♊ DA007
Barren ♌ DA008, PA006
Barren ♍ DA009
Barren Fields ♑ LI098
Barren Mountains ♄ AB241
Barren Signs ♒ PT325
Barren Signs ♈ PT325
Barren Signs ♊ LI089
Barren Signs ♌ LI089, PT325
Barren Signs ♍ LI089
Barren Signs ♏ PT325
Barren Signs ♑ PT325
Bars (Taverns, Malt-Houses) ♍ LI096
Bartender ☽ LI081
Bartenders ♄ RA050
Barvaria (Part) ♒ DA013
Base Trades ♄ DA017
Basel, Switzerland ♍ DA009, LI096, PA074
Basement ♉ LI094
Bashful ♃ LI062
Basil ♂ CU

Basil ♃ DA020, LI064, RA052
Basil ♏ CU
Basil, Royal ☿ AB236
Basil, Sweet ♂ GA068
Basilisk (= Monster) ♄ LI060, RA051
Bastard-(English-)Rhubarb ♂ GA068
Bat ☽ RA064
Bat ♄ RA050
Bat (= Stick or Cudgel) ♄ LI060
Batavia, Holland ♂ DA021, LI068
Bath Loving ♀ LI074
Baths ☽ DA027, LI082
Bats ♂ AB247
Bavaria ♄ DA018, LI061, RA051
Bavaria ♏ PA075
Bavaria, Northern ♏ LI097
Bavaria, West & South ♒ LI099
Bay ☉ CU
Bay ♌ CU
Bay Tree ☉ RA057
Bay Tree ♃ GA068
Bayberry Tree ♃ LI064
Bazaars ☿ AB242
Bead, Glass (=Bugle) ♀ CU
Beads Strung ☽ AB243
Beans ☿ AB243, DA025, LI079
Beans ♀ GA070
Beans (Broad) ♀ CU
Beans (French) ♀ CU
Bear ♂ LI068
Bear ♄ LI060, RA051
Beard, Flaxen or Sandy ♃ DA019
Beard, Heavy ☽ GA072
Beard, Little ☿ GA071
Beard, Little ♈ DA005
Beard, Much ☉ GA069
Beard, Much ♃ GA067
Beard, Thin ☿ AB249
Beard, Thin ♄ DA018, GA066
Beard, Thin & Spare ☿ DA025
Beard, Thin ♑ PA008

Beard, Long ☽ AB249
Beard, Small ♃ AB249
Bearsfoot ♄ DA018, LI059, RA050
Bearwards ♂ LI067
Beasts of Burden ☽ AB246
Beasts, Destructive ♂ AB246
Beasts, Domesticated ☽ AB246
Beasts, Mad ♂ AB246
Beasts, Obedient to Man ☽ AB246
Beasts, Wild ♂ AB246
Beautiful Things 11th House AB276
Beauty ♀ PA109
Becafico Bird (Ficedula) ♀ LI075
Bedhangings ♀ DA024
Bedrooms ♀ PA015, RA060
Beds ♀ DA024, LI075, PA015, RA060
Beech Tree ♃ LI064
Bees ☿ LI079
Bees ♃ LI064, RA053
Bees 6th House LI558
Beetles ☿ LI079
Beetles ♄ AB246
Beets (Red) ♄ CU
Beets (White) ♃ CU, GA068
Beggarly ☽ GA072, LI081
Beggarly ♂ in 1st House GA046
Beggars ☽ PA017
Beggars ♄ DA017, GA067, LI059, PA011, RA050
Beginning ♈ DA005
Beginning, Lean & Weak ♊ DA007
Beginning, Lean & Weak ♏ DA011
Beginning, Wreathed ♉ DA006
Beginning, Gross & Strong ♌ DA008
Behemence ♄ AB250
Belleric myrobalan (Fruit) ♄ AB243
Bellis perennis ♀ in ♋ CU
Belly ☽ DA026, PT321, RS015
Belly ♀ RS014
Belly ♍ DA009, RS015
Belly 6th House AB277, RS015
Belly 9th House RS097

Belly Disease ♍ RS017
Belly, Fluxes ☽ LI247, RS021
Belly, Inferior Parts ♎ DA010
Belly, Looseness ♄ DA018
Belly, Lower 6th House LI245
Belly, Part ♎ RS015
Belly, Part 7th House RS015
Belly, Upper ♋ LI245
Bellyaches ♍ DA009, LI246
Beloved of Friends ⊗ in 11th House GA062
Beloved of Women ♀ in 1st House GA046
Benedictus ♂ LI068
Beneficent ☿ PT361
Beneficent ♀ PT357
Beneficent ♃ PT347
Benefices 9th House LI055, PA045
Benevolent ♃ DA019
Benjamin ☉ LI341
Berberis vulgaris ♂ CU, GA068
Berga, Spain ♑ DA012
Bergamo ♈ LI094
Berges ♑ PA076
Berula erecta ♀ GA070
Berula erecta ♄ RA050
Beryll (Stone) ♀ DA023, LI075, RA060
Besieged City, Town, Fort 4th House LI379
Besieged Towns' Ammunition 5th House LI379
Besieged Towns' Army 5th House LI379
Best and Easiest Things ♃ AB241
Bestial ♈ DA005, PA004
Bestial ♉ DA006, PA004
Bestial ♌ DA008, PA006
Bestial ♑ DA012
Beta ♃ CU, GA068
Beta ♄ CU, GA067
Beta altissima ♄ CU
Betony ♃ DA020, LI064, RA052
Betony (Water) ♃ GA068
Betony (Water) ♃ in ♋ CU
Betony (Wood) ♃ CU
Betony (Wood) ♈ CU

Betula alba ♀ CU
Betula pendula ♃ RA053
Betula pendula ♀ CU, GA070
Betula spp. ♃ LI064
Beverages ☽ AB245
Bewitched 12th House LI464
Bezoar ♃ DA019, LI064, RA053
Bicorporeal ♊ AB231
Bicorporeal ♍ AB231
Bicorporeal ♐ AB231, PA008
Bicorporeal ♓ AB231
Bidens tripartita ♃ CU
Bidens tripartita ♋ CU
Bifoil = Two-Blade Grass ♄ GA067
Bilberries ♃ CU
Bile ☿ PT321
Bile [Choler], Black ♄ AB017, DA017
Bile, Red (Red Choler) ♂ RS020
Bile, Yellow ♂ AB247
Bile, Yellow (Yellow Choler) ☉ RS020
Birch ♀ CU, ♀ GA070
Birch ♃ LI064, RA053
Birch, Silver ♀ CU
Birds of Prey ♂ RA055
Birds, All Red Ones ♂ AB247
Birds, Aquatic ☿ AB247
Birds, Aquatic ♄ AB247
Birds, Carnivorous, Curved Bill ♂ AB247
Birds, Grain Eating ♃ AB247
Birds, Nocturnal ♂ AB247
Birds, Nocturnal ♄ AB247
Birds, not Black ♃ AB247
Birds, Straight Beaks ♃ AB247
Birdsfoot Trefoil ♄ GA067
Birth, When Will It Be? 5th House GA266, LI231
Bishop Weed (Aegopodium) ♀ GA070
Bishops ♃ DA019, GA067, LI063, PA108
Bishops 9th House LI055, PA045
Bistort (Herb) ♄ CU, GA067
Bithwind ♄ RA050
Bithynia, Asia Minor ♋ PA074

Bitter ♂ AB240, DA020
Bitter ♄ DA017, LI059
Bitter ♈ DA005
Bitter ♐ DA011
Bitter Fruit ♂ AB244
Bitter Sweet ☿ CU
Bitter Sweet ♃ AB240
Bitter Taste ♂ LI067
Bitter Trees ♂ AB244
Black ♄ DA017, PT193
Black ♎ LI086
Black ♑ LI086
Black 5th House PA043
Black 6th House AB277, LI054, PA044
Black 7th House PA044
Black 8th House AB277
Black & White 5th House LI053, PA043
Black Animals ♄ AB246
Black Bile ☿ AB247
Black Jaundice ♄ LI059
Black Mixed with Yellow ♄ AB240
Black Stones ♄ LI060
Black-Blue ♍ LI086
Black-Hair ♄ PT305
Blackberry ☿ LI272
Blackberry ♄ LI272
Blackberry ♀ in ♈ CU
Blackbird ☿ RA062
Blackbird ♀ RA060
Blackbird ♄ LI060, RA050
Blacksmiths ♂ AB254
Blackthorn ♄ GA067
Bladder ☽ LI082, PA018, RS015
Bladder ♄ DA017, PA127, PT319, RS014
Bladder ♎ DA010, RS015
Bladder ♏ DA010, LI097, RS015
Bladder 7th House LI245, RS015
Bladder 8th House LI054, RS015
Bladder Abscesses ♎ LI096, RS017
Bladder Disease ☽ RA064
Bladder Disease ♀ RA061

Bladder Pain ♄ RA051
Bladder Pains ♄ LI246
Bladder Stones ☽ DA026
Bladder Stones ♂ LI067, RS020
Bladder Stones ♏ DA011, LI246, PA008
Bladder Ulcers ♎ RS017
Blasphemous ♂ in 3rd House GA049
Blisters ♂ LI067, RS020
Blites (Chenopodiaceae) ♀ GA070
Blondstone ♂ DA021
Blood ♃ AB247, PA012
Blood Corruption ♃ LI063, RA053
Blood Corruption ♊ DA007, LI094, RS017
Blood Corruption ♎ DA010, LI096, RS017
Blood Diseases ♃ DA019
Blood, Excess ♐ DA011
Blood Fluxes (Dysentery) ♂ LI540, PA128, RS020
Blood Fluxes (Dysentery) ♄ PT327
Blood Fluxes (Dysentery) ♎ DA010
Blood, Heated ♐ LI097, RS018
Blood Putrefaction ♃ LI246, RS019
Blood Putrefaction ♊ PA005
Blood, Spitting of ♂ PT327
Bloodstone ♂ LI068, RA055
Bloodthirsty ♂ PT353
Bloodwort (Sanguinaria) ♃ GA068
Bloody ♂ LI540
Bloody-Minded ♂ LI540
Blue ☿ LI086
Blue ♃ RA052
Blue ♒ LI086
Blue 1st House AB277
Blue and White ☽ AB240
Blue Bottle ♄ CU
Blue, Tending to White ♀ RA060
Blue-Black ♍ LI086
Boar ☉ RA058
Boasters ☿ GA071, LI077, PA016
Boasters ♂ LI540
Boastful ♂ PA093
Body, All Parts "Brevity" ♍ PA006

Body, Big & Strong ♃ DA020
Body, Big-Boned ♂ GA068
Body, Bow-Legged ♏ PA008
Body, Comely ☉ DA022
Body, Comely & Handsome ♀ GA070
Body, Deformed ♄ in 1st House GA046
Body, Delicate & Straight ♎ DA010
Body, Disproportioned ♑ DA013
Body, Diversely Proportioned ♓ DA014
Body, Dry & Lean ♑ DA012
Body, Fat (Somewhat) ♏ PA008
Body, Fat or Fleshy ♃ DA020
Body, Fleshy ♓ PA009
Body, Full Fleshy ☉ GA069, PA014
Body, Full, Well-Set ♏ DA011
Body, Hairy ♏ PA008
Body, Handsome ♒ DA013
Body, Handsomely Composed ♃ GA067
Body, Healthy ☉ DA022
Body, Ill-Composed ♓ DA014
Body, Ill-Composed, Undecent ♓ PA009
Body, Infirm & Sickly ☉ in 12th House GA063
Body, Large & Full ♌ PA006
Body, Large & Lusty ♌ DA009
Body, Lean & Spare ♈ PA004
Body, not Too Fat ♀ AB249
Body, Plump ☽ PA017
Body Proportions Diverse ♏ DA011
Body Shape 1st House PA041
Body, Small ♑ DA012
Body, Sometimes Dropsical ♓ PA009
Body, Spare, Lean & Slender ♑ PA008
Body, Straight ☿ PA016
Body, Straight ♐ DA012
Body, Straight & Upright ☿ GA071
Body, Straight & Well-Set ♊ DA007
Body, Strong & Able ♂ GA068, PA012
Body, Strong & Active ♊ PA005
Body, Strong, Well-Propor, Tall ♐ PA008
Body, Subtle & Spare ♍ DA009
Body, Well-fFramed ♎ DA010

Body, Well-ordered ♀ DA024
Body, Well-proportioned ♎ DA010
Body, Well-proportioned ♄ DA012
Body, Well-set ♌ PA006
Body, Well-shaped ♒ DA013
Body, Well-shaped ♀ PA015
Body with Upper Parts Bigger ♋ DA008
Boggy Places ☽ LI082
Bogs ☽ RA064
Bohemia ♌ DA008, LI096, PA074
Bohemia ☉ LI072, RA058
Boil, Core (=Botch) ♓ DA014
Boils (Medical) ♓ DA014, LI099, RS018
Boils, Internal (Pushes) ☉ DA022
Boils, Uterine (Pushes) ☉ DA022
Bold ♂ AB250, DA021, LI066
Bold ☉ DA022
Bologna ♉ LI094, PA073
Bondage ♃ in 12th House GA062
Bone Marrow ♃ AB247
Bone Pain ♄ LI246, RA051
Bones ☿ DA025
Bones ♄ AB247, LI579, PA011, PT319, RS014
Bones, Big ♂ PA012
Bononia [= Bologna] ♉ DA006, LI094, PA073
Books ♃ AB242
Books 9th House AB276, LI055
Books, Selling of ☿ AB254
Boot-licking ♃ LI063
Borage ♃ CU, DA020, LI064, RA052
Borago officinalis ♃ RA052
Bores ♄ AB252
Borrowing 2nd House AB276
Bosnia ♑ DA012
Botches (Core of a Boil) ♓ DA014
Bountiful ☉ GA069
Bountiful ♀ LI541
Bow-Legged ♏ PA008
Bowel Obstructions ♍ LI096, RS017
Bowels ☽ PA018, RS015
Bowels ♄ AB248

Bowels ♍ DA009, LI096, RS015
Bowels 6th House RS015
Bowels, Gas ☿ RS021
Bowling Alleys ☿ DA026, LI079, RA062
Box ♄ LI059, RA050
Brabant ♊ DA007, LI094, PA073
Brackbird ♀ LI075
Braggart ☿ LI078
Braggart ♂ LI066
Braggart ☿ in 9th House GA059
Brain ☉ LI247, PT319, RA057, RS014
Brain ☽ DA026, LI247, PA018, RS015
Brain ☿ LI247, RA061, RS015
Brain Disease ☉ LI071, RA058, RS020
Brain Disease ☿ LI078, PA017, RA062
Brain Distempers 1st House RS100
Brain, Penetrating ☿ GA071, PA016
Brains ☿ DA025
Brains ☉ AB247
Bramble ♂ AB244, DA021, GA068, RA054
Brandenburg ♑ DA012, LI098, PA076
Brasier (Profession) ♏ LI451
Brass ♀ DA023, LI075, RA060
Brass Household Vessels ♀ AB243
Brass, Fine ♃ AB243
Brassica napa ♂ GA068
Brassica nigra ♂ CU, RA054
Brassica oleracea ☽ GA072
Bratislava, Czech. ([V/W] ratislav[a/e]) ♍ DA009, PA075
Brawlers ♂ DA020
Brawling with Spouse ☋ in 7th House GA056
Brawls ♂ in 7th House GA055
Braziers ☉ GA069, LI071
Break-Outs ☽ RS021
Breaking Out ♓ LI099
Breast ♌ DA008
Breast Cancer ♋ LI095
Breast Defects ♋ PA005
Breast Disease ♋ RS017
Breast Large (=Voice Large) ♊ DA007
Breast Pains ♋ LI245

Breast, Lower ♌ LI246
Breasts ☽ AB248, DA026
Breasts ♋ DA007, LI095, RS015
Breasts 4th House GA050, LI052, PA043, RS015
Breath, Bad 1st House LI245
Breath, Shortness of ♃ PA128
Breath, Stinking ☉ RS020
Breathing (Exercise?) ♍ LI096
Breme ♒ LI099, PA076
Bremen, Germany ♒ DA013
Brescia, Italy ♉ LI094, PA073
Brewers ☽ GA072, LI081
Brewers ♄ GA067, LI059
Brewers ♏ LI451
Brewers ♓ LI451
Briars ♂ RA054
Bribe Takers ♃ RA052
Bribery 5th House AB276
Bribery 11th House AB276
Brick Burning Places ♂ PA013
Brick Burning Places ♈ LI093
Bricklayers ♄ RA050
Brickmakers ♄ GA067, LI059, RA050
Bridal Chambers ♀ DA024, LI075, PA015
Brief in Speech ☉ LI070
Brigandage ♂ AB254
Bright ♂ AB250
Brimstone ♂ DA020, LI068, RA055
Brindisi (Brundusium) ♍ DA009, LI096, PA074
Briony ♂ GA068
Bristol, England ♌ DA009, LI096
Britain ♂ PT135
Britain ♈ PT135
Brixia, Italy [= Brescia] ♉ DA006, LI094, PA073
Broken ♌ DA008
Broken ♑ DA012
Broken a Bit ♓ DA014
Brook-Lime ♂ CU, GA068
Brooks ☽ RA064
Brooks ♋ DA008, LI095
Brooks, Little ☽ LI082

Broom ♂ GA068
Broom-Men ♄ LI059, RA050
Broom-Rape ♂ GA068
Brothers ☉ AB249
Brothers ☿ DA025
Brothers 3rd House AB275, GA048, LI052, PA042
Brothers & Sisters Comely ♀ in 3rd House GA049
Brothers of Middle Age ♂ AB249
Brothers, Younger ☿ AB249
Brothers-in-Law 9th House AB276
Brown ♃ DA019
Brown ♏ LI086
Brown Hair ♐ PA008
Brown, Swarthy ♑ LI086
Bruges (Brussels) ♊ LI094, PA074
Brundusium [= Brindisi] ♍ DA009, LI096, PA074
Brunswick, Germany ♈ PA073
Brussels, Belgium ♊ DA007, LI094, PA074
Bryonia dioica ♂ CU, GA068
Bryony ♂ CU
Buckthorn (Purging) ♄ CU
Buckthorn-Plantain ♄ GA067
Buda, Hungary ♐ LI098, PA075
Budapest ♐ DA012
Bugle (Plant) ♀ CU, GA070
Buglosse (Herb) ♃ DA020, LI064, RA052
Buildings ♄ AB254, DA018, LI555, PA108
Buildings of Honor ☉ PA014
Buildings, Ruined ♄ PA011
Buildings, Ruinous ♄ DA018, RA051
Buildings, Decrepit ♄ LI060
Buildings, Magnificent ☉ DA023, RA058
Buildings, Stately ☉ PA014
Bulgaria ♑ DA012, LI098, PA076
Bull ☉ LI071, RA058
Bull ♀ RA060
Bupleurum rotundifolium ♄ GA067
Burdock ♀ GA070
Burdock ♄ LI059, RA050
Burdock (Greater) ♀ CU
Burgander (Bird) ♀ RA060

Burgundy ♈ DA006, LI094
Burgundy ♋ DA007, PA074
Burial Grounds ♄ LI060
Buried Treasure 8th House AB276
Burn ♂ PT037
Burnet ☉ CU, GA069
Burning ♂ LI067, PT321, RS020
Burns ♐ RS018
Bushy Places ♑ LI098
Business ☿ PA110
Business ♂ AB245
Business going to Ruin ♂ AB250
Business in Large Animals ☿ in 12th House GA063
Business Matters, Engaged in ☽ AB254
Business with Women as Clients ♀ PA015
Business, Abandoned 9th House AB276
Business, Success in 10th House AB275
Businessmen ☿ PT335
Busy about Unproductive Things ☿ in 12th House GA063
Busybody ☿ AB250, GA071, PA016
Busybody ♀ GA070
Butcher's Broom ♂ CU, GA068
Butchers ♂ AB254, GA068, LI067, PA013, RA054
Butchers ♈ LI450
Butomus umbellatus ♄ CU
Butter-Bur ☉ CU, GA069
Buttery ♍ LI096
Buttocks (Hamms) ♎ DA010, RS015
Buttocks (Hamms) ♀ DA023, RS014
Buttocks (Hamms) ☿ PT321
Buttocks (Hamms) ♄ AB248
Buttocks (Hamms) ♉ DA007
Buttocks (Hamms) ♑ RS015
Buttocks (Hamms) ♐ LI097, RS015
Buttocks (Hamms) 7th House RS015
Buttocks (Hamms) 9th House RS015
Buttocks (Hamms) 10th House GA060, RS015
Buttocks, Hurts ♐ RS018
Buttocks, Diseases ♎ LI246
Buyer of Property 1st House LI220
Buyers ☿ DA025

Buzzard ☉ LI072, RA057
Bythwind (Herb) ♄ LI059

-- C --

Cabbage ☽ DA026, GA072, LI082, RA063
Cabbage ☿ LI272
Cabbage ♄ LI272
Cadiz ♋ LI095
Caesarean Section ♃ AB252
Caesarea, Palestine ♈ DA006, LI094
Cajeta, Italy [= Latium] ♎ DA010, PA075
Calabria, Italy ♓ DA014, LI099, PA076
Calamint ☿ CU, GA071
Calamintha ascendens ☿ CU, GA071
Calamities ♂ in 2nd House GA047
Calandra (Bird) ☿ RA062
Calculators ☿ AB254, PT359
Calenture ♂ PA013
Calf ♀ LI075, RA060
Calumination ☽ AB250
Caluminous ☿ AB250
Calumnities 6th House AB276
Calumnities ☋ in 1st House GA046
Calumnities Prodigious ☋ in 7th House GA056
Calves 11th House AB277
Calves of Legs ♒ LI246
Calves, Thick ♀ AB249
Camel ☽ AB246
Camel ☿ AB246
Camerino, Italy [=Camerinum] ♏ DA011
Cammock ♂ RA054
Cammock (Herb) ♂ LI068
Campana (Plant) ☉ LI071
Campan[i]a, Italy ♉ DA006, LI094, PA073
Campan[i]a, Italy ♀ DA024, LI076, RA060
Cancer ♀ PT431
Cancer ♋ LI245
Cancer (Disease) ♋ RS017
Candle-Maker ♄ GA067, RA050
Cane ☉ LI071

Canes ☽ AB244
Canes & Things Growing in Water ☿ AB244
Canker ♄ DA017, PA011
Canker ♏ DA011
Cannabis sativa ☽ AB244
Cannabis sativa ♄ CU, GA067, LI059, RA050
Cannot obtain Hopes ☋ in 11th House GA062
Cantharides (Spanish Fly) ☉ LI072
Cantharides (Spanish Fly) ♂ DA021, LI068
Capable of Learning ☿ LI541
Capacity for Change ☽ PT361
Capers ♄ LI059, RA050
Capers Tree ♄ DA018
Capiscum frutescens ♂ CU
Capivity ☉ in 12th House GA063
Cappadocia, Asia Minor ♏ PA075
Capsella bursa-pastoris ♄ CU, LI059, RA050
Captains ♂ GA068, LI067, PA109
Captives 12th House LI463
Captivity ♄ AB254
Captivity ♄ in 10th House GA060
Captivity ♄ in 12th House GA062
Captivity 12th House GA062
Captivity, Indicates for Wizar ☽ AB254
Capture ♂ PT183
Capua, Italy ♈ DA006, LI094, PA073
Caraway ☿ AB243, CU, GA071
Carbuncle (Stone) ☉ DA022, RA057
Carbuncles (Inflammation) ♂ DA021, RS020
Cardamine pratensis ☽ CU
Cardiac Affections ♃ PT429
Cardiac Passion ☉ LI247
Cardinal ♑ PA008
Cardinals ♃ LI063
Cards ♀ LI556
Cards 5th House LI169
Carduus Benedictus ♂ CU, DA021, GA068, LI068, RA054
Carduus eriophorus ♂ GA068
Carduus heterophyllus ♄ GA067
Carduus marianus ♃ GA068
Careless ☽ LI081

Careless ♀ PT357
Careless ♃ GA067, LI063
Careless ♄ PA108
Careless of Body ♄ PT341
Carinibia* ♍ DA009
Carnelian Stone (Cornelian) ♀ DA023, LI075
Carolstad[e] ♉ DA006, LI094
Carpenters ♂ GA068, LI067, PA013, PT337, RA054
Carpenters, Ship ♄ RA050
Carriers ☿ GA071, LI078, PA016, RA061
Carrion Crows ☽ AB247
Carrot ☿ GA071
Carrot (Wild) ☿ CU
Cart-Maker ♈ LI450
Carters ♄ LI059, RA050
Carthage ☽ PT153, PT153
Carthage ♋ DA008, PA074, PT153, PT153
Carthamus tinctorius ☉ GA069, RA057
Carthamus tinctorius ♄ CU
Cartilege (Gristle) ♃ LI246, RS014
Carum carvi ☿ AB243, CU, GA071
Caspia ♎ DA010, PA075
Castanea sativa ♃ CU
Castles ♌ DA008, LI095
Castles 4th House LI052, PA043
Castor Oil Plant ♄ AB244
Castoreum (from Castor Bean) ♂ DA021, LI068, RA054
Cat ☽ RA064
Cat ♄ AB246, LI060, RA051
Catalonia ♏ LI097, PA075
Cataracts ☉ LI247
Catarrhs ☉ RA058, RS020
Catarrhs ♄ RA051
Cathars (Purges) ☉ DA022
Cathars (Purges) ☽ DA026
Cathars (Purges) ☿ DA025
Catmint = Catnip ♀ CU
Catnip = Nep ♀ GA070
Cattle 6th House AB275
Cattle 12th House AB275
Cattle Broker ♐ LI451

Cautery 3rd House AB276
Cautious in Friendship ♃ AB250
Cavalry ♂ AB252
Caves ♄ DA018, LI060, PA011, RA051
Cedar ☉ DA023, LI071, RA057
Ceiling of Houses ♈ LI093
Celandine [= Sallendine] ☉ DA023, GA069, LI071, RA057
Celandine (the Greater) ☉ CU
Celandine (the Greater) ♌ CU
Celandine (the Lesser) ♂ CU
Celebrated and Wealthy Citizen ☽ AB252
Celebrated in All Classes 10th House AB276
Cellars ♉ DA007
Cellars of Houses ♉ LI094
Cellars of Houses ♋ DA008, LI095
Celtica, Gaul ♐ PA075
Centaurea calcitrapa ♂ GA068
Centaurea cyanus ♄ CU
Centaurea jacea ♄ CU
Centaurea scabiosa ♄ CU, GA067
Centaurium erythraea ☉ CU, GA069
Centaurium erythraea ♃ DA020, LI064
Centaury ☉ CU, GA069
Centaury ♃ DA020, LI064
Cesena, Italy ♊ LI094
Ceterach (Finger-Fern) ♄ LI059
Chaldaea ☉ DA022, LI072, PT143, RA058
Chaldaea ♌ DA008, PA074, PT143
Challenges Honor to Himself ♂ GA068
Chamaemelum nobile ☉ CU
Chamber Within a Chamber ♎ LI096
Chambers ♎ LI096
Chameleon ☽ RA064
Chamomile ☉ CU
Chamomile (Camomel) ☉ GA069
Champions ♂ LI629
Chancellors ♃ LI063, RA052
Chandlers ♄ GA067, RA050
Changeable ☿ AB250
Changeable ♎ AB231, AB264
Changeable ♏ AB231

Changeable ♐ AB231
Changes in Querent's Life 1st House GA242, LI134
Character ☽ PT333
Character ☿ PT333
Charcoal Burning Places ♂ PA013
Charitable ♃ AB250
Charity ♃ LI062
Charity, Much ♃ GA067
Charming ♀ PT357
Charwomen ☽ GA072, LI081
Chaste ♃ AB250
Chaste but Sensual ☉ AB250
Cheapness & Dearness 7th House AB276
Cheaters ♂ LI066
Cheaters ♃ RA052
Cheating ☿ GA071, LI078
Cheating ♀ AB250
Cheats ♃ PA012
Cheeks ♈ RS015
Cheeks 1st House RS015
Cheeks Cherry ♎ DA010
Cheeks Cherry-Colored, Dimples ♀ DA024
Cheeks, Fat ♀ AB249
Cheerful ☽ AB250
Cheerful ♀ LI074, PT357
Cheerful ♂ AB250
Cheerful ♎ DA010
Cheese Storage ♍ LI096
Cheetahs, Trained ♃ AB246
Cheiranthus cheiri ☽ CU
Chelidonium majus ☉ CU, RA057
Chelidonium majus ♌ CU
Chemistry ♂ PA109
Chemists ♂ PA013
Chemists ♐ LI451
Chenopodium bonus-henricus ☿ CU
Cherries (Winter) ♀ CU
Cherry Tree ♀ GA070
Cherry Tree ♃ LI064, RA053
Chervil ♃ CU
Chess ♀ AB250

Chestnut Color ☿ PA016
Chestnut Tree ♂ DA021, LI068
Chestnut Tree ♃ CU
Chests ☉ AB248
Chests ♊ DA007, LI094
Chick Peas ☉ LI273
Chick Peas ♂ LI273
Chick Peas ♃ AB243
Chick Peas? (Cichpease) ♀ GA070
Chicken (Ancona, Italian Type) ♈ PA073
Chicks ☽ AB247
Chickweed ☽ CU
Chickweed ♀ GA070
Chiefs ☉ AB252
Child (= Barn) ☉ DA022
Child of Querent's Wife 11th House LI139
Child, Foreigner's 11th House AB276
Child, Gender of Unborn? 5th House GA266, LI230, PA065
Child, Servant's 11th House AB276
Childhood ☿ AB248, PT443
Childhood ♈ AB230
Childhood ♊ AB230
Childhood ♉ AB230
Childless ♄ in 5th House GA051
Children ♃ AB249
Children ♋ DA008
Children 5th House AB275, GA051, LI053, PA043, PT409
Children 11th House PT409
Children Apt for Study ☿ in 5th House GA052
Children Causing Grief ♂ in 5th House GA052
Children Causing Much Joy ♀ in 5th House GA052
Children Denied ☋ in 5th House GA052
Children, Destroyed ☋ in 5th House GA052
Children, Disobendient ☋ in 5th House GA052
Children, Dutiful & Obedient ♃ in 5th House GA051
Children, Few ♂ in 5th House GA052
Children, Few ♈ DA005
Children, Few ♎ DA010
Children, Few ♑ DA012
Children, Few ♒ DA013
Children, Few & Weak ♐ DA011

Children, Few but Honorable ☉ in 5th House GA052
Children, Friendly & Beneficent ☽ in 11th House GA062
Children, Illegitimate ♂ in 5th House GA052
Children, Ingenious ☿ in 5th House GA052
Children, Ingenious ♃ in 5th House GA051
Children Live Cruel Lives ☋ in 5th House GA052
Children, Long-Lived & Fortunate ☊ in 5th House GA052
Children, Many ♀ PT185
Children, Many ☽ in 5th House GA052
Children, Many ♀ in 5th House GA052
Children, Many ☊ in 5th House GA052
Children, Many & Fortunate ♀ in 11th House GA062
Children, Prosperous ♀ in 5th House GA052
Children's Condition 5th House GA051
Children's Prosperity ⊗ in 5th House GA052
Children's Qualities 5th House GA051
Children, Well-Behaved 10th House AB275
Children Will a Woman Have? 5th House DA103, GA264, LI222, PA065
Chimney Sweeps ♄ LI059
Chimneys ♂ DA021, LI068, PA013
Chimneys, Near ♌ DA008, LI095
Chin ♈ RS015
Chin 1st House RS015
Chin Cough ♄ RA051
Chin, Area Under 2nd House RS015
Chin, Area Under ♉ RS015
Chinost* (Schinos = Mastic) ☽ RA063
Chives ♂ CU
Choler ☉ LI247
Choler, Black ♄ DA017
Choler, Red ☉ DA022
Choler, Red ♂ DA020, RS020
Choler, Yellow ☉ RS020
Choleric ♈ PA004
Choleric ♌ PA006, PA006
Choleric ♐ PA008
Choleric Passion ♂ PA013
Cholic ☽ DA026, LI081, PA130, RS021
Cholic ♄ PA127, PT327
Cholic ♍ DA009, LI096
Cholic 9th House RS100

Cholic (Gripping of the Guts) 9th House RS100
Choristers ♀ GA070, LI074
Christian (Name) ☿ LI341
Christian Churches ♃ AB242
Chrysolite ☉ DA022, LI072, RA057
Chrysolite ♀ DA023, LI075, RA060
Church Income 9th House PA045
Church Living 9th House LI055
Church Position (Does Querent Get?) 9th House GA287, LI432
Churches ♃ PA012, RA053
Churchman ♐ LI451
Churchmen 9th House GA058
Churchyards ♄ DA018, LI060, PA011, RA051
Cich-Pease (Chick Peas?) ♀ GA070
Cichorium endivia ☽ RA063
Cichorium endivia ♃ CU, GA068
Cichorium intybus ♃ CU, GA068
Cinnabar ♂ AB243
Cinnamon ☉ DA023, LI071, RA057
Cinnamon ♂ LI272
Cinquefoil ☉ DA023, LI071, RA057
Cinquefoil ♃ CU, GA068
Circumcisers ♂ AB254
Circumspect ☉ PA109
Cisterns ♋ LI095
Cities 4th House LI052, PA043
Citron (Pomecitron) ☉ LI071
Citron or Myrobalan Tree ♄ AB244
Civet Cat ☽ RA064
Civet Cat ☿ RA062
Civet Cat ♀ RA060
Civetor (Plant) ♀ DA024
Civil Faction ♂ PT183
Civilians ♃ PA108
Claiming a Right 7th House AB276
Clary ☽ CU
Clary (Plant) ♀ GA070
Clary (Wild) ☽ CU
Clean in Appearance ♀ GA070
Cleanly ♀ LI541
Cleanly Dressed ♀ LI074

Cleavers ☽ CU
Cleavers (Goosegrass) ♄ GA067
Clement ☿ LI341
Clergy 9th House LI055
Clergymen ♃ GA067, PA012
Clergymen 9th House PA045
Clergymen Broken ♃ PA012
Clerks ☿ GA071, LI078, RA061
Clerks, Troublesome ☿ PA016
Cleves, Germany ♑ LI098
Clivia (African Amaryllis) ♑ PA076
Closet ♍ LI096
Clotbur ♄ LI059
Clothes 5th House AB275
Clothes Occupations ♀ LI075
Clothes, Fine ♀ AB250
Clothes, Green ♀ AB254
Clothes, White ♀ AB254
Clothiers ♃ GA067, LI063, RA052
Clothing ♃ AB245
Clothing Merchants ♀ PT337
Clouds, Dark ♄ RA051
Cloudy Weather ♄ LI060, RA051
Cloves ♃ DA019, LI064, RA052
Clown's Woundwort ♄ CU, GA067
Clowns ♄ GA067, LI059, PA011, RA050
Cnicus benedictus ♂ CU, GA068, RA054
Coachmen ☽ GA072, LI081
Coachmen ♄ RA050
Coal Miners ♄ RA050
Coal Mines ♄ LI060
Coal Pits ♄ PA011, RA051
Coarseness ♂ AB241
Coblentz, Germany[= Confluente] ♌ DA009
Cock (Bird) ☉ AB247, LI072, RA057
Cockatoo ☿ RA062
Cockatrice ♂ LI068, RA055
Cockle ☽ LI082, RA064
Cocks Head (Red Clover) ♀ GA070
Coffers ♊ DA007, LI094
Cogitation ☿ LI077

Cognition Deep ♄ DA018
Cognition Deep ☿ in 1st House GA046
Coiners ☉ RA056
Coiners ☿ PA095
Coins Struck with Name & Number ☿ AB243
Coins, Selling of ☿ AB254
Coition ♀ AB245
Colchicum autumnale ♄ CU
Colchis ♋ DA008, PA074
Colchis [= Phasiana] ♓ DA014
Cold & Barren ♍ PA006
Cold & Dry ♉ PA004
Cold & Dry ♑ PA008
Cold & Dryness ☿ AB232
Cold & Moist ♋ PA005
Cold & Moist ♓ PA009
Cold & Wet ♒ AB264
Cold & Wet ♓ AB264
Cold Rheumatic Diseases ☽ LI082
Cold Stomach ☽ LI082
Colds ♓ LI099
Colewort ☽ DA026, GA072, LI082, RA063
Colewort ♃ CU
Collapse of Buildings ♄ PT327
Colliers ♄ GA067, LI059, RA050
Cologne, Germany (Agrippina) ♐ DA011, PA075
Colonels ♂ GA068, LI067
Colonia, Italy ♐ DA011, PA075
Color ♀ PT337
Color 1st House LI050
Color Mixed ☿ PT193
Color of Skin 1st House GA045
Colored Herbs ♀ AB244
Colt's Foot ♀ CU, GA070
Columbine ☽ GA072
Columbine ♀ CU
Colutea Orientalis ☿ CU
Comagena, Syrian Province ♏ PA075
Comata, Part, Transalpine Gaul ♍ DA009
Combs, Manufacture of ☿ AB254
Comestio (Devouring) of Mouth Flesh ☉ DA022

Comfort 11th House LI559
Comfrey ♄ CU, GA067
Comfrey ♑ CU
Commander-in-Chief 10th House LI055, PA046
Commanding ♂ PT353
Commanding ♈ DA005
Commanding ♉ DA006
Commanding ♊ DA007
Commanding ♋ DA008
Commanding ♌ DA008, PA006
Commanding ♍ DA009
Commentaries 3rd House AB276
Commerce ☿ LI627
Commerce 11th House AB275
Commerce, Success in 10th House AB275
Commissioners ☿ LI078, RA061
Commodities Broker ♉ LI451
Common Halls ☿ RA062
Common Halls (Room) ☿ DA026, LI079
Common People ☽ DA026, LI081, PA018, PA110
Common People 1st House LI050
Common People (Eclipses) 1st House PA041
Common People (Mundane) 1st House PA041
Common Shores ☽ LI082, RA064
Commonwealths ☉ LI556, PA109
Compassionate ♃ PT347
Compassionate ♀ PT357
Complete ♃ AB241
Complex Flavors ☿ AB240
Complexion 1st House GA045, LI050, PA041
Complexion, A Little Swarthy ♌ PA006
Complexion, Between Yellow & Black ☉ DA022
Complexion, Brown ♂ PA012
Complexion, Brown ♈ DA006
Complexion, Brown (Greenish) ☿ AB249
Complexion, Brown or Ruddy ♍ DA009
Complexion, Clear White ☽ AB249
Complexion, Dark ☿ PA016
Complexion, Dark & Sallow ♏ DA011
Complexion, Dark & Swarthy ☿ GA071
Complexion, Dusky ♈ DA006

Complexion, Fair ♀ PA015
Complexion, Highly Colored ♂ DA021
Complexion, Honey-Colored ☉ GA069
Complexion, Lovely ♀ GA070
Complexion, Muddy ♄ PA010
Complexion, Obscure White W/Red ☉ DA022
Complexion, Occupations ♀ LI075
Complexion, Olive or Chestnut ☿ GA071
Complexion, Pale ♄ PA010
Complexion, Pale ♓ DA014, PA009
Complexion, Pale & Sickly ♋ PA005
Complexion, Red & White ☽ DA027
Complexion, Reddish-White ♀ AB249
Complexion, Ruddy ♃ PA011
Complexion, Ruddy & Pleasant ♃ GA067
Complexion, Ruddy, Sanguine ♌ PA006
Complexion, Ruddy-Brown ♂ GA068
Complexion, Saffron-Colored ☉ GA069
Complexion, Sanguine ♊ PA005
Complexion, Sanguine ♐ PA008
Complexion, Sanguine ♒ PA009
Complexion, Sanguine or Mixed ♃ DA019
Complexion, Swarthy ♈ DA006
Complexion, Swarthy ♉ PA004
Complexion, Swarthy ♄ PA010
Complexion, Swarthy ♏ PA008
Complexion, Swarthy or Black ♄ DA018
Complexion, Swarthy or Pale ♄ GA066
Complexion, Swarthy-Dusky ♈ PA004
Complexion, Tanned Like Leather ♂ DA021
Complexion, Tawny ☉ PA014
Complexion, White (Yellowish) ☉ AB249
Complexion, White or Pale ☽ GA072
Composed ☽ LI081
Compostella, Italy ♓ DA014, LI099, PA076
Compounds of Two Things ☿ AB241
Concealment of Disease ♃ PT329
Conceited ♃ LI540
Conceited ♎ LI538
Conceits (Imaginings) ☿ RS021
Conception 5th House LI223

Conception (When?) 5th House GA264, LI223
Conclusion, Happy 11th House LI559
Concubines ♀ DA024
Concubines 7th House AB275
Condemner of Arts ♎ LI538
Condemner of Women ♄ LI058
Conduct in Office (Ruler) 10th House AB276
Conduit Head (Places Near) ♒ DA013
Conduit, Water ☽ LI214
Conduit, Water ♄ LI214
Conferences ♃ LI064
Confidence 11th House GA061, LI056
Confident ♂ LI066, PA109
Confluence ♌ PA074
Confluentia ♌ LI096
Confused Opinions ♂ AB250
Confusion ♄ AB250
Confusion & Waste of Patrimony ☋ in 4th House GA051
Congestion ☿ RS021
Conium maculatum ♂ RA054
Conium maculatum ♄ CU, GA067, RA050
Conquerers ♂ RA054
Conquerors ♂ GA068, LI067, PA013
Conscience, Good ♃ in 3rd House GA049
Constables ☉ RA057
Constables, Troublesome ☉ PA014
Constance, Germany ♄ DA018
Constance, Germany ♑ DA012, PA076
Constant ♃ GA067
Constant in Religion ♒ LI538
Constantia ♄ LI061, RA051
Constantinople, Turkey ♋ DA008, LI095, PA074
Constipation ☽ RS021
Constipation ♄ DA018
Constitution, Good ♌ in 6th House GA054
Constitution, Healthful ☉ GA069
Consumption ☉ RS020
Consumption ☿ PT187
Consumption ♄ LI059, PA011, PA127, PT181, RA051, RS019
Consumption of Lights ♄ DA017
Contemporaries' Deaths 7th House AB276

Contemptuous ♂ PT353
Contention ♂ AB254, LI066, PA109
Contention ♂ in 7th House GA055
Contention 2nd House PA042
Contention 7th House AB275
Contention 8th House AB276
Contentions between Spouses ☋ in 7th House GA056
Contentions from those Close ☿ in 4th House GA051
Contentions with Ambassadors ♄ in 5th House GA051
Contentions with Father ♂ in 4th House GA050
Contentions with Messengers ♄ in 5th House GA051
Contentions with Public Enemies ♄ in 7th House GA054
Contests 7th House GA054
Contracts ☿ LI556
Controversies ♂ LI556
Controversies 7th House GA054
Controversies with Magistrates ☉ in 7th House GA055
Convallaria majalis ☿ CU
Conventions ♃ LI064
Conversation Excellent ♃ GA067
Convocations ♃ DA020, LI064
Convulsion Fits ☽ LI082, RS021
Convulsions ☽ DA027, RA064
Convulsions ♃ LI246, PA128, RA053, RS019
Convulsions ♌ LI095, RS017
Cony ♀ RA060
Conyza canadensis ♀ CU
Cooks ♀ DA024
Cooks ♂ GA068, LI067, PA013, PT337, RA054
Cooks ♐ LI451
Cool ♄ PT035
Coopers' Places ♎ LI096
Copper ♀ DA023, LI075, RA060
Copper ♂ AB243
Coppersmiths ☉ GA069, LI071
Coral ☿ AB243
Coral ♀ RA060
Coral Tree ♃ LI064, RA053
Coral, White & Red ♀ DA023, LI075
Corduba, Spain ♊ LI094, PA074
Corduba (Spain) ♊ DA007

Coriander ☿ AB243
Coriander ♀ DA024, LI075
Corinth, Greece ♍ DA009, PA074
Cormorant ♂ LI068, RA055
Cornelian (= Carnelian Stone) ♀ DA023, LI075
Corneola (Stone) ♀ RA060
Cornfield ♉ DA007, LI094
Cornfield 4th House LI052
Corporature Large ☉ GA069
Corpulent ☽ GA072
Corpulent ♃ GA067
Corylus avellana ☿ CU, GA071, RA062
Corylus avellana ♃ LI064, RA053
Costmary ♃ CU, GA068
Cotton, Co-ruler of ♀ AB244
Coughs ☉ RS020
Coughs ☽ RA064
Coughs ♋ DA008, PA005
Coughs ☿ DA025, LI247, PA017, PT187
Coughs ♃ PA012
Coughs ♄ DA018
Coughs ♓ DA014
Coughs, Chin ♄ LI246
Coughs, Dry ☿ RS021
Coughs, Rotten ☽ RS021
Coughs, Rotten ♋ LI095, RS017
Couhlearia officinalis ♃ CU, GA068
Council rooms ☿ AB242
Councillors ☿ AB252
Councillors ☿ in 10th House GA060
Counselors ♃ LI063, PA012, RA052
Countenance, Bold ♂ PA012
Countenance, Confident ♂ GA068
Countenance, Fierce ♂ DA021
Counterfeits ☿ PA095
Countesses ☽ GA072, LI081
Counties (Noblemen) 10th House LI055
Counting Friends 2nd House AB276
Courage ♂ LI066
Courageous ♂ LI540, PA093
Courageous ♌ DA009

Courteous ☉ GA069, GA069, PA014
Courtesy ♀ LI556
Courtezans ♀ AB252
Courtiers ☉ DA022, GA069, LI071
Courtiers, Honest ☉ PA014
Courts ☉ RA058
Courts of Justice ♃ DA020, LI064, PA012, RA053
Courts of Princes ☉ DA022, LI072, PA014
Cousins 3rd House LI052
Coveting Unlawful Beds ♀ LI074
Covetous ♄ DA018, GA066, LI058
Covetous ♍ LI538
Covetous ♏ LI538
Cow Parsnip (Heracleum) ☿ GA071
Cow-House ♑ LI098
Cowardice ♃ PT349
Cowards ♀ LI541
Cowards ♂ PA093
Cowherds ♄ LI059, RA050
Cowherds 6th House LI053
Cowslip ♀ CU, GA070
Cowslip ♈ CU
Coxcomb ☿ GA071
Crab ☽ LI082, RA064
Crab ♀ RA060
Crabfish ☉ LI071
Cracking of Pedigree ☉ GA069
Craconi, Poland [=Krakow] ♈ PA073
Crafty ☿ DA025, PA110
Crafty ♄ PA092
Crafty ♌ DA008
Crafty ♎ LI538
Crafty ♐ DA011
Cramps ♃ DA019, LI063, PA128, RA053, RS019
Cramps ☉ DA022, LI071, RA058, RS020
Cramps ♒ PA009, RS018
Cranes ☽ AB247
Cranes ☿ LI079, RA062
Cranes ♄ LI060, RA050
Cranesbill ♂ GA068
Crataegus monogyna ♂ CU, GA068

Creatures, Nocturnal ☿ AB246
Credulous ☿ LI078
Credulous (I.E., Believing) ♃ in 3rd House GA049
Creeping ♋ DA007
Creeping Animals ♄ LI060
Cremisum ♌ PA074
Cremona, Cisalpine Gaul ♌ DA008, LI096, PA074
Crete ☿ PT139
Crete ♍ DA009, PA074, PT139
Crickets ☿ AB247
Criminal Tricks ☿ GA071
Crimisium = Crimisus, Sicily? ♌ DA009
Crimson, Dark ♎ LI086
Cringing Companion ♃ GA067
Crithum maritimum ☿ GA071
Crithum maritimum ♃ CU
Croatia (Illyris) ♍ DA009, LI096
Croatia (Illyris) ♑ PA076
Croatia (Illyris) ♒ LI099
Croceal (Color) ☽ DA026
Crocodile ☉ AB246, LI071, RA058
Crocodile ♄ LI060, RA051
Crocus ☉ in ♌ CU
Crooked ♄ DA018
Crooked ♑ DA012
Crooked ♓ DA014
Crookedness ♂ in 6th House GA053
Crop Abundance ♃ PT183
Crop Yields Good ♀ PT187
Crosses with Servants ♄ in 6th House GA053
Crosswort ♄ CU, GA067
Crow ♀ RA060
Crow ♂ LI068, RA055
Crow ♄ LI060, RA050
Crowfoot ♂ CU, GA068
Crude Phlegm ♄ AB247
Crudities ♄ RS019
Cruel ♂ DA021, LI540, PA093
Cruel ♌ LI538
Cruel ♍ DA009, LI538
Cruel ♑ DA012

Crystals ♃ DA019, LI064, RA053
Crystals ☽ AB243, DA026, LI082, RA064
Cubebs (a Pepper) ☿ DA025, LI079, RA062
Cuckoo ☽ LI082
Cuckoo ♄ LI060, RA050
Cuckoo-Pint ♂ CU, GA068
Cuckoo-Pint ♀ RA060
Cucumber ☽ AB243, CU, RA063
Cucumis sativus ☽ AB243, CU, RA063
Cucurbita pepo ☽ CU, LI082, RA063
Cudgel or Stick (= Bat) ♄ LI060
Cudweed ♀ CU
Cudweed ♄ GA067
Cullen, Scotland ♃ DA020, LI065, RA053
Cuma, Asia Minor ♍ PA074
Cumin ☉ LI273
Cumin ♂ LI273
Cumin ♄ DA018, LI059, RA050
Cunning 9th House LI429
Cunning Animals ☿ LI079
Cure, Method of 11th House S2-43
Curiosity ☿ DA025
Curious ☿ LI077
Curious about Occult Knowledge ☿ GA071
Curriers ♂ PA013, RA054
Curriers ♄ DA017, GA067, RA050
Cuscuta epithymum ♄ CU, GA067
Customs, Changes in ☿ PT187
Cut-throats ♂ PA013, RA054
Cutlers ♂ DA021, GA068, PA109, RA054
Cutlers of Swords ♂ LI067
Cutting Hair ☽ AB254
Cyclades Islands ♉ DA006, PA073
Cyclamen hederifolium ♂ CU
Cydonia oblonga ♄ CU, GA067
Cynoglossum officinale ☿ CU, GA071
Cyperus longus ♂ CU
Cypress ♀ AB244, RA060
Cypress Tree ☿ LI272
Cypress Tree ♄ DA018, LI059
Cyprus ♀ DA024, LI076, RA060

Cyprus ♄ RA050
Cyprus ♉ DA006, LI094, PA073
Cysts (Wens) ♉ RS016
Cytisus scoparius ♂ GA068

-- D --

Daffodil ☉ LI272
Daffodil ♀ CU, LI075, RA060
Daffodil ♂ LI272
Daffodil, White & Yellow ♀ DA024
Daffodil, Yellow ♂ CU
Dairy-House ♍ LI096
Daisy ♃ DA020, LI064, RA053
Daisy ♀ CU, GA070
Daisy ♋ CU
Dalmatia, Yugoslavia ♐ DA011, LI098, PA075
Damage and Loss from Journeys ♄ in 9th House GA058
Damage and Loss from Voyages ♄ in 9th House GA058
Damage by Fire ♂ in 4th House GA050
Damage from Large Animals ♃ in 12th House GA062
Damage from Servants ☿ in 6th House GA053
Damage from Small Animals ♄ in 6th House GA053
Damage to Large Animals ♄ in 12th House GA062
Damascus ♌ DA008, LI096, PA074
Damsels ♀ DA024
Dancers ♀ PA110
Dancing ♀ AB250, PA094
Dancing Schools ♀ DA024, LI075, PA015, RA060
Dandelion ♃ CU, GA068
Danger from Disease ♄ in 7th House GA054
Danger from Falls ♄ in 10th House GA060
Danger from Small Journeys ♂ in 3rd House GA049
Danger in Small Journeys ♄ in 3rd House GA048
Danger of Being Murdered ♂ in 7th House GA055
Danger of Drowning ☽ in 8th House GA057
Danger of Drowning ☉ in 8th House GA057
Danger of Exile ☋ in 10th House GA061
Danger of False Testimonies ☽ in 8th House GA057
Danger of Imprisonment ♂ in 10th House GA060
Danger of Imprisonment ☋ in 10th House GA061

Danger of Loss from Servants ☽ in 12th House GA063
Danger of Loss of Estate ☉ in 7th House GA055
Danger of Loss of Goods ♃ in 8th House GA057
Danger of Loss of Reputation ☉ in 7th House GA055
Danger of Persecution ♂ in 10th House GA060
Danger of Poverty ☋ in 2nd House GA048
Danger of Stabbing ♂ in 7th House GA055
Danger of Violent Death ☽ in 7th House GA055
Danger of Violent Death ☽ in 8th House GA057
Danger of Violent Death ♂ in 8th House GA057
Danger of Violent Death ☽ in 12th House GA063
Danger of Violent Death ♄ in 8th House GA056
Danger of Violent Death ☋ in 8th House GA057
Danger of Violent Falls ♄ in 7th House GA054
Danger to Brothers ♄ in 3rd House GA048
Danger to Native's Life ♄ in 7th House GA054
Danger to Wife & Children ♀ in 8th House GA057
Dangers to Life (but Escape) ☉ in 8th House GA057
Daphne mezereum ♄ CU
Dark ♑ DA012
Dark Black 7th House LI054
Dark Red ♂ AB240
Dark-Skinned ♄ PT305
Darnel ♄ CU, GA067
Date Palms ☉ AB244
Dates ♀ AB243
Datura stramonium ♃ CU
Daucus carota ☿ CU, GA071
Dauphine, France ♎ DA010, PA075
Day-Laborers ♄ GA067, LI059, PA011, RA050
Day-Laborers 6th House LI053
Dead (What Happens to the?) 4th House AB275
Deadly Fears 8th House LI558
Deafness ♄ LI246, PA011, RA051, RS019
Deafness (Surdity) ♑ DA012
Dealing in Colors ♀ AB254
Dealing in Pictures ♀ AB254
Dearness & Cheapness 7th House AB276
Death ♄ AB252, PT181
Death 7th House PT429
Death 8th House LI054, PA045

Death by Natural Causes ♃ in 8th House GA057
Death by Sword or Iron ♂ DA021
Death in Childbed ♃ AB252
Death in Younger Years ☽ in 7th House GA055
Death not Violent ☿ in 8th House GA057
Death not Violent ♀ in 8th House GA057
Death of Children ♄ in 5th House GA051
Death of Contemporaries 7th House AB276
Death of Enemies (in War) 2nd House LI368
Death of Father Before Native ♄ in 4th House GA050
Death of Mother Before Native ♄ in 4th House GA050
Death of Querent When? 8th House GA283, LI409
Death of the Native 8th House GA056
Death of Wives ☋ in 7th House GA056
Death, Feigning 8th House AB275
Death, Its Causes 8th House AB275
Death, Kind of 8th House LI054
Death, Swift ♂ PT183
Death, Violent ♂ PT183
Death (What Succeeds It?) 4th House AB275
Death (What Manner?) 8th House GA284, LI412
Debates ♂ LI556
Debt ♄ PA108
Debt 2nd House LI378
Debt 12th House AB275
Debts from Gambling ♂ in 5th House GA052
Debts from Ill Company ♂ in 5th House GA052
Deceit 6th House AB276
Deceitful ☿ LI541
Deceitful ♄ DA018, LI539, PA108
Deceitful ♊ LI538
Deceitful ♏ DA011
Deceivers ☿ PA095
Deceivers ♂ AB250
Deceivers ♄ PA092
Decent ♀ LI541
Deception by Women ☿ in 6th House GA053
Deception in Matters of Faith ♄ in 3rd House GA048
Decorous ♀ PT357
Deeds 8th House GA056
Deep Color, Mixed Reddish Yellow ☽ AB240

Deeply Interested in Business ☿ AB250
Deer ☉ AB246
Deer ♃ AB246, LI064
Defects of Body 6th House AB275
Defendant in Lawsuit 7th House LI054
Deformity of Saturn Here 1st House PA041
Delicate Child ♀ AB249
Delicious ♃ AB240
Delight 5th House GA051, LI053, PA043
Delight from Women ☊ in 7th House GA055
Delight in Agriculture ☽ in 4th House GA051
Delight in Buildings ☽ in 4th House GA051
Delight in Curious Arts ☿ in 5th House GA052
Delighting in Journeys ☽ DA027
Delights in Civil Recreations ☊ in 5th House GA052
Delights in Peregrinations ☽ in 9th House GA059
Delirium ☿ RS021
Delphinate = Dauphine, France ♎ DA010, PA075
Demons ♄ AB252
Denial 7th House AB276
Denies Marriage ♀ in 8th House GA057
Denmark ☽ DA027, LI083, RA064
Denmark ♈ DA006, LI094, PA073
Dens ♄ DA018, LI060, RA051
Density ☽ AB241
Depilatory ☿ AB243
Deportment Good ☿ LI541
Depraved ♀ PT357
Depraved ♄ PA092
Deprivation of Common Sense ☿ DA025
Deprivation of Honor ☋ in 10th House GA061
Derthona, Italy [= Tortona] ♑ DA012
Descendants 4th House AB275
Descurainia sophia ♄ CU
Deserts ☽ LI082, PA018, RA064
Deserts ♄ DA018, LI060, PA011, RA051
Deserts ♌ DA008, LI095
Deserts Full of Wild Beasts ♄ AB242
Desire to Rule ☉ LI070
Desires to Journey Often ☽ in 5th House GA052
Desires Travel ☿ GA071

Desiring to Benefit Others ♃ LI062
Desirous of Delights ♀ PA110
Desirous of Honors ☉ DA022
Desirous of Peace ☽ GA072
Desirous of Rule ☉ GA069
Desirous of Sovereignty ☉ GA069
Desirous to Benefit Others ♃ GA067
Desolate Roads ♄ AB242
Destroys Riches ♄ in 2nd House GA047
Destruction of Brothers ☋ in 3rd House GA049
Destruction of Dwelling ♄ in 4th House GA050
Destruction of Hopes ♄ in 11th House GA061
Destruction of Kindred ☋ in 3rd House GA049
Destruction of Lands ♄ in 4th House GA050
Destruction of Sisters ☋ in 3rd House GA049
Destructions ♄ RA051
Detriment ☋ LI173
Devil's Bit ♀ GA070
Devil's Milk (Herb) ♂ DA021, LI068, RA054
Devoted to Religion/Good Works ♃ AB250
Devotees ♄ AB252
Devouring(Comestio)Mouth Flesh ☉ DA022
Devout ♃ AB250
Devout ♃ in 3rd House GA049
Dexterity ☿ LI541
Dexterity, Manual ☿ AB254
Diabetes ♀ LI075, RS021
Diambra (Drug) ☿ LI079
Diamond ☉ RA057
Diamond ♃ AB243
Diarrhea ☽ RS021
Diarrhea (Lask) ☽ DA027
Dice ♀ LI556
Dice 5th House LI169
Dictamnus albus ☉ RA057
Dictamnus albus ♀ CU
Dictatorial ♄ PT341
Differences with Parents ☽ in 4th House GA051
Digestion ♋ LI095
Digestion, Poor ♋ LI245
Digestion, Weak ♋ RS017

Digestive Faculty ♃ PA012, S2-46
Diggers of Metals ♄ PA108
Digitalis Purpurea ♀ CU, GA070
Dignified ♃ PT347
Dignities ♃ DA019
Dignity ☉ PA109, PT363
Dignity ☉ in 1st House GA046
Dignity ☽ in 1st House GA046
Dignity 10th House GA059, LI055, PA046
Dill ☿ CU, GA071
Diminution of Substance ♂ in 11th House GA061
Dimpled Chin ♀ PA015
Dimples ♀ DA024
Dining Room 10th House LI202
Dining Room ☉ DA023, LI072, RA058
Dining Room ♀ RA060
Dipsacus fullonium ♀ CU, GA070
Dipsacus pilosus ♂ CU
Dirty Places ♄ LI060
Disagreeable ♄ AB240
Disagreeable Smelling Fruit Trees ♄ AB244
Disaster to Eyes If Ill Luck 2nd House AB275
Discernment, Sharp 9th House AB275
Discord ♂ PA093
Discord ♄ AB250
Discord Among Friends ♄ in 11th House GA061
Discrete ♃ PA012
Discrete ♄ GA066
Discrete ♌ LI538
Discrete ♍ PA006
Discrete Wife ♃ in 7th House GA055
Discretion ☿ LI077
Disdainful ☉ LI070
Disdainful ♃ LI540
Disease 6th House GA053, PA044
Disease 12th House AB275
Disease of the Mind ☉ in 6th House GA053
Disease (Chronic or Acute?) 6th House GA270, LI247
Disease (Curability or not?) 6th House GA053
Disease (Mental or Physical?) 6th House GA269, LI264
Disease (Quality & Cause?) 6th House GA053

Disease (Recover or Die?) 6th House DA112, GA271, LI253
Disease (What is the Cause?) 6th House GA271, LI259, S2-36
Disease (What Part is Affected?) 6th House GA269, LI243
Diseases, Few ♀ in 1st House GA046
Diseases, Few ♌ in 6th House GA054
Diseases, Few but Venereal ♀ in 6th House GA053
Diseases, Hot & Dry ♂ in 6th House GA053
Diseases, Long & Chronic ☉ in 6th House GA053
Diseases, Long & Tedious ☉ in 12th House GA063
Diseases, Many ☽ in 6th House GA054
Diseases, Many ♂ in 12th House GA063
Diseases, Many ♄ in 6th House GA053
Diseases, Many ☋ in 6th House GA054
Diseases of Genitals ♄ in 7th House GA054
Diseases of Many Kinds ☽ AB252
Diseases, Corruption ♊ PA005
Diseases, Defects of Gastric ♍ PA007
Diseases, Dislocations ♊ PA005
Diseases, Ill Digestion ♋ PA005
Diseases, Peracute ☉ PA014
Dishonest ♓ LI538
Dismissal from Office 3rd House AB276
Disobedient Children ♄ in 5th House GA051
Dispersion ♀ AB241
Disputant ☿ GA071, LI077
Disputants in All Sects ☿ AB253
Disputants in Assembly ♂ AB252
Disputation ☿ AB254
Dissembler ♄ in 9th House GA058
Dissembling ♃ LI540
Dissembling ♄ GA067
Dissenters ♂ LI540
Dissipation 6th House AB276
Distant Places 5th House AB276
Distemper of the Gall ♂ PA013
Distempered Fancies ♊ LI094, RS017
Distempers 9th House RS100
Distempers (Mad, Sudden) ♂ LI067
Distempers, Melancholy ♄ PA011
Distribution of Water ♄ AB254
Ditch-Diggers ♄ RA050

Ditchers ♄ LI059
Ditches with Rushes ♋ DA008, LI095
Dittander (Karse) ♀ CU
Dittander (Karse) ♂ DA021, LI068
Dittany ☉ RA057
Dittany (White) ♀ CU
Dittany of Crete ♀ CU
Diurnal ♈ PA004
Diurnal ♊ PA005
Diurnal ♌ PA006
Diurnal ♎ PA007
Diurnal ♐ PA008
Diurnal ♒ PA009
Divedapper (Bird) ☽ RA064
Divination ☿ LI077
Divination ♍ LI451
Divine Law, Strenuous in ☽ AB254
Diviners ☿ DA025, GA071, LI078, RA061
Diviners ♄ in 9th House GA058
Divining Well ☿ LI541
Dock (Common) ♃ CU, GA068
Docks (i.e., Place) ☽ RA064
Doctors of Civil Law ♃ LI063
Documents ☿ PT335
Dodder ☉ AB244
Dodder of Thyme ♄ CU, GA067
Doe ♃ LI064, RA053
Does not Fear God ♂ GA068
Dog ☽ RA064
Dog ☿ RA062
Dog ♀ RA060
Dog ♂ AB246
Dog ♄ LI060, RA051
Dog Hunger* ♄ LI059, RS019
Dog Rose ☽ CU
Dog's Grass ♃ CU, GA068
Dog's Mercury ☿ CU
Dog's Tooth Violet ☽ CU
Dog, Domestic ☿ AB246
Doing Good ♃ AB254
Dolphin ♃ RA053

Dolphin ♀ LI075, RA060
Dolts ☿ LI541
Domelike (Tholous) ♍ LI096
Domestic Animals ♃ AB246
Domestical ♈ DA005
Domestical ♉ PA004
Domestical ♑ DA012
Domineering ☉ GA069, LI070
Doting ☿ DA025, PA130
Double Chin ♀ AB249
Doubt 9th House GA058
Dove's Foot ♂ CU
Dove, Stock ♀ LI075, RA060
Dove, Stock ♃ LI064, RA053
Dove, Turtle ☉ AB247
Doves 6th House LI558
Down or Cotton Thistle ♂ CU, GA068
Downcast Look ♄ AB249, GA066
Dowries ♀ LI556
Dowry 8th House GA056, LI054
Dowry ♀ DA024, PA109
Draba incana ☽ CU
Dragon ♃ LI064
Dragon ♄ RA050
Dragon (Snap?) ♄ LI059
Dragonwort ☿ DA025, LI079, RA062
Draughts ♀ AB250
Dreams 9th House GA058, LI055, PA045
Dreams, Deceitful ☋ in 9th House GA059
Dreams, False or Frivolous ♂ in 9th House GA058
Dreams, Many, According to Sign ☽ in 9th House GA059
Dreams, Pornographic ♀ in 9th House GA058
Dreams, Prophetic ♃ in 9th House GA058
Dreams, Prophetic ☊ in 9th House GA059
Dreams, Interpretation of 9th House AB275
Dress 11th House AB275
Drink 5th House AB276
Drinking ☽ PT321
Drinking ☉ AB245
Drinking Water ☽ AB245
Dropsy (= Edema) ☽ DA026, LI082, RS021

Dropsy (= Edema) ♄ DA018, PA011, RA051
Dropwort ♀ CU
Drosera anglica ♋ CU
Drosera anglica ☉ CU
Druggists ♀ PT337
Drugs ♂ AB245
Drugs Cold & Dry ♄ AB245
Drugs, Evil Effects on Body 8th House AB275
Drunkards ♂ DA020
Drunkards ☽ LI081, PA017
Drunkards ♀ PA094
Drunken ♂ PT353
Drunken ☽ GA072
Dry ♂ PT037
Dry ☿ PT039
Dry ♄ PT035
Dry Cough ☿ LI079, RA062
Dry Good Merchant ♀ RA058
Dryness ♂ AB241
Dryness ☿ PT187
Dryness ♄ AB241
Duchesses ☽ GA072
Ducks ☽ AB247, LI082, RA064
Duckweed (Lemna) ☽ GA072
Duels 7th House PA044
Duels (Adversary's Second) 8th House LI054
Duels (Querent's Second) 2nd House LI051
Duggs ♀ PA129
Dukedoms 10th House LI055
Dukes 10th House LI055, PA046
Dukes ☉ DA022, GA069, LI071, PA109, RA056
Dull ♃ LI063
Dull Capacity ♃ GA067
Dullness of the Market 8th House AB276
Dumb ♋ DA007
Dumb ♓ DA014
Dumbness ☿ LI079, RS021
Dunghills ♑ LI098
Durra ♃ AB243
Dust ♄ DA017, LI060
Dust Color ♃ AB240

Dwelling of the Native 4th House GA050
Dwellings ♄ AB245
Dyers ♂ LI067, PA013, RA054
Dyers of Black Cloth ♄ LI059, RA050
Dyes ♀ PT337
Dysentery (Bloody Flux) ♂ LI540, PA128, RS020
Dysentery (Bloody Flux) ♄ PT327
Dysentery (Bloody Flux) ♎ DA010

-- E --

Eager for Education ♃ AB250
Eager for Knowledge, Power ☉ AB250
Eager for Pleasure ☿ AB250
Eager for Victory ☉ AB250
Eager for Wealth ♃ AB250
Eager to Buy Slaves & Girls ☿ AB250
Eagle ☉ AB247, LI072
Eagle ♀ LI075, RA060
Eagle ♂ LI068
Eagle ♃ LI064, RA053
Ear Diseases 1st House RS100
Ear Noises ♄ RS019
Ear Ringing ♄ RS019
Ear, Left ☿ RA061
Ear, Left ♂ LI246, PA013, RS014
Ear, Left ♃ AB248, DA019
Ear, Left, Diseases ♃ RA053
Ear, Left, Infirmities ♃ RS019
Ear, Right ♄ AB248, DA017, PA011, PA127, RS014
Ear, Right, Noise ♄ LI246
Earls ☉ DA022, GA069, LI071
Earls 10th House LI055, PA046
Ears 1st House LI245, RS015
Ears ♈ DA005, RS015
Ears, Large ♄ GA066, PA010
Ears, Small ♂ AB249
Ears, Thick ☿ AB249
Earth ♄ AB247
Earthquakes ☿ PT187

Earthy ♉ PA004
Easily Frightened ☽ GA072, LI081
Easily Worked Soil ♃ AB241
East ♈ LI093
East ♌ LI095
East ♐ LI097
East 1st House LI364
East Northeast 2nd House LI364
East Southeast 12th House LI364
East Winds ☉ LI072
East Winds ♄ LI060
Easterly ♐ PA008
Eating ☉ AB245
Eaves of Houses ♒ DA013
Ecclesiastical Dignitaries ♃ PA108
Ecclesiastical Honors ☉ in 9th House GA058
Ecclesiastical Honors ♃ in 9th House GA058
Ecclesiastical Men ♃ LI063, RA052
Ecclesiastical Preferments ☉ in 9th House GA058
Ecclesiastical Preferments ♀ in 2nd House GA047
Echium vulgare ☉ CU, GA069
Echium vulgare ♃ RA052
Edema (Dropsy, Hyposarca, Leucophlegmatica) ☽ DA026, LI082, RS021
Edema (Dropsy, Hyposarca, Leucophlegmatica) ♀ RS020
Edema (Dropsy, Hyposarca, Leucophlegmatica) ♄ DA018, PA011, RA051,
    RS019
Edith ☉ LI341
Edmund ☿ LI341
Educated Men ☿ GA071
Education 1st House AB275
Eel ☽ LI082, RA064
Eel ♄ LI060, RA051
Effeminate ♀ PA094, PT357
Egg White ☿ LI272
Egg White ♄ LI272
Eggplant ♂ AB244
Eglantine ♃ CU
Egoistic ♃ AB250
Egypt ☿ DA026, LI080, RA062
Egypt ♄ AB242
Egypt, Higher ♓ DA014, PA076

Egypt, Lower ☿ PT155
Egypt, Lower ♊ PA074, PT155
Egypt, Northern ♓ LI099
Ejection ♎ DA010
Elder ☿ LI079
Elder ♀ CU, GA070
Elder (Dwarf) ♀ CU
Elderly Age ♃ PT447
Eleanor ☽ LI341
Elecampane ☿ CU, GA071
Elegance ☿ AB250
Elegance ♀ PT185
Elegant ♀ LI541
Elegant ♀ in 1st House GA046
Elephant 12th House LI056
Elephant ☽ AB246
Elephant ♃ LI064, RA053
Elephant ♄ LI060, RA051
Elephantiasis ♄ PT327
Elephants' Houses ♄ AB242
Elizabeth ♄ LI341
Ellen ☽ LI341
Elm Tree ♄ CU, GA067
Elm Tree ♌ PA074
Eloquence ☿ LI077
Eloquent ☿ AB250, GA071, PA094
Eloquent ♀ PA094, PT357
Eloquent ♃ AB250
Elymus ♃ CU, GA068
Embassies ☽ PA110
Embroiderers ♀ DA023, GA070, LI074, PA015, RA058
Emerald, Jewel (Smaragde) ☿ RA062
Emerald, Jewel (Smaragde) ♀ AB243, RA060
Emerald, Jewel (Smaragde) ♃ DA019, LI064, RA053
Emerald, Jewel (Smaragde) ☽ AB243
Emerods (= Hemorrhoids) ♏ DA011
Eminence ♃ LI540
Emir and His Conduct in Office 10th House AB276
Emir, Mandate of 2nd House AB276
Empericks ♃ RA052
Emperors ☉ GA069, LI071, PA014, RA056

Empires 10th House LI055, PA046
Employees 6th House LI174
Employees (Just or not?) 6th House GA272, PA067
Empty Places ☉ AB241
Emulous, E.G. Emulating ☿ PT361
End Lean & Weak ♉ DA006
End, Lean & Weak ♌ DA008
End of the Sickness 4th House S2-34
End Strong & Gross ♏ DA011
End-of-the-Matter 4th House GA050, LI052, PA043
Ending, Gross & Strong ♊ DA007
Ending, Weak ♈ DA005
Endive ☽ DA027, LI082, RA063
Endive ☿ LI272
Endive ♃ GA068
Endive ♄ LI272
Endive (Wild Chicory) ♃ CU
Enemies are Clerks ☿ in 12th House GA063
Enemies are Sollicitors ☿ in 12th House GA063
Enemies, Many ☽ in 12th House GA063
Enemies, Many ☊ in 12th House GA063
Enemies' Assistants 8th House PA045
Enemies, Private 12th House GA062, PA047
Enemies, Private (How Identify?) 12th House DA122, GA293, LI460
Enemies, Private (Quality of) 12th House GA293, LI460
Enemies, Public 7th House GA054, PA044
Enemies, Public? 7th House GA278, LI383
Enemies, Secret 12th House LI460
Enemy 6th House AB276
Enemy 11th House AB275
Enemy 12th House AB275
Enemy in War 7th House LI368
Enemy's Death (in War) 2nd House LI368
Engineers ♂ LI629
England ♈ DA005, LI094, PA073
England (Part) ♊ DA007
England, West & Southwest ♊ LI094
Engravers ☿ DA025, PA110
Engravers ♀ RA058
Engrossed in Own Affairs ♄ AB250
Enjoys Novelties ☽ GA072

Enjoys Peregrinations ☽ in 9th House GA059
Enslavement ♂ PT183
Enslaving People by Treachery ♄ AB250
Enslaving People by Violence ♄ AB250
Enticement ♀ PA015
Entrails ☽ RS015
Enula (Plant) ☉ DA022, LI071
Envious ☿ LI541
Envious ♄ DA018, GA066, LI058, PA092
Envy ♄ DA018
Envy 12th House AB276
Epilepsy ☽ DA027, LI082, PA018, PT365, RA064, RS021
Epilepsy ☿ DA025, PT365
Epilepsy ♂ LI246
Epilepsy ♄ RA051
Epilepsy ♈ DA005, LI093, RS016
Epilepsy 1st House RS100
Epilobium angustifolium ♄ CU
Epilobium hirsutum ♄ CU
Epistles 3rd House GA048, LI052
Epithimium (Dodder of Thyme) ♄ GA067
Equisetum arvense ♄ CU, GA067, RA050
Equitable ♃ PA092
Erect Gait & Figure ☽ AB249
Erfurt, Germany ♍ DA009, PA075
Erigeron acer ♂ CU
Ermine ☿ AB246
Ermine ♄ AB246
Erotic ♀ PT357
Erphord = Erfurt, Germany ♍ PA075
Errors in Faith ♄ in 9th House GA058
Errors in Religion ♄ in 9th House GA058
Eruca sativa ♀ CU, GA070
Eryngium maritimum ♀ GA070
Eryngium maritimum ♎ CU
Eryngo ♀ GA070
Eryngo ♎ CU
Erysimum cheiranthoides ♂ CU, GA068
Erysipelas (Streptococcus) ♂ LI246, PA013, PT431
Erythronium dens canis ☽ CU
Escaped 6th House AB276

Estate 2nd House GA047
Estate 4th House LI210
Estate of Dead Persons 8th House PA045
Estate of Deceased 8th House LI054
Ethiopia ♒ DA013
Ethiopia [=Trogloditica[m]] ♀ PT157
Ethiopia [=Trogloditica[m]] ♄ AB242
Ethiopia [=Trogloditica[m]] ♎ DA010, PA075, PT157
Etruria, Italy ♎ PA075
Eunuchs ♄ AB252
Eunuchs, Affairs of 6th House AB276
Euphorbia helioscopia ♂ CU
Euphrasia officinalis ☉ CU, GA069, LI071, RA057
Euphrasia officinalis ♌ CU
Eveweed ♂ CU
Evil Conduct ♂ AB250
Evil Demon 12th House PT275
Evil Faith ☋ in 9th House GA059
Evil from Voluptuous Courses ☋ in 5th House GA052
Evil Oppression by Government ♄ AB254
Evil-Speaker ♄ PT341
Evils from Persons of Renown ☽ in 8th House GA057
Evils from Private Enemies ♄ in 12th House GA062
Evils of Intellect ☿ LI079
Examining the Querent 2nd House AB276
Excel in Inventions ☿ in 5th House GA052
Excellent Spirits ☽ AB250
Excess of the Flowers 5th House RS100
Exchangers of Money ☿ LI078
Exchangers of Money ♀ GA070
Exchequer 11th House LI056, PA046
Excitability ☽ PT361
Excrement ☽ RS197
Excrement Retention ☽ RS021
Execution ♂ AB254
Exercise? (=Breathing) ♍ LI096
Exile ♄ AB250, PT181
Exile ♄ in 12th House GA062
Exile 12th House AB275, LI460
Expenditure 8th House AB275
Expensive ♀ LI074

Expensive ☉ LI070
Expensive Mistresses ♀ in 2nd House GA047
Experience ♄ DA018
Experience in Occult Matters ☿ in 9th House GA059
Experienced ☿ PT359
Expertness in Religious Law 3rd House AB275
Exphord = Erfurt, Germany ♍ DA009
Expulsion ☽ RS192
Explusion ♃ PA128
Extreme Cold & Dryness ♄ AB231
Extreme Heat & Dryness ♂ AB231
Exulcerations ♂ RS020
Eye Damage Likely ☋ in 1st House GA046
Eye Defects ♂ in 8th House GA057
Eye Disease ☽ PA018
Eye Disease ☉ DA022, LI071, PA129, RA058
Eye Fluxes ☉ DA022
Eye, Full ♀ DA023
Eye, Full with Sharp Sight ☉ PA014
Eye Hurts ☽ RS021
Eye Impediments ♏ DA011
Eye Impediments (15-18° ♐) DA011
Eye Infirmities ☉ RS020
Eye Inflammation ☉ PA014
Eye, Left ☽ AB248
Eye, Left (Men) ☽ DA026, LI247, PA018, RS015
Eye, Left (Women) ☉ DA022, LI247, PA014, RA057
Eye, Left, Diseases (Men) ☽ RA064
Eye Pains 1st House RS100
Eye, Piercing & Sharp ♂ GA068
Eye Problems 1st House RS100
Eye Rheums ☽ RS021
Eye, Right ☉ AB248, PA129, RS014
Eye, Right (Men) ☉ DA022, LI247, PA014, RA057
Eye, Right (Women) ☽ DA026, LI247, PA018, RS015
Eye, Right, Diseases (Women) ☽ RA064
Eye, Sharp ♂ PA012
Eyebright (Plant) ☉ CU, DA023, GA069, LI071, RA057
Eyebright (Plant) ♌ CU
Eyebrows ♈ RS015
Eyebrows 1st House RS015

Eyebrows, Black ♈ DA006
Eyebrows, Joined ☽ AB249
Eyebrows, Joined ☿ AB249
Eyebrows, Joined ♄ AB249
Eyebrows, Little ♀ DA023
Eyebrows, Lowering ♄ GA066, PA010
Eyes ♈ DA005, RS015
Eyes 1st House LI245, RS015
Eyes, Big ♌ PA006
Eyes, Black ♀ PA015
Eyes, Black or Grey ☿ DA025
Eyes, Blood-Shot ☉ RS020
Eyes, Bright & Piercing ♊ DA007
Eyes, Comely & Gray ♃ GA067
Eyes, Fair ☿ GA071, PA016
Eyes, Fine, Large Iris ♀ AB249
Eyes, Full ♉ PA004
Eyes, Full, Dark, Hazel or Black ♀ GA070
Eyes, Grey ☽ GA072, PA017
Eyes, Great Goggled ☉ GA069
Eyes, Hazel ♂ GA068
Eyes, Large ♃ AB249
Eyes, Large ♌ DA008
Eyes, Large ♍ DA009
Eyes, Large & Grey ♃ PA012
Eyes, Little ♄ GA066, PA010
Eyes, Redness ☉ RS020
Eyes, Secretions ☉ LI247
Eyes, Sharp Grey ♂ AB249
Eyes, Sharp & Piercing ☉ GA069
Eyes, Small ♂ AB249
Eyes, Small ♄ AB249, DA018
Eyes, Sore ♌ LI095, RS017
Eyes, Sparkling or Sharp ♂ DA021
Eyes, Uneven Size ☽ GA072
Eyesight ☉ DA022, LI247, PT319

-- F --

Face ♈ DA005, RS015
Face 1st House LI050, RS015

Face Wheals ♈ DA005
Face Wounds ♂ LI246
Face, a Little Swarthy ♊ PA005
Face, Big ♉ PA004
Face, Broad ♏ PA008
Face, Evil ♐ DA012
Face, Fair ♒ DA013
Face, Fine and Round ♀ AB249
Face, Full ♃ DA019
Face, Full-Faced ☽ DA026
Face, Good & Large ♓ DA014
Face, Goodly & Fair Round ♀ DA023
Face, Handsome ♋ PA005
Face, Large ☉ PA014
Face, Large ♓ PA009
Face, Lean ♄ DA018
Face, Long ☿ DA025
Face, Long ♈ DA006
Face, More Oval Than Round ♍ PA006
Face, Oval ♃ PA012
Face, Oval ♈ PA004
Face, Oval & Clear ♒ PA009
Face, Puffy ♈ DA005
Face, Round ☽ AB249, DA026, GA072
Face, Round ☉ DA022
Face, Round ♀ PA015
Face, Round ♂ PA012
Face, Round ♃ AB249
Face, Round ♋ DA008, PA005
Face, Round ♎ DA010
Face, Round & Pale ☽ PA017
Face, Sour ♄ AB249
Face, Thin & Lean ♑ DA012
Face, Unpleasant ♄ DA018
Face, Well-Favored ♎ DA010
Faculty of Reflection ☿ AB245
Faenza, Italy [= Faventia] ♑ DA012
Failure 9th House AB276
Failure in Business ♄ AB250
Faint-Hearted ☽ DA026
Fainting ☉ DA022, LI247

Fair ☉ DA022
Fair ♊ DA007
Fair ♍ DA009
Fair ♎ DA010
Fair ♒ DA013
Fair in Dealings ♃ GA067
Fair Lodgings ♀ LI075
Fair Stature ☽ LI081
Fair Stature ♀ LI074
Fair Yellow or Bright Flaxen ☉ GA069
Fair-Spoken ♀ PA094
Fairness Mean ♑ DA012
Fairs ☿ LI079
Fairs (Commerce) ☿ DA026
Faithful ☉ LI070
Faithful ♃ DA019, GA067, GA067, LI062
Faithless ♀ LI074
Falcon ☉ AB247
Falcon ☿ AB247
Falling from Heights ♂ DA021
Fallow Ground ♑ LI098
Falls from Animals ♐ DA011
Falls from Horses ♐ LI097, RS018
Falls from Horses & the Like ♐ PA008
False ☿ LI077, PA095
False Pregnancy 5th House RS100
False Testimony ♂ AB250
Falsehearted ♀ PA094
Falsifying ☿ AB250
Fame ♀ PT185
Fame ♃ PT183
Family Noble & Long-Lived ♌ in 4th House GA051
Famous ☉ PA109
Famous Magistrateship ☉ DA022
Fancy ☿ LI247
Fancy Sharp & Subtle ☿ GA071
Fancy, Ingenious ♊ PA005
Fantasies ♄ LI059
Fantasy ☿ DA025, RS015
Far-Sightedness ☿ AB250
Farmers 6th House LI053

Farmers ♂ PT337
Farmers ♑ LI451
Farming ♄ AB254
Farming Profit ♄ LI555
Farms 4th House LI202
Fars ♃ AB242
Fastidious ♀ PT357
Fat ♓ DA014
Fat ☉ AB247, LI273
Fat ☽ GA072
Fat ☽ in 1st House GA046
Fat ♀ AB240
Fat ♂ LI273
Fate 9th House AB275
Father 4th House GA050
Father Honorable ♃ in 4th House GA050
Father's Accumulated Wealth 5th House AB275
Father's Brothers & Sisters 6th House PA044
Father's Burial, What Said 5th House AB275
Father's Condition 4th House GA050
Father's Death Hastened ♂ in 4th House GA050
Father's Estate If Inherit? 4th House GA262, LI210
Father's Substance 5th House GA051
Fathers 4th House LI052, PA043
Fathers ♄ AB249, DA017, GA067, LI059, PA011, PT241, RA050
Fathers ☉ AB249, PT241
Fatigue ♃ AB252
Fatness ♀ DA023, RS014
Faventia, Italy [= Faenza] ♑ DA012
Faverel (Wooly) ☽ CU
Favors from Great Personages ☊ in 1st House GA046
Favors from Magistrates ♃ in 11th House GA061
Favors from Princes ♀ in 10th House GA060
Fear 8th House LI054, PA045
Fear 9th House GA058
Fear 12th House AB275
Fear ♄ PT181
Fear ♄ in 12th House GA062
Fear of Poverty ☋ in 2nd House GA048
Fearful ☽ DA026
Fearful ♀ LI541, PA094

Fearful ♃ LI540, PA093
Fearful ♄ AB250, DA018, PA092
Fearful of Enemies ☿ AB250
Fearing Nothing ♂ PA012
Fearless ♂ GA068, LI540, PA093
Fearless ♐ LI538
Fears God ♀ in 9th House GA058
Feasts ♀ AB254
Feasts 5th House AB276
Feasts, Marriage 7th House AB275
Feathers ♄ AB247
Feedlot ♈ LI093
Feet 12th House AB277, GA062, LI056, PA047, RS015
Feet ☿ PA017, RS015
Feet ♓ DA014, LI099, RS015
Feet, Big ♄ AB249
Feet, Long ♊ DA007
Feet, Long, Well Shaped ☿ AB249
Feet, Swelling ♓ LI246
Feigned Courtesy ♃ PA093
Feigning Death 8th House AB275
Fellowship ♀ PA109
Fel[d]kirth, Austria ♎ DA010
Feminine ♉ PA004
Feminine ♋ PA005
Feminine ♍ PA006
Feminine ♏ PA007
Feminine ♑ PA008
Feminine ♓ PA009
Fennel ☿ GA071
Fennel ☿ in ♍ CU
Fenugreek ☉ LI272
Fenugreek ☿ CU
Fenugreek ♀ AB243
Fenugreek ♂ LI272
Fern ☿ GA071
Fern ♄ LI059, RA050
Fern (Brake or Bracken) ☿ CU
Fern (Royal) ♄ CU, GA067
Ferrara ♈ DA006, LI094, PA073
Ferraria, Spain ♂ DA021, LI068

Fertility ♀ PT187
Fertilizing Winds ♃ PT037
Fervence (City)* ♑ PA076
Fervent Faith ☉ in 9th House GA058
Fesse, Morocco [=Fez] ♏ PA075
Fetters 3rd House AB276
Feverfew ☉ CU
Feverfew ♀ CU, GA070
Feverfew ♃ DA020, RA053
Fevers ♂ AB252, PT429, RA055
Fevers ♃ AB252, LI063
Fevers of the Blood ♈ DA005
Fevers of the Blood ♌ DA008
Fevers, Burning ♂ LI246
Fevers, Burning ♌ PA006
Fevers, Chronic ♃ RS019
Fevers, Continuous (Synochus) ♃ RS019
Fevers, Hot ♐ DA011
Fevers, Intermittant ♂ LI067, PT183
Fevers, Pestilential ♂ RS020
Fevers, Pestilential ♌ DA008
Fevers, Pestilential ♐ LI097, RS018
Fevers, Putrid ♂ PA128
Fevers, Recurring ☿ PT187
Fevers, Recurring ♂ LI579
Fevers, Recurring (Quotidian) ☽ RS021
Fevers, Rotten ☉ RS020
Fevers, Sharp ♂ DA020, PA013
Fevers, Tropical ♂ LI246
Fevers, Violent ♌ LI095
Fevers, Violent Burning ♌ RS017
Feversend (Herb) ♃ LI064
Few Diseases ♃ in 6th House GA053
Few Enemies ☊ in 7th House GA055
Fez ♏ LI097
Fez, Morocco [Fesse] ♏ PA075
Ficedula (Becafico Bird) ♀ LI075
Fickle ☽ PA017
Fickle ☿ PT361
Ficus garica ♀ RA060
Ficus garica ♃ AB244, CU, LI064, RA053

Fiddlers ♀ LI074, PA015, RA058
Field ☽ DA027
Field-Vine ☿ LI272
Field-Vine ♄ LI272
Fields 4th House AB275, LI052
Fields ☽ LI082, PA018, RA064
Fierce ♂ LI540
Fierce (Breme) ♒ LI099, PA076
Fiery ♐ PA008
Fig ♀ DA024
Fig ♃ RA053
Fig Tree ♀ RA060
Fig Tree ♃ AB244, CU, LI064
Figs ♀ AB243, LI075
Figs, Dry ☉ LI273
Figs, Dry ♂ LI273
Figure, Fine ☿ AB249
Figure, Fine ♃ AB249
Figwort ♀ CU, GA070
Filanginella uliginosa ♀ CU
Filanginella uliginosa ♄ GA067
Filbert Tree ☿ DA025, LI079, RA062
Filipendula ♀ GA070
Filipendula ulmaria ♃ CU
Filipendula vulgaris ♀ CU
Fines 12th House AB275
Finger Swelling ☿ RS021
Finger, Fore- ♃ RS014
Finger, Little ☿ RS015
Finger, Middle ♄ RS014
Finger, Ring ☉ RS014
Finger-Fern ♄ LI059
Fingers 3rd House LI052, RS015
Fingers ☿ DA025, LI247, PA130
Fingers ♊ RS015
Fingers & Hands ♀ AB248
Fingers, Long ☿ GA071
Fingers, Long ♂ AB249
Fingers, Short ♀ AB249
Fingers, Short ♄ AB249
Fir Tree ♃ CU

Fire from the Heart Thru Body ♐ AB230
Fireplaces ♂ AB242
Fireplaces ♌ LI095
Fires ♂ PT185
Fires in Minerals & Plants ♌ AB230
Fires in Ordinary Use ♈ AB230
Firestone ☿ DA025
Firewood ♂ AB242
Firmness ☽ PT361
Fish, Hurtful ♂ RA055
Fish, Large ☉ AB246
Fish-Mongers ☽ LI081
Fishermen ☽ GA072, LI081, PA110
Fishers ☽ DA026
Fisherwomen ☽ LI081
Fishponds ☽ DA027, LI082, PA018, RA064
Fishponds ♓ DA014, LI099
Fistulas ☉ DA022
Fistulas ♀ PT431
Fistulas ♂ DA021, LI067, LI246, PA013, PT327, RA055, RS020
Fistulas ♄ RA051
Fistulas ♄ in 7th House GA054
Fistulas ♏ DA011, LI097, PA008, RS018
Fistulas ♐ DA011, LI246, PA008, RS018
Five-Leaved Grass ☿ RA062
Flag (Yellow) ☽ CU
Flanders ☿ DA026, LI080, RA062
Flanders ☽ DA027, LI083, RA064
Flanders ♊ DA007, LI094, PA073
Flank ☿ RS182
Flank 7th House LI245
Flatulence (Guts, Croaking) ♍ RS017
Flax ☿ CU, LI272
Flax ☽ AB244
Flax ♃ DA020, LI064, RA052
Flax ♄ LI272
Flaxweed ♂ CU, GA068
Flaxweed ♄ GA067
Fleabane (Canadian) ♀ CU
Fleabane (Small) ♀ CU
Fleas ♄ AB246

Fleawort ☿ LI272
Fleawort ♄ GA067, LI272
Flesh ♀ PT321, RS014
Fleur-de-Lys (Garden/Blue) ☽ CU
Flies ♄ AB247
Flirts ♀ LI541
Flixweed ♄ CU
Florence ♈ DA006, LI094, PA073
Flower-de-Luce ☽ GA072
Flowers ♀ AB236
Fluellein ☽ CU, GA072
Flux ♄ RS019
Flux of the Stomach ♀ PA129
Flux, Bloody (Dysentery) ♂ LI540, PA128, RS020
Flux, Bloody (Dysentery) ♄ PT327
Flux, Bloody (Dysentery) ♎ DA010
Fluxes of the Belly ☽ LI082
Fluxes of the Rheums ♉ DA006
Fly Cantharis ☉ LI072
Fly Cantharis ♂ DA021, LI068
Foeniculum vulgare ☿ GA071
Foeniculum vulgare ☿ in ♍ CU
Folly 8th House AB276
Fond of Bazaars ♀ AB254
Fond of Commerce ♀ AB254
Fond of Discussion ♃ PT347
Fond of Ornaments ♀ AB250
Fond of Wine ♀ AB250
Food 5th House AB276
Food 11th House AB276
Food, Selling ☽ AB254
Foods ☉ AB245
Foods, Dryer Than Cold ☿ AB245
Foods, Equally Cold & Moist ☽ AB245
Foods, Pleasant to Taste ♀ AB245
Foolish ☉ LI070
Fools ☿ PA095
Foot (Sot) ☽ LI081
Foot Botches ♓ RS018
Foot Breaking Out ♓ RS018
Foot Disease ♓ LI099, RS018

Foot Itch ♓ RS018
Foot Scabs ♓ RS018
Foot-Gout ♄ LI059
Foot-Races ☿ PA248
Footaches ♓ RS018
Footmen ☿ GA071, LI078, PA016, RA061
Forehead, Broad ☉ PA014
Forehead, Broad ♄ PA010
Forehead, Broad ♄ GA066
Forehead, Broad & High ☉ GA069
Forehead, High ☿ GA071
Forehead, High & Large ♃ GA067
Forehead, Fine ♂ AB249
Forehead, High ☿ DA025, PA016
Forehead, High ♉ DA006
Forehead, High & Large ♃ PA012
Forehead, Large ♉ PA004
Forehead, Narrow ☿ AB249
Foreign Affairs 7th House LI558
Foreign Countries 9th House LI055
Foreign Travel 7th House AB276
Foreigner's Child 11th House AB276
Forests ♌ DA008, DA008, LI095
Forgers ☿ PA095
Forges ♂ LI068
Forgetful ☽ AB250
Forgetful ☿ PT361
Forgetfulness ☽ RS198
Forkfish ☿ LI079, RA062
Forkfish ♂ LI068, RA055
Form 1st House LI050
Fortitude ☉ LI556
Fortresses 3rd House AB276
Forts ♌ LI095
Fortunate Brothers ♃ in 3rd House GA049
Fortunate in Father's Kindred ☊ in 6th House GA054
Fortunate in Hopes ⊗ in 11th House GA062
Fortunate in Large Animals ☊ in 12th House GA063
Fortunate in Small Journeys ☿ in 3rd House GA049
Fortunate Journeys ☊ in 3rd House GA049
Fortunate Kindred ♃ in 3rd House GA049

Fortunate Kindred ♌ in 3rd House GA049
Fortunate Small Journeys ♃ in 3rd House GA049
Fortune 2nd House GA047
Fortune ⊗ in 10th House GA061
Fortune, Admirable ♃ in 2nd House GA047
Fortune, Damaged ☋ in 2nd House GA048
Fortune from Princes ♃ in 4th House GA050
Fortune from Small Animals ♃ in 6th House GA053
Fortune Grows ♌ in 10th House GA061
Fortune in Large Animals ♄ in 12th House GA062
Fortune Increased from Mother ♀ in 10th House GA060
Fortune Tellers ☿ AB254
Fortune, Greater ♃ PA011
Foul ♓ DA014
Fountains ☽ DA027, LI082, PA018, RA064
Fountains ♀ DA024, LI075, RA060
Fowl, Domestic ♃ AB247
Fox ☿ AB246, LI079, RA062
Fox ♂ LI068
Foxfish ☿ RA062
Foxglove ♀ CU, GA070
Fracture of Knees ♑ RS018
Fragaria vesca ♀ CU, GA070
Fragaria vesca ♃ LI064, RA052
Fragrant Herbs ♀ AB244
Frame, Big Boned ♈ PA004
France ☉ PT135
France ♂ PT135
France ♈ DA005, LI094, PA073, PT135
France ♌ PT135
France, Southwest ♍ LI096
Francolin (Partridge) ♃ AB247
Franconia ♉ DA006, PA073
Frangula alnus ♀ CU
Frangula alnus ♋ CU
Frank Look ♃ AB249
Frankfurt ♎ LI097
Frankfurt am Main ♎ DA010, PA075
Frankfurt Upon Oder ♏ DA011, LI097, PA075
Frankincense ♂ LI273
Frankincense ☉ DA023, LI071, LI273, RA057

Frankincense ♀ RA060
Frankness ☽ PT361
Fraud 12th House AB276
Fraud ♄ AB250
Fraudulent ♓ LI538
Fraudulent Transactions ♄ AB254
Fraxinus excelsior ☉ CU, GA069, LI071, RA057
Fraxinus excelsior ♀ RA060
Fraxinus excelsior ♃ LI064, RA053
Freestone (Fruit) ♃ DA019, LI064, RA053
Freiburg, Germany ♎ DA010
Freising, Germany [= Frisinga] ♎ PA075
Frejus, France [= Forum Julium] ♏ DA011, LI097, PA075
French Wheat ♀ LI075
Frenetic ☿ LI077
Frenetic ☿ in 9th House GA059
Frenzies ☽ RA064
Frenzies ♂ RA055, RS020
Frenzy ☿ PA130, RA062
Fribourg ♎ LI097
Friday ♀ AB241, LI076
Friday Night ☽ AB241
Friend of Good Government ♃ AB250
Friend's Falseness 11th House LI056
Friend's Fidelity 11th House LI056
Friendliness ♃ AB250
Friendliness ♀ AB250
Friendly ♂ AB250
Friendly ☉ AB250
Friends 3rd House AB275
Friends 5th House AB275
Friends 11th House AB275, LI056, PA046
Friends, Agreement 11th House LI459
Friends Become Enemies ♂ in 7th House GA055
Friends, Counting of 2nd House AB276
Friends, Faithful ♀ in 11th House GA062
Friends, Faithful & Honest ♃ in 11th House GA061
Friends, False ♂ in 11th House GA061
Friends, Ingenious & Prudent ♀ in 11th House GA062
Friends, Many ☽ in 11th House GA062
Friends, Many in Younger Years ♀ in 11th House GA062

Friends of Native 11th House GA061
Friends, Sickness of 8th House AB276
Friends (Quality of?) 11th House GA291, LI459
Friendship 11th House AB275, LI056, PA046
Friendship between Neighbors 7th House LI370
Friendship with Princes ♌ in 11th House GA062
Friendship (Is Offer Real?) 11th House DA123
Friesing, Germany [= Frisinge] ♎ DA010
Frisinga = Freising, Germany ♎ PA075
Frisinge = Freising, Germany ♎ DA010
Frivolous ☿ AB250
Frogs ☽ LI082, RA064
Fruit of a Tree ♃ AB236
Fruit with Rough Skin ♂ AB244
Fruitful Signs ♉ DA006
Fruitful Signs ♋ LI089
Fruitful Signs ♏ DA011, LI089
Fruitful Signs ♓ DA014, LI089
Fruits ♃ AB245
Fruits of the Earth ♄ PA108
Fugitives 7th House LI054, PA044
Fugitives 12th House AB276
Fugitives (Found or not?) 7th House GA279, LI319
Fugitives (Where? What Distance?) 7th House GA280, LI323
Full Manhood ☉ AB248
Fumaria officinalis ☿ RA062
Fumaria officinalis ♃ LI064, RA052
Fumaria officinalis ♄ CU, GA067, LI059, RA050
Fumitory ☿ RA062
Fumitory ♃ DA020, LI064, RA052
Fumitory ♄ CU, DA018, GA067, LI059, RA050
Furious ♂ LI066
Furious ♉ PA004
Furnaces ♂ DA021, LI068, PA013, RA055
Fursbush = Furze = Gorse ♂ GA068

-- G --

Gain 2nd House PA042
Gain ⊗ in 1st House GA046
Gain from Arts & Sciences ☿ in 2nd House GA047

Gain from Business ⊗ in 2nd House GA048
Gain from Church Affairs ⊗ in 9th House GA059
Gain from Clerkship ☿ in 2nd House GA047
Gain from Embassies ☿ in 2nd House GA047
Gain from Employment ⊗ in 2nd House GA048
Gain from Father's Kin ♃ in 6th House GA053
Gain from Friends ⊗ in 2nd House GA048
Gain from Inheritance ♃ in 8th House GA057
Gain from Lands, Inheritances ♌ in 4th House GA051
Gain from People Dealt with ♀ in 7th House GA055
Gain from Public Employment ♌ in 5th House GA052
Gain from Servants ⊗ in 6th House GA054
Gain from Small Animals ☽ in 6th House GA054
Gain from Small Animals ⊗ in 6th House GA054
Gain from the Dead ♀ in 8th House GA057
Gain from Writing ☿ in 2nd House GA047
Gains Estate from Wife ♃ in 7th House GA055
Gains Riches ☽ in 1st House GA046
Galangal (Ginger Family) ♂ LI273
Galangal (Ginger Family) ☉ LI273
Galatia ♓ PA076
Galatia, Asia Minor ♓ DA014
Galega officinalis ☿ in ♌ CU
Galingale ♂ CU
Galium aparine ☽ CU
Galium aparine ♄ GA067
Galium cruciata ♄ CU, GA067
Galium odoratum ♂ CU
Galium verum ♀ CU, GA070
Gall 5th House RS015
Gall 6th House RS015
Gall ☿ DA025, RS015
Gall ♂ DA020, LI067, LI246, PA013, RA054, RS014
Gall ♌ RS015
Gall ♍ RS015
Gall Bladder ☿ AB247
Gall Bladder ♂ AB248
Gall Overflow ♂ RA055
Gall Stoppage ☿ DA025
Gall-Oak ♄ CU
Gall-Stones (?) ♎ LI246

Gallia ♌ DA008
Gallia ♍ DA009
Gallia comata (Part) ♍ PA074
Gallia togata ♌ PA074
Gambling (Win or Lose?) 5th House GA267
Games ♀ AB254
Gamesters (Synonym Prostitute) ♀ LI074, RA058
Gamesters (Synonym Prostitute) ♂ LI067, RA054
Gamesters (Synonym Prostitute) ♓ LI451
Gaming 5th House GA051
Gaming ♀ AB254, LI556
Garamantes, Africa ♓ DA014, PA076
Garbage (Rubbish) ♄ DA017, LI060
Garbage (Rubbish Heaps) 8th House AB276
Gardeners ♄ GA067, LI059, RA050
Gardening ♉ LI451
Gardens ♀ DA024, LI075, RA060
Gardens ♃ PA012, RA053
Gardens ♏ DA011, LI097
Gardens 4th House LI052
Gardens, Fine ♀ PA015
Garlic ☉ LI273
Garlic ♂ AB244, CU, DA021, GA068, LI068, RA054
Garrets ♎ LI096
Gas (Bowels) ☿ RS021
Gas (Intestinal) ♍ DA009
Gascovia (Basque Region) ♐ DA012
Gaunt ♏ LI097
Gaunt at Somme (France) ♏ DA011
Gaunt at Somme (France) ♑ DA012
Gazelle ☉ AB246
Gedrosia, Persia ♑ DA012
Geese ☽ LI082
Geese 6th House LI558
Gem, Precious 12th House AB276
Gender of Unborn Child 5th House LI053
Generals ☉ AB252
Generals ♂ DA020, GA068, PA013
Generals of Armies ♂ LI067, RA054
Generosity ♀ AB250
Generosity ♌ DA009

Generous ♂ LI540
Generous ♃ AB250, GA067, PT347
Generous in Distributing Food ☽ AB250
Generous Things ☉ AB241
Genital Diseases ♀ DA023
Genital Diseases ☽ RA064, RS021
Genital Diseases ♄ in 7th House GA054
Genital Diseases ♏ PA008, RS018
Genital Stones ♂ LI246
Genital Stones ♏ LI097, RS018
Genitals ☽ LI082
Genitals ♀ AB248, DA023, LI247, PA129, RS014
Genitals ♂ LI246, PA128, PT319
Genitals ♏ DA010, LI097, RS015
Genitals 7th House LI245
Genitals 8th House GA056, LI054, PA045, RS015, RS097
Genitals, Diseases of Men's ♂ LI067
Genitals, Women's ☽ DA026
Genoa ♋ DA008, LI095, PA074
Gentian (Autumn) ♂ CU
Gentianella amarella ♂ CU
Gentile ♀ PA110
Gentle ♀ DA023
Gentlemen ☉ GA069, LI071, RA056
Gentlemen ♃ LI555
Gentlemen of Quality ☉ PA014
Gentleness ☿ AB250
Geographical Desirability 1st House GA242, LI132
Geometers ☿ LI541, PA094
Geometricians ☿ AB254
Geometry ☽ AB254
George ♄ LI341
Geranium ♂ GA068
Geranium molle ♂ CU
Geranium robertianum ♀ CU, GA070
Germander ☿ GA071
Germander ♂ CU
Germany ♂ PT135
Germany ♈ DA005, LI094, PA073, PT135
Gethulia ♏ PA075
Geum urbanum ☽ DA026, GA072, RA063

Geum urbanum ♃ CU
Ghent ♌ PA074
Ghouls ♄ AB252
Giddiness ☽ LI248
Giddiness ☉ RA058
Giddiness ☿ LI078, RS021
Giffon ♂ LI068
Gifted ☿ PT361
Gifts 5th House LI558
Gifts & Legacies from the Dead ☊ in 8th House GA057
Gifts from Friends ♀ DA024
Gifts from Rulers ♃ PT183
Gifts from Women ♀ DA024
Gifts Given by Princes ☉ in 3rd House GA049
Gifts of Friends ♀ PA109
Gilliflowers ♃ LI064, RA052
Ginger ☉ DA022, LI071, RA057
Ginger ♂ DA021, LI068, RA054
Ginger (Asarum) ♂ LI068
Giraffe ☽ AB246
Given to All Manner of Learning ♍ PA006
Given to Evil Company ♀ PA094
Given to Excessive Venery (i.e., sex) ♀ AB250
Given to Vain Pleasures ♀ in 1st House GA046
Gives Good Advice ☿ LI541
Giving in Marriage 7th House AB275
Gladiole (Water) ♄ CU
Gladwin ♄ CU
Gladwin, Stinking ♄ GA067
Glass ♂ LI216
Glass Maker ♌ LI451
Glaucoma ♄ PT321
Glechoma hederacea ♀ CU, GA070
Glittering ♃ AB240
Gloomy ♄ PT341
Glory ♃ LI062
Glory ☉ in 10th House GA060
Glovers ♀ GA070, LI074, RA058
Glow-Worms ☉ LI071
Glycyrrhiza glabra ☿ CU, GA071
Glycyrrhiza glabra ♃ RA053

Gnats ♂ LI068
Gnats ♄ LI060
Goat ☽ RA064
Goat ♀ RA060
Goat's Beard ♃ CU
Goat's Thorn ♂ CU
Goats ☉ LI071
Goats ♀ LI075
Goats ♂ LI068
Goats ♄ AB246
Goats 6th House LI053, PA044
Goats, Mountain ☉ AB246
God 9th House PT273
God-Fearing ♃ PT347
Godliness ♃ LI062
Godly ♃ DA019
Gold ☉ DA022, LI071
Gold ♀ AB250
Gold & that Coined for Kings ☉ AB243
Gold Brocades, Receiving ☉ AB254
Gold Brocades, Selling ☉ AB254
Gold Household Vessels ♀ AB243
Golden Herb ♄ LI059
Goldenrod ♀ CU, GA070
Goldsmiths ☉ GA069, LI071, PA014, RA056
Goldsmiths Work ♀ AB254
Goldsmiths Work ♃ AB254
Gonorrhea ♀ DA024, LI075, PA015, RA061, RS020
Gonorrhea ♏ LI097, RS018
Gonorrhea 10th House RS100
Good ♀ LI541, PT357
Good Carriage ☿ LI541
Good Contracts ⊗ in 7th House GA056
Good Demon 11th House PT273
Good Disposition ♀ AB250
Good Disposition ♃ AB250
Good from Kindred ☽ in 6th House GA054
Good from Relgious Kindred ☽ in 3rd House GA049
Good from Servants ☽ in 6th House GA054
Good from Women ♌ in 7th House GA055
Good Government ♃ AB254

Good Journeys ☉ in 3rd House GA049
Good Journeys with Kin ☽ in 3rd House GA049
Good Judgment ☉ LI070
Good Manners ♀ in 1st House GA046
Good Marriages ⊗ in 7th House GA056
Good Memory for Stories ☿ AB250
Good Nose ☿ AB249
Good Nose ♂ AB249
Good Understanding ☿ in 4th House GA050
Good-for-Nothing ☿ LI541
Good-Hearted ☽ AB250
Good-Natured ♀ AB250
Goods, Moveable 2nd House GA047
Goods of Deceased Persons 8th House GA056
Goods of Father 4th House LI210
Goose ☽ RA064
Gooseberry ♀ CU
Gooseberry ♃ LI064, RA053
Goosegrass (Cleavers) ♄ GA067
Gorlick ♋ DA008, PA074
Gorse ♂ GA068
Gosshawk ☉ LI072
Gossip ☿ LI077
Goth[o]land [= Gotland, Sweden] ♂ DA021, LI068
Gotland, Sweden [= Goth[o]land] ♂ DA021, LI068
Gourds ☽ DA026, LI082, RA063
Gout ♄ AB252, LI246, RA051, RS019
Gout ♒ PA009
Gout ♓ DA014, LI099, PA010
Gout, Foot ☽ RS021
Gout, Foot ☿ LI079, RA062, RS021
Gout, Foot ♄ DA018
Gout, Foot 7th House RS100
Gout, Hand ☿ LI079, RA062, RS021
Gout, Hand ♄ DA018, LI059, RS019
Gout, Wrists ☽ RS021
Gout, Wrists & Feet ☽ LI082
Gouts, Hot ♂ RS020
Goutweed ♄ CU, GA067
Government ☉ LI556
Government Abilities ♂ LI540

Government Employment 10th House LI175
Government with Council Nobles 10th House AB275
Governors ♃ LI540
Gracia, Spain ☿ RA062
Grain Fields ♍ LI096
Grains ☿ AB245
Grammarians ☿ LI078
Granada ♋ DA007, PA074
Granaries ♍ LI096
Grandchildren ♃ AB249
Grandfathers ♄ AB249, DA017, GA067, LI059, PA011, RA050
Grandparents 4th House AB275
Grapes ♀ AB243, GA070
Grass ☽ AB244
Grasshopper ♄ LI060
Gratiola officinalis ♂ CU
Grave ☉ GA069
Grave ♃ DA019, PA012
Grave ♄ GA066, PA092
Grave (Manner) ♌ LI538
Grave (Manner) ♄ AB250, LI058
Grave Digging ♄ AB254
Grave in Moderation ♃ LI540
Grave-Robbers ♂ AB254
Gravel ♏ RS018
Gravelly Fields ♎ LI096
Gravers ♀ GA070, LI074
Gravity ☉ LI070
Gravity Lacking in Words ☉ GA069
Gray ☿ LI079
Gray Colored Cloths 1st House LI051
Great ♍ DA009
Great Patrimony ☉ in 4th House GA050
Greece ☿ DA026, LI080
Greece ♂ AB242
Greece ♍ DA009, PA074
Greece (Part) ♑ DA012, PA076
Greece, Near Thebes ♎ LI097
Greece, Southern ♍ LI096
Green ♀ DA023
Green ♃ RA052, RA052

Green ♌ LI086
Green ♐ LI086
Green 2nd House AB277, LI052, PA042
Green 12th House AB277, LI056, PA047
Green & Black 8th House LI054, PA045
Green & Red ♃ LI086
Green & White 9th House LI055, PA045
Green (Winter) ♄ CU
Green Sickness (Anemia) ☽ PA018, RS021
Green, Pale ☽ DA026, LI082, RA063
Green-Russet ♋ LI086
Greenish ♀ AB240
Grey Mixed with Sky Color ☿ DA025
Greyhound ☿ LI079
Grief ♄ in 6th House GA053
Gripping of the Guts 9th House RS100
Gristles ♃ DA019, PA128, RS014
Grocers ♀ LI628
Groin ♎ RS015
Groin ♏ LI246
Groin 7th House RS015
Groin 8th House LI245
Gromwell (Lithospermum) ♀ GA070
Grooms ♂ AB254
Grooms ♄ RA050
Gross ♃ LI063
Gross ♈ DA005
Gross ♉ DA006
Gross Capacity ♃ GA067
Ground Ivy (Ale-Hoof) ♀ GA070
Ground Pine (Common) ☿ GA071
Ground Pine (Common) ♂ CU
Grounds, Bushy ♉ DA006
Grounds, Full of Water ♓ DA014, LI099
Grounds, Plain ♉ DA006
Grounds, Rising Above ♐ DA012
Grounds, with Many Springs ♓ DA014, LI099
Grounds, with Waterfowl ♓ DA014, LI099
Groundsel (Common) ♀ CU, GA070
Growing Hair ☽ AB254
Growth ☽ RS198

Guesna* ♉ DA007, PA073
Guests ♀ LI628
Guidance, Correct 5th House AB276
Guile ☿ LI541
Gum laudanum ♀ RA060
Gundgavia, Hungary ♎ DA010
Gunmakers ♂ DA021
Gunners ♂ GA068, LI067, PA013, RA054
Gut, Diseases ♍ LI246
Guts ☽ PA018
Guts ♍ RS015
Guts 6th House RS015
Guts, Croaking ♍ RS017
Guts, Small 7th House LI245

-- H --

Hackneymen ☽ GA072, LI081
Hail ♄ PT181
Hair ♄ AB247
Hair, Abundant Curly Reddish ♃ AB249
Hair, Black ♑ DA012, PA008
Hair, Black ☿ DA025
Hair, Black ♉ DA007, PA004
Hair, Black or Dark ♄ GA066
Hair, Black or Dark ♍ DA009
Hair, Black or Very Brown ♍ PA006
Hair, Blackish ♋ DA008
Hair, Bright & Fair ♒ PA009
Hair, Bright Brown ☽ GA072
Hair, Brown ♃ PA012
Hair, Brown ♐ DA012
Hair, Brown and Sad ☿ GA071, PA016
Hair, Chestnut-Colored ♃ GA067
Hair, Crisp ☉ DA022
Hair, Curly ☉ DA022
Hair, Curly ♂ GA068
Hair, Curly ♃ DA019
Hair, Cutting ☽ AB254
Hair, Dark ♊ DA007
Hair, Dark Brown ♊ PA005

Hair, Dark Brown ♋ PA005
Hair, Dark Flaxen ♌ PA006
Hair, Dark or Black ♄ PA010
Hair, Fine and Long ☿ AB249
Hair, Flaxen & Curling ☉ PA014
Hair, Good, with Locks ☽ AB249
Hair, Growing ☽ AB254
Hair, Inclined to Red ♈ PA004
Hair, Lank ♂ AB249
Hair, Light Brown ♎ DA010
Hair, Long ☉ AB249
Hair, Lots & Black ♄ AB249
Hair, Much ☽ GA072
Hair, Much ♍ DA009
Hair, Much ♑ DA012
Hair, Much & Curling ♌ PA006
Hair, Much & Curling ♏ PA008
Hair, Red ♂ AB249, DA021, GA068, LI636, PT311
Hair, Red or Sandy, Curly ♂ PA012
Hair, Sad ♏ DA011
Hair, Sad, Brown Black ♏ PA008
Hair, Sandy-Flaxen ♂ GA068
Hair, Soft & Gentle ♃ GA067
Hair, Swarthy or Black ♄ DA018
Hair, Thick ☿ GA071
Hair, Thick ☽ PA017
Hair, Wan & Obscure ♑ DA012
Hair, Whitish Bright ♒ DA013
Hair, Yellow ♌ PA006
Hair, Yellow or Flaxen ♌ DA009
Hair, Yellowish Inclining Flax ♎ PA007
Halls ☉ LI072, RA058
Halls ♊ DA007
Halls (Formal Rooms) ☿ PA017
Halls in Houses ♊ LI094
Hamburg ♒ DA013, LI099, PA076
Hamlets of Leadworkers ♃ AB242
Hamms (see *Buttocks*)
Hand ☿ DA025, LI247
Hand Diseases ♊ LI094, RS017
Hand Gout ☿ LI079, RA062, RS021

Hand Gout ♄ DA018, LI059, RS019
Hand Gross ♉ DA007
Hand Swelling ☿ RS021
Hand, Brawny Part ☽ RS015
Hand, Plain of Mars ♂ RS014
Handicraft ♂ LI556
Hands ☿ PA017, RS015
Hands ♊ DA007, LI245, RS015
Hands 3rd House AB277, LI052, PA042, RS015
Hands, Coarse ♄ AB249
Hands, Long ☿ GA071
Hands, Long ♊ DA007
Hands, Short & Fleshy ☽ GA072, PA017
Hands, Short & Thick ♉ PA004
Hands & Fingers ♀ AB248
Handsome ☿ AB249
Handsome ♃ GA046
Handsome Face ♀ AB250
Handsome, Comely Countenance ♐ PA008
Hangings ♀ LI075, PA015
Hangmen ♂ GA068, LI067, PA013, ṘA054
Hankering After Management ☉ AB250
Hankering After Wealth ☉ AB250
Hankering After Worldly Affair ☉ AB250
Happiness ♀ PT185
Happiness ♃ PT183
Happiness 11th House AB275
Happy ♃ DA019
Happy in Chosen Profession ⊗ in 10th House GA061
Harbors ☽ LI082
Harbors 12th House AB275
Hard ♂ AB241
Hard Stones ♄ AB243
Hardness ♄ AB241
Hare ☿ AB246, RA062
Hare ♄ LI060, RA051
Hare Lip ♈ LI093, RS016
Hares 6th House LI053
Harlots 12th House LI559
Harnias ♀ LI075
Harsh ☉ PT363

Harsh with Opponents ☉ AB250
Hart ☿ RA062
Hart ♀ LI075, RA060
Hart ♃ LI064, RA053
Hart's Tongue ♃ CU, GA068
Harvests, Poor 5th House AB276
Hasford ♊ DA007, LI094
Hashish-Prepared as Confection ♂ AB243
Hassia (Country)* ♑ DA012, LI098, PA076
Hated by Princes ♄ in 9th House GA058
Hater of Sordid Men ☉ GA069
Hater of Sordid Persons ♃ GA067
Hater of Work ☽ GA072
Hates Work ☽ LI081
Hating Sordid Actions ♃ LI062
Hatred 6th House AB276
Hatred Between Brothers ♂ in 3rd House GA049
Hatred Between Brothers ♄ in 3rd House GA048
Haunches ♎ DA010, LI096
Haunches ♐ DA011
Haunter of Taverns ♀ GA070
Havens of the Sea ☽ DA027, LI082
Hawk ☉ RA057
Hawk ♂ LI068, RA055
Hawkweed ♄ CU, GA067
Hawthorn ♂ CU, GA068
Hay-Ricks ♍ LI096
Hazel Nut ☿ CU, GA071, RA062
Hazel Nut ♃ LI064, RA053
Head ☉ AB248, RS014
Head ♂ PA128
Head ♈ DA005, LI245, RS015
Head 1st House AB277, LI050, RS015
Head Colds ☿ LI079
Head Pains 1st House RS100
Head, Diseases of ♃ LI246
Head, Diseases of ♈ PA004
Head, Heaviness ♃ RS019
Head, Large ☉ AB249, DA023
Head, Large ♄ AB249
Head, Large ♂ AB249

Head, Large ♌ DA008, PA006
Head, Right, Noise ♄ LI246
Head-Boroughs ☉ RA057
Headache ♃ DA019, PT429
Headache ♈ LI093, PA004, RS016
Headache 1st House RS100
Headstrong ♂ LI540, PT353
Health ♀ PT185
Health ♃ PT183
Health 1st House LI129
Health, Indifferent ☽ in 1st House GA046
Health of Body ☽ in 6th House GA054
Health of Body ☊ in 6th House GA054
Health of Querent's Child 5th House LI053
Healthy ♀ PT357
Hearing ♄ AB248, LI269
Hearing and Touch ♃ AB248
Heart 5th House AB277, GA051, LI053, PA043, RS015
Heart 11th House RS097
Heart ☉ DA022, LI247, PA014, PT319, RA057, RS014
Heart ♌ DA008, LI095, RS015
Heart (Navel) Diseases ♀ RS020
Heart (with the Sun) ♃ AB247
Heart Disease ☉ LI071, RS020
Heart Disease ♌ RS017
Heart Disease 11th House RS100
Heart Palpitation ♃ RA053
Heart Palpitations ♃ LI063, RS019
Heart Palpitations ☉ PA014, RA058, RS020
Heart Passion ♌ RS017
Heart Problems ♌ LI095
Heart, Trembling ☉ LI247
Heart Weakness ♌ RS017
Heart, Wringings at ♃ LI246
Heart-Burning ☉ PA129
Heart's Ease ♄ CU
Heat ♃ PT037
Heat ♌ AB264
Heat Inclining to Moisture ♉ AB264
Heaviness ♄ AB241
Hedera helix ☉ RA057

Hedera helix ☽ GA072
Hedera helix ♃ LI064, RA053
Hedera helix ♄ CU
Hedonists ♀ LI541
Heels ♓ DA014
Heidelberg ♍ DA009, LI096, PA075
Height ♄ AB248
Heilbronn, Germany ♎ DA010, PA075
Heirs 8th House LI054
Heletropion (Tree) ☉ LI071
Heliotrope ☉ DA023, GA069
Heliotropion (Stone) ☉ RA057
Hellas ♍ PT159
Hellbore ♄ DA018, LI059, RA050
Hellbore (Black) ♄ CU
Hellbore (White) ♄ CU
Helleborus ☉ LI273
Helleborus ♂ LI273
Helleborus niger ♄ CU, RA050
Helvetia ♉ DA006
Hematites (Stone) ☿ LI272
Hematites (Stone) ♄ LI272
Hemlock ♂ DA021, LI068, RA054
Hemlock ♄ CU, DA018, GA067, LI059, RA050
Hemorrhages ♂ PT431
Hemorrhoids ♂ PT327
Hemorrhoids ♄ DA018, LI059, RS019
Hemorrhoids ♄ in 7th House GA054
Hemorrhoids 8th House LI054
Hemorrhoids (Emerods) ♏ DA011
Hemorrhoids (Pyles in the Ars) ♏ RS018
Hemp ☽ AB244
Hemp ♄ CU, DA018, GA067, LI059, RA050
Hempseed ♄ AB243
Henbane ♄ CU, DA018, GA067, LI059, RA050
Henry ☽ LI341
Henry, Good (Herb) ☿ CU
Hens 6th House LI558
Hens, Water ♂ AB247
Hepatic Diseases ♀ PT431
Hepatitis (Jaundice) ♌ DA008

Hepatitis (Yellow Jaundice) ♂ LI246, PA128
Hepatitis (Yellow Jaundice) ♌ LI095
Heracleum ☿ GA071
Herb Christopher ♄ CU
Herb Grace (Rue) ☉ LI071, RA057
Herb Grace (Rue) ♄ DA018, LI059
Herb Robert ♀ CU, GA070
Herb True-Love ♀ CU, GA070
Herbage, Quality of 7th House LI207
Herbipolis ♉ DA006, LI094
Herbs of Dry Places ♂ LI067
Herbs with Sharp Pointed Leaves ♂ LI067
Herdsmen ♄ LI059, RA050
Hereditaments 4th House GA050
Heretic ☋ in 9th House GA059
Heritages, Apportioning ♄ AB254
Hermaphrodite ☿ LI079
Hermitages ♓ LI099
Herniaria glabra ♄ GA067
Hernias ♀ RS021
Hernias ♏ DA011
Herons ☽ AB247
Herpes 12th House RS100
Hesperis matronalis ♂ CU
Hibernal ♑ AB231
Hibernal ♒ AB231
Hibernal ♓ AB231
Hidden Things 3rd House AB276
Hidden Treasure 8th House AB276
Hidden Treasure & Much Gain ☉ in 4th House GA050
Hides, Selling of ☿ AB254
Hiding Places, Thieves 3rd House AB276
Hiera (Drug) ☿ LI079
Hiera (Herb) ☿ RA062
Hieracium murorum ♄ CU, GA067
Hieracium stoloniferum ☽ GA072
High ☉ GA069
High & Sandy Ground ♈ PA004
High and Thin Stature ☿ LI078
High Ground ♐ LI098
High Places ♊ LI094

High-Constables ☉ LI071
High-Minded ♃ AB250, PT347
High-Sheriffs ☉ LI071
Higher Sciences ☽ AB254
Highwaymen ♂ AB254, RA054
Highways ☽ DA027, LI082, PA018, RA064
Hills ♊ DA007, LI094
Hills ♐ DA012, LI098
Hillsides ♎ LI096
Hilly Ground ♈ DA006, LI093
Hilly Places ♒ DA013, LI099
Hind ☽ RA064
Hinder Regions ♂ AB247
Hips ♐ LI246, RS015
Hips 8th House RS097
Hips 9th House GA058, LI055, PA045, RS015
Hircania (Near Caspian Sea) ♊ DA007, PA073
Hisarum* ♒ PA076
Hispalis (Seville, Spain) ♓ DA014, PA076
Historical Study ☽ DA026
Historiographers ☿ LI556
History ☽ LI557
History, Study of ☽ PA110
Hoarseness ☿ DA025, LI079, PA017, RA062, RS021
Hogherds 6th House LI053, PA044
Hogs 6th House LI053
Hogs ☽ RA064
Hogs ♄ LI060, RA051
Holds Head Forward ♄ GA066
Holes ♄ LI060, RA051
Holes (Places) ♄ DA018
Holland ☽ DA027, LI083, RA064
Holland ♋ DA008, LI095, PA074
Holland [= Batavia] ♂ LI068
Holly ♄ CU
Hollyhocks ♀ CU
Honest ♒ DA013
Honest ☉ DA022, GA069, PA014
Honest ♃ LI540, PA092
Honest ♉ DA006
Honest ♌ DA008

Honest ♃ in 3rd House GA049
Honest ♀ in 3rd House GA049
Honest Men ♃ DA019
Honest Siblings ⊗ in 3rd House GA049
Honesty, Natural ♃ LI555
Honey ☉ RA057
Honey Color 5th House LI053
Honeysuckle ☿ GA071
Honeysuckle ♂ in ♋ CU
Honor 10th House GA059, LI055, PA046
Honor ☉ LI556, PA109, PT363
Honor ♀ PT185
Honor ☉ in 1st House GA046
Honor & Dignity in Old Age ☉ in 4th House GA050
Honor & Riches from Friends ☊ in 11th House GA062
Honor from Vulgar People ☽ in 5th House GA052
Honor in Old Age ☉ in 7th House GA055
Honorable ♃ LI062, PT347
Honorable, Trusty Custodian ♃ AB250
Honored Within Family ♃ in 6th House GA053
Honors ☊ in 1st House GA046
Honors from Great Persons ☽ in 10th House GA060
Honors from Great Persons ☽ in 11th House GA062
Honors from Great Persons ☉ in 11th House GA061
Honors from Women ♀ in 10th House GA060
Hoopoo = Hoopoe (Bird) ♃ AB247
Hopes 11th House GA061, LI056, PA046
Hopes Achieved ♀ in 11th House GA062
Hopes Fulfulled ☉ in 11th House GA061
Hopes to be Prosperous ☽ in 11th House GA062
Hopes, Vain & Deceitful ♂ in 11th House GA061
Hopes (Shall They Be Obtained?) 11th House DA120, GA292, LI458, PA071
Hops ♂ CU, GA068
Horary, Asking Questions 1st House AB276
Hordeum vulgare ☽ AB243
Hordeum vulgare ☉ LI071, RA057
Hordeum vulgare ♃ AB243
Hordeum vulgare ♄ CU, GA067
Horehound ☿ GA071
Horehound ♂ DA021, LI068, RA054
Horehound (Black) ☿ CU

Horehound (White) ☿ CU
Horn ♄ AB247
Horse ☉ RA058
Horse Injuries ♐ RS018
Horse Tail ♄ CU
Horse-Races 12th House LI175
Horsemanship ♂ LI556
Horseradish ♂ CU, GA068
Horses ☉ LI071
Horses ♂ LI068
Horses ♄ AB246
Horses 12th House LI056
Horses, Lost 12th House LI467
Horses, Stolen 12th House LI467
Horses, Arab ☉ AB246
Horses, Injuries from ♐ LI097
Horsetail ♄ DA018, GA067, LI059, RA050
Hospitality 3rd House LI557
Hostage Negotiator ♎ LI451
Hot ♂ AB241
Hot & Dry ♈ PA004
Hot & Dry ♌ PA006
Hot & Dry ♐ PA008
Hot & Moist ♊ PA005
Hot & Moist ♎ PA007
Hot & Moist ♒ PA009
Hot Tempered, Quickly Recovers ☉ AB250
Hotel Operators ♄ LI059
Hottonia palustris ♄ CU
Hound's Tongue ☿ CU, GA071
House Flies ♂ LI068
House for Four-Footed Beasts ♐ LI098
House Leek (S[e/i]engreen or Wall Pepper) ♃ CU, GA068
House Leek (S[e/i]ngreen) ☿ LI272
House Leek (S[e/i]green) ♄ LI272
House of Commons 11th House LI056
House to Be Purchased 4th House PA064
Housebreaking ♂ AB254
Household Goods 2nd House LI557
Household Requisites 2nd House AB275
Houses ☉ LI072

Houses ♄ LI555
Houses 4th House AB275, GA050, LI052, PA043
Houses, Bridechambers ♀ DA024
Houses, Common Halls ☿ DA026
Houses, Condition 4th House LI206
Houses, Dark Places ♑ LI098
Houses, Dining Rooms ☉ DA023
Houses, Eaves ♒ DA013, LI099
Houses, [Great] Halls ☉ DA023
Houses, Living Rooms ☉ DA023
Houses, Low ♉ DA006
Houses, Low Areas ♑ LI098
Houses, Near Chimneys ♌ DA008
Houses, Near the Fire ♐ DA012
Houses, Near the Ground ♑ LI098
Houses, Near Muddy/Marshy Ground ♏ DA011
Houses, Near Orchards ☿ AB242
Houses, Near Water ♏ DA011
Houses, Near Water ♓ LI099, DA014
Houses, Near Well or Pump ♓ DA014
Houses of Bleachers ☿ AB242
Houses of Offices ♄ RA051
Houses of Painters ☿ AB242
Houses, Roof ♒ DA013, LI099
Houses, Ruined ♏ LI097
Houses, Ruins of ♏ DA011
Houses, Standing Water ♓ DA014
Houses, Surrounding Moats ♓ DA014
Houses, Upper Rooms ♎ LI096
Houses, Upper Rooms ♐ DA012
Houses, Upper Rooms ♒ DA013, LI099
Houses, Upper Rooms Near Fire ♐ LI098
Houses, Walls ♊ DA007
Houses with Cattle Implements ♉ DA006, LI094
Hul, Sweden ♎ PA075
Human ☉ LI070
Human ♊ DA007, PA005
Human ♎ DA010, PA007
Human ♒ DA013, LI538, PA009
Human ♐ DA011
Humane ☉ GA069

Humble ☉ PT363
Humidity ☿ PT039
Humidity ♀ PT037
Humidity ♃ PT037
Humors, Dropsical ♋ RS017
Humulus lupulus ♂ CU, GA068
Hungary ♃ DA020, LI065, RA053
Hungary ♐ DA011, LI098, PA075
Hunstmen ☽ GA072
Hunting 1st House LI365
Hunting Ground ♎ LI096
Huntsmen ☽ LI081
Huntsmen ☉ LI071
Hurricanes ☿ PT187
Hurts by Iron ♂ LI067, RS020
Husbandmen ♄ DA017, GA067, LI059, PA011, RA050
Husbandry ♄ PA108
Husbandry ♉ LI451
Hyacinth ♃ DA019, LI064, RA053
Hyacinth (Stone) ☉ DA022, LI072, RA057
Hyaena ☿ LI079, RA062
Hydrocotyle vulgaris ♀ CU
Hyoscyamus niger ♄ CU, GA067, LI059, RA050
Hypericum androsaemum ♄ DA018, LI059
Hypericum ascyron ☉ GA069
Hypericum perforatum ☉ CU, GA069, RA057
Hypericum perforatum ♃ RA052
Hypericum perforatum ♌ CU
Hypochondria ☉ AB247
Hypochondria ♍ PA007
Hypocistis ☿ LI272
Hypocistis ♄ LI272
Hypocrite ♃ GA067, PA012
Hypocrite ♓ LI538
Hypocrite ♄ in 3rd House GA048
Hypocrite ♄ in 9th House GA058
Hyposarca see Edema
Hyssop ☽ RA063
Hyssop ♃ CU, GA068
Hyssop ♋ CU
Hyssop (Hedge) ♂ CU

Hyssopus officinalis ☽ RA063
Hyssopus officinalis ♃ CU, GA068
Hyssopus officinalis ♋ CU

-- I --

Iberis ♄ GA067
Ibis ☿ RA062
Icicle (Stiria) ♄ LI061
Idiot ☿ GA071, LI078
Idle ☽ GA072, LI081
Idle ♀ DA023
Idolators ♂ AB253
Idumea (Livonia, Estonia) ♏ PA075
Ignorance Concealed ♄ AB250
Ignorant ♃ GA067, LI063
Ignorant ♂ AB250
Ilex aquifolium ♄ CU
Iliac Passion (Sciatica) ♄ DA017, RA051
Ill-Favored ♄ LI539
Illecebrum verticillatum ☿ LI272
Illecebrum verticillatum ♄ CU, GA067
Illustrators ♀ LI074
Illustrious Actions ☉ PA109
Illyris, Croatia/Bosnia ♑ DA012, PA076
Imagination ☿ DA025, LI247, PA017, RS015
Imagination, Strong ☿ GA071
Imagination, Strong ♄ GA066
Imaginings (=Conceits) ☿ RS021
Immodest ♀ GA070
Immovable ♂ LI066
Immovable Goods 4th House LI558
Impatient of Servitude ♂ LI540
Impediment ☋ LI173
Impetuous ☿ PT361
Impetuous ♂ PT353
Impious ♂ LI540, PT353
Implacable ♄ DA018
Imposing Will on the Ignorant ☉ AB250
Imposters 12th House LI559
Impostumes (see *Abscess*)

Impostumes of the Stomach ♋ RS017
Impotency ♀ LI075, RS021
Impotency ♄ PA011
Impotency ♀ in 6th House GA053
Imprisonment ♄ DA018, PT181
Imprisonment 12th House GA062, LI056, PA047
Imprisonment ♂ in 7th House GA055
Imprisonment ☽ in 8th House GA057
Imprisonment ♄ in 10th House GA060
Imprisonment ☉ in 12th House GA063
Imprisonment Because of Religion ☉ in 3rd House GA049
Imprisonment for Crimes ♂ in 12th House GA062
Imprisonment from Enemies ☽ in 12th House GA063
Imprisonment from Women ♀ in 12th House GA063
Imprisonments ♄ in 6th House GA053
Improvement; Warm Weather ♋ AB264
Impudent ♏ LI538
Incendiary ♂ GA068, PA013
Incest ♀ GA070
Incestuous ♀ LI074
Inclined to Love & Sensuality ♀ AB250
Inconstant ☽ GA072
Inconstant ☿ DA025, LI078
Inconstant ♎ LI538
Inconstant ☽ in 1st House GA046
Increase of Fortune by Friends ♃ in 11th House GA061
Increase of Patrimony ♃ in 4th House GA050
Incredulous ♂ in 3rd House GA049
India ☿ RA062
India ♄ AB242, PT141
India ♑ DA012, PA076, PT141
Indifference ♃ PT349
Indifference ♄ PT341
Indifferent ♂ PT353
Indifferent ♀ PT357
Indigence, Extreme 8th House AB275
Indulgent ♃ LI062
Industrious ☉ DA022, LI070, PT363
Industrious to Acquire Honor ☉ GA069
Industrious to Acquire Repute ☉ GA069
Infamous ♀ LI541

Infancy ☽ PT443
Infancy to Old Age (Quarters) ☽ AB248
Infertility ♀ LI247
Infidelity ♂ in 9th House GA058
Inflammation, Subcutaneous ♂ DA021
Inflammation, Mucous Membranes ♄ RA051
Inflammation, Mucous Membranes ☉ RA058, RS020
Inflammations ♂ RS020
Inflammations ♃ RS019
Information 9th House AB276
Infortune, Greater ♄ PA010
Infortune, Lesser ♂ PA012
Ingenious ☽ GA072
Ingenious ☿ DA025
Ingenious ♈ LI538
Ingenious ♐ DA011
Ingenious Workmen ☿ DA025
Ingolstadt, Germany ♄ DA018, LI061, RA051
Ingolstadt, Germany ♒ DA013, LI099, PA076
Inheritances ♄ DA018, LI555, PA108
Inheritances 4th House GA050, LI052, PA043
Inheritances 8th House AB275
Inheritances & Honors ♌ in 8th House GA057
Inheritances from Friends ♄ in 8th House GA056
Inheritances from Relatives ♄ in 8th House GA056
Inhumane ♂ GA068, LI066
Injury from four-footed Animals ♐ RS018
Injury from Animals ♂ DA021
Inland Journeys 3rd House LI052
Innkeepers ♀ PT337
Inobedient Family ♄ in 6th House GA053
Inquirers Into Nature ☿ PT359
Insects, Poisonous ♄ AB246
Insipid ☽ AB240
Insolent ♂ PT353
Inspiring ♃ AB250
Instep ♓ RS015
Instep 12th House RS015
Intellect ☿ LI077, PA017
Intelligence 3rd House AB275
Intelligent ☉ AB250

Intelligent ♃ AB250
Intemperate ♂ DA020
Internal Organs, Diseases of 6th House AB275
Internal Organs, Diseases of ♄ AB252
Interpretation ☿ PT335
Interpretation of Dreams ♃ AB254
Interpreter of Dreams ♄ in 9th House GA058
Interpretation of Visions & Dreams 9th House AB275
Intestinal Diseases ♀ LI075
Intestine, Small ☽ LI247
Intestines ♃ AB248
Intestines 6th House LI053
Intestines (Entrails) ☽ PA130, RS015
Intolerant ♂ PA093
Inula conyza ♀ CU
Inula helenium ☿ CU, GA071
Inventing Destructive Machines ☿ LI541
Inventive ☿ LI077, PT359
Inventors ☿ DA025, PA110
Involuntary Movements (Starts) ♃ RS019
Iran, Middle [=Sogdiana] ♒ PA076
Iraq ☿ AB242
Ireful ♂ DA021, LI540
Ireful ♈ DA005
Ireful ♌ DA008
Ireful ♏ DA011
Ireland ♉ DA006, LI094, PA073
Iris florentiana ☽ GA072
Iris foetidissdma ♄ CU, GA067
Iris germanica ☽ CU
Iris pseudacorus ☽ CU, GA072
Iron ♂ AB243, LI068, PT321, RA055
Iron Slag ♄ AB243
Ironworkers ♂ LI556, PT337
Irreverent ♂ GA068
Irrigation ☽ LI214
Irrigation ♄ LI214
Irrigation Channels ☿ AB242
Isabel ♀ LI341
Isatis tinctoria ♄ GA067
Islam ♀ AB253

Islands ♀ AB242
Italy ☉ DA022, LI072, PT135, RA058
Italy ♌ DA008, LI096, PA074, PT135
Italy, Campania ♉ LI094, PA073
Italy, Campània ♀ LI076
Itch ♃ RS019
Itch ♈ DA005
Itch ♑ LI098, RS018
Itch ♐ LI246
Itch ♓ DA014, LI099
Itch about the Knee ♑ LI246
Ivy ☉ RA057
Ivy ☽ GA072
Ivy ♃ LI064, RA053
Ivy ♄ CU

-- J --

Jacinths ☉ AB243
Jack Daw ☿ RA062
Jack-of-All-Trades ☽ LI081
Jackal ☿ AB246
Jailers ♂ PA013, RA054
Jamaica ♎ PA075
James ☉ LI341
Janitors (Broom-Men) ♄ LI059, RA050
Jasione montana ☿ CU
Jasminum officinale ♃ in ♋ CU
Jasper ♂ DA021, LI068, RA055
Jasper, Green ♀ RA060
Jaundice ♌ DA008, PA006
Jaundice ♂ RS020
Jaundice ♄ DA018
Jaundice, Black ☿ RS021
Jaundice, Black ♄ DA017, LI246, PA127, RA051, RS019
Jaundice, Yellow ♂ DA020, LI246, PA128, RA055
Jaundice, Yellow ♌ LI095, RS017
Jaw Pains 1st House RS100
Jealosies ☋ in 7th House GA056
Jealous ♀ PA094
Jealous ♄ GA067, LI058, PA092, PT341

Jerboe ♄ AB246
Jerusalem ☉ AB242
Jerusalem ♍ DA009, LI096, PA074
Jessamine (White Jasmine) ♃ in ♋ CU
Jester ♓ LI451
Jesting ♀ AB250
Jesuits ♄ GA067, LI059, PA011, RA050
Jet-Black ♄ AB240
Jewellers ♀ GA070, LI074, PA015, RA058
Jewellers ♂ PT337
Jewellers ♑ LI451
Jewels ♀ LI556
Jewels 3rd House AB275
Jewels Set in Silver & Gold ♀ AB243
Jewels Worn by Man ♃ AB243
Jews ♄ AB253, DA017, PA108
Joan ♄ LI341
Job (Does Querent Get It?) 10th House DA117, GA288, LI444, PA071
Job (Remain in Employment?) 10th House GA289, LI447
Jocose ♀ PA094
John ♃ LI341
Joint Aches ♄ RA051
Joints ♎ LI246
Jollity ♀ GA070
Journey, Short (How Good?) 3rd House GA256, LI195, PA063
Journeys ☿ DA025
Journeys by Water 3rd House AB276
Journeys, Desired ☽ in 1st House GA046
Journeys, Long 9th House GA058, LI137, PA045
Journeys, Long (Prosperous or not) 9th House GA285, LI422, PA070
Journeys, Many ☿ in 9th House GA059
Journeys, Many ☽ in 9th House GA059
Journeys, Many ⊗ in 9th House GA059
Journeys, Many & Cross ♂ in 9th House GA058
Journeys, Many & Profitable ☉ in 9th House GA058
Journeys, Wretched & Unfortunat ☋ in 9th House GA059
Journeys Small, Inland 3rd House GA048, PA042
Joy ♀ AB250
Joy 5th House AB275
Judaea ♂ PT143
Judaea ♈ LI094, PT143

Judenburg ♐ DA012
Judges ♃ DA019, GA067, LI063, PA012, RA052
Judges 10th House AB276, LI055, PA046
Judgment ☉ GA069
Judgment Composed ☉ DA023
Juglanns regia ☉ CU, GA069
Juglanns regia ☿ LI079, RA062
Juglanns regia ♀ RA060
Juliacum, Germany [= Juliers] ♑ DA012, PA076
Julian ♄ LI341
Juliers, Germany [= Juliacum] ♑ DA012, PA076
Juniper Tree ☉ CU
Juniperus communis ☉ CU
Juniperus sabina ♂ CU
Juniperus sabina ♄ RA050
Jurors ☽ LI403
Just ♃ DA019, GA067, LI062, PA092, PT347
Justice ☉ PT363
Justice ♃ LI555
Justices of Peace ☉ LI071

-- K --

Katherine ♂ LI341
Keen ♂ PT353
Keeps Away from Bad-Heartednes ☿ AB250
Keeps Away from Discord ☿ AB250
Keeps Away from Strife ☿ AB250
Keeps Away from Trickery ☿ AB250
Keeps Promises ☉ GA069
Keeps Secrets ☉ GA069
Keeps Secrets ☿ AB250
Khurasan, Iran ♃ AB242
Kidney Absesses (Impostume) ♎ LI096, RS017
Kidney Disease ♀ LI075
Kidney Disease ♃ RA053
Kidney Disease ♎ PA007, RS017
Kidney Gravel ♎ DA010
Kidney Heat (Fever) ♎ DA010, PA007
Kidney Pains ♀ RS020
Kidney Stones ♂ LI067, RA055, RS020

Kidney Stones ♎ LI246, RS017
Kidney Stones ♏ DA010
Kidney Ulcers ♎ PA007, RS017
Kidneys ♀ PA129, RS014
Kidneys ♂ AB248, DA020, PT319, RS014
Kidneys ♎ LI096, RS015
Kidneys 7th House GA054, RS015
Kidneys 10th House RS097
Kidneys to Hips 7th House PA044
Kidneywort ♀ GA070
Kidneywort ♀ in ♎ CU
Kind ♃ PT347
Kindred 3rd House GA048, LI052, PA042
King Among Kings ☽ AB250
King's Allies 11th House LI056
King's Ammunition 11th House LI056
King's Associates 11th House LI056
King's Attendants ♄ AB252
King's Council 11th House PA046
King's Counsellors 11th House GA061, LI056
King's Evil ☽ RS021
King's Evil ♉ DA006, RS016
King's Favorites 11th House GA061, LI056
King's Money 11th House LI056
King's Servants 11th House GA061, LI056
King's Soldiers 11th House LI056
King's Treasure 11th House LI056
Kingdom, State of 1st House PA041
Kingdoms 10th House LI055, PA046
Kingdoms ☉ LI556, PA109
Kingly ♌ PA006
Kings ☉ AB252, DA022, GA069, LI071, PA014, RA056
Kings ☽ AB252
Kings ♃ AB252
Kings 10th House AB276, LI055
Kings and Sultans Palaces ☉ AB242
Kingship 10th House GA059, PA046
Kinswomen ♀ DA024
Kitchen ♏ DA011, LI097
Kite (Bird) ♂ LI068, RA055
Knapweed ♄ GA067

Knapweed (Common) ♄ CU
Knapwort (Harshweed) ♄ CU
Knautia arvensis ☿ CU
Knee Disease ♑ PA009, RS018
Knee Fractures ♑ DA012, LI098, PA009
Knee Fractures & Strains ♑ RS018
Knee Injuries ♑ LI098
Knee Sprains ♑ PA009
Knee Strains ♑ DA012
Knees 10th House AB277, GA060, LI055, PA046, RS015
Knees ♄ AB248
Knees ♑ DA012, LI098, RS015
Knotgrass ☿ LI272
Knotgrass ♄ CU, GA067, LI272
Knowledge 3rd House AB275
Knowledge 9th House LI429
Knowledge in All Sciences 9th House GA058
Knowledge of Genealogy 4th House AB275
Knowledge of Many Things ♄ DA018
Knowledge Used for Bad Purpose ♄ AB254
Knowledgeful ☉ AB250
Krakow, Poland [= Craconi] ♈ PA073

-- L --

Labdanum = Rockrose ♀ LI075
Labor, Unclean ♄ PA108
Laboratories ♂ PA013
Laborers ☉ DA022
Laborers ♄ RA050
Laborious ♄ DA018, LI539, PT341
Laborious ♉ LI538
Lacerne ♉ PA073
Lackies ☽ DA027, PA110
Lacking Malice ♃ PA092
Lactuca sativa ☽ CU, GA072
Lactuca virosa ♂ CU
Ladies ☽ DA026, GA072, LI081
Ladies Thistles (Carduus) ♃ GA068
Lady's Bedstraw ♀ CU, GA070
Lady's Mantle ♀ CU, GA070, LI075

Lady's Smock ☽ CU
Lagoecia cuminoides ☉ AB247
Lairs of Wild Beasts ♄ AB242
Lakes, Stinking ♏ DA011, LI097
Lameness ♂ in 6th House GA053
Lameness ♒ DA013
Lameness ♓ LI099, PA010, RS018
Lameness of the Foot ♓ DA014
Lamentation ♄ AB250
Lamium ♀ CU, GA070
Lancing of Abscesses 3rd House AB276
Land, Measuring ☽ AB254
Land, Quality of 4th House GA259, LI205
Landa ♎ PA075
Landable Fortune ☉ in 4th House GA050
Landeshure ♎ PA075
Landlord or Landlady 7th House LI208
Lands 4th House GA050, LI052, PA043
Lands, Newly Plowed ♈ LI093
Landshaett [Ger. = Landshut] ♎ DA010
Landshut [Ger. = Landshaett] ♎ DA010
Lang De Boeuf ♃ CU
Laon [Fr. = Laudam = Laudunum] ♎ DA010
Lapidaries ♀ DA023, GA070, LI074
Lapis Lazuli ☉ AB243
Lapis Lazuli ♀ LI075, RA060
Lapis Lazuli ♄ DA017, LI060, RA051
Lapwing ♂ LI068
Lapwing ♄ LI060, RA050
Larder ♏ DA011, LI097
Large Cattle 12th House LI056
Large Stature ☉ LI070
Lark ☉ RA057
Lark ☿ RA062
Lark ♃ AB247, RA053
Lark (Bird) ♃ LI064
Larkwort ♃ DA020, LI064
Larnyx ☿ RS015
Laryngitis ☿ RS021
Lascivious (= Luxurious) ♀ DA023, PT357
Lascivious (= Luxurious) ♈ DA005

Lascivious (= Luxurious) ♉ DA006
Lascivious (= Luxurious) ♌ DA008
Lascivious (= Luxurious) ♑ DA012
Lascivious (= Luxurious) ♓ DA014
Lasciviousness (= Luxury) ♀ LI265
Lask (Diarrhea) ☽ DA027
Laskwort ♃ RA052
Lassitude in the Limbs ♄ RS019
Latin Ware ♀ DA023
Latrine Duty ♄ RA050
Latten Ware ♀ LI075
Laudam [= Laon = Laudunum / France] ♎ DA010
Laughing ♀ AB250
Laughing ♃ AB250
Laurel ☉ DA022, LI071
Laurel Tree ☉ DA023, LI071
Laurence ☉ LI341
Laurus nobilis ☉ CU
Laurus nobilis ♃ GA068
Laurus nobilis ♌ CU
Lavandula angustifolia ☉ RA057
Lavandula angustifolia ☿ CU, GA071
Lavender ☉ RA057
Lavender ☿ CU, GA071
Lavender (Cotton) ☿ CU
Law Makers ♃ PT335
Law Making ♂ AB254
Law Positions ♃ DA019
Law, Changes in ☿ PT187
Lawlessness ♂ PT185
Lawsuit (Who Wins?) 7th House GA277, LI369
Lawsuits ♂ LI556
Lawsuits 7th House AB275, GA054, PA044
Lawsuits without a Case 8th House AB276
Lawsuits (Defendant's Friends) 8th House LI054
Lawsuits (Querent's Assistants) 2nd House LI051
Lawsuits (Querent's Friends) 2nd House LI051
Lawyers ☿ GA071, LI139, PA016
Lawyers ♃ AB252, DA019, LI063, PA012, RA052
Lawyers 9th House GA058
Lawyers 10th House LI055

Lawyers, Pettyfogging ☿ PA016
Lazy ☽ GA072
Lazy ♀ AB250, GA070, LI074
Lead ♄ AB243, DA017, LI060, RA051
Lead Color ♄ AB240, PA010
Lead Monoxide (Litharge) ♄ AB243
Leaders ♂ AB252
Leaders ♃ PT347
Leadership ♂ PT353
Lean ☿ DA025
Lean ♄ DA018
Lean Rather Than Fat ♎ PA007
Lean, Spare Body ♈ PA004
Learned ☿ PT359
Learned ♃ AB250
Learned Men ☿ RA061
Learning ☿ LI077
Learning 9th House LI055
Learning without a Teacher ☿ GA071, PA016
Learning (Benefit to Querent?) 9th House GA286, LI429
Leather Worker ♂ LI067
Leather Worker ♄ LI059
Leaves of a Tree ☽ AB236
Leaves, Thick & Juicy ☽ LI082
Lecherous ♑ LI538
Lechery ♀ LI556
Leech ☉ GA069
Leeks ☉ LI273
Leeks ♂ AB244, DA021, LI068, RA054
Leeks, House (Singreen) ☿ LI272
Leeks, House (Singreen) ♄ LI272
Left Ear ♂ LI067, PT319
Left Ear ♃ LI063
Left Eye (Men) ☽ LI082
Left Eye (Women) ☉ LI071
Left Side ☽ RS015
Left Side Diseases ☽ LI081, RS021
Left Side of Body ☽ PT321
Leg from Knee to Ankle 11th House LI245
Leg Injuries ♒ RS018
Leg Swelling ☿ RS021

Leg Tumors ♒ DA013
Legacies 8th House GA056, LI054, PA045
Legates ☽ DA027
Legs 11th House GA061, LI056, PA047
Legs ♂ AB248
Legs ♒ DA013, LI098
Legs, Crooked ♄ AB249
Legs, Diseases of ♒ PA009
Legs, Short ♉ DA007
Legs, Small ☿ DA026
Legs, Upper Part ♑ RS015
Legs, Upper Part 10th House RS015
Leipsig ♉ PA073
Leisure 8th House AB276
Lemna minor ☽ GA072
Lemon Tree ☉ DA023, LI071, RA057
Lending 2nd House AB276
Length ♂ AB241
Length of Life (Nativities) 1st House AB275
Length of Life (Querent) 1st House GA242, LI129, PA062
Lens culinaris ☿ LI272
Lens culinaris ♀ CU
Lens culinaris ♄ AB243, LI272
Lentil Shaped Stones ♂ AB243
Lentils ☿ LI272
Lentils ♀ CU
Lentils ♄ AB243, LI272
Leonurus cardiaca ♀ GA070
Leonurus cardiaca ♀ in ♌ CU
Leopard ♂ AB246, LI068
Leopards, Trained ♃ AB246
Lepidium campestre ♂ GA068
Lepidium sativum ♀ CU
Lepidium sativum ♂ DA021
Leprosy ♄ DA017, LI059, PA011, RA051
Leprosy ♈ DA005
Leprosy ♑ DA012, LI098, RS018
Leprous or Scurvy Eruption ♄ RA051
Lethargy ☿ DA025, LI078, PA130, RA062, RS021
Lethargy ♈ PA004
Letter Carriers ☽ GA072, LI081

Letters 3rd House GA048, LI052, PA042
Lettuce ☽ DA026, GA072, LI082
Lettuce (Common Garden) ☽ CU
Lettuce (Great Wild) ♂ CU
Leucanthemum vulgare ♀ CU, GA070
Leucanthemum vulgare ♃ DA020, LI064, RA053
Leucanthemum vulgare ♋ CU
Leucophlegmatia ☽ RS021
Leucophlegmatia ♀ RS020
Level Ground ☽ AB241
Levisticum ☉ GA069
Levisticum officinale ☉ in ♉ CU
Levites ♃ RA052
Levity in Appropriate Places ☽ AB250
Lewd ♀ LI074
Lewdness (Priapism) ♀ GA070, RS021
Lewdness (Priapism) ♏ RS018
Liars ☿ GA071, LI077, PA016, PT361
Liars ♄ LI058
Liberal ♀ PA094
Liberal ♃ DA019, LI062, PA092, PT347
Liberality 10th House AB275
Libidinous ☿ in 6th House GA053
Library ☿ PA017, RA062
Licentious ♂ AB250
Lichen (Dog) ♃ CU
Lichen (Dog) ♋ CU
Licorice ☿ CU, GA071
Licorice ♃ LI064, RA053
Liepsig ♉ DA006, LI094
Lieutenants ☉ LI071
Life 1st House AB275, LI050, PA041
Life of the Native 1st House GA045
Life, Best Part 1st House GA242, LI134
Life Fortunate & Powerful ♌ in 1st House GA046
Life, Long ♃ in 1st House GA046, GA046
Life, Long ♃ in 8th House GA057
Life, Long ☉ DA022
Life, Long ☉ in 1st House GA046
Life, Long & Healthful ♌ in 8th House GA057
Life, Long & Healthful ♀ in 1st House GA046

Life, Quality of 1st House GA242, LI135
Life, Short ♂ in 1st House GA046
Life, Short ☽ in 12th House GA063
Life, Short ♄ in 1st House GA046
Life, Short ☋ in 1st House GA046
Light-Minded ☿ PT361
Lightness ☽ AB241
Lightning ♂ LI068
Lights ♋ RS015
Lights 4th House RS015
Lignum ☉ LI071
Lignum aloes (Plant) ☉ DA023
Ligustrum vulgare ☽ GA072
Lilum candidum ☽ CU
Lily ♀ LI075, RA060
Lily of the Valley ☿ CU
Lily of the Valley ♀ DA024
Lily, Water ☉ AB236
Lily, Water ☽ CU, GA072
Lily, Water ♀ DA024, LI075
Lily, White & Yellow ♀ DA024
Lily, White Garden ☽ CU
Limbs 7th House RS097
Limbs, Strong ♈ PA004
Limbs, Wanting ♓ DA014
Linaria vulgaris ♂ CU, GA068
Linaria vulgaris ♄ GA067
Lindama* ♈ PA073
Linden Tree ☽ DA026, LI082
Linden Tree ♃ CU
Linen-Drapers ♀ GA070, LI074, PA015, RA058
Linguist ☿ in 1st House GA046
Lingwort ♂ DA021, LI068, RA054
Linnet ☿ RA062
Linseed ☽ RA063
Linseed ♄ AB243
Linsie-Woolsie Colors ☿ DA025
Lintz ♌ DA008, LI096, PA074
Linum usitatissimum ☽ AB244
Linum usitatissimum ☿ CU, LI272
Linum usitatissimum ♃ LI064, RA052

Linum usitatissimum ♄ LI272
Lion ☉ AB246, LI071, RA058
Lion ♂ AB246
Lions, Trained ♃ AB246
Lips, Cherry ♀ PA015
Lips, Red ♀ DA024
Lips, Thick ♄ AB249, DA018, GA066, PA010
Lips, Thick ♉ PA004
Lips, Thin ☿ PA016, GA071
Lips, Thin ♂ AB249
Lisbon, Portugal ♎ DA010, LI097, PA075
Lisping ☿ PA017
Listera ovata (Bifoil) ♄ GA067
Literate Men ☿ LI078
Litharge (Lead Monoxide) ♄ AB243
Lithospermum prostratum ♀ GA070
Lithuania ♑ DA012, PA076
Litigation ♂ AB250
Little Acquisition of Property 5th House AB275
Little Broken ♓ DA014
Little Conjugal Happiness ☽ AB250
Live in Pomp & Glory ♃ in 4th House GA050
Livelihood 2nd House AB275
Liver ☽ DA026
Liver ♀ DA023, LI247, PT321, RS014
Liver ♋ DA007, RS015
Liver ♃ DA019, LI063, PA012, RA052, RS014
Liver ♌ RS015
Liver ♎ RS015
Liver 4th House RS015
Liver 5th House LI053, RS015
Liver 6th House LI245
Liver 7th House RS015
Liver (Together with Venus) ♂ AB247
Liver (Women) ☽ LI082, RA064, RS015
Liver Disease ♀ DA023
Liver Disease ♃ PA128
Liver Distempers ♃ RS019
Liver Heat ♃ RS019
Liver Infirmities ♃ RA053
Liver Inflammation ♃ DA019, LI246, PA012

Liver Pains (Man) 5th House RS098
Liver Weakness ♀ LI247
Liver, Cold ☉ DA022
Liverwort ♃ DA020, GA068, LI064
Lives Free of Controversy ♀ in 7th House GA055
Living Room ☿ PA017
Livonia, Latvia/Estonia ♎ DA010, LI097, PA075
Loadstone ♂ DA021, LI068, RA055
Loadstone ♄ DA017, LI060, RA051
Loans (Shall Querent Obtain?) 2nd House GA251, LI173
Lobster ☽ LI082, RA064
Locusts ☿ LI079
Locusts (Plague) ♂ PT185
Locusts (Plague) ♄ PT181
Lodgings, Fair ♀ DA024, PA015
Lofty ☉ GA069, PA014
Lofty Houses ♀ AB242
Logician ☿ GA071, LI077
Loin Disease ♀ PA015
Loin Disease ♎ RS017
Loin Heats ♎ RS017
Loins ♀ DA023, PA015, RS014
Loins ♎ DA010, LI096, RS015
Loins 7th House GA054, RS015
Lolium temulentum ♄ CU, GA067
Lombardy ♂ DA021, LI068
Lombardy ♊ DA007, LI094
Lombardy (Part) ♊ PA073
London ♊ DA007, LI094, PA074
Long & Narrow Chin ♑ PA008
Long Face ♑ PA008
Long Illnesses ♄ PT181
Long Journeys 9th House GA058, LI055
Long Life ☉ DA022
Long Life ♃ in 8th House GA057
Long Periods of Time 12th House LI176
Long Visage ♐ PA008
Longevity 11th House AB275
Longing for Approval ☿ AB250
Longing for Power & Government ☉ AB250
Longing for Power, Reputation ☿ AB250

Lonicera periclymenum ☿ GA071, GA071
Lonicera periclymenum ♂ in ♋ CU
Looking Downward ♄ PA010
Loosestrife ☽ CU, GA072
Loquacious ☽ AB250
Lords Major 11th House LI056
Lorraine ♉ DA006, LI094, PA073
Loss ☋ in 1st House GA046
Loss & Damage from Servants ♀ in 6th House GA053
Loss & Damage from Women ♀ in 12th House GA063
Loss from Great Persons ♄ in 10th House GA060
Loss from Servants ☉ in 12th House GA063
Loss from Servants ♂ in 12th House GA062
Loss from Small Animals ☉ in 6th House GA053
Loss from Small Animals ☋ in 6th House GA054
Loss from Wives ♂ in 4th House GA050
Loss in Lands, Buildings ☋ in 4th House GA051
Loss of Estate by Authorities ☉ in 8th House GA057
Loss of Estimation or Credit ☋ in 4th House GA051
Loss of Goods ☋ in 8th House GA057
Loss of Honor ☋ in 10th House GA061
Loss of Property 6th House AB275
Loss of Reputation ☋ in 10th House GA061
Loss or Damage 2nd House LI051
Loss or Damage in Lawsuits 2nd House PA042
Losses 7th House AB275
Lost 6th House AB276
Lost Items Recoverable? 7th House GA280, LI356, PA069
Lost Property 12th House AB276
Lote-Fruit Trees ♃ AB244
Lotus corniculatis ♄ GA067
Lovage ☉ GA069
Lovage ☉ in ♉ CU
Lovain ♊ DA007, LI094, PA074
Love ♀ LI556, PA109
Love 7th House LI054
Love 11th House AB275
Love Between Brothers & Sister ♀ in 3rd House GA049
Love Matters 7th House PA044
Love-Toys ♀ in 5th House GA052
Lover of Arts ♊ LI538

Lover of Arts ♍ LI538
Lover of Dancing ♀ PT357
Lover of Delight ♀ DA023
Lover of Delights ♀ in 1st House GA046
Lover of Elegance & Amusement ☽ AB250
Lover of Fair Dealing ♃ LI062
Lover of God ☉ in 9th House GA058
Lover of Honor ☉ PA109
Lover of Learning ♊ LI538
Lover of Learning ♍ LI538
Lover of Magnificence ☉ LI070
Lover of Mirth ♀ LI073
Lover of Novelties ☽ PA017
Lover of Ornaments ♀ DA023
Lover of Peace ☽ GA072
Lover of Pleasure ♃ PT347
Lover of Property ♄ PT341
Lover of Religion ☉ in 9th House GA058
Lover of Sciences ☽ LI081
Lover of Slaughter ♂ LI066
Lover of the Arts ♀ PT357
Lover of the Body ♄ PT341
Lover of Women ☽ AB250
Lovers ☉ DA022
Lovers ♀ PA110
Loving to All ♃ PA092
Low Houses ♉ LI094
Lower Belly 6th House LI053
Lower Part of Fire ☉ AB247
Lubeck ♋ DA008, PA074
Lucas ♋ DA008
Lucerne ♉ DA006
Lucy ☉ LI341
Lugwort ☿ DA025
Lugwort ♃ DA020
Lunaria ☽ GA072, RA063
Lunatic Passions ☽ RS021
Lung Disease ☿ PA017
Lung Disease ♃ PA012
Lung Disorders 4th House RS100
Lung Inflammation ♃ DA019, LI063, RA053, RS019

Lungs ☽ AB247
Lungs ♃ DA019, LI246, PA012, PT319, RS014
Lungs ♋ LI245
Lungs 4th House LI052, PA043
Lungs (Lights) ♋ RS015
Lungs (Lights) 4th House RS015
Lungs, Defluctions of ♋ PA005
Lungwort ☿ LI079, RA062
Lungwort ♃ CU, GA068, LI064, RA052
Lupin ♂ in ♈ CU
Lust ♀ DA024, RA061, RS021
Lustful ♀ LI541
Lustful ♂ AB250
Lute, Playing ♀ AB254
Luxurious (Lascivious) ♀ DA023, PT357
Luxurious (Lascivious) ♈ DA005
Luxurious (Lascivious) ♉ DA006
Luxurious (Lascivious) ♌ DA008
Luxurious (Lascivious) ♑ DA012
Luxurious (Lascivious) ♓ DA014
Luxury (Lasciviousness) ♀ LI265
Lydia, Asia Minor ♓ DA014, PA076
Lying ☽ AB250
Lying ☿ AB250
Lying ♄ GA067
Lymph accumulation, Swelling ☽ RS021
Lynnet (Bird) ☿ LI079
Lyons ♍ DA009, LI096, PA074
Lysimachia nummularia ☿ GA071
Lysimachia nummularia ♀ CU
Lysimachia vulgaris ☽ CU, GA072

-- M --

Mace (Plant) ♃ DA019, LI064, RA052
Macedonia ♄ PT139
Macedonia ♑ DA012, LI098, PA076, PT139
Mad ♂ PT353
Madder ♂ CU
Madder (Typographic error as Naddir) ♂ GA068
Madness ☿ LI078, PA017, RA062, RS021

Madness ♂ DA020, PA013, RS020
Madness ♄ RS019
Magdeberg, Germany ♋ DA008, LI095, PA074
Magic (Subtle Arts) ☿ DA025
Magicians ♄ AB252
Magistracy 10th House GA059, LI055
Magistrates ☉ AB252, GA069, LI071
Magnanimous ☉ DA022
Magnanimous ♃ DA019, GA067, LI062, PT347
Magnates ♃ AB252
Magnesia ♀ AB243
Magnet (Perhaps? = Adamant) ☉ LI072
Magnet (Perhaps? = Adamant) ♂ DA020, LI068
Magnetic Iron ♂ AB243
Magnetite ♂ DA021
Magnetite ♄ DA017
Magnificent ♃ PT347
Magpie ♂ RA055
Maidenhair Fern ☿ CU, GA071
Maidenhair Fern ♀ DA024, LI075, RA060
Maids 6th House AB275
Maids ♀ GA070
Maize ☉ AB243
Majesty ☉ LI070
Majors ☉ LI071
Maker of Crowns ♀ AB254
Maker of Diadems ♀ AB254
Malaria (Quartane Agues or Tertian Fever) ♂ LI067, PA128, PT183, RS020
Malaria (Quartane Agues or Tertian Fever) ♄ LI059, PA011, PT181, RA051,
    RS019
Malaria (Quartane Agues or Tertian Fever) ♑ DA012
Malcontent ☽ PA017
Male Genital Diseases ♂ RS020
Male Genital Wounds ♂ RS020
Malefic, Greater ♄ GA066
Malevolent Plotter ♄ AB250
Malicious ☿ PA095
Malicious ♄ GA066, LI058
Malicious Turbulence ☿ LI541
Malicious Undermining 12th House LI056
Malignant ♄ LI539

Mallow ☿ LI272
Mallow ♀ CU, GA070
Mallow ♄ LI272
Malt-houses ♍ LI096
Maltsters ☽ GA072, LI081
Maltsters ♄ GA067, LI059
Malus ♀ GA070
Malva sylvestris ☿ LI272
Malva sylvestris ♀ CU, GA070
Malva sylvestris ♄ LI272
Man ♃ AB246
Man (Male) ☉ LI304
Mandate of Emir 2nd House AB276
Mandragora officinarum ☽ LI082
Mandragora officinarum ☿ CU
Mandragora officinarum ♄ LI059, RA050
Mandrake ☽ DA026, LI082
Mandrake ☿ CU
Mandrake ♄ DA018, LI059, RA050
Manhood, Mature ♂ PT445
Manhood, Young ☉ PT445
Manly Countenance ♌ PA006
Manna (Shrub) ♃ LI064
Manna (Shrub) ☉ AB244
Manors 4th House LI202
Mansions of the Nobility ♃ AB242
Mantua ♉ DA006, LI094, PA073
Manual Dexterity ♂ LI540
Manual Labor ♂ LI629
Manufacture of Combs ☿ AB254
Manufacturing Perfumes ♀ AB254
Manuscript Illuminators ♀ GA070
Many Brothers & Sisters ☽ in 3rd House GA049
Many Children ♃ in 5th House GA051
Many Journeys ⊗ in 3rd House GA049
Many Professions ☽ LI081
Many Public Enemies ☿ in 7th House GA055
Many Public Enemies ☊ in 7th House GA056
Maple Tree ♃ CU
Marble ♃ DA019, LI064, RA053
Marble ☉ AB243

Marble ♀ RA060
Marcasite ☽ RA064
Marcasite ♀ DA023, LI075
Marcasite ☿ DA025, LI079, RA062
Marcasite ♃ AB243
March Grounds ♋ LI095
March, France [= Marchia] ♑ DA012
Marchia, France [= March] ♑ DA012
Margaret ☉ LI341
Marigold ☉ DA022, GA069, LI071, RA057
Mariners ☽ GA072, LI081, PA110
Marjoram ☉ LI272
Marjoram ☿ DA025, LI079, RA062
Marjoram ♂ LI272
Marjoram (Sweet) ☉ RA057
Marjoram (Sweet) ☿ GA071
Marjoram (Sweet) ♃ RA052
Marjoram (Sweet) ☿ in ♈ CU
Marjoram (Wild) ♃ DA020, RA052
Marjoram (Wild) ☿ CU
Market, Dullness of the 8th House AB276
Markets ☿ DA026, LI079, PA017, RA062
Marquesses ☉ DA022, GA069, LI071, RA056
Marriage ♀ DA024, PA109
Marriage ♂ AB250
Marriage 7th House GA054, LI054, PA044
Marriage (Describe the Partner) 7th House GA275, LI308
Marriage (If So, When?) 7th House GA274, LI307
Marriage (More Than Once?) 7th House GA274, LI307
Marriage (Shall the Querent?) 7th House GA273, LI307
Marriage (Shall They Agree After?) 7th House GA275, LI309
Marriage (Who Dies First?) 8th House GA285, LI411, PA070
Marriage (Will They or Won't They?) 7th House DA105, GA275, LI302,
  PA067
Marriage Feasts 7th House AB275
Marriage, Happy ♀ PT185
Marriage, Honorable ♃ in 7th House GA055
Marriage, Pleasurable ♃ in 7th House GA055
Marriage, Unhappy ☍ in 7th House GA056
Marriage to Widow ♀ in 8th House GA057
Marriages or Engagements, Many ♀ in 7th House GA055

Marrow ☉ LI273
Marrow ♂ LI273
Marrow ♄ AB247
Marrow of the Back ☽ RS015
Marrow, Spinal Decay 1st House RS100
Marrubium vulgare ☿ CU
Marrubium vulgare ♂ RA054
Marseilles ♈ DA006, LI094
Marsh Mallow ♀ CU
Marshals ♂ GA068, LI067, RA054
Marshy Ground ♋ DA008
Martial ♂ DA020
Mary ☽ LI341
Masculine ♈ PA004
Masculine ♊ PA005
Masculine ♌ PA006
Masculine ♎ PA007
Masculine ♐ PA008
Masculine ♒ PA009
Masons ♄ PA108
Masters of the Mint ☉ RA056
Masterwort ♂ CU, GA068
Mastic (Pistacia lentiscus) ♃ DA020, LI064
Mastic (Pistacia lentiscus) ♌ PA074
Mastiff ♂ LI068, RA055
Mastix ♃ RA053
Material Want ♂ in 2nd House GA047
Mathematical Propensity ☽ in 9th House GA059
Mathematical Skill ♄ in 9th House GA058
Mathematicians ☿ GA071, LI078, PA016, PT361, RA061
Mathematics ☿ DA025, PA094
Mathematics ☿ in 9th House GA059
Mathematics Freak ☿ in 1st House GA046
Matrix Passions ☽ RS021
Matter Which Preceded? 12th House AB276
Matthew ☿ LI341
Maud ☉ LI341
Mauritania ♏ PA075
Mayors ♃ LI555
Mayweed, Stinking ♀ CU
Mazovia, Poland (Province) ♑ PA076

Meadowsweet ♃ CU
Mean-Spirited ♄ PT341
Means to Attain Riches 2nd House LI168
Measles ☽ LI082, RA064, RS021
Measles ♃ RS019
Measuring by Bulk ♀ AB254
Measuring by Length ♀ AB254
Measuring by Weight ♀ AB254
Measuring Land ☽ AB254
Measuring Water ☽ AB254
Mecca ☿ AB242
Mechanic ☿ LI078
Mechanical Trade 10th House LI174
Mechlin, Belgium ♑ DA012, LI098, PA076
Meddling ☿ LI541
Media, Asia Minor ♀ DA024, LI076, PT141
Media, Asia Minor ♉ PT141
Media, Asia Minor ♒ DA013, LI099, PA076
Mediastinum ♋ RS015
Mediastinum 4th House RS015
Medicine 6th House LI558
Medicine 11th House S2-43
Medicine (C.F. Zael) 4th House S2-40
Medicine, Practice of ☽ AB254
Medina ☿ AB242
Medium Tall ♀ AB249
Medlars ♄ AB243, GA067
Meissen, Germany ♐ DA011, PA075
Melancholic Infirmities ♄ LI246
Melancholy ♄ AB250, GA066, RA051
Melancholy ♉ PA004
Melancholy ♍ LI246, PA006
Melancholy ♑ DA012, PA008
Melancholy Diseases ☿ DA025
Melancholy Thistle (Carduus) ♄ GA067
Melilot ☿ GA071
Melissa officinalis ☉ DA022, GA069, LI071, RA057
Melissa officinalis ♃ CU, RA052
Melissa officinalis ♋ CU
Melon ☽ AB244, DA026, LI082, RA063
Members of Generation ☽ RA064

Memory ☿ DA025, LI580, PA017, RS015
Memory, Deep ♄ DA018
Memory, Defects ☿ RA062
Memory, Excellent ☿ in 4th House GA050
Memory, Good ☿ in 1st House GA046
Memory Loss or Defects ☿ RS021
Memory Problems ☿ LI079
Menstrual Cycle ☽ PA130
Menstrual Diseases ☽ RS021
Menstrual Flow (Flower) Excess 5th House RS100
Menstrual Flow, Irregular 5th House RS098
Menstrual Problems ☽ RA064
Menstrual Retention ☽ RS021
Menstruation ☽ DA026, LI082, PA018
Mental Disorders ☽ in 6th House GA054
Mental Disorders ☉ in 6th House GA053
Mentha ♀ GA070
Mentha ♃ RA053
Mentha aquatica ♀ CU
Mentha piperata ♀ CU
Mentha pulegium ♀ CU, GA070
Mentha spicata ♀ CU
Mentz ♊ DA007
Mercers ♀ GA070, LI074
Merchandizing Addict ☿ in 1st House GA046
Merchant in Dry Goods (Mercer) ♀ RA058
Merchants ☿ AB252, DA025, GA071, LI077, PA110, PT335, RA061
Merchants ♒ LI451
Merchants ♃ AB252
Merchants 11th House LI175
Merciful ♀ LI541
Mercurialis annua ☽ CU
Mercurialis annua ♀ GA070
Mercurialis perennis ☿ CU, RA062
Mercury ☿ DA025
Mercury (Element) ☿ RA062
Mercury (French) ☽ CU
Mercury (Herb) ☿ RA062
Mercury (Herb) ♀ GA070
Mercy ♀ LI556
Meridional ♎ DA010

Merriment 5th House GA051, LI053, PA043
Merry ♀ PA094
Mesenteries (Mesenterion) ♍ LI096, RS015
Mesenteries (Mesenterion) 6th House RS015
Mesenterion 6th House RS015
Mesenterion ♍ RS015
Meseriacks ♂ PA013
Meseriacks, Impediments in ♍ LI246
Mesopotamia ☿ PT141
Mesopotamia ♍ DA009, LI096, PA074, PT141
Message ☽ DA026
Messenger (Status of Message?) 5th House GA267, LI235
Messengers ☽ DA026, LI081, PA110
Messengers ☿ GA071, LI078, PA016, RA061
Messengers 3rd House LI052, PA042
Messengers 5th House AB276, GA051
Messengers of Republics 5th House LI053
Messina ♏ LI097, PA075
Metal Diggers ♄ LI555
Metal Tailing ♄ DA017
Metallic Dross ♄ LI060, RA051
Metals ♄ PA108
Meum athamantigum ☿ in ♋ CU
Meum athamantigum ♀ GA070
Mezereon Spurge ♄ CU
Middens 8th House AB276
Middle Age ♃ AB248
Middle Stature ♂ LI067
Midriff 6th House RS015
Midriff ♍ RS015
Midwives ☽ GA072, LI081
Migraines ☽ RA064
Migraines ☿ PA130
Migraines ♂ DA021, LI067, RA055, RS020
Migraines ♈ DA005, LI093, RS016
Migrations 3rd House AB275
Milan, Italy ♋ DA008, LI095
Milan, Italy ♍ PA074
Mild ♃ DA019
Mild and Gentle Beasts ♃ LI064
Military ♂ PT353

Military Journeys, Fortunate ♂ in 9th House GA058
Milky Colored ♀ DA023
Millers ☽ LI081
Millet ♀ DA024
Millstone ☿ DA025, LI079
Mind, Perplexed ☋ in 1st House GA046
Mind, Qualities 1st House GA045
Mind, Sincere & Good ☉ DA022
Minding Own Business ♃ PT347
Mine (Mineral) 4th House LI215
Miners ♄ DA017, GA067, LI059
Mines 4th House LI558
Mines ☉ AB241
Mines ♄ PA108
Ministers ☿ LI078
Ministers ♃ LI063
Mint ♀ GA070
Mint ♃ DA020, LI064, RA053
Mint (Garden or Spear) ♀ CU
Mint (Pepper) ♀ CU
Mint (Water) ♀ CU
Minters of Money ☉ GA069, LI071, PA014
Miracles 9th House AB276
Mirth ♀ GA070
Miscarriages ♀ PT321
Miscarriages ♂ PT329
Miscarriages 5th House RS100
Mischievous in Speech ☿ PA095
Miserly ♄ AB250
Misers ♄ PA108
Misery 12th House AB275
Mislaid Object (Where is It?) 4th House GA262, LI202, PA064
Misnia = Meissen, Germany ♐ DA011, PA075
Misplaced Jealosy ♀ LI074
Missions ☽ AB254
Mistletoe ☉ CU, GA069
Mistress ♀ DA024
Mistress of the House ☽ LI557
Mistrustful ♄ GA067, LI058
Mithraists and Magians ☉ AB253
Mithridate Mustard (Pennycress) ♂ GA068

Mixed 7th House AB277
Mixed Colors ☽ LI086
Mixed Colors ☿ DA025, LI079
Moats ♓ LI099
Modena, CA Gaul [= Mutina] ♐ DA011, PA075
Moderate ♃ AB241
Moderate Brilliancy ☽ AB240
Moderate Cold & Moisture ☽ AB232
Moderate Cold & Moisture ♀ AB232
Moderate Heat & Dryness ☉ AB232
Moderate Heat & Moisture ♃ AB231
Moderate Things ☿ AB241
Moderately Cold & Moist Foods ♀ AB245
Moderation ♃ AB241
Moguntia[cum], Germany ♊ PA074
Moist ♍ DA009
Moist Places ☽ AB242
Moisture ☽ AB241, PA110
Moisture & Thunder ♍ AB264
Mole ♄ LI060, RA051
Molestation of Wives ♂ in 4th House GA050
Monachium [Monaco] ♏ DA011, PA075
Monaco [Monachium] ♏ DA011, PA075
Monarchs ☉ RA056
Monday ☽ AB241, LI083
Monday Night ♃ AB241
Money Lent 2nd House LI051, PA042
Money Squandered ♄ in 2nd House GA047
Money Wasted ♄ in 2nd House GA047
Money, Apportioning ♄ AB254
Moneywort ☿ GA071
Moneywort ♀ CU
Monks ♄ GA067, LI059, PA011, RA050
Monster (= Basilisk) ♄ LI060
Mont ♊ LI094
Montsferat ♒ DA013, LI099, PA076
Moonstone ☽ AB243
Moonwort (Lunaria) ☽ GA072
Moors ♄ PA108
Moors (Islam) ♄ DA017
Morality ♃ LI555

Moravia, Czechoslovakia ♐ DA011, LI098, PA075
Moribund ♄ AB252
Morphew (Skin Eruption) ♂ DA021
Morphew (Skin Eruption) ♄ DA017, RA051
Morus nigra ☿ CU, GA071
Morus nigra ♃ LI064, RA053
Mosaics ♂ AB243
Mosbach, Germany ♎ PA075
Mosel ♒ DA013, PA076
Moslems ♄ DA017, PA108
Mosphachium (City)* ♎ DA010
Mosques ☿ AB242
Mosques ♃ AB242
Moss ♄ DA018, GA067, LI059, RA050
Most Agreeable ♀ AB241
Most Beautiful ♀ AB241
Most Delicious ♀ AB241
Most Expert ☉ AB241
Most Pungent ♀ AB241
Mother 10th House GA059
Mother, Prenatal Fancies of 12th House AB275
Mother's Condition & Quality 10th House GA059
Mother's Life Short ♄ in 10th House GA060
Mother's Life Short ☋ in 10th House GA061
Mothers ☽ AB249, DA027, PT241
Mothers ♀ AB249, DA024, LI074, PT241, RA058
Mothers 10th House LI055, PA046, PT251
Motherwort ♀ GA070
Motherwort ♀ in ♌ CU
Mount Lebanon ☉ AB242
Mountains ♄ DA018, LI060
Mountains ♊ DA007, LI094
Mountains, Rich in Minerals ☉ AB241
Mountaintops ♎ LI096
Mountebacks ♃ PA012, RA052
Mournful ♄ DA018
Mourning ♄ PT181
Mouse ♄ AB246, LI060, RA051
Mousear (Hieracium) ☽ GA072
Mouth ☉ AB248
Mouth Disease ☉ DA022, LI071, RA058, RS020

Mouth, Great ♉ DA006
Mouth, Large ♉ PA004
Mouth, Sore 1st House LI245
Mouth, Wide ☿ AB249
Mouth, Wide ♄ AB249
Moveable ♑ PA008
Moveable Goods 2nd House LI051, PA042
Moves Frequently ☽ LI081
Moves Often ☽ GA072
Moving from Place to Place 6th House AB276
Much Given to Drinking ☽ in 5th House GA052
Much Given to Revelling ☽ in 5th House GA052
Much Thought and Talk ☽ AB250
Mucus Membrane Inflammation ♄ LI246
Mucus [= Salt Phlegm] ♋ DA008, LI095, RS017
Mucus [= Salt Phlegm] ♓ DA014, LI099, RS018
Muddy Ground ♏ LI097
Muddy Places ♄ LI060
Mugwort ♀ DA024, GA070
Mugwort (Common) ♀ CU, LI075
Mulberries ☉ AB244
Mulberry Tree ☿ CU, GA071
Mulberry Tree ♃ LI064, RA053
Mule ☿ RA062
Mule ♂ LI068
Mullein ♄ GA067
Mullein (Black) ♄ CU
Mullein (Great) ♄ CU
Mullet ☿ LI079
Multiple Marriages ♀ in 7th House GA055
Murder ♂ LI066, PT185
Murder 8th House AB275
Murder, Sudden for a Trifle 7th House AB276
Murderer ♂ in 4th House GA050
Murderers ♂ PA013, RA054
Murmuring ♄ LI058
Muscles ♃ RS014
Muscovia ♑ DA012
Muscovia ♒ DA013, LI099, PA076
Mushroom (Garden) ☿ in ♈ CU
Mushrooms ☽ DA026, LI082, RA063

Music ♀ in 5th House GA052
Musical ♀ LI074
Musical Propensity ☽ in 9th House GA059
Musicians ♀ DA023, GA070, LI074, PA015, RA058
Musicians ♎ LI451
Musing of Great Things ♄ PA092
Musk ♀ AB254
Musk (Civet) ☉ LI071
Musk (Civet) ♀ LI075
Musk (Plant) ☉ DA022, RA057
Musk (Plant) ♀ DA024, RA060
Muskmelon ☽ RA063
Mussel ☽ RA064
Mustard ♂ AB244, GA068, RA054
Mustard (Black) ♂ CU
Mustard (Hedge) ♂ CU, GA068
Mustard (White) ♂ CU
Mustard Seed ♂ DA021, LI068
Mutable ☽ DA027, GA072
Mutable ☽ in 1st House GA046
Mute Signs ♋ LI089
Mute Signs ♏ LI089
Mute Signs ♓ LI089
Myrrh ☿ LI272
Myrrh ♄ LI272
Myrrh Tree ☉ DA023, LI071
Myrrhis odorata ♃ CU
Myrtle Tree ☿ CU
Myrtle Tree ♀ LI075, RA060
Myrtle Tree ♄ AB236
Myrtus communis ☿ CU
Myrtus communis ♀ LI075, RA060
Myrtus communis ♄ AB236

-- N --

Nabatea (S.E. of Palestine) ♄ AB242
Nabatean Glass ☽ AB243
Naddir (Typographic error for Madder) ♂ GA068
Nails ♄ AB247
Naive ♃ LI540

Nantes ♉ DA006, LI094, PA073
Naples ♈ DA006, LI094, PA073
Narbonne ♐ DA011, LI098, PA075
Narcissus ♀ AB236
Narcissus ♃ AB236
Narcissus pseudonarcissus ♀ CU, LI075, RA060
Narcissus pseudonarcissus ♂ CU, LI272
Narcotics ♄ AB245
Narrow Streets of Common People ☽ AB242
Nasamonia, Libya ♓ DA014
Native Honored for Clerkship ☿ in 5th House GA052
Native Honored for Ingenuity ☿ in 5th House GA052
Native Honored for Skill ☿ in 5th House GA052
Native Land 1st House AB275
Natural Power ☽ AB245
Navel ☿ RS182
Navel ♃ RS014
Navel ♎ DA010, RS015
Navel 7th House RS015
Navel (Heart) Diseases ♀ RS020
Navigation ☽ DA026, LI557
Navigation ♄ LI555
Navigators ☽ PA110
Neat ♀ PT357
Neat Dresser ♀ GA070
Neat Man ♀ LI073
Neck ☽ AB248
Neck ♀ PA015
Neck ♉ DA006, LI245, RS015
Neck 2nd House AB277, GA047, LI052, PA042, RS015
Neck Disease ♀ PA015
Neck, Handsome ♀ AB249
Neck, Long ♈ DA006, PA004
Neck, Long ♑ DA013
Neck, Short ♄ AB249
Neck, Short ♏ DA011, PA008
Neck, Short & Fat ♉ DA006
Necromancers ☿ AB254, LI077
Negligent ♃ LI540, PA093
Negligent ♄ LI539, PA092
Negotiations ☿ LI556

Neighbors 3rd House GA048, LI052, PA042
Neighbors (Accord with) 3rd House GA253, LI188
Nep = Catnip ♀ GA070
Nepeta cataria ♀ CU, GA070
Nephritis ♂ PT429
Nerve Disease 12th House RS100
Nerve Weakness 1st House RS100
Nerves ☉ AB247, RS014
Nettle ♂ DA021, GA068, RA054
Nettle (Common) ♂ CU, LI067
Never Contented ♄ LI058
New Arts ☿ DA025
New Colors ☿ DA025
News 3rd House AB276, LI192
News-monger ☿ LI078
Next World, Concern for 11th House AB275
Nice ☽ RA064
Nicholas ☽ LI341
Nicotiana tabacum ♂ CU, GA068
Nigella sativa ☿ CU
Niggards ♄ PA092
Night Owl ☽ RA064
Night Raven ☽ RA064
Night-Farmers ♄ LI059
Night-Worms ☉ LI071
Nightengale ☉ LI072, RA057
Nightengale ☿ AB247, RA062
Nightengale ♀ LI075, RA060
Nightmares ♄ in 9th House GA058
Nightowl ☽ LI082
Nightshade ♄ CU, DA018, GA067, LI059, RA050
Nipple, Left ♌ RS015
Nipple, Left 5th House RS015
Nipples ♀ DA023, LI247, RS014
Nipples ♋ DA007, LI095, RS015
Nipples 4th House RS015
No Concern for Future ☽ LI081
Nobility 1st House AB276
Nobility ☉ LI556, PA109
Noble ☉ AB241
Noble ♂ PA093, PT353

Noble ♃ AB250, GA067, PA012
Noble Actions ♃ AB254
Noble Brothers ☉ in 3rd House GA049
Noble Matrons ☽ AB252
Noble Men ♃ PA108
Noble-Born ☉ RA056
Noblemen (=Counties) ♃ DA019
Noblemen (=Counties) 10th House LI055
Nobles ☽ AB252
Nobles ☉ AB252, PA109
Nobles ♀ AB252
Nobles ♃ AB252
Nocturnal ♉ PA004
Nocturnal ♋ PA005
Nocturnal ♍ PA006
Nocturnal ♏ PA007
Nocturnal ♑ PA008
Nocturnal ♓ PA009
Nonconformist, Religious ☿ GA071
Nonconformist, Religious ♄ GA067
Nonmonogamous ♑ LI538
Noor Hen ☽ RA064
Norimberge [= Nuremberg, Ger.] ♊ DA007, LI094
Nori[m/n]berge [= Nuremberg, Ger.] ☽ DA027, LI083, RA064
Normandy, France ♓ DA014, LI099, PA076
North ♋ LI365
North ♏ LI097
North ♑ AB231
North ♒ AB231
North ♓ AB231
North 4th House LI053
North Northeast 3rd House LI364
North Northwest 5th House LI364
North Wind ♑ AB231
North Wind ♒ AB231
North Wind ♓ AB231
North Winds ☽ LI082
North Winds ♃ LI064
Northeast ♌ LI365
Northeast ♏ LI365
Northern ♋ LI095

Northern ♓ LI099
Northwest ♒ LI365
Northwest ♓ LI365
Northwestern Countries ♂ AB242
Norway ♏ PA075
Norway, Woods ♏ LI097
Nose ♈ RS015
Nose 1st House RS015
Nose Diseases 1st House RS100
Nose, Flat ♄ GA066, PA010
Nose, Long ☿ GA071, PA016
Nose, Lumpish ♄ DA018
Nose, Pretty, Short, Round ♑ PA008
Nose, Thick & Prominent ♃ AB249
Nose, Thin, Long & Sharp ☿ DA025
Nostril ♀ AB248
Nostril ♂ AB248
Nostril, Left ♀ RS014
Nostril, Right ♂ RS014
Nostrils ☿ RS182
Nostrils, Wide ♉ DA006
Not Intellectually Strong ☽ AB250
Not Quarrelsome ♀ AB250
Notables 10th House AB276
Notaries ☿ PA110
Novaria, Italy [= Milan] ♍ PA074
Novgorod, Russia ♉ DA007, LI094
Nullet ☿ RA062
Numidia, Africa ♋ PA074
Nuremberg, Germany ☽ DA027, LI083
Nuremberg, Germany ♊ LI094, PA074
Nurses ☽ AB249, GA072, LI081
Nut ☿ DA025
Nut Trees ♄ AB244
Nutmeg ♃ DA019, LI064, RA052
Nutriment 2nd House AB275
Nymphaea alba ☽ CU, GA072

-- O --

Oak ♃ RA053

Oak Tree ♃ CU, GA068, LI064
Oak-Gall Tree ♄ AB244
Oats ☿ GA071
Obedient ♎ DA010
Obedient ♏ DA011
Obedient ♐ DA011
Obedient ♑ DA012
Obedient ♒ DA013
Obedient ♓ DA014
Obeys Nobody Willingly ♂ GA068
Objects, Densest ☽ AB241
Objects, Lightest ☽ AB241
Objects, Most Moist ☽ AB241
Objects, Thickest ☽ AB241
Obscene ♂ LI066
Obstinacy 7th House AB276
Obstinate ☉ PT363
Obstinate ♄ DA017
Obstruction of Meseriacks ♍ RS017
Obstructions ♃ RA053
Obstructions (Oppilations) ☽ LI580, PA018, RS017
Obstructions of the Gut ♍ DA009
Occupation 10th House LI450
Ocre ♂ LI068
Ocymum basilicum ♂ CU, GA068
Ocymum basilicum ♃ DA020, LI064, RA052
Ocymum basilicum ♍ LI096, PA074
Ocymum basilicum ♏ CU
Offensively Acid ♄ AB240
Office ☉ LI556
Office 10th House LI055
Office Buildings ♄ LI060, RA051
Office from Great Person ☽ in 3rd House GA049
Office, Dismissal from 3rd House AB276
Office, Return to 10th House LI448
Officers in Armies ♂ LI067, PA013
Officers in Authority 10th House LI055
Offices Given by Princes ☉ in 3rd House GA049
Officials ☉ AB252
Officials of the Treasury 11th House AB276
Often Entangled in Love Matters ♀ GA070, LI074

Often Removing 3rd House LI052
Oily Berries ♀ AB244
Old Age ♄ AB248, PT447
Old Age ♒ AB231
Old Age ♑ AB231
Old Age ♓ AB231
Old Age, Native is Honored ☉ in 7th House GA055
Old Buildings ♄ AB242
Old Gold ☿ AB243
Old Men ♄ DA017, GA067, LI059, PA011, RA050
Old Things 3rd House AB276
Older Brothers ♄ AB249
Olive ♀ DA024, LI075
Olive ♃ LI064
Olive Tree ♃ RA053
Olive Tree ♄ AB244
Olives ♄ AB243
One-Blade (Smilacina) ☉ GA069
Onion ☉ LI273
Onion ☽ LI082
Onion ♂ AB244, CU, DA021, GA068, LI068, RA054
Ononis spinosa ☿ GA071
Ononis spinosa ♂ CU, LI068
Onopordum acanthium ♂ CU, GA068
Opacity ☽ AB241
Open Countenance ☿ AB250
Ophioglossum ♋ CU
Ophioglossum vulgatum ☽ CU, GA072
Ophioglossum vulgatum ☿ DA025, LI079, RA062
Oppilations (Obstructions) ☽ PA130, RS021
Opponents ♂ AB252
Opposition in Duels 7th House LI054
Opposition in Lawsuits 7th House LI054
Opposition in Quarrels 7th House LI054
Opposition in War 7th House LI054
Oppression ♂ LI556
Oppression of Native's Enemies ☋ in 12th House GA063
Oppressors ♂ LI066
Opthalmia ☉ RS020
Orach ♀ CU
Orage (Herb) ♄ DA018, LI059, RA050

Orange ☉ AB243
Orange Tree ☉ DA023, LI071, RA057
Orange, Sweet ♀ DA024
Oratories ♃ DA020, RA053
Orators ☿ GA071, LI078, PA016, RA061
Orators ♃ PT337
Orators ♎ LI451
Oratory ♃ LI064
Orcades [=Orkney Islands] ♑ LI098, PA076
Orchades [=Orkney Islands] ♑ DA012
Orchards ♏ DA011, LI097
Orchards 4th House LI052
Orchid ♀ CU
Orchina ♌ DA008
Orchis ♀ CU
Orderly ♃ LI540, PA092
Ordinaries ☿ DA026, RA062
Ordinary Vessels ♃ AB242
Oregano ☿ CU
Organs of Speech ☿ AB248
Organs, Internal Diseases of 6th House AB275
Organy (Wild Marjoram) ♃ DA020, LI064, RA052
Origanum (Oregano?) ♀ AB243
Origanum dictamnus ♀ CU
Origanum majorana ☉ RA057
Origanum majorana ☿ GA071
Origanum majorana ♃ RA052
Origanum majorana ☿ in ♈ CU
Origanum vulgare ☿ CU, RA062
Origanum vulgare ♃ RA052
Orkney Islands [= Orc[h]ades] ♑ DA012, LI098, PA076
Ornaments ♀ DA024, PA109
Ornaments 11th House AB275
Ornaments, Gold ♀ AB254
Ornaments, Silver ♀ AB254
Orpiment (Yellow Arsenic) ☉ AB243
Orpine ☽ CU, GA072
Orsim(Place)* ♎ DA010
Oryza sativa ☉ CU
Oryza sativa ♃ AB243
Os Sacrum ♐ RS015

Os Sacrum 9th House RS015
Osmunda regalis ♄ CU, GA067, RA050
Ostrich ♂ LI068
Ostrich ♄ LI060, RA050
Otter ☽ LI082, RA064
Out-House ♎ LI096
Out-Lawed People 7th House LI054
Outwardly Dissembling ♄ LI058
Ovarian Ulcers ♎ PA007
Ovaries, Running of ♏ PA008
Ovary ♀ PA015
Over-Anxious for Comfort ☽ AB250
Over-Anxious for Health ☽ AB250
Overwork 6th House AB275
Overworked ♄ AB252
Ovum ♀ LI247
Ovum ♏ S2-56
Owl ♀ LI075
Owl ♂ LI068, RA055
Owl ♄ LI060, RA050
Owl, Night ☽ LI082
Owners of Estates ♄ AB252
Ox ♃ RA053
Ox-House ♑ LI098
Oxalis acetosella ♀ CU
Oxen ☽ AB246
Oxen ♃ AB246, LI064
Oxen ♄ AB246
Oxen 12th House LI056
Oxford ♑ DA012, LI098, PA076
Oxiana, Sarmatia ♒ DA013
Oxyria digyna ♀ CU
Oyster ☽ LI082, RA064
Oyster-Wives ☽ LI081

-- P --

Paces Dark, Near Ground ♑ DA013
Padua ♈ DA006, LI094, PA073
Paeonia officinalis ☉ GA069, LI071, RA057
Paeonia officinalis ♃ LI064, RA053

Paeonia officinalis ⊙ in ♌ CU
Paeony ⊙ DA023, GA069, LI071, RA057
Paeony ♃ LI064, RA053
Paeony ⊙ in ♌ CU
Pain, Acute Abdomenal (Cholic) ☽ RS021
Pain, Acute Abdomenal (Cholic) 9th House RS100
Painful ♄ PA092
Painters ♀ DA024, GA070, LI074, PA015, PT337, RA058
Painters ♊ LI451
Palaces ⊙ DA022, LI072, PA014, RA058
Palaces ♃ PA012, RA053
Palaces, King's ♌ LI095
Pale Colored ♄ DA017
Pale Green ☽ DA026
Palermo ♉ LI094
Palestine ♈ DA006, PA073, PT157
Pallbearers ♄ RA050
Palm Tree ☽ RA063
Palm Tree ⊙ DA023
Palm Tree ☿ LI272
Palm Tree ♄ LI272
Palpitations ⊙ LI071, PA129
Palpitations 11th House RS100
Palpitations of the Heart ⊙ RA058
Palpitations of the Heart ♃ RA053
Palsy ☽ DA026, RS021
Palsy ♄ DA018, RS019
Palsy ♓ DA014
Palsy 5th House GA051
Pamphilia, S. Asia Minor ♓ DA014, PA076
Panorme, Sicily ♉ DA006
Panormus [= Palermo] ♉ LI094
Panther ☽ RA064
Panther ♀ LI075, RA060
Panther ♂ LI068, RA055
Papaver rhoeas ☽ CU, GA072, RA063
Papaver rhoeas ♄ RA050
Papaver somniferum ☽ CU
Papia, Italy ♍ DA009
Papis, Italy ♍ PA074
Paralysis see Apoplexy

Parents 4th House AB275
Parents Have Short Life ♂ in 10th House GA060
Parents, Honorable ♃ in 4th House GA050
Parietaria officinalis ☿ CU, GA071
Paris ☿ DA026, LI080
Paris ♍ DA009, LI096, PA074
Paris quadrifolia ♀ CU, GA070
Parks ♌ DA008, LI095
Parliamentarians ♃ PA108
Parlors ☉ RA058
Parma ♉ LI094, PA073
Parrot ☿ LI079, RA062
Parsley ☿ RA062
Parsley (Common) ☿ CU, GA071
Parsnip ♀ GA070
Parsnip ♄ LI059, RA050
Parthia ♀ RA060
Parthia, Iran ♀ DA024, LI076
Parthia, Iran ♉ DA006, LI094, PA073
Partner (as in Business) 7th House LI369
Partner's Money (Benefit Querent?) 8th House GA284, LI412
Partners 7th House GA054
Partnership 7th House AB275
Partnerships (Shall They Agree?) 7th House GA276, LI369
Partridge ☽ AB247
Partridge ♀ LI075, RA060
Partridge ♃ LI064, RA053
Partridge (Francolin) ♃ AB247
Party at Home 1st House LI147
Party at Home 4th House LI147
Party at Home 7th House LI147
Party at Home 10th House LI147
Party Far from Home 3rd House LI147
Party Far from Home 6th House LI147
Party Far from Home 9th House LI147
Party Far from Home 12th House LI147
Passion ♂ AB245, LI067
Passions of the Womb ♀ DA024
Pastimes 5th House LI169
Pasture ♈ LI093
Pasture ♉ DA006

Pasture 4th House LI052
Pasture with No Houses Near ♉ LI094
Pastureland not Sown ♉ AB230
Patience ♀ AB250
Patience ♄ LI058
Patient ☉ AB250
Patient ♃ AB250
Patient (Medical) 1st House S2-41
Patient (Medical) 10th House S2-40
Patient (Inquiry After) 7th House S2-28
Patrimony 4th House GA050
Patronage, usually Religious 9th House LI055
Paunch ♄ RS014
Paunch, Large with Folds ☉ AB249
Paymaster ♄ AB254
Pea Hen ♃ LI064
Peace (Mundane & Eclipses) 7th House PA044
Peace or War 7th House LI054
Peace-Loving ☽ LI081
Peaceful ♒ AB231
Peaceful ♑ AB231
Peaceful ♓ AB231
Peaceful Existence ♃ PT183
Peacemaker ♃ AB250
Peach ♀ DA024, RA060
Peach Tree ♀ CU, GA070
Peach Tree ♃ AB244
Peaches ♀ LI075
Peacock ☉ LI072
Peacock ♃ AB247, LI064, RA053
Peacock ♄ LI060, RA050
Pear Tree ♃ AB244, LI064, RA053
Pear Tree ♀ CU, GA070, RA060
Pear, Wild ♂ AB244
Pearls ☽ AB243
Pearls ♀ AB243
Pearls, Dealing in ♀ AB254
Peas ☿ AB243
Pecten ☿ RS182
Pedagogue ♎ LI451
Pelican ♀ LI075, RA060

Pellitory of Spain ☿ CU
Pellitory of the Wall ☿ CU, GA071
Peltigera canina ♃ CU
Peltigera canina ♋ CU
Penile Erection, Pathol. ♏ LI097
Penis ♀ S2-56
Penis ♄ AB248
Penis ♏ RS015
Penis 8th House RS015
Pennycress (Thlaspi) ♂ GA068
Pennyroyal ♀ CU, GA070
Pennywort (Common Marsh) ♀ CU
Pensions ☉ LI556
Penury ♌ in 12th House GA063
People, Common ☽ DA026
Pepper ☉ RA057
Pepper ♂ CU, DA021, LI068, RA054
Pepper ♄ AB243
Pepper (Guinea) ♂ CU
Peppermint ♀ CU
Pepperwort (Lepidium) ♂ GA068
Peregrinations ☽ PA110
Perfection, Anxiety for in All ☿ AB254
Perfidious ☿ LI541
Performing High Matters ♃ LI540
Perfume ♀ AB250, PT337
Perfume 11th House AB275
Perfume Merchants ♀ PT337
Perfumers ♀ GA070, LI074, PA015, RA058
Pergamo ♈ DA006
Perils in Younger Years ☉ in 7th House GA055
Peripneumonia ♃ RS019
Periwinkle ♀ GA070
Periwinkle (Great) ♀ CU
Perjured ♂ GA068, PA013
Perjurer ♂ LI066
Perjury ☿ GA071, PA016
Persia ♀ PT141
Persia ♃ DA020, LI065, RA053
Persia ♉ DA006, LI094, PA073, PT141
Person Low in Stature ♓ PA009

Person, Tall & Slender ♍ PA006
Persons Employed by Native 6th House GA053
Persons, Trafficed with 7th House GA054
Pertinaceous ♄ LI539
Perturbations ♂ in 7th House GA055
Perusium caput histria ♉ DA006
Pestilence ♂ PA128, PT431
Pestilence ♌ LI095, RS017
Pestilent Airs ♂ LI068
Petasites hybridus ☉ CU, GA069
Peter ♂ LI341
Petroselinum crispum ☿ CU, GA071, RA062
Pets ☿ LI541
Petty ♄ PT341
Pettyfoggers ☿ RA061
Peucedanum officinale ☿ CU
Peucedanum ostruthium ♂ CU, GA068
Pewter ♃ RA053
Pewterers ☉ GA069, LI071, PA014
Pharaonic Glass ☉ AB243
Pharmacists ♀ LI628
Pharmacists ♂ LI067
Pharmacists ♏ LI451
Phasania [= Phasiana = Colchis] ♓ DA014
Phaseolus vulgaris ♀ CU
Pheasant ♃ LI064, RA053
Philanderer ♑ LI538
Phillip ☉ LI341
Philosophers ☿ AB254, GA071, LI078, PA016, RA061
Philosophical Skill ♄ in 9th House GA058
Philosophy ☿ DA025
Philosophy 9th House AB275
Phlegm ☽ AB247
Phlegm ♄ PT319
Phlegm, Salt [= Mucus] ♋ DA008, LI095, RS017
Phlegm, Salt [= Mucus] ♓ DA014, LI099, RS018
Phlegmatic ☽ in 1st House GA046
Phlegmatic ♋ PA005
Phlegmatic ♏ PA007
Phlegmatic ♓ PA009
Phoenicia ☉ DA022, LI072, PT143

Phoenicia ♌ DA008, PA074, PT143
Phoenix ☉ LI072, RA057
Phyllitis scolopendrium ♃ CU, GA068
Physalis alkekengi ♀ CU, GA070
Physicians ☉ AB252
Physicians ♂ DA021, GA068, LI067, PA013, RA054
Physicians ♏ LI451
Physicians (C.F. Zael) 1st House S2-40
Physicians 7th House LI054, PA044, S2-41
Physicians 10th House S2-24
Piacenza, Cis-Alpine AC Gaul [= Placentia] ♎ DA010
Picea abies ♃ CU
Picris echioides ♃ CU
Picture Drawers ♀ GA070, LI074, PA015, RA058
Piedmont ♒ DA013, LI099, PA076
Piercing Eye ♈ PA004
Piety 9th House AB275
Pigeon ☿ AB247
Pigeon ♀ RA060
Pigeon ♃ AB247
Pigeon, Wild (Stock Dove) ♀ LI075, RA060
Pigeon, Wild (Stock Dove) ♃ LI064, RA053
Pigs ☽ RA064
Pigs ♄ RA051
Pigs 6th House LI558
Pigs, Wild ♂ AB246
Pike ♂ LI068, RA055
Piles (Disease) ♏ LI097
Pilewort ♄ GA067
Pilfering ☿ GA071
Pilgrimage 9th House LI422
Pilgrims ☽ GA072, LI081
Pimpernel ☉ GA069
Pimpernel ☿ RA062
Pimpernel ♃ DA020, LI064, RA052
Pimpinella major ☽ CU
Pimpinella saxifraga ☽ CU
Pimples (Pushes, Whelks) ☉ LI071
Pimples (Pushes, Whelks) ♂ DA021
Pimples (Pushes, Whelks) ♈ LI093, PA004, RS016
Pimples (Pushes, Whelks) ♋ DA007

Pimples, Facial ☉ RS020
Pimples, Facial ♌ DA008
Pimples, Facial ♑ DA012
Pine Tree ♂ CU
Pine Tree ♃ LI064, RA053
Pine Tree ♄ DA018, LI059, RA050
Pinus sylvestris ♂ CU
Pinus sylvestris ♃ LI064, RA053
Pinus sylvestris ♄ LI059, RA050
Piper cubeba ☿ DA025, LI079
Piper nigrum ☉ RA057
Piper nigrum ♂ CU, LI068, RA054
Piper nigrum ♄ AB243
Pipers ♀ LI074, PA015, RA058
Piping of Water ☽ LI214
Piping of Water ♄ LI214
Piracy ☿ PT187
Piracy ♂ PT185
Pirapirasta* ☿ LI272
Pirapirasta* ♄ LI272
Pirates ♂ LI629
Pisa, Italy ♋ DA008, PA074
Pisa, Italy ♒ DA013
Pisaurun, Italy [= Pesaro] ♒ LI099
Pis[s]mires (Ants) ☿ LI079, RA062
Pistacia lentiscus ☽ RA063
Pistacia lentiscus ♃ DA020, LI064
Pistacia lentiscus ♌ PA074
Pistoria, Italy [= Pistorium] ♏ DA011, PA075
Pistorium [= Pistoria, Italy] ♏ DA011, PA075
Pitch ☉ AB243
Pitch Dark ♄ AB240
Pitiful ♀ DA023, PA094
Pitiless ♂ PT353
Pity ♀ PA109
Placenta ♎ LI097, PA075

Places (Arable Land) ♉ PA005
Places (Barren) ♑ PA009
Places (where Brick Burned) ♂ DA021, LI068
Places (Brooks) ♋ PA006
Places (Castles) ♌ PA006
Places (Caves) ♓ PA010
Places (Chests) ♊ PA005
Places (Cisterns) ♋ PA006
Places (Coffers) ♊ PA005
Places (to Cool Water) ☽ AB242
Places (Corn-Fields) ♍ PA007
Places (Cow-Houses) ♑ PA009
Places (Dairy) ♍ PA007
Places (Fallow Ground) ♑ PA009
Places (Fish-Ponds) ♓ PA010
Places (Forests) ♌ PA006
Places (Forts) ♌ PA006
Places (Gardens) ♏ PA008
Places (where Grain is Stored) ♍ PA007
Places (Great & Navigable Rivers) ♋ PA006
Places (Halls or Dining Rooms) ♊ PA005
Places (where Hawking/Hunting) ♎ PA007
Places (High) ♊ DA007
Places (Hills) ♊ PA005
Places (Hilly) ♒ DA013
Places (Hilly & Uneven) ♒ PA009
Places (with Husbandry Tools) ♑ DA013
Places (Inaccessible) ♌ DA008, LI095, PA006
Places (King's Palaces) ♌ PA006
Places (where Minerals Are) ♒ PA009
Places (Moats Around Houses) ♓ PA010
Places (Moist) ♋ PA006
Places (Moist Moorish Grounds) ♓ PA010
Places (Moorish Grounds) ♏ PA008
Places (Mountainous Places) ♊ PA005
Places (Muddy) ♄ DA019
Places (Muddy, Dirty, Stinking) ♄ RA051
Places (Near Church Altars) ♃ DA019
Places (Near Conduit Head) ♒ DA013
Places (Near Rivers) ♋ DA008
Places (Near Small Springs) ♒ DA013

Places (Neat) ♃ LI064
Places (Newly Dug) ♒ LI099
Places (with Old Wood) ♑ DA013
Places (of Oratory) ♃ PA012
Places (Orchards) ♏ PA008
Places (Out - Lone Houses) ♎ PA007
Places (Pastures) ♉ PA005
Places (Plain Ground) ♉ PA005
Places (Private, Unfrequented) ♈ PA004
Places (Quagmires) ♏ PA008
Places (Ruinous Houses near Water) ♏ PA008
Places (the Sea) ♋ PA006
Places (Sinks) ♋ PA006
Places (Small Cattle Feeding) ♈ PA004
Places (Springs) ♋ PA006
Places (Stables) ♐ PA008
Places (Steep & Rocky) ♌ DA008
Places (Steep Rocks) ♌ PA006
Places (Stinking) ♄ DA018
Places (Stinking Lakes) ♏ PA008
Places (Stone Quarries) ♒ DA013, PA009
Places (Storehouses) ♊ PA005
Places (Study Where Books Are) ♍ PA007
Places (Threshold) ♑ DA013
Places (for Tools of Husbandry) ♑ PA009
Places (where Travellers Meet) 7th House AB276
Places (Uneven) ♒ LI099
Places (Uneven Ground) ♒ DA013
Places (Upland, Hilly Grounds) ♐ PA008
Places (Wainscot) ♊ PA005
Places (Wash Houses) ♋ PA006
Places (Water Mills) ♓ PA010
Places (Water-courses) ♋ PA006
Places (Wells Near Houses) ♋ PA006
Places (Windmills) ♎ PA007
Places (where Wood is Cut) ♎ LI096
Places (where Wood Was Cut Recently) ♎ PA007
Places (Woods) ♌ PA006
Places in Houses (with Books) ♍ LI096
Places in Houses (Ceiling) ♈ PA004
Places in Houses (Cellars) ♋ PA006

Places in Houses (Cellars) ♉ PA005
Places in Houses (Chambers) ♎ PA007
Places in Houses (Chimneys) ♌ PA006
Places in Houses (Cisterns) ♓ PA010
Places in Houses (Closet/Books) ♍ PA007
Places in Houses (Dining Room) ♊ PA005
Places in Houses (East Part) ♈ PA004
Places in Houses (Eaves) ♒ PA009
Places in Houses (where Fire is) ♌ PA006
Places in Houses (Garrets) ♎ PA007
Places in Houses (Kitchen) ♏ PA008
Places in Houses (Larder) ♏ PA008
Places in Houses (Living Room) ♊ PA005
Places in Houses (Low) ♉ PA005
Places in Houses (Low Rooms) ♉ PA005
Places in Houses (Near Ground) ♑ PA009
Places in Houses (Near Threshold) ♑ PA009
Places in Houses (Roofs) ♒ PA009
Places in Houses (Sinks) ♏ PA008
Places in Houses (Standing Water) ♓ PA010
Places in Houses (Turrets) ♎ PA007
Places in Houses (Upper Rooms) ♎ PA007
Places in Houses (Upper Rooms) ♐ PA008
Places in Houses (Upstairs/Fire) ♐ PA008
Places in Houses (Vaults) ♉ PA005
Places in Houses (Wash-House) ♏ PA008
Places in Houses (Wells) ♓ PA010
Places in Houses (about Window) ♒ PA009
Places of Worship ♀ AB242
Plague ♂ DA020, LI067, PA013, RA055, RS020
Plague ♃ RS019
Plague ♌ LI095, RS017
Plain Ground ♉ LI094
Plains ☽ AB241
Plaintiff 1st House LI403
Plantago coronopus ♀ CU
Plantago coronopus ♄ GA067
Plantago lanceolata ♀ CU
Plantago major ♀ CU, GA070
Plantain ♀ CU, GA070
Plantain (Buck's Horn) ♀ CU

Plantain (Ribwort) ♀ CU
Planting ☽ DA026, PA239
Planting ♄ PA239
Plants Bearing Husks or Pods ☿ LI079
Plants with No Seeds/Berries ♍ AB230
Plants with Spreading Leaves ☽ DA027
Plastering in Houses ♈ LI093
Plastering in Houses ♊ DA007, LI094
Plasy 12th House RS100
Plasy ♄ RA051
Players ♀ GA070, LI074
Playhouses ♀ RA060
Playrooms ♊ DA007, LI094
Plays 5th House LI053
Plays ♀ LI556
Plays ♀ in 5th House GA052
Pleasant ♀ LI541, PT357
Pleasant ♃ AB241
Pleasant Faced ♂ AB250
Pleasant Man ♀ LI073
Pleasure 5th House AB275, GA051, LI053, PA043
Pleasure ♀ GA070, RA058
Pleasure-Seeking ♀ DA023, PA094
Pleasures Destroyed ☋ in 5th House GA052
Pleura, Diseases of ♋ PA005
Pleurisy ♃ DA019, LI063, PA012, RA053, RS019
Pleurisy ♋ DA008
Pleurisy ♌ LI095, RS017
Pleurisy 4th House RS100
Pleurisy, Bastard ☉ RS020
Plotters ☿ LI541
Plotters ♄ PT341
Ploughman's Spikenard ♀ CU
Plowmen ♄ RA050
Plumbers ♄ GA067, LI059, RA050
Plump ♀ PT311
Plums ♀ CU, DA024, GA070, LI075
Plutocrats ♀ AB252
Pneumonia ♃ PT429
Pneumonia 4th House RS100
Podagra (see *foot gout*)

Podex (Anus) ♄ AB248
Poet ♎ LI451
Poetic Propensity ☽ in 9th House GA059
Poetical ♀ LI541
Poetry ☿ AB254
Poets ☿ GA071, LI078, PA016, RA061
Poets ♀ DA024, PA110
Poison ♀ PT431
Poison 8th House LI054
Poison Pen ☿ GA071
Poisoning 8th House AB275
Poisonous Drugs ♄ AB245
Poland ♀ RA060
Poland, Greater ♀ DA024
Poland, Greater ♉ LI094, PA073
Poland, Lessor ♈ PA073
Polemonium Caeruleum ☿ CU
Political ☿ LI077
Politician ♍ LI451
Polonia ♀ LI076
Polonia ♈ DA006, LI094
Polonia the Great ♉ DA006
Polygonatum multiforum ♄ CU, GA067
Polygonum ♂ CU, GA068, LI068, RA054
Polygonum ♃ DA020
Polygonum ♄ CU
Polygonum bistorta ♄ CU, GA067
Polypodium vulgare ♃ in ♌ CU
Polypodium vulgare ♄ DA018, GA067, LI059, RA050
Polypody ♃ in ♌ CU
Polypody ♄ DA018, GA067, LI059, RA050
Polyps (Polypus) ♈ LI093, RS016
Polypus (Disease) ♈ LI093, RS016
Pomecitron (Citron) ☉ DA022, LI071, RA057
Pomegranites ☿ CU, LI272
Pomegranites ♀ RA060
Pomegranites ♃ LI064, RA053
Pomegranites ♄ LI272
Pomegranites, Bitter ♂ AB244
Pomegranites, Bitter ♄ AB243
Pomegranites, Sweet ☽ AB244

Pomegranites, Wild ♃ AB243
Pompion (Pumpkin) ☽ DA026, LI082, RA063
Pools ☽ PA018, RA064
Poor Harvests 5th House AB276
Pope's Legates ☽ LI081
Popinian (Bird)* ☿ LI079
Popinjay ☿ RA062
Poplar (Black) ♄ CU
Poplar (White) ♄ CU
Poplar Tree ♄ GA067
Poppy ☽ DA026, GA072, LI082, RA063
Poppy ♄ DA018, LI059, RA050
Poppy (White or Opium) ☽ CU
Poppy (Wild) ☽ CU
Populus ♄ GA067
Populus alba ♄ CU
Populus nigra ♄ CU
Porphyrio (Bird) ☿ RA062
Port Towns ☽ LI082, RA064
Portion of Wife or Sweetheart 8th House PA045
Portland, England ♑ PA076
Ports ☽ DA027
Portugal ♓ DA014, LI099
Portulaca oleracea ☽ GA072
Posnania, Poland ♉ DA006, PA073
Possessions ♄ DA018
Posture (Inclining, Head Forward) ♄ DA018
Posture (not Very Straight) ♓ DA014
Posture (Stooping in Shoulders) ♓ PA009
Potentilla anserina ♀ CU
Potentilla erecta ☉ CU, GA069
Potentilla reptans ☉ DA023, LI071, RA057
Potentilla reptans ♃ CU, GA068
Potters ♄ DA017, LI059
Potters Vessels ♂ AB242
Pourcontrell (Fish) ☿ RA062
Poverty ♄ AB250, PT181
Poverty ♃ in 12th House GA062
Poverty 2nd House LI051, PA042
Poverty 6th House AB276
Poverty 8th House AB275

Poverty or Wealth of Nation 2nd House LI051
Powerful ♂ PT353
Powerful ☉ in 1st House GA046
Pox ♃ RS019
Pox ♏ PA008
Practice of Medicine ☽ AB254
Praecordiacs (Over Heart) ♋ RS015
Praecordiacs (Over Heart) 4th House RS015
Prague ♌ LI096, PA074
Pragus ♌ DA008
Praise 11th House AB275, LI056
Prattler ☿ GA071, LI077
Prattler ♀ GA070
Prattler ♂ GA068, LI066, PA012
Prayer 11th House AB275
Precious Things ♀ DA024
Precipitate ☿ PT361
Preferment ☉ LI556
Preferment 10th House GA059, LI055, PA046
Preferments from Great Persons ⊗ in 10th House GA061
Pregnancy 5th House LI226, PA043
Pregnant (Is the Querent?) 5th House GA265, LI226
Pregnant Women ☽ AB252
Pregnant Women 5th House LI053
Prejudiced about Large Animals ☋ in 12th House GA063
Prelates ♃ LI555, PA108
Premature Births ♀ PT321
Prenatal Fancies of Mother 12th House AB275
Preserves True Friends ☿ AB250
Pretender to Knowledge ☿ GA071
Pretending Friendship ♂ in 11th House GA061
Pretending to Knowledge ☿ LI078
Priapism ♀ PA129, RA061, RS021
Priapsim ♏ RS018
Price of House 10th House LI208
Price of Land 10th House LI208
Prickings ♃ RA053
Pride ♀ AB250
Pride 8th House AB276
Prideful ♃ PA093
Priests ♃ GA067, LI063, RA052

Prime Officers 10th House LI055
Primrose ♀ CU, GA070
Primula veris ♀ CU, GA070
Primula veris ♈ CU
Primula vulgaris ♀ CU, GA070
Princely Dignities ☉ DA022
Princely Fame after Death ☉ in 4th House GA050
Princes ☉ DA022, GA069, LI071, PA014, RA056
Princes ♃ GA067
Princes 10th House LI055
Princes by Usurping ♂ GA068
Princes Ruling by Tyranny ♂ LI067
Principal Magistrate ☉ LI071
Principalities ♃ DA019
Printer ☿ LI078
Printer ♍ LI451
Printers ☿ GA071
Prison ♂ AB254
Prison ♄ LI555
Prison 3rd House AB276
Prison 6th House AB276
Prison 12th House AB275
Prison for Wizards ☽ AB254
Prisoner (When Freed?) 12th House GA293, LI461, PA072
Prisoners 12th House AB276, LI461
Prisons ♄ PA108
Private Enemies 12th House LI056
Privet ☽ GA072
Privy Parts ♏ DA010, LI246
Privy Parts 8th House GA056, LI054
Privy Parts, Diseases of ♏ PA008
Prodigal ☽ DA026, LI081
Prodigal ♂ DA021
Prodigal ♃ GA067, LI540, PA093
Prodigal ♂ in 1st House GA046
Profession 10th House AB275, GA059, LI055, PA046
Profession of Children 2nd House AB275
Profession What to Follow? 10th House GA290, LI450
Professors of Philosophy ☿ PA110
Proficient in Mathematics ☿ in 10th House GA060
Profit ♀ PT187

Profit by Church Business ♃ in 10th House GA060
Profit by Inventions ☉ in 10th House GA060
Profit by Judicial Offices ♃ in 10th House GA060
Profit by Negotiation ♃ in 10th House GA060
Profit from Friends ♀ in 11th House GA062
Profit from Inventions ♀ in 9th House GA058
Profit from Journeys ☊ in 9th House GA059
Profit from Martial Matters ♂ in 10th House GA060
Profit from Office 11th House LI559
Profit from Religion ☊ in 3rd House GA049
Profit from Rental of Property 10th House LI208
Profit or Gain 2nd House LI051
Profit or Loss 2nd House LI170
Profit or Loss from Small Cattle 6th House LI053
Profits from Martial Ventures ♂ in 11th House GA061
Profound in Imagination ♄ LI058
Promoter of Mischief ♂ GA068
Promotion (Preferment) 10th House PA046
Promotion through Friends 11th House LI559
Prone to Venery ♀ LI074
Propense to Astrology ☽ in 9th House GA059
Propense to Study ☽ GA072
Propensity toward Mathematics ☿ in 3rd House GA049
Property, Increase ♀ PT185
Property Managers ♄ PT335
Property of Oppressors 12th House AB276
Property, Wife's 8th House AB275
Proportion, Good or Equal ♍ DA009
Prosperity ♃ PT183
Prosperity ⊗ in 2nd House GA048
Prosperity of Father's Kin ⊗ in 6th House GA054
Prosperity of Uncles & Aunts ⊗ in 6th House GA054
Prosperous Journeys ⊗ in 3rd House GA049
Prostitutes (= Gamesters) ♀ LI074
Prostitutes (= Gamesters) ♂ LI067
Prostitutes (= Gamesters) ♓ LI451
Prostitutes (= Gamesters) 12th House LI559
Prostitution ♄ LI555
Protection by Friends ⊗ in 2nd House GA048
Proud ☉ GA069, LI070
Proud ☿ DA025

Proud ♃ LI540
Provident ☉ DA022
Provokes Others ♂ LI540
Prudent ☉ GA069, LI070
Prudent ☿ PA094, PT361
Prudent ♂ GA068, PA012
Prudent ♃ GA067, LI062
Prudent ☿ in 1st House GA046
Prudent ♃ in 1st House GA046
Prudent in Own Affairs ♂ LI066
Prunella vulgaris ♀ CU, GA070
Prunella vulgaris ♃ LI064
Prunus domestica ♀ CU, GA070
Prunus persica ♀ CU, GA070, RA060
Prunus persica ♃ AB244
Prunus spinosa ♄ CU
Prussia ♋ DA008, LI095, PA074
Pteridium aquilinum ☿ CU
Ptisick (Tuberculosis) ☿ PA130, RA062, RS021
Ptisick (Tuberculosis) ♋ DA007, LI095, RS017
Ptisis ♄ RS019
Pubes ♂ AB248
Public Employment ☉ LI556
Public Enemies 7th House LI054
Public Enemies, Many ♅ in 7th House GA056
Public Matters, Important 1st House AB276
Puglia, Italy ♌ LI096, PA074
Pulicaria dysenterica ♀ CU
Pulmonaria officinalis ☿ LI079, RA062
Pulmonaria officinalis ♃ CU, GA068, LI064, RA052
Pulpits ♃ AB242
Pulse ♃ LI246, PA128, RA053, RS014
Pulse ♄ LI059, RA050
Pulse, High and Swift ♂ RS020
Pulse, Low ♀ RS021
Pulses ♃ DA019
Pumpkin ☽ CU, DA026, LI082, RA063
Pumps ♓ LI099
Pungent but not Poisonous ♂ AB245
Pungent, Evil Smelling Trees ☿ AB244
Pungent, Trees ♂ AB244

Punica granatum ☿ CU
Punica granatum ♀ RA060
Punica granatum ♃ RA053
Purchase of Land by Querent 4th House DA100, GA258, LI204, PA064
Pure White tending to Straw ♀ AB240
Purges (Cathars) ☽ DA026
Purges (Cathars) ☉ DA022
Purges (Cathars) ☿ DA025
Purging (Scouring) 10th House RS100
Purple ☉ LI071
Purple ♀ LI086
Purple ♃ DA019, LI063, RA052
Purple (Some Say) ☉ DA022
Purple-Yellow ☉ LI086
Purslane ☽ GA072
Pushes ♈ RS016
Pushes (Pimples) ♂ DA021
Pushes (Pimples) ♈ LI093
Pushes (Pimples) ♋ DA007
Pushes in the Face ♌ DA008
Pushes in the Face ♑ DA012
Pushes in the Interior Parts ☉ DA022
Pushes in the Womb ☉ DA022
Putrefying Animals ♄ RA051
Putrefying Creatures ♄ LI060
Pye (Bird) ☿ LI079
Pye (Bird) ♀ LI075, RA060
Pye (Bird) ♂ LI068
Pyles in the Ars ♏ RS018
Pyrola minor ☽ CU
Pyrus sativa ♀ CU, GA070, RA060
Pyrus sativa ♃ AB244, LI064, RA053

-- Q --

Quack-salvers ♃ RA052
Quagmires ♏ DA011, LI097
Quality & Nature of Grounds 4th House LI052
Quality of Life ♀ PT185
Quarreling with Siblings ☋ in 3rd House GA049
Quarreller ♂ DA020, PA013

Quarrels ♂ LI556
Quarrels ♂ in 7th House GA055
Quarrels ♄ in 7th House GA054
Quarrels 2nd House PA042
Quarrels 7th House PA044
Quarrels with Eminent Women ☿ in 7th House GA055
Quarrels with Kindred ♂ in 10th House GA060
Quarrelsome ♂ AB250, GA068, LI540
Quarrelsome ♄ PA092
Quarries ♒ DA013, LI099
Quarries 4th House LI575
Quarrymen ♂ PT337
Quartan[e] Agues Fevers (Malaria) ♄ DA012, PT181, RA051
Queens ☽ DA026, GA072, LI081, PA110
Queens ♀ AB252
Quercus infectoria ♄ CU
Quercus robur ♃ CU, GA068, LI064, RA053
Querent 1st House LI147
Querent's Friends (Eclipses) 2nd House PA042
Querent's Friends (Mundane) 2nd House PA042
Querent's Life 1st House PA041
Querent's Wealth 2nd House PA042
Quick = sighted ♌ PA006
Quick-tempered ♂ PT353
Quicksilver ☿ AB243, DA025, LI079
Quiet ☉ DA022
Quiet Man ♀ LI073
Quince ☿ LI272
Quince ♀ AB244
Quince ♄ LI272
Quince Tree ♄ CU, GA067
Quinsy (Tonsillitis) ♀ PA129
Quinsy (Tonsillitis) ♉ PA005, RS016
Quotidian (Recurring) Fever ☽ RS021
Quotidian (Recurring) Fever ☿ PT187
Quotidian (Recurring) Fever ♂ DA020, LI579

-- R --

Rabbit ☽ LI082
Rabbit ♀ LI075, RA060

Rabbits 6th House LI053, PA044
Races, Foot ☿ PA248
Rachel ♃ LI341
Radish ☉ LI273
Radish ♂ AB244, CU, DA021, GA068, LI068, RA054
Ragwort ♀ CU, GA070
Raisins ♀ DA024, LI075
Raisins ♃ LI064
Ram ☉ LI071, RA058
Rampion (Sheep's) ☿ CU
Ranger, Park 6th House LI053
Rank, Advancement in 1st House AB276
Ranunculus auricomus ♂ CU, GA068
Ranunculus ficaria ♄ GA067
Ranunculus ficaria ♂ CU
Rapaceous ♂ DA021
Rapacious ♂ PT353
Rape (Plant) ☽ DA026, LI082
Rapeseed ☽ RA063
Raphanus sativus ♂ CU, GA068, RA054
Rapontick = Rhapontic ♂ GA068
Raptors ♂ LI068, RA055
Rascals ☿ PT361
Rash ♂ AB250, DA021, GA068, LI066, PA093, PT353
Rash ♂ in 3rd House GA049
Raspberry ♀ CU
Rational ♒ DA013
Rationality ☿ PA017
Ratisbon[e], Germany ♓ DA014, LI099, PA076
Rats ☽ RA064
Rattle Grass ☽ CU, GA072
Raven ♂ LI068, RA055
Ravenna ♄ DA018, LI061, RA051
Ravenna ♌ DA008, LI096, PA074
Ravenous ♂ LI066
Ravenous ♄ DA018
Ravenous & Bold Animals ♂ LI068
Ravens ♄ AB247
Re-algar (Arsenic Monosulpide) ☉ AB243
Ready ☿ PA094
Ready to Punish ♄ PT341

Ready Understanding ♊ PA005
Real Estate 4th House AB275
Reason ☿ PA097
Reception Room ☿ PA017
Recklessness ♃ AB250
Reclaiming Land ♄ AB254
Rectitude 5th House AB276
Red ♂ DA020, LI067, PT193, RA054
Red ♌ LI086
Red 3rd House LI052, PA042
Red 4th House AB277, LI052, PA043
Red 10th House AB277
Red & Green ♃ LI086
Red & White 10th House LI055, PA046
Red Arsenic ♃ AB243
Red Beets ♄ GA067
Red Brambles ♂ LI068
Red Clover ♀ GA070
Red Hair ♂ AB249, DA021, GA068, LI636, PT311
Red Lead (Paint Pigment) ♂ DA021
Red Marble ☿ RA062
Red Sanders (Herb) ♂ DA021, LI068, RA054
Red Things ♂ AB241
Red-White ♈ LI086
Red-White ♊ LI086
Reddish Flowers ☉ LI071
Redness of Face ♂ RS020
Reeds ☽ AB244
Reeds ☿ LI079
Refuge for Thieves ♈ LI093
Relations 3rd House AB275
Relations-in-Law 3rd House AB275
Relationship Satisfaction ♀ PT185
Reliever of Poor ♃ LI062
Religion 9th House AB275, GA058
Religion ♃ AB254, PA108
Religion, Changeable ♂ in 9th House GA058
Religion, Strenuous in ☽ AB254
Religious ♃ AB250, DA019, LI062, PA092
Religious ♀ in 3rd House GA049
Religious ♀ in 9th House GA058

Religious ♃ in 3rd House GA049
Religious ☊ in 3rd House GA049
Religious ☊ in 9th House GA059
Religious ♉ DA006
Religious ♒ DA013
Religious Conventions ♃ DA020
Religious Dissenter ☿ GA071
Religious Dissenter ♄ GA067
Religious Men 9th House LI055
Religious of Various Sects ♄ AB252
Religious Sects 9th House LI558
Religious Siblings ⊗ in 3rd House GA049
Removal from One House to Another 1st House LI212
Removals 3rd House GA048
Remove or Abide? 4th House GA260, LI212
Removing from Place to Place 3rd House PA042
Renown ☉ PA109
Renown 10th House GA059
Rent Collector ♊ LI451
Renter, of Land or House 1st House LI208
Repining ♄ GA067, LI058
Reporter of Own Acts ♂ GA068
Reproaches ♃ in 12th House GA062
Reproduction ♀ PA129
Reproductive Diseases ♀ RA060, RS014, RS020
Reproductive Problems, Men ♃ RA053
Reproductive System Diseases ☽ RS021
Reproductive Tract Diseases ♀ LI247
Reproving Evil-Doers ☉ AB250
Reputation 10th House LI213
Reputation Destroyed ♂ in 4th House GA050
Reseda luteola ♂ GA068
Reserve ♄ LI058
Resolute ☉ DA022
Resourcefulness ☽ PT361
Respected by People ☽ AB250
Responsible ♃ AB250
Rest-Harrow ♂ CU, LI068
Rest-Harrow ☿ GA071
Restaurant 5th House GA051, LI169
Restaurant ☿ LI079

Restless ☉ GA069, LI070
Result of Taking Property 4th House LI208
Retail Supplier ♄ GA067, RA050
Retention ♄ PA011, RS102
Retentive Power ♄ AB245
Reveals Secrets ☽ AB250
Revelling 5th House GA051
Revengeful ♂ LI540, PA093
Revenue ☿ PT187
Reverence ☉ PT363
Reverencing Aged Men ♃ LI062
Revilers of Demons ♄ AB252
Revilers of Ghouls ♄ AB252
Revilers of Magicians ♄ AB252
Revolution ☉ AB241
Rhamnus catharticus ♄ CU, GA067
Rhapontic ♂ GA068
Rhaponticum sive rha ♂ GA068
Rheims, France ♓ DA014, LI099, PA076
Rheine, Germany [= Rhene] ♍ DA009
Rhene (Part) [= Rheine, Ger.] ♍ DA009
Rhetia (Tyrol) ♉ DA006, PA073
Rhetoric ☿ DA025
Rheum ☿ PA130
Rheum & Defluction, Diseases ♉ PA005
Rheum palmatum ♂ CU, GA068
Rheum palmatum ♃ RA052
Rheum rhaponticum ♂ CU, GA068
Rheumatic Diseases (Cold) ☽ RS021
Rheumatism ♄ PA127, PT181
Rheumes in the Eyes ☽ LI082
Rheums ☽ DA026, RS021
Rheums ☉ DA022
Rheums ♄ DA017, LI059, PA127
Rheums, Fluxes ♉ RS016
Rhinanthus ☽ CU, GA072
Rhine (Part) ♍ PA074
Rhodes ♍ DA009, LI096, PA074
Rhubarb ♂ CU, GA068
Rhubarb ♃ DA020, LI064, RA052
Rhus coggyria ♃ CU

Rib Diseases ♃ RS019
Rib Diseases ♌ RS017
Ribes uva-crispa ♀ CU
Ribes uva-crispa ♃ LI064, RA053
Ribs ♃ DA019, LI063, PA012, RS014
Ribs ♋ DA007, RS015
Ribs ♌ DA008, LI095
Ribs 4th House RS015
Ribs, Disease of ♋ PA005
Rice ☉ CU
Rice ♃ AB243
Rich ♃ DA019
Rich and their Syncophants ♃ AB252
Rich from Inheritance ⊗ in 8th House GA058
Rich Men ♃ LI555, PA108
Rich or Poor 2nd House GA249, LI167, PA062
Richard ♃ LI341
Rich & Eminent Parents ♀ in 4th House GA050
Riches ☉ DA022
Riches ♃ PA105
Riches ⊗ PA105
Riches 2nd House GA047
Riches ☊ in 1st House GA046
Riches and Honors from Religion ☊ in 9th House GA059
Riches from Great Persons ⊗ in 10th House GA061
Riches from Lands and Houses ♃ in 4th House GA050
Riches, Great ♃ in 10th House GA060
Riches, Great ☊ in 2nd House GA048
Riches, Increased ☉ in 1st House GA046
Riches, Increased ♃ in 2nd House GA047
Riches, Never Settled ☽ in 2nd House GA048
Riches through Women ♀ in 2nd House GA047
Riches with Wives ☊ in 7th House GA056
Riches without Labor ♃ in 4th House GA050
Riches (Ecclesiastical Source) ☊ in 2nd House GA048
Riches (Means to Attain) 2nd House GA250, LI168
Riches (When in Life Attained) 2nd House GA250, LI171
Ridgebone, Prickling & Shooting ♃ LI246
Right Ear ♄ LI059, PT319
Right Eye (Men) ☉ LI071
Right Eye (Women) ☽ LI082

Right Side ☉ RS014
Right Side of Body ☉ PT319
Ring-Dove ☉ AB247
Rings, Silver ☽ AB254
Ringworm ♂ LI067, RS020
Ringworm ♃ RS019
Ringworm ♈ DA005, LI093, RS016
Rioting ♀ GA070
Riotous ♀ LI074
Ripest Things ♀ AB241
Rising from Low to High ☉ in 10th House GA060
Rivers ☽ DA027, LI082, PA018, RA064
Rivers ♋ DA008
Rivers Full of Fish ♓ DA014, LI099
Rivers, Great ♋ LI095
Rivers, Near ♋ LI095
Roads 9th House AB276
Roads with Trees ☽ AB242
Roadside Fires ♂ AB242
Robber ♂ PA093
Robbery ☿ PT187
Robbery ♂ PT185
Robert ♂ LI341
Robust ♄ PT305
Rocket Cress ♀ CU, GA070
Rocket Cress ♂ AB244
Rockrose (Labdanum) ♀ LI075
Rocky Places ♌ LI095
Roger ☉ LI341
Roman Empire ☉ RA058
Romandiola [French-Speaking Switzerland?] ♄ DA018, LI061, RA051
Rome ♌ DA008, LI096, PA074
Rome ♏ LI097, PA075
Roof of House ♒ DA013
Room within a Room ♎ LI096
Rooms, Low ♉ DA007, LI094
Rooms, Wainscot ♊ LI094
Root of Scarcity ♄ CU
Roots of a Tree ♄ AB236
Rosa Solis ☉ DA023, GA069, LI071, RA057
Rose ♀ RA060

Rose ♂ AB236
Rose ♃ AB244
Rose, Damask ♀ CU, GA070
Rose, Fresh ☿ LI272
Rose, Fresh ♄ LI272
Rose, Red ♃ GA068
Rose, White ☽ GA072
Rose, White ♀ DA024, LI075
Rosemary ☽ RA063
Rosemary ☉ CU, DA023, GA069, LI071, RA057
Rosmarinus officinalis ☽ RA063
Rosmarinus officinalis ☉ CU, GA069, LI071, RA057
Rotten Coughs ☽ LI082
Rotten Fevers ☉ LI071, RA058
Rottenburg, Germany ♐ DA012
Rotting Places ♏ LI097
Rouge ♂ AB243
Rough-Hewn ♄ LI539
Round, Lovely Beautiful Face ♎ PA007
Royal Palaces ♃ AB242
Rubbish ♄ DA017, LI060
Rubbish Heaps 8th House AB276
Rubia ♂ GA068
Rubia tinctorum ♂ CU
Rubus fructicosus ☿ LI272
Rubus fructicosus ♀ in ♈ CU
Rubus fructicosus ♄ LI272
Rubus idaeus ♀ CU
Ruby ☉ LI072, RA057
Ruby (Stone) ☉ DA022
Ruddy Sanguine Complexion in Youth ♎ PA007
Rude ♄ PA092
Rue ☉ GA069, LI273
Rue ♂ AB244, LI273
Rue ♄ DA018, LI059, RA050
Rue ☉ in ♌ CU
Rue (Herb Grace) ☉ LI071
Rue (Herb Grace) ♄ DA018, LI059
Rue, Goat's ☿ in ♌ CU
Rue, Wild ♂ AB244
Ruined Houses ♏ LI097

Ruining Prospects by Anxiety ☿ AB250
Ruining Prospects by Misfortune ☿ AB250
Rule ☉ PA109
Ruler ♃ PA108
Rumex acetosa ♀ CU, GA070
Rumex acetosella ♀ CU
Rumex alpinus ♂ CU
Rumex obtusifolius ♃ CU, GA068
Rumors 3rd House LI052, PA042
Rumors True or False? 3rd House DA095, GA256, LI193
Runaways 7th House PA044
Ruptures ♄ RS019
Ruptures ♏ DA011, LI097, RS018
Rupturewort ♄ GA067
Ruscus aculeatus ♂ CU, GA068
Rushes ♄ GA067
Rushes ♋ LI095
Russet ♑ LI086
Russet-Green ♋ LI086
Russia ♉ DA006, LI094, PA073
Ruta graveolens ☉ GA069
Ruta graveolens ☉ in ♌ CU

-- S --

Sabaud[i]a, Italy ♎ DA010
Sabina ♌ DA008
Sable ♄ AB246
Sad ♄ PA092
Saffron ☉ DA022, GA069, LI071, RA057
Saffron ♃ DA020, LI064, RA053
Saffron 11th House LI056
Saffron ☿ LI272
Saffron ♄ LI272
Saffron (Meadow) ♄ CU
Saffron (Wild,Safflower) ♄ CU
Saffron Color ♂ RA054
Sage ♃ GA068
Sage ♄ LI059, RA050
Sage (Common Garden) ♃ CU
Sage, Box ♄ DA018

Sage, Wood ♀ CU, GA070
Sailors ☽ DA026, GA072, LI081, LI557
Sailors ♄ RA050
Sailors ♒ LI451
Sailors & Passengers (Lord of) 1st House PA062
Saint Lucas ♋ LI095
Salix Alba ☽ CU, GA072
Salix Alba ♄ AB244, RA050
Sallendine = Celandine ☉ RA057
Sallow Tree ♄ DA018
Salsola kali ♂ CU
Salt ☽ AB240
Salt ♓ DA014
Saltpeter ☉ LI273
Saltpeter ♂ LI273
Saltwort ♂ CU
Salty Taste ☽ DA026
Saltzburg, Austria ♒ DA013
Salutary Things ☉ AB245
Salvia officinalis ♃ CU, GA068
Salvia officinalis ♄ RA050
Salvia sclarea ☽ CU
Salvia sclarea ♀ GA070
Salvia verbenaca ☽ CU
Samaria ♒ PA076
Sambucus ebulus ♀ CU
Sambucus nigra ☿ LI079
Sambucus nigra ♀ CU, GA070
Samphire ☿ GA071
Samphire (Rock or Small) ♃ CU
Sandy Fields ♎ LI096
Sandy Ground ♈ DA006, LI093
Sandy Growing Herbs ☿ LI079
Sandy Soil ☿ AB241
Sanguinaria (Bloodwort) ♃ GA068
Sanguine ♃ DA019
Sanguine ♎ PA007
Sanguine ♒ PA009
Sanguisorba minor ☉ CU, GA069
Sanicle ♀ DA024, GA070
Sanicle ♂ CU

Sanicula europaea ♀ GA070
Sanicula europaea ♂ CU
Santolina chamaecyparissus ☿ CU
Saponaria officinalis ♀ CU, GA070
Sapphire ♃ LI064, RA053
Sapphire ♄ DA017, LI060, RA051
Sapphire ♀ DA023, RA060
Sapphire, Blue ♀ LI075
Saracen's Consound (Senecio) ♄ GA067
Sardinia ♊ DA007, PA073
Sarmatia, Russia-Poland ♂ DA021, LI068
Sarmatia, Russia-Poland ♒ DA013
Sarsaparilla ♂ CU
Satiety ☽ LI082
Sativus ♃ CU
Saturday ♄ AB241, LI061
Saturday Night ♂ AB241
Satureia hortensis ☿ CU, GA071
Satureia montana ☿ CU, GA071
Saturnine Friends ♄ in 11th House GA061
Satyrian ♀ RA060
Satyrion (Aphrodisiac Orchid) ♀ DA024
Sauce-Alone (Jack-in-Hedge) ☿ CU
Sauce-Alone (Jack-in-Hedge) ♃ GA068
Savage ☉ PT363
Savage ♂ PT353
Savine ♂ CU
Savine ♄ LI059, RA050
Savine Tree ♄ DA018
Savory (Summer) ☿ CU, GA071
Savory (Winter) ☿ CU, GA071
Savory Herbs ♀ AB245
Savory Herbs & Garden Stuff ☿ AB244
Savoy ♎ LI097
Saw-Pit ♎ LI096
Saxifrage (Great Burnet) ☽ CU
Saxifrage (Small Burnet) ☽ CU
Saxifrage, Burnet ☽ GA072
Saxifrage, White ☽ GA072
Saxony ♄ DA018, LI061, RA051
Saxony ♑ DA012, PA076

Saxony, Southwest ♑ LI098
Scabbiness ♋ LI245
Scabiosa columbaria ☿ CU
Scabious ☿ GA071
Scabious (Field) ☿ CU
Scabious (Lesser Field) ☿ CU
Scabs ♄ LI246, RA051
Scabs ♑ DA012, LI098, PA009, RS018
Scabs ♓ DA014, LI099
Scammony ♂ DA021, LI068
Scandalous ♀ LI074
Scandals ☋ in 1st House GA046
Scandals ☋ in 7th House GA056
Scarlet ☉ LI071
Scarlet (Clear Red) ☉ DA022
Scars ♂ LI579, PA013
Scars on the Face ♂ LI067, RS020
Scavengers ♄ GA067, LI059, RA050
Schismatical ♃ LI063
Scholars ♃ PA012, RA052
School Teacher ♍ LI451
Schoolmasters ☿ GA071, LI078, PA016, RA061
Schools ☿ DA026, LI079, PA017, RA062
Schools 3rd House AB276
Sciatica (Iliaca Passion) ☽ LI082, RA064, RS021
Sciatica (Iliaca Passion) ♄ DA017, LI246, RA051
Sciatica (Iliaca Passion) ♐ LI246, PA008
Sciatica (Iliaca Passion) ♑ DA012
Sciatica (Iliaca Passion) 6th House RS100
Sciatica-Cress (Iberis) ♄ GA067
Science ♃ AB242
Science 9th House LI429
Sclavonia, Around Bulgaria ♐ DA011
Scorn 12th House AB276
Scornful ♃ LI540
Scorpions ♂ LI068
Scorpions ♄ AB246, LI060, RA051
Scotland ♋ DA007, LI095, PA074
Scouring 10th House RS100
Scribes ☿ DA025, PT335
Scriveners ☿ LI078, RA061

Scrofula (King's Evil) ☽ LI082, RA064, RS021
Scrofula (King's Evil) ♉ LI094, RS016
Scrofula (King's Evil) 2nd House LI245, RS100
Scrophularia auriculata ♃ GA068
Scrophularia auriculata ♃ in ♋ CU
Scrophularia nodosa ♀ CU, GA070
Sculptors ☿ GA071, LI078, PA016, RA061
Sculpture Propensity ☽ in 9th House GA059
Scurfs (Disease) ♑ LI246
Scurvy ♂ PT327
Scurvy ♄ PA011
Scurvy-Grass ♃ CU, GA068
Sea ☽ DA027, PA110
Sea ♋ LI095, DA008
Sea Banks ♋ LI095
Sea Birds ☽ LI082
Sea Calf ☉ RA058
Sea Ports ☽ RA064
Sea Tangle (Herb) ☽ RA063
Sea-blue ♃ DA019, LI063
Sea-bluish ☽ DA026
Sea-calf ☉ LI071
Sea-fox ☉ LI071
Sea-green ♃ DA019, LI063
Sea-green ☽ DA026
Seamsters ♀ RA058
Seamstresses (Sempsters) ♀ GA070
Searcher Into Mysteries ☿ LI077
Searcher of Novelties ☽ LI081
Searchers After Curiosities ☿ PA110
Secret ☉ DA022, LI070
Secret Enemies ♄ DA018
Secret Enemies 12th House GA062
Secret Informers 12th House LI056
Secret Knowledge ☿ LI077
Secretaries ☿ GA071, LI078, PA016, RA061
Secretaries ♄ LI059
Secretaries ☿ in 10th House GA060
Secretaries ♍ LI451
Secretion, Excess ♍ LI246
Secrets ♄ PA092

Secrets 3rd House AB276
Sectaries (Religious Dissenter) ☿ GA071
Sectarists (Religious Dissenter) ♄ GA067
Sedges ♋ LI095
Seditions 7th House LI558
Seditious ♂ DA020, LI066, PA109
Sedum acre ♃ CU, GA068
Sedum album ☽ CU
Sedum Telephium ☽ CU, GA072
Seed of a Tree ☿ AB236
Seed of Pistacia Terebinthus ♂ AB243
Seed of Turpentine Tree ♂ AB243
Seed, Reproductive ♀ DA023, LI247, PA015, RS014
Seed, Reproductive ♃ AB247, DA019, LI246, PT319, RS014
Seed, Reproductive ♏ S2-56
Seeds which Fly with the Wind ♃ AB244
Seekers of Mysteries ☿ PT361
Seeking a Good Name/Help Others ☉ AB250
Seeking Friendship ☿ AB250
Seeking Solitariness ♄ AB250
Selenite ☽ DA026, LI082, RA064
Self-Esteem Low ♄ LI539
Self-Undoing 12th House LI056
Selfheal ♃ DA020, LI064
Selfheal ♀ CU, GA070
Seller, of Property 7th House LI220
Sellers of Beer ♂ AB254
Sellers of Boars ♂ AB254
Sellers of Boxes ♂ AB254
Sellers of Cheetahs ♂ AB254
Sellers of Copper ♂ AB254
Sellers of Glass ♂ AB254
Sellers of Hounds ♂ AB254
Sellers of Sickles ♂ AB254
Sellers of Wolves ♂ AB254
Selling and Making Armor ♂ AB254
Selling Black Slaves ♄ AB254
Selling Books ☿ AB254
Selling Coins ☿ AB254
Selling Food ☽ AB254
Selling Grapes ♃ AB254

Selling Hides ☿ AB254
Selling Old Gold and Silver ♃ AB254
Selling Slaves ☿ AB254
Selling Sugar Cane ♃ AB254
Selling Things Made of Bone ♄ AB254
Selling Things Made of Copper ♄ AB254
Selling Things Made of Hair ♄ AB254
Selling Things Made of Iron ♄ AB254
Selling Things Made of Lead ♄ AB254
Semen ♀ PA015
Semen ♃ DA019, PT319, RS014
Semitertian Fever ☉ RS020
Sempervivum tectorum ☿ LI272
Sempervivum tectorum ♃ CU
Sempervivum tectorum ♄ LI272
Sempsters (Seamstresses) ♀ GA070
Sena ♉ LI094, PA073
Sena (Umbria) ♄ LI059
Senators ♃ GA067, LI063, PA012
Sene ♄ RA050
Senecio jacobaea ♀ CU, GA070
Senecio saracenicus ♄ GA067
Senecio vulgaris ♀ CU, GA070
Senna ☿ CU
Sensations ☽ PA096
Sense Deprivation ☿ LI247, PA130
Sensuality ♀ AB245, PA109
Separations from Spouse ♄ in 7th House GA054
Separations from Spouse ☋ in 7th House GA056
Septum (Mediastinum) ♋ RS015
Septum (Mediastinum) 4th House RS015
Sepulchres ♄ PA011, RA051
Serenity ♃ LI064
Sergeants ♂ GA068, LI067, PA013, RA054
Serious ♃ GA067
Seriousness 9th House AB275
Serpents ☿ LI079, RA062
Serpents ♃ RA053
Serpents ♄ LI060, RA051
Serpents, Venomous ♂ AB246
Servant among Servants ☽ AB250

Servant's Child 11th House AB276
Servants ☿ DA025
Servants 6th House GA053, LI053, PA044
Servants 12th House AB275
Servants Cause Loss & Damage ♀ in 6th House GA053
Servants, Evil ☋ in 6th House GA054
Servants, Faithful & Honest ♃ in 6th House GA053
Servants, Good, Faithful, Honest ♌ in 6th House GA054
Servants, Unfortunate ♂ in 6th House GA053
Servants (Just or not?) 6th House GA272, PA067
Service ☽ DA026
Service Tree ♄ GA067
Servitude ♌ in 12th House GA063
Sesame ♃ AB243
Sesame ♄ AB244
Severe ♄ LI058
Seville, Spain ♓ PA076
Sex Appeal ♂ PA013
Sex of Fetus 5th House PA043
Sextons ♄ GA067
Sextons of Churches ♄ LI059
Sexual Excess ♀ PA109
Sexual Organs 8th House AB277
Sezes, Italy [= Sezze] ♎ DA010
Sezze, Italy [= Sezes] ♎ DA010
Shame-faced ♃ DA019
Shameless ♂ AB250, DA021, LI540, PA093
Shameless ♄ PT341
Shameless ♀ in 12th House GA063
Shanks ♒ RS015
Shanks 11th House LI245, RS015
Shape 1st House LI050
Shark ♂ LI068, RA055
Sharp ☿ LI077
Sharp ♄ DA017, LI059
Sharp ♍ DA009
Sharp ♑ DA012
Sharp Intelligence/Understanding ☿ AB250
Sharp Minds ☿ LI541
Sharp Pen ☿ LI077
Sharp Taste ♂ DA020, LI067

Sharp Things ♂ AB241
Sharp Tongue ☿ LI077
Shedder of Blood ♂ in 4th House GA050
Sheep ☽ AB246
Sheep ☉ AB246
Sheep ♀ RA060
Sheep ♃ AB246, LI064, RA053
Sheep ♄ AB246
Sheep 6th House LI053, PA044
Sheep Feeding Grounds ♑ LI098
Sheep Pens ♑ LI098
Shellfish ☽ LI082, RA064
Shellfish ☉ RA058
Shellfish ♄ LI060, RA051
Shells ♀ AB243
Shepherd's Purse ♄ CU, DA018, LI059, RA050
Shepherd's Rod ♂ CU
Shepherds 6th House LI053, PA044
Shepherds ♂ AB254
Shepherds ♄ LI059, RA050
Shin ♒ LI246, RS015
Shin 10th House PA046
Shin 11th House LI245, RS015
Shingles (Disease) ♂ LI067, RA055, RS020
Shining ♀ AB240
Shining ♃ AB240
Ship ☽ LI157
Ship 1st House LI157
Ship at Sea 1st House PA062
Ship at Sea (Safety or Peril) 1st House GA242, LI157, PA062
Ship (Between Breast & Water) ♉ LI158
Ship (Between Water Lines) ♎ LI158
Ship Carpenter ♄ RA050
Ship Carpenter ♒ LI451
Ship (Crew's Quarters) ♏ LI158
Ship Painter ♒ LI451
Ship Trimmer ♒ LI451
Ship's Belly ♍ LI158
Ship's Bottom ♋ LI158
Ship's Breast ♈ LI158
Ship's Captain ♒ LI158

Ship's Cargo 1st House PA062
Ship's Crew ♐ LI158
Ship's Crew 1st House LI157
Ship's Ends ♑ LI158
Ship's Goods 1st House LI157
Ship's Master ♒ LI451
Ship's Oars ♓ LI158
Ship's Stern ♊ LI158
Ship's Storehouse ♑ LI098
Ship's Top, Above Water ♌ LI158
Shipbuilders ♂ PT337
Shipwreck of Patrimony ♄ in 4th House GA050
Shipwrecks ♂ PT185
Shipwrecks ♄ PT181
Shooting Pains ♃ RA053
Shopkeeper ♄ LI059
Shops ♂ DA021
Shores ☽ PA018
Short ♉ DA006
Short Fuse ♂ PA093
Short Journeys 3rd House AB275, LI187
Short Stemmed Trees ☽ AB244
Short, Full, Well-Set, Strong ♉ PA004
Shortness ♄ AB241
Shoulder Bone ♊ DA007
Shoulder Diseases ♊ LI094, RS017
Shoulders ♊ DA007, LI245, RS015
Shoulders 2nd House LI052
Shoulders 3rd House GA048, LI052, PA042, RS015
Shoulders, Back Part 5th House LI245
Shoulders, Broad ♈ PA004
Shoulders, Thick ♈ DA006
Shoulders, Thick ♓ DA014
Shoulders, Thick & Broad ♌ DA009
Shoulders, Thick and Crooked ♄ DA018
Shoveling Feet ♄ GA066
Shrewd ☿ PT359
Shrub Land ♉ LI094
Siblings Accord with 3rd House GA253, LI188, PA063
Sicilia ☉ RA058
Sicilia ♉ PA073

Sicily ☉ DA022, LI072, PT135
Sicily ♌ DA008, LI096, PA074, PT135
Sickly ♈ DA005
Sickly ♉ DA006
Sickly ♏ DA011
Sickly ♑ DA012
Sickly ♓ DA014
Sickness ♃ AB252
Sickness ♄ AB252
Sickness 6th House AB275, GA053, LI053, PA044
Sickness 7th House S2-40
Sickness, Long in Duration ♄ DA018
Sickness of Friends 8th House AB276
Side Disease ♌ RS017
Side, Left ☽ DA026, RS015
Side, Right ☉ DA022
Sides ☉ AB248
Sides ♃ DA019, PA012, RS014
Sides ♋ RS015
Sides ♌ DA008, LI095
Sides 4th House AB277, RS015
Sides 5th House LI053
Sight ☉ AB248, RS014
Sight, Darkness of ♎ DA010
Sight, Dim & Obscure ♑ DA012
Sigina* ♍ DA009
Silesia ♈ LI094, PA073
Silesia, Greater ♈ DA006
Silesia, Lower ♍ DA009, PA074
Silicy ♓ DA014, PA076
Silkmen ♀ GA070, LI074, PA015, RA058
Silver ☽ AB243, DA026
Silver ♀ AB250
Silver (Metal) ☽ LI082
Silver Color ☽ LI082, RA063
Silver Color ☿ PA016
Silver Cups, Rings, Bangles ☽ AB243
Silver Household Vessels ♀ AB243
Silver Marcasite ☿ RA062
Silver Metal ☽ RA064
Silver Rings ☽ AB254

Silverweed ♀ CU
Simon ☽ LI341
Simple (Pure in Heart) ☽ AB250
Simson (Blue) ♂ CU
Sinapis alba ♂ CU
Sincere ☉ GA069
Sincere in Faith ♃ in 9th House GA058
Sinew Disease 12th House RS100
Sinews ☉ DA022, LI579, PA129, PT319, RS014
Sinews ☿ DA025, RS015
Sinful ☿ PT361
Singer ♀ DA023
Singer ♓ LI451
Singing, Accompanying ♀ AB254
Single Purpose ♄ PT341
Singreen (= Sengreen, House Leek) ☿ LI272
Singreen (= Sengreen, House Leek) ♄ LI272
Sink-cleaners ♄ DA017
Sinks ♄ LI060, PA011, RA051
Sinks ♏ DA011, LI097
Sisters ♀ AB249
Sisters 3rd House AB275, GA048, LI052, PA042
Sisters, Elder ☽ AB249
Sisymbrium officinale ♂ CU, GA068
Sium sisarum ♀ CU
Skeptic ♃ GA067
Skeptic ☋ in 9th House GA059
Skill in All Branches of Relig ☽ AB254
Skin ♄ AB247
Skin and All Relating Thereto ☽ AB247
Skin Color 1st House GA045
Skin Eruption (Morphew) ♂ DA021
Skin Eruption (Morphew) ♄ DA017
Skirret ♀ CU
Sky Blue Mixed Darker Color ☿ AB240
Sky Color ♀ DA023
Slanderers ☿ PA095
Slanderous ♄ LI539
Slaughterhouses ♂ DA021, LI068, PA013, RA055
Slaves ☉ AB249
Slaves ☿ AB252

Slaves ♄ AB249
Slaves 6th House AB275
Slaves 12th House AB275, LI463, PT421
Slaves, Selling ☿ AB254
Slavonia, Croatia ♂ AB242
Slavonia, Croatia ♐ LI098, PA075
Sleep ♄ AB245
Sleepiness without Rest ♃ RS019
Slender ♎ DA010
Slighting a Good Name ♀ PA094
Sloe Bush ♄ CU
Sluggards ♀ LI541
Sluggish ♄ GA067, LI058
Small Cattle ♀ LI075
Small Cattle 6th House LI053
Small Journeys 3rd House LI052
Small Journeys, Prosperous ♀ in 3rd House GA049
Small of the Back ♀ RS014
Small Trees ♍ AB230
Smallage ☿ GA071
Smallage (Wild Celery) ☿ CU
Smallpox ☽ LI082, RA064, RS021
Smallpox ♂ PA013
Smallpox ♈ DA005, LI093, LI245, RS016
Smallpox of the Face ♂ RS020
Smaragd[e] (see *Emerald Jewel*)
Smell ♀ RS014
Smell ♂ PA013
Smell & Inhaling Organs ♀ AB248
Smell and Touch ♂ AB248
Smell, Sense of ♀ LI269, PT321
Smelters ♂ DA021
Smilacina bifolia ☉ GA069
Smilax ♂ CU
Smith's Shops ♂ LI068, RA055
Smiths ♂ DA021, GA068, LI067, PA013, PT337, RA054
Smithy ♂ PA013
Smooth Trees ♀ AB244
Smooth-Leaved Plants ♀ LI075
Smoothness ♀ AB241
Smoothness ♃ AB241

Smyrnium olusatrum ♃ CU, GA068
Snails ☽ LI082
Snakes, Large Black ♄ AB246
Snipe ♃ RA053
Snipe (Bird) ♃ LI064
Soapwort ♀ CU, GA070
Sober ♃ LI540, PA012
Sober ♄ GA066
Sober ♌ LI538
Sober Speech ♒ LI538
Societies ☉ AB252
Sodomite ♀ AB250
Soft ☽ GA072, LI081
Soft Stones ☽ DA026
Softest Things ♀ AB241
Sogdiana, Middle Iran ♒ DA013, PA076
Soil, Condition 4th House LI206
Soils with Abundant Water ♀ AB241
Solanum dulcamara ☿ CU
Solanum nigurm ♄ CU
Soldier (Common Water) ☽ in ♓ CU
Soldiers ♂ DA020, GA068, LI067, RA054
Soldiers 11th House PA046
Solicitors ☿ GA071, LI078, RA061
Solicitous ♄ LI058
Solicitous about Riches ☽ in 2nd House GA047
Solidago virgaurea ♀ CU, GA070
Solidity ♃ AB241
Solitariness ♄ GA066, PA010
Solitary ♂ AB250
Solitary ♄ DA018, LI539, PA092, PT341
Solomon's Seal ♄ CU, GA067
Some Levity ♃ AB250
Somewhat Bitter ☽ AB240
Sonchus arvensis ♀ CU
Sonchus oleraceus ♀ CU, GA070
Sonchus oleraceus ♂ GA068
Sonchus palustris ♀ CU
Song ♀ AB250
Songs, Composing ♀ AB254
Soothsayers ☿ PT335

Sophists ♃ PT337
Sorbus ♄ GA067
Sordid ♄ GA067, LI058, PT341
Sordid Professions ♄ LI555
Sore Throats ♉ DA006, LI094, RS016
Sorrel ♀ GA070
Sorrel (Common) ♀ CU
Sorrel (Mountain) ♀ CU
Sorrel (Sheep's) ♀ CU
Sorrel (Wood) ♀ CU
Sorrel Color 3rd House LI052
Sorrow ♄ in 6th House GA053
Sorrow ♄ in 12th House GA062
Sorrow ☗ in 1st House GA046
Sorrow ♌ DA008
Sorrow 6th House LI558
Sorrow 12th House LI056
Sorrow in Marriage ♄ in 7th House GA054
Sorrow in Younger Years ☽ in 7th House GA055
Sorrowful ♄ LI539
Sorrows 8th House PA045
Sorrows 12th House PA047
Sot (Fool) ☽ LI081
Soul 1% AB275
Soul, Character ☽ PT333
Soul, Character ☿ PT333
Soul-Evil (Foul-Evil?)* ♈ DA005
Soundness, of Things 11th House AB276
Sour ♄ LI059
Sour in Taste ♄ DA017
Sour-Sweet Taste ☉ LI071
South ♉ LI094
South ♋ AB230
South ♍ AB230
South ♌ AB230
South ♑ LI365
South 10th House LI364
South Southeast 11th House LI364
South Wind ♀ LI076
South Wind ♋ AB230
South Wind ♌ AB230

South Wind ♍ AB230
Southeast ♉ LI365
Southeast ♐ LI365
Southern ♍ LI096
Southern ♑ LI098, PA008
Southernwood ☿ CU, GA071
Southernwood (Field) ☿ CU
Southwest ♊ LI365
Southwest ♍ LI365
Sovereignty 10th House GA059, PA046
Sow-Thistle ♀ GA070
Sow-Thistle (Common) ♀ CU
Sow-Thistle (Tree) ♀ CU
Sow-Thistle Tree (Marsh) ♀ CU
Sowbread ♂ CU
Sower of Discord ♂ in 1st House GA046
Sowing ☽ PA239
Sowing ♄ PA239
Sowing Seeds ☽ DA026
Sown Crops ♑ AB230
Spain ♃ DA020, LI065, PT135, RA053
Spain ♐ DA011, LI098, PA075, PT135
Spanish Fly (Cantharides) ☉ LI072
Spanish Fly (Cantharides) ♂ DA021, LI068
Sparing ♄ LI539
Sparrow ♀ LI075, RA060
Spasms ♃ PT429
Spasms ♄ PT327
Speaking ☿ AB245
Spearmint ♀ CU
Speculative ☿ PT361
Speech ☿ LI247, PT321, RS015
Speech, Good ♊ DA007
Speech, Graceful ☿ in 1st House GA046
Speech, Loss ♑ DA012
Speech, Open ♂ LI540
Speech ,Slow ☉ DA023
Speech, Sober & Grave ♃ GA067
Spells 1st House AB276
Spendthrift ☉ GA069, LI070
Spendthrift ♀ GA070

Spendthrift ♂ PT353
Spendthrift ♃ GA067
Sperm ♀ DA023, LI247, RS014
Sperm ♃ AB247, DA019, LI246, PT319, RS014
Sperm ♏ S2-56
Sperm, Defective ♀ PA015
Spice Merchants ♀ PT337
Spices ♀ PT337
Spider ☿ LI079, RA062
Spignel (Broad-Leaved) ☿ in ♋ CU
Spignel (Plant) ♀ GA070
Spikenard (Plant) ☉ DA023, LI071
Spinach ♄ DA018, LI059, RA050
Spinacia Oleracea ♄ RA050
Spine 8th House LI245
Spinners of Gold and Silver ☉ RA056
Spires ♎ LI097, PA075
Spirit ☿ LI247
Spirit, Bold, Lofty, Undaunted ♂ GA068
Spirit, Great ☉ GA069
Spirited ♂ PT353
Spiritless ♀ LI541
Spirits ☿ DA025, RS015
Spiritual Offices ♃ DA019
Spiteful ♂ AB250
Spiteful ♍ LI538
Splay-Footed ♄ PA010
Spleen ☽ AB248
Spleen ♄ AB247, DA017, LI059, LI579, PA011, PT319, RA050, RS014
Spleen ♋ DA007, LI245, RS015
Spleen 4th House RS015
Spleen Obstructions ♄ RS019
Spleen Obstructions ♍ PA007
Spleenwort ♄ GA067
Spleenwort, white ☿ GA071
Sports 5th House LI169
Sports Injuries ♐ LI097, RS018
Spouse, Pleasant and Beautiful ♀ in 7th House GA055
Spring Flowers ♀ AB244
Spring, Small (Places Near) ♒ DA013
Springs ♋ DA008, LI095

Springs ☽ LI082, RA064
Springs (Water) ☿ AB242
Springs (Land Nearby) ♒ LI099
Spurge ♂ DA021
Sp[e]iers, Germany ♎ DA010
Squareness ♀ AB241
Squill ♂ CU
Squin[ances, ancy, cies, cy, zie, zle] (Woodruffe) ♉ DA006, PA005
Squin[ances, ancy, cies, cy, zie, zle] (Woodruffe) 2nd House RS100
Squin[ances, ancy, cies, cy, zie, zle] (Woodruffe) ♃ DA019, LI079, RA053, RS019
Squirrel ☿ LI079, RA062
St. Andrews (Scotland) ♋ DA008, PA074
St. Anthony's Fire ♂ LI246
St. John's Wort ☉ CU, DA022, GA069, LI071, RA057
St. John's Wort ♃ RA052
St. John's Wort ♌ CU
St. John's Wort (Tutsan) ♄ DA018, GA067, LI059
St. Peter's Wort (Hypericum) ☉ GA069
Stable & Firm Inheritance ♀ in 4th House GA050
Stable of Great Horses ♐ LI097
Stable of Small Beasts ♈ LI093
Stable Patrimony ⊗ in 4th House GA051
Stables ♉ DA006, LI094
Stables ♐ DA011
Stables (Horses, Asses, Camels) ♄ AB242
Stachys officinalis ♃ CU, RA052
Stachys officinalis ♈ CU
Stachys palustris ♄ CU
Stag ♃ LI064, RA053
Stageplays ♀ LI074
Stammering ☿ DA025, LI078, PA017, RA062, RS021
Stammering ♓ LI538
Stammers ☉ AB249
Standing Pools ☽ DA027, LI082
Staphylococcal Inflammation ♂ RS020
Star-Thistle (Centaurea) ♂ GA068
Starfish ☉ LI071, RA058
Stargard[e]* ♐ LI098, PA075
Starling ☿ AB247
Starting of the Members ♃ RS019

Starwort ♄ DA018, LI059, RA050
State of the Union 1st House LI050
Stateliness ☉ LI070
Stationers ☿ GA071, LI078
Stature 1st House LI050, PA041
Stature, Above Middle ☽ PA017
Stature, Comely ♃ DA019
Stature, High ☿ PA016
Stature, Indifferent ♑ PA008
Stature, Middle ♀ GA070
Stature, Middle ♂ GA068, PA012
Stature, Middle ♄ DA018, GA066, PA010
Stature, Middle ♈ PA004
Stature, Middle ♋ PA005
Stature, Middle ♌ DA008
Stature, Middle ♒ DA013
Stature, not Tall ♒ PA009
Stature, of Native 1st House GA045
Stature, Proper ♊ PA005
Stature, Short ♓ DA014
Stature, Short & Thin ☉ DA022
Stature, Small ♋ DA008
Stature, Somewhat above Middle ☽ GA072
Stature, Somewhat Short ♏ DA011
Stature, Straight, Small ♀ DA024
Stature, Strong, Well-composed ♒ PA009
Stature, Tall ☿ DA025
Stature, Tall & Handsome ♃ GA067
Stature, Tall & Upright ♃ PA011
Stature, Tall Indifferent ☿ GA071
Steel ♂ RA055
Stellaria media ☽ CU
Stellaria media ♀ GA070
Stem of a Tree ☉ AB236
Step-Father 3rd House AB276
Step-Mother 10th House AB276
Stephen ☉ LI341
Steppes ♉ LI094
Steps, Long ♂ AB249
Stetin = Stettin, Germany ♈ PA073
Stewards ☉ LI071

Stick or Cudgel (= Bat) ♄ LI060
Stimulating ☿ PT187
Stinking ♄ AB240
Stinking Places ♄ PA011
Stipends ☉ LI556
Stiria, Austria [= Styria] ♑ DA012, LI098, PA076
Stiria, Austria [= Styria] ♄ DA018, RA051
Stock ♃ RA053
Stock Dove (Wild Pigeon) ♀ LI075, RA060
Stock Dove (Wild Pigeon) ♃ LI064, RA053
Stomach ☽ AB248, DA026, PA018, PT321, RS015
Stomach ☉ AB247
Stomach ♀ RS014
Stomach ♋ LI095
Stomach ♌ DA008, RS015
Stomach 4th House GA050, LI245
Stomach 5th House LI053, RS015
Stomach Abscess (Impostumes) ♋ LI095, RS017
Stomach, Bottom ♍ RS015
Stomach, Bottom 6th House RS015
Stomach, Cold ☽ RS021
Stomach, Cold ☉ DA022
Stomach, Cold ♋ RS017
Stomach Disease ♀ DA023
Stomach Disorders ♋ RS017
Stomach Flux, I.E. Purge ☽ DA027
Stomach, Griping ☉ PA014
Stomach, Lower 4th House RS097
Stomach Problems 4th House RS100
Stomach Weakness ♀ LI247
Stomachaches ☽ LI081, RS021
Stone Cutters ♄ LI555
Stone Dressers ♂ PT337
Stone of Diverse Colors ☿ LI079
Stone Quarries ♒ DA013, LI099
Stone Quarries 4th House LI575
Stone, Black ♄ RA051
Stonecrop ☽ CU
Stones 8th House RS015
Stones ☽ LI082, RS015
Stones ♍ DA009

Stones ♏ RS015
Stones (Disease) ♄ PA011
Stones (e.g., Kidney) 8th House LI054
Stones, Black Colored ♄ DA017
Stones, Blue ♄ RA051
Stones Found in Ox-Gall ♃ AB243
Stones, Infirmities ♍ RS017
Stones, Kidney ♎ LI096
Stones, Multi-Colored ☿ DA025
Stones, Retention of (Disease) ♎ PA007
Stones, Soft ☽ LI082, RA064
Stones, White & Yellow ♃ AB243
Stones, Yellow and Green ☿ AB243
Stooping ♄ GA066
Storax Tree ☉ CU
Storehouse, Grain ♊ DA007
Storehouses for Grain ♊ LI094
Stork (Bird) ♃ LI064
Strains of the Knees ♑ RS018
Stranger 7th House LI154
Strangulation ♃ PT429
Strangury ♀ PA129
Stratiotes aloides ☽ in ♓ CU
Straw Color ♀ AB240
Strawberries ♃ DA019, LI064, RA052
Strawberries ♀ CU, GA070
Streams with Trees ☽ AB242
Strenuous in Divine Law ☽ AB254
Strenuous in Religion ☽ AB254
Streptococcus (Erysipelas) ♂ LI246
Strife ♄ in 7th House GA054
Strife with Friends ☋ in 11th House GA062
Strombi (Fish) ☉ RA058
Strong ☉ DA022
Strong ♈ DA005
Strong ♉ DA006
Strong ♌ DA008, DA009, PA006
Strong ♏ DA011
Strong ♒ DA013
Strong, Able Body ♏ PA008
Strong-Minded ♄ PT341

Stubborn ♂ PT353
Stubborn ♄ LI058, PA092
Students ♃ PA012, RA052
Students in University ♃ LI063
Studious ☽ PA017
Studious ☿ LI541, PA094
Studious ♄ GA066, LI058, PA092
Studious ♍ PA006
Studious for Own Profit ♄ LI539
Study ☿ PA017, RA062
Study ♍ LI096
Study of History ☽ DA026
Stupidity ♃ PT349
Stuttgart ♐ DA012
Styrax officinalis ☉ CU
Styria, Austria [= Stiria] ♑ DA012, LI098, PA076
Styria, Austria [= Stiria] ♄ DA018
Subaudia (Country?)* ♎ PA075
Subcutaneous Inflammation ☉ LI072
Subcutaneous Inflammation ♂ LI067
Subject to Scars in Face ♂ in 1st House GA046
Subjects of a Monarch 6th House LI174
Substance of Women 8th House LI139
Substance, Querent's 2nd House LI139
Subtle ☿ LI077, PA094
Subtle ♀ LI541
Subtle ♄ PA092
Subtle Arts (Magic) ☿ DA025
Success ☉ PT363
Successful ♀ PT357
Successful in Long Journeys ♃ in 9th House GA058
Succisa pratensis ♀ GA070
Succory ♃ GA068
Succory (Wild) ♃ CU
Suckling 2nd House AB275
Sudden Deaths ♂ PT183
Sudden Strokes ♂ PT429
Sudden Swooning ☉ LI071
Suestam = Suessa? = Sessa ♎ DA010
Suevia (German Tribe) ♈ LI094
Sugar ♃ DA019, RA052

Sugar Cane ☉ AB244
Sugar Plantations ♀ AB242
Sullen & Proud ♄ AB250
Sulphur ♃ AB243
Sultan's Rule 10th House AB275
Sumach ☿ LI272
Sumach ♃ CU
Sumach ♄ LI272
Sumptuous ♂ LI540
Sun Spurge ♂ CU
Sunday ☉ AB237, LI072
Sunday Night ☿ AB241
Sundew ☉ CU
Sundew ♋ CU
Superiority ☽ in 1st House GA046
Superstition ♃ PT349
Superstitious ♃ LI540, PA093
Superstitious ♄ DA018, LI539, PA093, PT341
Superstitious ♂ in 9th House GA058
Surdity (Deafness) ♑ DA012
Surfeits ☽ LI082, RA064, RS021
Surfeits by Alcohol ♎ LI246
Surfeits by Drinking or Eating ♎ LI246
Surgeons ♂ AB254, DA021, GA068, LI067, PA109, RA054
Surgeons ♏ LI451
Surveying 9th House AB275
Surveyors ☽ AB254
Surveyors ☿ AB254
Surveyors ♊ LI451
Suspicion 6th House AB276
Suspicious ♄ AB250, GA067, LI058, PA092
Suspicious ☊ in 9th House GA059
Swallow ☿ RA062
Swallow ♀ RA060
Swallow-Wort ♃ CU
Swallowing ☽ RS197
Swallows ☿ LI079
Swallows ♀ LI075
Swallows ♄ AB247
Swan ☽ RA064
Swan ☉ LI072, RA057

Swan ♀ LI075, RA060
Sweden ♈ DA006, PA073
Sweden, Northern ♉ DA006, LI094
Sweden, Southern ♒ DA013
Sweet ♃ AB240
Sweet ♊ DA007
Sweet ♒ DA013
Sweet Berries ♀ AB244
Sweet Conversation ♃ LI062
Sweet Flavor ♀ AB240
Sweet Maudlin (Achillea) ♃ GA068
Sweet Odors ♃ LI063
Sweet or Tall Herbs ♃ AB244
Sweet Oranges ♀ LI075
Sweet Smelling Flowers ♀ AB236
Sweet Smelling Plants ♀ LI075
Sweet Smelling Trees ♀ AB244
Sweet Smells ♃ DA019
Sweet Taste ♀ LI075
Sweethearts 7th House LI054
Swelling 8th House RS100
Swelling ☽ RS021
Swelling ♀ RS020
Swelling ♂ DA021
Swelling ♄ LI059
Swelling of Tissues ♄ LI246
Swelling, Abscess (Impostume) 4th House RS100
Swelling, Watery ♋ LI095
Swimming in the Head ♄ RS019
Swine 6th House LI558
Switzerland ♉ LI094
Swooning ☉ PA014, RS020
Swooning, Sudden ☉ RS020
Sycamore Tree ♀ CU
Sycamore, White ♀ DA024, LI075
Sycophant ♄ in 3rd House GA048
Symphytum officinale ♄ CU, GA067
Symphytum officinale ♑ CU
Synagogues ♃ AB242
Synochus putrida ♃ RS019
Synods ♃ DA020, LI064, RA053

Syphilis ♀ LI075, PA015, RA061, RS020
Syphilis ♏ DA010
Syracuse ♌ DA008, LI096, PA074
Syrenaica* (Ukraine?) ♊ PA074
Syria ♂ AB242, PT143
Syria ♈ DA006, LI094, PA073, PT143

-- T --

Taciturn ♄ LI539
Tagetes ☉ GA069
Tailoring ♀ AB254
Tailors ☿ GA071, LI078
Tailors ♂ LI067, PA013, RA054
Tainting of Potable Waters ♂ PT185
Takes Pleasure in Everything ♀ AB250
Tall ♂ AB249
Tall ♄ AB249
Tall ♊ DA007
Tall Stature ♃ LI063
Tall Trees with Oily Fruit ☉ AB244
Tall, Straight Body ♎ PA007
Tallness (Inclination Toward) ♎ DA010
Tamarinds ♂ DA021, LI068, RA054
Tamarisk ♄ DA018, LI059, RA050
Tamari[sk]? ♄ GA067
Tanacetum parthenium ♀ CU, GA070
Tanacetum parthenium ♃ RA053
Tanacetum vulgare ♀ CU, GA070
Tanners ♂ LI067, PA013, RA054
Tanners ♄ GA067, PA108
Tansy ♀ CU
Tansy, Garden ♀ GA070
Tansy, Wild ♀ GA070
Tapsters ☽ GA072
Tarangubin [= Tarentam] ☉ AB244
Taranto, Italy [= Tarentum] ♉ DA006, PA073
Taraxacum officinale ♃ CU, GA068
Tarentum, Italy [= Taranto] ♉ DA006, PA073
Tarragon ♂ CU
Tartar, Russia ♒ DA013, LI099

Tartaria ♒ PA076
Tarvisium, Italy [=Treviso] ♏ DA011
Taste ☽ DA026, LI247, RS015
Taste ☿ AB248
Taste ♀ RS014
Taste, Mixed Sour & Sweet ☉ DA022
Taste, Sense of ☽ PT321
Taste, Sense of ♀ LI269
Tasteless Flavors ☽ LI082
Taverns 5th House GA051, LI053, PA043
Taverns ♀ LI074
Taverns (Malt-Houses) ♍ LI096
Tawny ♎ LI086
Tax-Collectors ☿ AB252
Taxus baccata ♄ CU, LI059, RA050
Teachers ☿ PT335
Teachers' Houses ♃ AB242
Teaching Manners ☿ AB250
Teaching Revelation ☿ AB250
Teaching Theology ☿ AB250
Teaching, Logic ☿ AB250
Teak ♀ AB244
Tearful ♄ PT341
Teasel ♀ CU, GA070
Teeth ☉ AB248
Teeth ♄ DA017, LI059, PA011, RS014
Teeth, Distorted or Oblique Set ☉ DA023
Teeth, Separate/Crooked ☽ AB249
Teeth, Small ☿ AB249
Teeth, Small ♀ AB249
Temerity ♂ LI540
Temperate ♃ PT037
Temperate ♊ AB264
Temperature of the Body 1st House GA045
Tenacious ♃ LI063
Tenants 1st House LI206
Tenants 6th House LI053
Tender ☽ GA072, LI081
Tenderness to Children ♀ AB250
Tenderness to Friends ♀ AB250
Tends not to Marry ♀ in 9th House GA059

Tenements 4th House GA050, LI052
Tennis Courts ☿ DA026, LI079, PA017, RA062
Terrors 6th House AB276
Tertian Fevers (Malaria) ☉ RS020
Tertian Fevers (Malaria) ♂ LI067, PA128, PT183, RS020
Testament of Deceased 8th House LI174
Testicles ♀ S2-56
Testicles ♂ RS014
Testicles and Left Side ☽ RA064
Teucrium scorodonia ♀ CU, GA070
Teugruim chamaedrys ☿ GA071
Teugruim chamaedrys ♂ CU
Thankful ♃ LI062
Theaters ☉ DA022, PA014
Thebaida, Egypt [= Thebes] ♎ DA010
Thebes ♎ PA075
Thebes [= Thebaida] ♎ DA010
Theft ☿ AB250, GA071, LI078, PA016, PT187
Theft 7th House LI054, PA044
Theft (More Than One Thief?) 7th House DA129, GA282, LI339, PA069
Theft (When Will It Be Recovered?) 7th House GA282, LI356
Thief ☿ LI078, RA061
Thief ♂ DA020, GA068, LI067, PA013, RA054
Thief ♄ AB252
Thief 7th House AB276, LI054, PA044
Thief 12th House AB276
Thief is Brother ♂ LI364
Thief is Familiar ☿ LI364
Thief is Father ☉ LI364
Thief is Friend ☿ LI364
Thief is Kinsman ♂ LI364
Thief is Master ☉ LI364
Thief is Mistress ☽ LI364
Thief is Mother ☽ LI364
Thief is Servant ♄ LI364
Thief is Son ♂ LI364
Thief is Stranger ♄ LI364
Thief is Woman (Wife) ♀ LI364
Thief is Youth ☿ LI364
Thief (Age and Sex?) 7th House DA126, GA281, LI336, PA069
Thievery ♂ LI066

Thieves' Hiding Places 3rd House AB276
Thigh Behind the Knee 10th House LI245
Thigh Hurts ♐ RS018
Thighs ☿ DA025, RS182
Thighs ♃ AB248
Thighs ♎ DA010, LI246
Thighs ♐ DA011, LI097, RS015
Thighs 7th House LI245
Thighs 9th House AB277, GA058, LI055, PA045
Thighs 10th House LI055
Thighs, Back Part ♑ LI246
Things, Coldest ♄ AB241
Things, Hardest ♄ AB241
Things, Hidden 3rd House AB276
Things, in General Use ☉ AB245
Things, Lost 8th House AB276
Things, Manufactured of Silver ☽ AB243
Things, Most Powerful ♄ AB241
Things, Most Stinking ♄ AB241
Things, Newly Legitimized 10th House AB276
Things, Old 3rd House AB276
Things, Old 8th House AB276
Things, Profitable & Agreeable ♃ AB245
Things, Ruined 8th House AB276
Things Which Are Sound 11th House AB276
Thirroma (Place)* ♐ DA011
Thirst, Great ♂ RS020
Thistle ♂ DA021, GA068, LI067, RA054
Thistle, Down or Cotton ♂ GA068
Thlaspi arvense ♂ GA068
Tholous (Domelike) ♍ LI096
Thomas ♃ LI341
Thorn Trees ♂ LI068
Thorn-Apple ♃ CU
Thorns ♂ DA021
Thorns, Twigs, Bark of a Tree ♂ AB236
Thorny Places ♑ LI098
Thorny Trees ♂ AB244
Thorough Leaf ♃ LI064
Those who Dress in Black ♄ AB253
Those who Neglect Devotion 12th House AB276

Thought ☿ PT321
Thoughtful ☽ DA026
Thoughtful ☉ DA022, LI070
Thoughtful ☿ PT359
Thoughts Reserved ♏ DA011
Thrace ♑ LI098, PT139
Thrace ♄ PT139
Thrace [= Thravia] ♑ PA076
Thracia, Balkans ♑ DA012
Thravia [= Thrace] ♑ PA076
Three ♃ LI065
Three-Leaved Grass ☿ DA025, LI079
Thrifty ♄ LI539
Throat ♀ DA023, LI247, PA015, RS014
Throat ♃ AB248
Throat ♉ DA006, LI245, RS015
Throat 2nd House LI245
Throat Disease ♀ PA015
Throat Disease ♉ PA005
Throat Disease 2nd House RS100
Throat Next to Stomach 3rd House RS097
Throat Pain ♌ RS208
Throat, Fluxes of Rheum ♉ LI094
Throat-Bole ☿ RS182, RS182
Thrush ☿ RA062
Thrush ♀ LI075, RA060
Thrush ♄ LI060, RA050
Thumb, Mount of ♀ RS014
Thunder ♂ LI068
Thunder & Rain ♈ AB264
Thunder Lightning ♏ AB264
Thuringia, Germany ♑ DA012, PA076
Thursday ♃ AB241, LI065
Thursday Night ☉ AB241
Thuscia, Italy [= Etruria] ♎ DA010, PA075
Thyme ♀ CU, LI075, RA060
Thyme (Wild) ♀ CU
Thymus serpyllum ♀ CU
Thymus vulgaris ♀ CU, RA060
Th[o]roughwax (Bupleurum) ♄ GA067
Tides ☽ DA027

Tiger ♂ LI068, RA055
Tiger ♃ LI064
Tigure ♉ PA073
Tillage ♄ DA018, LI555
Tillage 4th House LI052, PA043
Timber, Felling ☽ PA240
Timber, Felling ♄ PA240
Timid ☽ AB250
Timid ♀ PT357
Timid ♄ AB250
Timorous ☽ GA072, LI081
Timorous ♄ GA067, LI058
Tin ☿ RA062
Tin ♃ AB243, DA019, LI064
Tine ♃ RA053
Tinners ♄ LI059
Tire-Makers ♀ LI628
Toad ♄ LI060, RA051
Tobacco ♂ CU, GA068
Toes ♓ RS015
Toledo, Spain ♐ DA011, LI098, PA075
Tongue ☿ DA025, LI247, PA017, PT321, RA061, RS015
Tongue (with Venus) ☿ AB248
Tongue Dryness ☿ RS021
Tongue Impediments ☿ DA025, PA130
Tongue Imperfections ☿ RS021
Tongue Problems ☿ LI079
Tongue-Evil ☿ LI079, RS021
Tonsil Inflammation ♉ LI094
Tonsilitis (Quinsy) ♀ PA129
Tonsilitis (Quinzies) ♉ PA005, RS016
Too Anxious about Women ☽ AB250
Too Much Marriage ☽ AB250
Too Uxorious ☽ AB250
Tool Shed ♑ LI098
Tooth Pains 1st House RS100
Toothache ♄ LI246, PA011, RA051
Toothache ♈ DA005, LI093, PA004, RS016
Topaz ☉ RA057
Topaz ☿ DA025, LI079, RA062
Topaz ♃ DA019, LI064, RA053

Tormentil ☉ CU, GA069
Torments ♂ in 7th House GA055
Tortoise ☽ LI082, RA064
Tortoise ♄ LI060, RA051
Tortona, Italy [= Derthona] ♑ DA012
Torture ♂ AB254
Torture ♄ AB254
Touch and Hearing ♃ AB248
Touch, Sense of ♃ PT319
Touchstone ♂ DA021, LI068, RA055
Toulouse, France ♍ DA009, PA074
Towns 4th House LI052, PA043
Towns ☽ DA027
Trabezond [= Trebizond] ♏ DA011
Tractable ☉ LI070
Trade 10th House LI055, PA046
Trademan's Shop ☿ PA017, RA062
Trader ♄ LI059
Trader in Large Animals ☿ in 12th House GA063
Trades ♂ LI556
Tradesmen ☿ RA061
Tradesmen's Shops ☿ DA025, LI079
Trafficker in Large Animals ☿ in 12th House GA063
Tragopogon pratensis ♃ CU
Trailing Plants ☽ AB244
Traitors ♂ LI066
Transgressions in Faith ♄ in 3rd House GA048
Trapezant [= Trebizond] ♏ PA075
Trash (Rubbish) ♄ DA017, LI060
Trash (Rubbish) Heaps 8th House AB276
Travel ☽ PT423
Travel ♂ AB250
Travel 9th House AB275
Travel Desires ☿ LI077
Travel, Foreign 7th House AB276
Travellers ☽ GA072, LI081
Treacherous ♂ GA068, LI066, PA013
Treacle ☿ DA026, LI079, RA062
Treacle Mustard (Erysimum) ♂ GA068
Treasure ♄ PA108
Treasure 3rd House AB276

Treasure 7th House AB276
Treasure, Buried 4th House LI202
Treasure, Buried 8th House AB276
Treasure, Hidden (Is It Obtainable?) 4th House GA260, LI215
Treasure, Hidden 4th House LI052, PA043
Treasure, Hidden 8th House AB276
Treasures or Riches Hidden ♃ in 4th House GA050
Treasury of Kingdom 11th House PA046
Treasury of Nation 11th House LI171
Treasury of the Sultan 11th House AB276
Treasury, Officials of the 11th House AB276
Trebozond, Turkey [Trapezant, Trabezond] ♏ DA011, PA075
Tree Coral ☿ AB243
Trees, BearingFruit with Soft Skin ♃ AB244
Trees, Bearing Hard Shell Fruit ♄ AB244
Trees, Large & Tall ♑ AB230
Trees, Prickly ♂ DA021
Trees, Shade & Spreading ☽ LI082
Trees, Soft to Touch ♀ AB244
Trees, Sweet Fruited ♃ AB244
Trees, Whose Fruit is Dried ☉ AB244
Trefoil ☿ CU, DA025, LI079
Trefoil, Meadow ☿ GA071
Tremblings ♄ LI059, RS019
Tremblings ♌ RS017
Tremblings & Qualms ♌ PA006
Trenches ♋ LI095
Trent ♒ DA013, LI099, PA076
Treviso, Italy [=Tarvisium] ♏ DA011
Tribulations 12th House LI056
Tribulations ☋ in 1st House GA046
Tricks ☿ PA016
Tricky ♂ AB250
Trientalis europaea ♄ CU
Trifle, Lost which not Found 6th House AB276
Trifler ☿ LI078
Trifolium repens ☿ CU, GA071
Trigonella foenum-graecum ☉ LI272
Trigonella foenum-graecum ☿ CU
Trigonella foenum-graecum ♀ AB243
Trigonella foenum-graecum ♂ LI272

Trim and Neat ♀ DA023
Trip Long or Short? 9th House DA113, GA286, LI424
Tripewomen ☽ LI081
Triticum ☽ AB243
Triticum ♀ CU, GA070
Triticum ♃ AB243, LI064, RA052
Triticum ♍ LI096
Trogloditica (Ethiopia) ♎ DA010
Troops ♂ AB252
Tropical ♈ AB231
Tropical ♋ AB231
Tropical ♎ AB231
Tropical ♑ AB231
Trouble ♄ in 12th House GA062
Trouble & Anxiety for Ancestor ☋ in 4th House GA051
Trouble from Crimes ♂ in 12th House GA062
Trouble in the Office 11th House AB276
Troubles about Riches ♂ in 2nd House GA047
Troubles from Servants ☉ in 6th House GA053
Troubles to Native's Mother ♀ in 8th House GA057
Troublesome ☉ GA069, LI070
Troublesome Wit ☿ GA071
True ♃ DA019
True-Hearted ♃ in 9th House GA058
Trunsole (typo for turnsole) ☉ GA069
Trust 11th House LI056
Trust, from Great Person ☽ in 3rd House GA049
Trust, Place of 10th House LI444
Trusting ♀ GA070
Trustworthiness 9th House AB275
Trustworthy ☉ GA069, LI070
Trusty ♄ AB250
Truth-Telling ♃ AB250
Truth-Telling ♄ AB250
Tuberculosis (Ptisick, Ptisis) ☽ LI082
Tuberculosis (Ptisick, Ptisis) ☿ PA017, RA062, RS021
Tuberculosis (Ptisick, Ptisis) ♄ RS019
Tuberculosis (Ptisick, Ptisis) ♉ LI094
Tuberculosis (Ptisick, Ptisis) ♋ LI095, RS017
Tuberculosis (Ptisick, Ptisis) 2nd House LI245
Tuesday ♂ AB241, LI068
Tuesday Night ♀ AB241

Tumors, Benign Skin ♉ LI094
Tumors, Especially Genital ♂ PT329
Tumultous ♂ LI540
Tumults 12th House AB275
Tunis ♋ DA008, LI095, PA074
Turbulent ♂ GA068, LI066
Turin ♀ RA060
Turin ♊ PA074
Turing ♀ LI076
Turing (Turin?)* ♀ DA024
Turkey ♌ LI096
Turkcy (Part) ♌ DA008, PA074
Turkish People ♂ DA021
Turnsole (Heliotropium) ☉ GA069
Turpentine Tree ♀ LI075, RA060
Turpentine Tree ♄ AB244
Turquoise ☿ AB243
Turtledove ♀ RA060
Turvisium ♏ PA075
Tussilago farfara ♀ CU, GA070
Tutsan (see *St. John's Wort*)
Tutty (Zinc Oxide) ♃ AB243
Twins (Shall She Have?) 5th House GA266, LI230
Two-Penny Grass ☿ DA025, LI079
Tympanies ☉ RS020
Tyrannical ♂ LI540, PT353
Tyrannous ♂ PA093
Tyranny ♂ LI556, PA109
Tyrants ☉ PA014, RA057
Tyrants ♂ DA021, GA068, LI067, RA054
Tyrol ♉ PA073

-- U --

Ugly ♄ AB249
Ulcers ♂ DA020
Ulcers ♓ DA014, LI099, RS018
Ulcers in the Bowels ♍ DA009
Ulex europaeus ♂ GA068
Ulmus minor ♄ CU, GA067
Ulmus minor ♌ PA074

Umbilicus rupestris ♀ GA070
Umbilicus rupestris ♀ in ♎ CU
Unchaste but Quickly Repentant ♂ AB250
Uncles 6th House GA053, LI053, PA044
Unconstant ☽ PA017
Unconstant ☿ LI541
Unconstant ♋ LI538
Undaunted ♂ PA012
Undependable ☿ PT361
Underground Brick Making ☽ AB242
Underground Canals ♄ AB242
Underground Vaults ♄ AB242
Undertakers ♄ LI059
Underwater Brick Making ☽ AB242
Undiscriminating ☿ PT361
Unexcelled in War ♂ GA068
Unfeeling ♄ PT341
Unfortunate Accident to Legs 6th House AB275
Unfortunate Children ♄ in 11th House GA061
Unfortunate in Large Animals ♂ in 12th House GA063
Unfortunate Journeys ☋ in 3rd House GA049
Ungodly ♂ in 3rd House GA049
Ungovernable ♂ LI066
Unhappy Life ♄ in 1st House GA046
Unhappy Marriage ☋ in 7th House GA056
Unicorn ♃ LI064, RA053
Unjust ☿ PT361
Unjust ♂ LI540
Unmovable ♂ GA068
Unpleasant Foreign Travel ☽ in 7th House GA055
Unpleasant Look ♄ PA010
Unreasonable ♂ LI066
Unruly ♂ PT353
Unsettled ☽ GA072
Unstable ☽ DA026
Unstable ☿ DA025, PA095, PT361
Unstable ♂ in 9th House GA058
Unstable in Religion ☋ in 9th House GA059
Unstable in Younger Years ♀ in 10th House GA060
Unsteadfast ☽ GA072, LI081
Unsteady ☿ PT361

Unsteady ♂ AB250
Unsuspicious ♀ GA070
Untainted ♃ GA067
Unthankful ♂ LI066
Untrustworthy ♂ AB250
Unwearied ☿ GA071
Unwilling to Believe Good ♄ AB250
Upholsterers ♀ GA070, LI074, RA058
Upper Part of Body, Big ♋ PA005
Upper Part of Fire ♂ AB247
Uprising ♂ PT183
Upstairs ♎ LI096
Urbine [= Urbino] ♏ LI097
Urbinium [= Urbino] ♏ PA075
Urbino ♏ PA075
Urbino [= Urbine] ♏ DA011
Urginea Maritma ♂ CU
Urination, Painful ♀ LI247, PA015
Urination, Painful ♏ LI246
Urination, Painful 8th House LI054
Urine Retention ☽ RS021
Urine Retention ♎ DA010, PA007
Urtica dioica ♂ CU, GA068, LI067, RA054
Useful Foods ♀ AB245
Userers ☿ LI078
Users of Iron Tools ♂ RA054
Usurers ☿ GA071, RA061
Usurpers ☉ PA014, RA057
Usurpers ♂ GA068, LI067, RA054
Usury ♄ LI555
Uterine Disease ♀ PA015
Uterine Disorder (Passion) ♀ DA024
Uterine Kindred ♀ AB249
Uterus ♀ DA023
Utrecht ♈ DA006, LI094
Uxorious ♃ AB250

-- V --

Vacant Places ☉ AB241
Vaccinium Myrtillus ♃ CU

Vacillating Riches ☽ in 2nd House GA048
Vagabonds ☽ DA026, GA072, LI081, PA110
Vaginal Discharge, White 5th House RS100
Vain Candor ♃ LI540
Vain Fears ♄ LI059
Vain Imaginings ☿ LI079
Vain-Glorious ♂ in 9th House GA058
Valachia, Poland [= Walachia] ♒ DA013, LI099
Valencia, Spain ♏ DA011
Valenciennes ♊ PA074
Valentia, Rome ♏ LI097, PA075
Valerian ♀ DA024, LI075, RA060
Valerian (Greek) ☿ CU
Valerian (True Wild) ☿ CU
Valerian, Garden ☿ GA071
Valeriana officinalis ♀ RA060
Valeriana officinalis ♄ GA067
Valiant ☉ DA022
Valiant ♂ LI066, PA093
Valiant ♌ PA006
Valiant ♐ LI538
Valleys ♄ DA018
Valleys, Hidden ♄ LI060
Valleys, Obscure ♄ RA051
Variable ♋ LI538
Varicose Veins ♒ PA009
Vein Diseases ♃ RS019
Vein, Coagulation ♒ LI099
Veins ☽ DA027
Veins ♂ AB247, DA020, PA128, PT319, RA054, RS014
Veins ♃ LI063, PA012, RS014
Venereal Disease ♀ DA023, LI075
Venice ♋ DA008, LI095, PA074
Ventricle ☽ LI580
Venturesome ♂ PT353
Veratrum viride ♄ CU
Verbascum ♄ GA067
Verbascum nigrum ♄ CU
Verbascum thapsus ♄ CU
Verbena officinalis ☉ RA057
Verbena officinalis ☿ RA062

Verbena officinalis ♀ CU, GA070, RA060
Verbena officinalis ♄ RA050
Vercellas, Italy ♊ PA074
Vermillion ♂ LI068
Vermillion (Stone) ♂ DA021
Vermillion, Red ♂ RA055
Vernal, Changeable ♈ AB230
Vernal, Changeable ♉ AB230
Vernal, Changeable ♊ AB230
Verona ♈ DA006, LI094, PA073
Veronica beccabunga ♂ CU, GA068
Veronica officinalis ☽ CU, GA072
Versatile ♂ PT353
Versatility ☽ PT361
Vertigo ☽ RA064
Vertigo ☿ LI078, PA017, RA062, RS021
Vertigo ♈ PA004
Vervain ☉ RA057
Vervain ☿ LI079, RA062
Vervain ♀ CU, DA024, GA070, RA060
Vervain ♄ DA018, LI059, RA050
Very Wet ♑ AB264
Vessels which Hold Water ♀ AB242
Veterinarian ♈ LI450
Veterinarian ♑ LI451
Veterinarian, Barnyard ♌ LI451
Veterinarian, Barnyard ♑ LI451
Veterinary Surgeons ♂ AB254
Vexations ♌ DA008
Vicia faba ♀ CU, GA070
Vicious ♈ DA005
Vicious ♏ DA011
Vicious ♑ DA012
Vicious ♓ DA014
Victim of Journeys ♂ in 2nd House GA047
Victim of Theft ♂ in 2nd House GA047
Victorious ♂ PA012
Victorious Over Enemies ♃ in 7th House GA054
Victorious Over Enemies ⊗ in 7th House GA056
Victory ♂ PA109
Victory 7th House LI054

Victory Over Private Enemies ♃ in 12th House GA062
Victory Overrides All ♂ GA068
Vienna ♀ RA060
Vienna (France) ♏ PA075
Vienna, Austria ♀ DA024, LI076
Vienna, Austria ♎ DA010, LI097, PA075
Vienna, Austria ♏ DA011, LI097
Vile ♀ in 12th House GA063
Villages 4th House LI202
Vilna, Lithuania [= Vilnius] ♑ DA012, PA076
Vilnius, Lithuania [= Vilna] ♑ DA012, PA076
Vinca Major ♀ CU, GA070
Vincentia* ♋ DA008, PA074
Vindell, England [=Portland] ♑ PA076
Vine Tree (Grapes) ☉ CU
Vine Tree (Grapes) ♀ GA070
Vines ☽ AB244
Vines ☉ AB244, DA022, LI071, RA057
Vines ♀ RA060
Vines ♃ LI064, RA053
Vineyards ♏ DA011, LI097
Vineyards ♒ DA013, LI099
Vineyards 4th House LI052
Vintners ☽ GA072, LI081
Vintners ♏ LI451
Viola odorata ♀ CU, GA070, RA060
Viola odorata ♃ LI064, RA053
Viola tricolor ♄ CU
Violence 6th House AB276
Violence ♂ PA109, PT183
Violent ☿ DA025
Violent ♂ AB250, DA021, LI066
Violent ♄ PT341
Violent ♏ PA007
Violent ♈ PA004
Violet ♀ RA060
Violet (Herb) ☽ AB236
Violet (Herb) ♃ DA020, LI064, RA053
Violet (Herb) ♀ CU, GA070, LI075
Violet (Plant) ♀ DA024
Violet (Water) ♄ CU

Viper's Bugloss ☉ CU, GA069
Virgins ☽ AB254
Virgins ♀ LI074, PA015, RA058
Virtue ♃ PA108
Virtuous ♀ GA070, LI074
Virtuous ♃ LI062
Visage 1st House GA045
Visage, "Full-Faced" ☽ DA026
Visage, Evil ♐ DA012
Visage, Fair ♒ DA013
Visage, Full ♃ DA019
Visage, Good Large ♓ DA014
Visage, Goodly & Fair Round ♀ DA023
Visage, Large ☉ GA069
Visage, Lean ♄ DA018
Visage, Long ☿ DA025, GA071, PA016
Visage, Long ♈ DA006
Visage, Long ♒ PA009
Visage, Oval ♃ GA067
Visage, Plump & Round ♀ GA070
Visage, Round ☽ DA026
Visage, Round ♂ GA068
Visage, Round ♋ DA008
Visage, Round ♎ DA010
Visage, Thin & Lean ♑ DA012
Visage, Unpleasant ♄ DA018
Visage, Well-favored ♎ DA010
Viscum album ☉ CU, GA069
Vision and Taste ☽ AB248
Visions 9th House GA058, LI055
Visions, Interpretation of 9th House AB275
Vital Spirit ☉ RS020
Vital Spirits ☉ PA014
Vital, Growing, Nutritive ♃ AB245
Vitex agnus castus ☽ RA063
Vitis vinifera ☉ CU, RA057
Vitis vinifera ♀ GA070, RA060
Vitis vinifera ♃ RA053
Vitriol ☽ DA026
Vitriol ☿ DA025, LI079
Vizirs ♃ AB252

Vocation 10th House LI558
Voice ☿ RS015
Voice, Big & Great ♌ DA009
Voice, Box ☿ RS015
Voice, Clear ☉ DA023
Voice, Fine ☿ AB250
Voice, Large (Arc. Breast) ♊ DA007
Voleteras, Italy [= Volterra] ♐ DA011, PA075
Volterra, Italy [= Voleteras] ♐ DA011, PA075
Voluptuous ♀ in 1st House GA046
Voluptuousness ♀ RA058
Vomit ☿ DA025
Vomit ♀ LI247
Vomiting 4th House RS100
Vomiting of the Blood ♂ RS020
Voyages 9th House GA058, LI055, PA045
Voyages, Unsuccessful ☿ PT187
Vratislavia = Bratislava, Czechoslovakia ♍ DA009, PA075
Vulture ♂ LI068, RA055
Vulva ☽ RS198
Vulva ♀ S2-56

-- **W** --

Wages Dues Shall Querent Receive 2nd House GA252, LI170
Wagtail (Bird) ♀ LI075
Wailing ♄ AB250
Wainscot Rooms ♊ DA007
Walachia, Poland [= Valachia] ♒ DA013, LI099
Walking from Place to Place ☽ DA026
Wall Rue (white Spleenwort) ☿ GA071
Wallflower ☽ GA072
Wallflower (Common) ☽ CU
Walls of Houses ♊ LI094
Walnut ☉ CU, GA069
Walnut ☿ LI079
Walnut ♀ DA024, RA060
Walnut Tree ☿ LI079, RA062
Walwort ♃ DA020, LI064, RA052
Wan in Color ♄ DA017
War ♂ PA109

War (Eclipses) 7th House PA044
War (Mundane) 7th House PA044
War Damage ♂ in 2nd House GA047
War, or Peace 7th House LI054
War, Victor in 7th House PA044
War-Mongers ♂ LI066
War-Mongers ♍ LI538
War (Shall (S)he Return Safely?) 7th House GA277, LI367
War (Shall the Castle Be Taken?) 7th House GA278, LI368
Wardrobe-Keepers ♀ LI628
Wardrobes ♃ DA020, LI064, RA053
Wardrobes ♀ DA024, LI075, RA060
Warfare ♂ LI556
Warhorses ♐ LI097
Warming, Moderate ♀ PT037
Warriners 6th House PA044
Warrior ♂ PA012
Wars ♂ LI066, PT183
Wary ☿ LI541, PA094
Wash-Houses ♋ DA008, LI095
Wash-Houses ♏ DA011, LI097
Wasps ♂ AB247
Waste, Hard and Stony Land ♂ AB241
Wastes Estate & Treasure ☉ in 12th House GA063
Wastes Money Seeking Curiosities ☿ GA071
Wastes Patrimony ☉ LI070
Wastes Patrimony ♃ GA067, LI063
Watch-Makers ♂ GA068, LI067, RA054
Water Pipes ☽ LI214
Water Pipes ♄ LI214
Water Serpents, Stinging ♂ RA055
Water Wagtail (Bird) ♀ RA060
Water, Measuring ☽ AB254
Water, Standing ♓ LI099
Water, Stinking, Alkaline ♓ AB230
Water, Sweet and Pure ♋ AB230
Water, Turbid ♏ AB230
Water-Bearers ☽ LI081
Water-Mills ♓ DA014
Water-Supply 4th House AB275
Water-Work ☽ LI214

Water-Work ♄ LI214
Watercress ☽ GA072
Waterflag = Flower-De-Luce ☽ GA072
Waterfowl ☽ RA064
Watermen ☽ GA072, LI081
Watermills ♓ LI099
Waters, Navigable ♋ DA008, LI095
Watery ♏ PA007
Wavering ☽ PA017
Wavering ☿ DA025, PA095
Wavering ♂ LI066
Waylayers ♂ DA021
Wayward ☿ DA025
Weakness ♄ PT327
Weakness in the Limbs ♄ RS019
Wealth 2nd House LI051, PA042
Wealth Accumulation ☉ in 2nd House GA047
Wealth Acquired thru Trickery ♄ AB250
Wealth by Work 1st House LI557
Wealth from Fish-Ponds ☽ in 4th House GA051
Wealth from Fishing ☽ in 4th House GA051
Wealth from Mills ☽ in 4th House GA051
Wealth of Father 5th House LI053, PA043
Wealth, Securing of the Ancient 5th House AB276
Wearing a Crown ☉ AB253
Weasel ☽ LI082
Weasel ☿ LI079, RA062
Weasel ♄ AB246
Weather (Cloudy) ♄ RA051
Weather (Dark) ♄ RA051
Weather (Gentle Showers, Winter) ♀ RA060
Weather (Pleasant) ♃ RA053
Weather (Seasonal) ☉ RA058
Weather (Storms, Hail) ☿ RA062
Weather (Temperate Heat, Summer) ♀ RA060
Weather T(hunder & Lightning) ♂ RA055
Weavers ♀ PT337
Wedlock ♀ DA024, LI556
Wednesday ☿ AB241, LI080
Wednesday Night ♄ AB241
Weeping ♄ AB250

Weld (Wold - Herb) ♂ GA068
Well-born Ladies 3rd House AB276
Well-known ☉ AB241
Well-minded ☉ GA069
Well-proportioned Body ♎ PA007
Well-spoken ♀ AB250
Well-spoken ♍ PA006
Well-spoken ♎ DA010
Wells ♄ AB242, LI060, RA051
Wells ♋ LI095
Wells ♓ LI099
Wens ♉ DA006, RS016
West ♎ AB231, LI365
West ♏ AB231
West ♐ AB231
West 7th House LI054
West Indies ☿ RA062
West Indies ♑ LI098
West Northwest 6th House LI364
West Southwest 8th House LI364
West Wind ♎ AB231
West Wind ♏ AB231
West Wind ♐ AB231
Western ♊ LI094
Western ♎ LI096, PA007
Western ♒ LI098, PA009
Western Winds ♂ LI068
Westphalia ♒ DA013, LI099, PA076
Wetemberg [Wurttemberg, Ger.] ♊ PA073
Wetenburgh [= Wurttemberg, Ger] ♊ DA007
Whale ♃ RA053
Wharfs ☽ RA064
Wharves ☽ PA018
What Happens to the Dead 4th House AB275
What Succeeds Death 4th House AB275
Whatever Warmer than 4th Degree ☉ AB245
Wheat ☽ AB243
Wheat ♀ CU, GA070
Wheat ♃ AB243, DA020, LI064, RA052
Wheat ♍ LI096
Wheatfield ♉ LI094

Whelks see Pimples
Where Implements of Cattle Are ♉ PA005
Where Querent May Best Live 1st House LI132
Where Writings Are Kept ♍ PA007
Whether Another Shall Be at Home 1st House GA242, LI147
Whether Querent Become Rich 2nd House LI167
Which Spouse Dies First 8th House PA070
White 1st House LI051, PA041
White 5th House AB277, PA043
White 9th House AB277
White ☽ DA026, LI082, RA063
White ♀ DA023, LI075, LI086
White ♃ PT193
White and Mixed Yellow & Brown ♃ AB240
White Clothes ♃ AB254
White Flowers ♀ LI075
White Glistening ♓ LI086
White Lead ♃ AB243
White Purge ♂ LI068
White Stones ☽ AB243
White-Red ♈ LI086
White-Red ♊ LI086
White-Yellow ♉ LI086
Whites 5th House RS100
Whiting (Fish) ♀ RA060
Whorehouses ♀ RA060
Whoremongers ♀ PA094
Wicked ♂ DA021
Wicked Acts ☿ LI077
Wicked People ♄ AB252
Widows ☽ DA027, LI557, PA110
Widows ♀ GA070, PA015
Wife ♀ DA024
Wife, Discrete ♃ in 7th House GA055
Wife, Good Behavior ♌ in 7th House GA056
Wife, Honest, Prudent ♌ in 7th House GA056
Wife, Noble and Virtuous ☉ in 7th House GA055
Wife, Quarrelsome ♂ in 7th House GA055
Wife, Rich and Fair ☽ in 7th House GA055
Wife, Shameless ♀ in 6th House GA053
Wife, Unobedient ♀ in 6th House GA053

Wife, Virtuous, Honest ♃ in 7th House GA055
Wife's Kindred 9th House GA058, LI055, PA045
Wife's Property 8th House AB275
William ♄ LI341
Willow Tree ☽ CU, GA072
Willow Tree ♄ AB244, DA018, LI059, RA050
Willowherb ♃ LI064
Willowherb (Hairy) ♄ CU
Willowherb (Rosebay) ♄ CU
Wills 8th House GA056, LI054, PA045
Wily ☿ LI541
Wimpina(City)* ♎ DA010
Wind Diseases ♊ DA007
Wind in the Veins ♊ PA005
Wind-Cholic ☽ RA064
Wind-Cholic ♍ LI246, RS017
Windiness ♃ DA019, LI063, RA053, RS019
Windiness in the Veins ♃ LI246
Windiness in the Veins ♊ LI094, RS017
Windmills, Nearby ♎ LI096
Winds Melancholic ♒ RS018
Winds, Destructive Storms ♒ AB230
Winds, Melancholy ♒ LI099
Winds, Quiet Air ♊ AB230
Winds, When They Blow 2nd House AB276
Windy ♐ AB264
Windy Weather ☿ LI079
Wine 10th House AB276
Wine ♀ PT337
Wine-Bibbers, Dressed in Red ♂ AB253
Winter Gilliflowers = Wallflower ☽ GA072
Wintergreen ☽ CU
Wisdom 9th House LI429
Wise ♃ LI062
Wise ☿ DA025, LI541, PT359
Wit Good ♊ DA007
Wit Wholly for Its Own End ♍ DA009
Witchcraft 1st House AB276
Witches 12th House LI056
Withdraws from Bad Friends ☿ AB250
Withering ♄ PT181

Without Honesty ♂ GA068
Without Modesty ♂ GA068
Wittenburg[h], Germany ♋ DA008, LI095, PA074
Wittiness ☿ PA110
Witty ☽ GA072
Witty ☿ GA071, LI077, PA016
Witty ♀ PA094
Witty ♈ LI538
Witty ♊ LI538
Witty ♍ PA006
Wives ☽ DA027
Wives ♀ AB249, GA070, LI074, PA015, RA058
Wives 7th House LI054
Wizards, Captivity ☽ AB254
Wizards, Deception of Prison ☽ AB254
Wizened ♄ AB249
Woad ♄ GA067
Woers ♀ LI541, PA094
Wold (Weld - Reseda) ♂ GA068
Wolf ♂ AB246, LI068, RA055
Wolf ♄ LI060, RA051
Wolfbane ♄ DA018, LI059, RA050
Womb ☽ PT321
Womb ♀ AB248, DA023, LI247, PA015, RS014
Womb ♃ AB248
Womb ♏ RS015
Womb 5th House RS097
Womb 7th House LI245
Womb Defects ♏ LI097, RS018
Womb Diseases ♀ RS020
Womb Impediments 5th House RS098
Womb Suffocation ♀ RS020
Women 7th House AB275
Women ☽ GA072, LI081
Women ♀ GA070, LI304, PA015, RA058
Women, Affairs of 6th House AB276
Women, Chaste ♉ DA006
Women, Friendship of 11th House AB275
Women, Honest & Chaste ♒ DA013
Women-Loving ♀ LI541
Women, Pregnant 5th House PA043

Women, Religious & Chaste ♌ DA008
Women Tailors ♀ LI074, PA015
Women, Young ♀ DA023
Women's Genitals ☽ DA026
Women's Tailors ♀ RA058
Wood-working Place ♑ LI098
Woodbine ☿ GA071
Wooden Cups, Sellers of ♂ AB254
Woodruffe (Squin[cy, zle, ancy, ances]) ♂ CU
Woodruffe (Squin[cy, zle, ancy, ances]) ♃ DA019, LI063, RS019
Woodruffe (Squin[cy, zle, ancy, ances]) ♉ DA006, PA005
Woodruffe (Squin[cy, zle, ancy, ances]) 2nd House RS100
Woodruffe (Sweet) ♂ CU
Woods ♄ DA018, LI060, PA011, RA051
Woods ♌ DA008, LI095
Woods, Quality of 10th House LI206
Wool ♄ AB247
Wool Merchant ♑ LI451
Woolen Drapers ♃ GA067, LI063, RA052
Woolly Thistle (Carduus) ♂ GA068
Words Few ♄ DA018
Workaholic ♄ PT341
Works for Riches ♄ LI539
Works of Beauty ♀ AB254
Works of Magnificence ♀ AB254
Works to Get Money from Wills ☿ in 8th House GA057
Worms ☽ RS021
Worms ♂ LI068
Worms ♍ LI096, RS017
Worms ♓ DA014, LI099, PA076
Worms in Children & Men ☽ LI082
Wormseed (Treacle) ♂ CU
Wormwood ♂ CU, GA068
Wormwood (Roman) ♂ CU
Wormwood (Sea) ♂ CU
Worn-outness ☉ AB241
Worship of the Gods ☿ PT187
Wound in Face if Mars Here 1st House PA041
Wounds ♂ DA021, LI067, PA013
Wounds to Hands & Feet ♂ in 8th House GA057
Wounds to Hands & Feet ♂ in 12th House GA063

Wounds, especially Head & Face ♂ PA128
Wrath ♄ AB254
Wrath of Leaders ♂ PT183
Wratislave = Bratislava, Czech. ♍ DA009, PA075
Wren ♀ LI075, RA060
Wrestlers ☿ AB252
Wrists ♊ RS015
Writers 12th House AB276
Writing ☿ DA025
Writings ☿ LI139
Wurttemberg, Germany [Wetemberg, Wetenburgh] ♊ DA007, PA073

-- Y --

Yarrow ♀ CU, GA070
Yellow ☉ DA022, LI071, RA057
Yellow ☽ DA026
Yellow ♀ PT193
Yellow ♂ DA020, LI067, RA054
Yellow ♐ LI086
Yellow 3rd House AB277, LI052, PA042
Yellow 11th House AB277, LI056, PA047
Yellow Flowers ☉ LI071
Yellow Green ♃ DA019, LI063
Yellow in White of Eye ☉ AB249
Yellow Jaundice ♂ LI067, PA013
Yellow Purple ☉ LI086
Yellow Sulphur ☉ AB243
Yellow White ♉ LI086
Yellow, Mixed ♃ RA052
Yellow, Pale ☽ LI082, RA063
Yemen ♄ AB242
Yew ♄ CU, LI059, RA050
York ♋ DA008, LI095, PA074
Young Scholars ♃ LI063
Young Women ♀ DA023
Youth ♀ PT443
Youth ♂ AB248
Youth ♋ AB230
Youth ♌ AB230
Youth ♍ AB230

Youth & Adolescence ♀ AB248
Youthful Vigor ☉ AB245

-- Z --

Zanzibar ♄ AB242
Zealand ☽ DA027, LI083, RA064
Zealand ♋ LI095, PA074
Zealous ♃ in 9th House GA058
Zealous ♄ LI539
Zealous in Affects ♀ GA070
Zinc Oxide ♃ AB243
Zurich ♉ DA006

Planetary Rulerships

*Indicates that the meaning of a word is unknown.

Sun ☉

Adamant (Stone) LI072
Adamine DA022
Aetites (Stone in Eagles' Nests) DA022, RA057
Affable GA069, LI070
Aiming at High Things PA014
Alice LI341
Allium cepa LI273
Allium sativum LI273
Aloes LI071, RA057
Amber (Plant) DA022, LI071, RA057
Ambitions LI556
Ambitious DA022, PA109
Andrew LI341
Angelica GA069
Animals, Nocturnal AB246
Animals, Wild, White Hooved AB246
Anne LI341
Armenia AB242
Aromaticus* RA057
Arrogant LI070
Arsenic Monosulphide AB243
Arsenic, Yellow AB243
Arsenick (Arsesmart) DA023, LI071
Arsesmart (Arsenick) DA023, LI071
Arteries PA014
Artonicum (Arsenick) DA023, LI071
Ash Tree CU, DA023, GA069, LI071, RA057
Ass, Wild AB246
Authorities, Petty PA014
Authority Figures LI556

Baboon RA058
Baldness DA022
Balm DA022, GA069, LI071, RA057
Barin (= Bairn = Barn) DA022
Barley DA023, LI071, RA057
Barn (Barin = Child) DA022
Barons GA069, LI071
Bay CU
Bay Tree RA057
Beard Much GA069
Benjamin LI341
Bile, Yellow (Yellow Choler) RS020
Boar RA058
Body, Comely DA022
Body, Full, Fleshy GA069, PA014
Body, Healthy DA022
Bohemia LI072, RA058
Boils, Internal (Pushes) DA022
Boils, Uterine (Pushes) DA022
Bold DA022
Bountiful GA069
Brain LI247, PT319, RA057, RS014
Brain Disease LI071, RA058, RS020
Brains AB247
Braziers GA069, LI071
Breath, Stinking RS020
Brief in Speech LI070
Brothers AB249
Buildings of Honor PA014
Buildings, Magnificent DA023, RA058
Buildings, Stately PA014
Bull LI071, RA058

Burnet CU, GA069
Butter-Bur CU, GA069
Buzzard LI072, RA057
Cabunkle (Stone) RA057
Campana (Plant) LI071
Cane LI071
Carbuncle (Stone) DA022
Cardiac Passion LI247
Carthamus tinctorius GA069, RA057
Cataracts LI247
Catarrhs RA058, RS020
Cathars (Purges) DA022
Cedar DA023, LI071, RA057
Celandine = [Sallendine]   DA023,
  GA069, LI071, RA057
Celandine (the Greater) CU
Centaurium erythraea CU, GA069
Centaury CU, GA069
Chaldaea   DA022, LI072, PT143,
  RA058
Chamaemelum nobile CU
Chamomile [Camomel] CU, GA069
Chaste But Sensual AB250
Chelidonium majus CU, RA057
Chests AB248
Chick Peas LI273
Chiefs AB252
Child (= Bairn) DA022
Choler LI247
Choler, Red DA022
Choler, Yellow RS020
Chrysolite DA022, LI072, RA057
Cinnamon DA023, LI071, RA057
Cinquefoil DA023, LI071, RA057
Circumspect PA109
Citron (Pomecitron) LI071
Cock (bird) AB247, LI072, RA057
Coiners RA056
Comestio (Devouring) of Mouth Flesh
  DA022
Commonwealths LI556, PA109

Complexion Between Yellow & Black
  DA022
Complexion Honey-Colored GA069
Complexion Obscure White W/Red
  DA022
Complexion Saffron-Colored GA069
Complexion Tawny PA014
Complexion White (Yellowish)
  AB249
Constables RA057
Constables, Troublesome PA014
Constitution Healthful GA069
Consumption RS020
Coppersmiths GA069, LI071
Corporature Large GA069
Coughs RS020
Courteous GA069, PA014
Courtiers DA022, GA069, LI071
Courtiers, Honest PA014
Courts RA058
Courts of Princes   DA022, LI072,
  PA014
Crabfish LI071
Cracking of Pedigree GA069
Cramps   DA022, LI071, RA058,
  RS020
Crocodile AB246, LI071, RA058
Cumin LI273
Daffodil LI272
Date Palms AB244
Deer AB246
Desire to Rule LI070
Desirous of Honors DA022
Desirous of Rule GA069
Desirous of Sovereignty GA069
Devouring (Comestio) Mouth Flesh
  DA022
Diamond RA057
Dictamnus albus RA057
Dignity PA109, PT363
Dining Rooms DA023, LI072, RA058

Disdainful LI070
Diseases, Peracute PA014
Dittany RA057
Dodder AB244
Domineering GA069, LI070
Dove, Turtle AB247
Drinking AB245
Drosera anglica CU
Dukes   DA022, GA069, LI071, PA109, RA056
Eager for Knowledge, Power AB250
Eager for Victory AB250
Eagle AB247, LI072
Earls DA022, GA069, LI071
East Winds LI072
Eating AB245
Echium vulgare CU, GA069
Edith LI341
Emperors   GA069, LI071, PA014, RA056
Empty Places AB241
Enula (Plant) DA022, LI071
Euphrasia officinalis CU, GA069, LI071, RA057
Expensive LI070
Eye Disease DA022, LI071, PA129, RA058
Eye Fluxes DA022
Eye Infirmities RS020
Eye Inflammation PA014
Eye, Full with Sharp Sight PA014
Eye, Left (Women) DA022, LI247, PA014, RA057
Eye, Right AB248, PA129, RS014
Eye, Right (Men) DA022, LI247, PA014, RA057
Eyebright (Plant)   CU, DA023, GA069, LI071, RA057
Eyes, Blood-Shot RS020
Eyes, Great Goggled GA069
Eyes, Redness RS020

Eyes, Secretions LI247
Eyes, Sharp & Piercing GA069
Eyesight DA022, LI247, PT319
Face, Large PA014
Face, Round DA022
Fainting DA022, LI247
Fair DA022
Fair Yellow or Bright Flaxen GA069
Faithful LI070
Falcon AB247
Famous PA109
Famous Magistrateship DA022
Fat AB247, LI273
Fathers AB249, PT241
Fenugreek LI272
Feverfew CU
Fevers, Rotten RS020
Figs, Dry LI273
Finger, Ring RS014
Fish, Large AB246
Fistulas DA022
Fly, Spanish (Cantharides) LI072
Foods AB245
Foolish LI070
Forehead, Broad PA014
Forehead, Broad & High GA069
Fortitude LI556
France PT135
Frankincense DA023, LI071, LI273, RA057
Fraxinus excelsior   CU, GA069, LI071, RA057
Friendly AB250
Full Manhood AB248
Galangal (Ginger Family) LI273
Garlic LI273
Gazelle AB246
Generals AB252
Generous Things AB241
Gentlemen GA069, LI071, RA056
Gentlemen of Quality PA014

Giddiness RA058
Ginger DA022, LI071, RA057
Glow-worms LI071
Goats LI071
Goats, Mountain AB246
Gold DA022, LI071
Gold & That Coined for Kings AB243
Gold Brocades, Receiving AB254
Gold Brocades, Selling AB254
Goldsmiths GA069, LI071, PA014,
   RA056
Good Judgment LI070
Gosshawk LI072
Government LI556
Grave GA069
Gravity LI070
Gravity Lacking in Words GA069
Hair, Crisp DA022
Hair, Curly DA022
Hair, Flaxen & Curling PA014
Hair, Long AB249
Halls LI072, RA058
Hankering after Management AB250
Hankering after Wealth AB250
Hankering after Worldly Affair
   AB250
Harsh PT363
Harsh with Opponents AB250
Hater of Sordid Men GA069
Hawk RA057
Head AB248, RS014
Head, Large AB249, DA023
Head-Boroughs RA057
Heart DA022, LI247, PA014, PT319,
   RA057, RS014
Heart-burning PA129
Heart Disease LI071, RS020
Heart Palpitations PA014, RA058,
   RS020
Heart, Trembling LI247
Hedera helix RA057

Heletropion (Tree) LI071
Heliotrope DA023, GA069
Heliotropion (Stone) RA057
Helleborus LI273
Herb Grace (Rue) LI071, RA057
High GA069
High-constables LI071
High-sheriffs LI071
Honest DA022, GA069, PA014
Honey RA057
Honor LI556, PA109, PT363
Hordeum vulgare LI071, RA057
Horses LI071, RA058
Horses, Arab AB246
Hot=Tempered, Quickly Recovers
   AB250
Houses LI072
Houses, Dining Rooms DA023
Houses, Living Rooms DA023
Houses, [Great] Halls DA023
Human LI070
Humane GA069
Humble PT363
Huntsmen LI071
Hyacinth (Stone) DA022, LI072,
   RA057
Hypericum ascyron GA069
Hypericum perforatum CUm GA069,
   RA057
Hypochondria AB247
Illustrious Actions PA109
Imposing Will on the Ignorant AB250
Industrious DA022, LI070, PT363
Industrious to Acquire Honor GA069
Industrious to Acquire Repute GA069
Inflammation: Mucous Membranes
   RA058, RS020
Intelligent AB250
Italy DA022, LI072, PT135, RA058
Ivy RA057
Jacinths AB243

James LI341
Jerusalem AB242
Judgment GA069
Judgment Composed DA023
Juglanns regia CU, GA069
Juniper Tree CU
Juniperus communis CU
Justice PT363
Justices of Peace LI071
Keeps Promises GA069
Keeps Secrets GA069
Kingdoms LI556, PA109
Kings   AB252, DA022, GA069,
    LI071, PA014, RA056
Kings and Sultans Palaces AB242
Knowledgeful AB250
Laborers DA022
Lagoecia cuminoides AB244
Lapis Lazuli AB243
Large Stature LI070
Lark RA057
Laurel DA022, LI071
Laurel Tree DA023, LI071
Laurence LI341
Laurus nobilis CU
Lavandula angustifolia RA057
Lavender RA057
Leech GA069
Leeks LI273
Left Eye (Women) LI071
Lemon Tree DA023, LI071, RA057
Levisticum GA069
Lieutenants LI071
Life Long DA022
Lignum LI071
Lignum aloes (Plant) DA023
Lily, Water AB236
Lion AB246, LI071, RA058
Liver, Cold DA022
Lofty GA069, PA014
Long Life DA022

Longing for Power & Government
    AB250
Lovage GA069
Lover of Honor PA109
Lover of Magnificence LI070
Lovers DA022
Lower Part of Fire AB247
Lucy LI341
Magistrates AB252, GA069, LI071
Magnanimous DA022
Magnet (Perhaps? = Adamant) LI072
Maize AB243
Majesty LI070
Majors LI071
Man (Male) LI304
Manhood, Young PT445
Manna (Shrub) AB244
Marble AB243
Margaret LI341
Marigold   DA022, GA069, LI071,
    RA057
Marjoram LI272
Marjoram (Sweet) RA057
Marquesses DA022, GA069, LI071,
    RA056
Marrow LI273
Masters of the Mint RA056
Maud LI341
Melissa officinalis DA022, GA069,
    LI071, RA057
Mind, Sincere & Good DA022
Mines AB241
Minters of Money   GA069, LI071,
    PA014
Mistletoe CU, GA069
Mithraists and Magians AB253
Moderate Heat & Dryness AB232
Monarchs RA056
Most Expert AB241
Mount Lebanon AB242
Mountains Rich in Minerals AB241

242 Planetary Rulerships ⊙ *Sun*

Mouth AB248
Mouth Disease   DA022, LI071,
  RA058, RS020
Mulberries AB244
Musk (Civet) LI071
Musk (Plant) DA022, RA057
Myrrh Tree DA023, LI071
Nerves AB247, RS014
Night-worms LI071
Nightengale LI072, RA057
Nobility LI556, PA109
Noble AB241
Noble-born RA056
Nobles AB252, PA109
Obstinate PT363
Office LI556
Officials AB252
One-blade (Smilacina) GA069
Onion LI273
Opthalmia RS020
Orange AB243
Orange Tree DA023, LI071, RA057
Origanum majorana RA057
Orpiment (Yellow Arsenic) AB243
Oryza Sativa CU
Paeonia officinalis GA069, LI071,
  RA057
Paeony   DA023, GA069, LI071,
  RA057
Palaces   DA022, LI072, PA014,
  RA058
Palm Tree DA023
Palpitation of the Heart RA058
Palpitations ,LI071, PA129
Parlors RA058
Patient AB250
Paunch, Large with Folds AB249
Peacock LI072
Pensions LI556
Pepper RA057
Petasites hybridus CU, GA069

Pewterers GA069, LI071, PA014
Pharaonic Glass AB243
Phillip LI341
Phoenicia DA022, LI072, PT143
Phoenix LI072, RA057
Physicians AB252
Pimpernel GA069
Pimples LI071
Pimples, Facial RS020
Piper Nigrum RA057
Pitch AB243
Pleurisy, Bastard RS020
Pomecitron (Citron) DA022, LI071,
  RA057
Potentilla erecta CU, GA069
Potentilla reptans   DA023, LI071,
  RA057
Preferment LI556
Princely Dignities DA022
Princes   DA022, GA069, LI071,
  PA014, RA056
Principal Magistrate LI071
Proud GA069, LI070
Provident DA022
Prudent GA069, LI070
Public Employment LI556
Purges (Cathars) DA022
Purple LI071
Purple (Some Say) DA022
Purple-yellow LI086
Pushes in the Interior Parts DA022
Pushes in the Womb DA022
Quiet DA022
Radish LI273
Ram LI071, RA058
Re-algar (Arsenic Monosulpide)
  AB243
Reddish Flowers LI071
Renown PA109
Reproving Evil-doers AB250
Resolute DA022

Restless GA069, LI070
Reverence PT363
Revolution AB241
Rheums DA022
Rice CU
Riches DA022
Right Eye (Men) LI071
Right Side RS014
Right Side of Body PT319
Ring-dove AB247
Roger LI341
Roman Empire RA058
Rosa solis DA023, GA069, LI071, RA057
Rosemary CU, DA023, GA069, LI071, RA057
Rosmarinus officinalis CU, GA069, LI071, RA057
Rotten Fevers LI071, RA058
Ruby LI072, RA057
Ruby (Stone) DA022
Rue GA069, LI273
Rue (Herb Grace) LI071
Rule PA109
Ruta graveolens GA069
Saffron DA022, GA069, LI071, RA057
Sallendine = Celandine RA057
Saltpeter LI273
Salutary Things AB245
Sanguisorba minor CU, GA069
Savage PT363
Scarlet LI071
Scarlet (Clear Red) DA022
Sea Calf LI071, RA058
Sea-fox LI071
Secret DA022, LI070
Seeking a Good Name/Help Other AB250
Semitertian Fever RS020
Sheep AB246

Shellfish RA058
Sicily DA022, LI072, PT135, RA058
Side, Right DA022
Sides AB248
Sight AB248, RS014
Sincere GA069
Sinews DA022, LI579, PA129, PT319, RS014
Slaves AB249
Smilacina Bifolia GA069
Societies AB252
Sour-wweet Taste LI071
Speech Slow DA023
Spendthrift GA069, LI070
Spikenard (Plant) DA023, LI071
Spinners of Gold And Silver RA056
Spirit, Great GA069
St. John's Wort CU, DA022, GA069, LI071, RA057
Stammers AB249
Starfish LI071, RA058
Stateliness LI070
Stature, Short & Thin DA022
Stem of a Tree AB236
Stephen LI341
Stewards LI071
Stipends LI556
Stomach AB247
Stomach Griping PA014
Stomach, Cold DA022
Storax Tree CU
Strombi (Fish) RA058
Strong DA022
Styrax officinalis CU
Subcutaneous Inflammation LI072
Success PT363
Sudden Swooning LI071
Sugar Cane AB244
Sunday AB237, LI072
Sundew CU
Swan LI072, RA057

Swooning PA014, RS020
Swooning, Sudden RS020
Tagetes GA069
Tall Trees with Oily Fruit AB244
Tarangubin=tarentam (Plant) AB244
Taste, Mixed Sour & Sweet DA022
Teeth AB248
Teeth, Distorted or Oblique Set
  DA023
Tertian Fever RS020
Theaters DA022, PA014
Thief is Father LI364
Thief is Master LI364
Things in General Use AB245
Thoughtful DA022, LI070
Thursday Night AB241
Topaz RA057
Tormentil CU, GA069
Tractable LI070
Trees Whose Fruit is Dried AB244
Trigonella foenum-graecum LI272
Troublesome GA069, LI070
Turnsole (Heliotropium) GA069
Trustworthy GA069, LI070
Tympanies RS020
Tyrants PA014, RA057
Usurpers PA014, RA057

Vacant Places AB241
Valiant DA022
Verbena officinalis RA057
Vervain RA057
Vine Tree (Grapes) CU
Vines AB244,DA022,LI071,RA057
Viper's Bugloss CU, GA069
Visage, Large GA069
Viscum album CU, GA069
Vital Spirits PA014, RS020
Vitis vinifera CU, RA057
Voice Clear DA023
Walnut CU, GA069
Wastes Patrimony LI070
Wearing a Crown AB253
Weather: Seasonal RA058
Well-minded GA069
Well-known AB241
Whatever Warmer than 4th Degree
  AB245
Worn-outness AB241
Yellow DA022, LI071, RA057
Yellow Flowers LI071
Yellow in White of Eye AB249
Yellow Purple LI086
Yellow Sulphur AB243
Youthful Vigor AB245

Moon D

Abraham's Balm (Agnus-Castus) RA063
Abscess (Apostem) DA026, LI082, RS021
Accounting AB254
Adaptable AB250
Adder's Tongue CU, GA072
Adherents of Prevailing Religion AB253
Agaricus campestris RA063
Agencies AB254
Agnus-Castus (Vitex) RA063
Alewives LI081
Allium cepa LI082
Ambassadors PA110
Anemia (= Green Sickness) PA018, RS021
Apoplexy LI081, RA064, RS021
Apostem (Abscess) DA026, LI082, RA064, RS021
Appetite RS015
Aquilegia Vulgaris GA072
Arrach (Garden) CU
Arthritis RS021
Ash-color DA026
Atriplex hortensis CU
Aunts, Maternal AB249
Azarbaijan AB242
Baboon RA064
Barley AB243
Bartender LI081
Bat RA064
Baths DA027, LI082
Beads Strung AB243
Beard Heavy GA072
Beard, Long AB249
Beasts of Burden AB246
Beasts, Domesticated AB246
Beasts, Obedient to Man AB246
Beggarly GA072, LI081

Beggars PA017
Belly DA026, PT321, RS015
Belly, Fluxes LI247, RS021
Beverages AB245
Bladder LI082, PA018, RS015
Bladder Disease RA064
Bladder Stones DA026
Blue And White AB240
Body, Plump PA017
Boggy Places LI082
Bogs RA064
Bowels PA018, RS015
Brain DA026, LI247, PA018, RS015
Brassica oleracea GA072
Break-outs RS021
Breast AB248, DA026
Brewers GA072, LI081
Brooks RA064
Brooks, Little LI082
Business Matters, Engaged in AB254
Cabbage DA026, GA072, LI082, RA063
Calumination AB250
Camel AB246
Canes AB244
Cannabis sativa AB244
Capacity for Change PT361
Captivity, Indicates for Wizar AB254
Cardamine pratensis CU
Careless LI081
Carrion Crows AB247
Carthage PT153
Cat RA064
Cathars (Purges) DA026
Celebrated and Wealthy Citizen AB252
Chameleon RA064
Character PT333
Charwomen GA072, LI081
Cheerful AB250
Cheiranthus cheiri CU

Chicks AB247
Chickweed CU
Chinosta (schinos = mastic) RA063
Cholic DA026, LI081, PA130, RS021
Cichorium endivia RA063
Civet Cat RA064
Clary CU
Cleavers CU
Coachmen GA072, LI081
Cockle LI082, RA064
Cold Rheumatic Diseases LI082
Cold Stomach LI082
Colewort DA026, GA072, LI082, RA063
Columbine GA072
Common People DA026, LI081, PA018
Common Shores LI082, RA064
Complexion Clear White AB249
Complexion Red & White DA027
Complexion White or Pale GA072
Composed LI081
Conduit, Water LI214
Constipation RS021
Convulsion Fits LI082, RS021
Convulsions DA027, RA064
Corpulent GA072
Coughs RA064
Coughs, Rotten RS021
Countesses GA072, LI081
Crab LI082, RA064
Cranes AB247
Croceal (Color) DA026
Crystals AB243, DA026, LI082, RA064
Cuckoo LI082
Cucumber AB243, CU, RA063
Cucumis sativus AB243, CU, RA063
Cucurbita pepo CU, LI082, RA063
Cutting Hair AB254
Deep Color Mixed Reddish Yellow

AB240
Delighting in Journeys DA027
Denmark DA027, LI083, RA064
Density AB241
Deserts LI082, PA018, RA064
Desirous of Peace GA072
Diarrhea (Lask) DA027, RS021
Diseases of Many Kinds AB252
Divedapper (Bird) RA064
Divine Law, Strenuous in AB254
Docks (i.e., Place) RA064
Dog RA064
Dog Rose CU
Dog's Tooth Violet CU
Draba incana CU
Drinking PT321
Drinking Water AB245
Dropsy (= Edema) DA026, LI082, RS021
Drunkards LI081, PA017
Drunken GA072
Duchesses GA072
Ducks AB247, LI082, RA064
Duckweed (Lemna) GA072
Easily Frightened GA072, LI081
Edema (Dropsy/leucophlegmatica) DA026, LI082, RS021
Eel LI082, RA064
Eleanor LI341
Elephant AB246
Ellen LI341
Embassies PA110
Emerald, Jewel AB243
Endive DA027, LI082, RA063
Enjoys Novelties GA072
Entrails RS015
Epilepsy DA027, LI082, PA018, PT365, RA064, RS021
Erect Gait & Figure AB249
Erythronium dens canis CU
Excellent Spirits AB250

Excitability PT361
Excrement RS197
Excrement Retention RS021
Expulsion RS192
Eye Disease PA018
Eye Hurts RS021
Eye Rheums RS021
Eye, Left AB248
Eye, Left (Men) DA026, LI247, PA018, RS015
Eye, Left, Diseases (Men) RA064
Eye, Right (Women) DA026, LI247, PA018, RS015
Eye, Right, Diseases (Women) RA064
Eyebrows, Joined AB249
Eyes, Gray GA072, PA017
Eyes, Uneven Size GA072
Face, Full-Faced DA026
Face, Round AB249, DA026, GA072
Face, Round & Pale PA017
Faint-Hearted DA026
Fair Stature LI081
Fat GA072
Faverel (Wooly) CU
Fearful DA026
Fevers, Recurring (Quotidian) RS021
Fickle PA017
Fields DA027, LI082, PA018, RA064
Firmness PT361
Fish Ponds DA027, LI082, PA018, RA064
Fish-Mongers LI081
Fishermen GA072, LI081, PA110
Fishers DA026
Fisherwomen LI081
Flag (Yellow) CU
Flanders DA027, LI083, RA064
Flax AB244
Fleur-de-Lys (Garden/Blue) CU

Flower-de-Luce GA072
Fluellein CU, GA072
Fluxes of the Belly LI082
Food, Selling AB254
Foods Equally Cold & Moist AB245
Foot (Sot) LI081
Forgetful AB250
Forgetfulness RS198
Fountains DA027, LI082, PA018, RA064
Frankness PT361
Frenzies RA064
Friday Night AB241
Frogs LI082, RA064
Galium aparine CU
Geese LI082
Generous in Distributing Food AB250
Genital Diseases RA064, RS021
Genitals LI082
Genitals, Women's DA026
Geometry AB254
Geum urbanum DA026, GA072, RA063
Giddiness LI248
Giraffe AB246
Goat RA064
Good-Hearted AB250
Goose RA064
Gourds DA026, LI082, RA063
Gout, Foot RS021
Gout, Wrists RS021
Gout, Wrists & Feet LI082
Grass AB244
Green Sickness (Anemia) PA018, RS021
Green, Pale DA026, LI082, RA063
Growing Hair AB254
Growth RS198
Guts PA018
Hackneymen GA072, LI081

Hair, Bright Brown GA072
Hair, Cutting AB254
Hair, Good, with Locks AB249
Hair, Growing AB254
Hair, Much GA072
Hair, Thick PA017
Hand, Brawny Part RS015
Hands Short & Fleshy GA072, PA017
Harbors LI082
Hater of Work GA072
Hates Work LI081
Havens of the Sea DA027, LI082
Hedera helix GA072
Hemp AB244
Henry LI341
Herons AB247
Hieracium stoloniferum GA072
Higher Sciences AB254
Highways DA027, LI082, PA018, RA064
Hind RA064
Historical Study DA026
History LI557
History, Study of PA110
Hogs RA064
Holland DA027, LI083, RA064
Hordeum vulgare AB243
Hunstmen GA072
Huntsmen LI081
Hyssop RA063
Hyssopus officinalis RA063
Idle GA072, LI081
Inconstant GA072
Infancy PT443
Infancy to Old Age (Quarters) AB248
Ingenious GA072
Insipid AB240
Intestine, Small LI247
Intestines PA130, RS015
Iris florentiana GA072
Iris germanica CU

Iris pseudacorus CU, GA072
Irrigation LI214
Ivy GA072
Jack-of-All-Trades LI081
Jurors LI403
King Among Kings AB250
King's Evil RS021
Kings AB252
Lackies DA027, PA110
Lactuca sativa CU, GA072
Ladies DA026, GA072, LI081
Lady's Smock CU
Land, Measuring AB254
Lask (Diarrhea) DA027
Lazy GA072
Leaves of a Tree AB236
Leaves Thick & Juicy LI082
Left Eye (Men) LI082
Left Side RS015
Left Side Diseases LI081, RS021
Left Side of Body PT321
Legates DA027
Lemna minor GA072
Letter Carriers GA072, LI081
Lettuce DA026, GA072, LI082
Lettuce (Common Garden) CU
Leucophlegmatia (dropsy) RS021
Level Ground AB241
Levity in Appropriate Places AB250
Lightness AB241
Ligustrum vulgare GA072
Lilum Candidum CU
Lily, Water CU, GA072
Lily, White Garden CU
Linden Tree DA026, LI082
Linseed RA063
Linum Usitatissimum AB244
Little Conjugal Happiness AB250
Liver DA026
Liver (Women) LI082, RA064, RS015

Lobster LI082, RA064
Loosestrife CU, GA072
Loquacious AB250
Lover of Elegance & Amusement AB250
Lover of Novelties PA017
Lover of Peace GA072
Lover of Sciences LI081
Lover of Women AB250
Lunaria GA072, RA063
Lunatic Passions RS021
Lungs AB247
Lying AB250
Lymph Accumulation, Swelling RS021
Lysimachia vulgaris CU, GA072
Malcontent PA017
Maltsters GA072, LI081
Mandragora officinarum LI082
Mandrake DA026, LI082
Many Professions LI081
Marcasite RA064
Mariners GA072, LI081, PA110
Marrow of the Back RS015
Mary LI341
Mastic (chinosta) RA063
Matrix Passions RS021
Measles LI082, RA064, RS021
Measuring Land AB254
Measuring Water AB254
Medicine, Practice of AB254
Melon AB244, DA026, LI082, RA063
Members of Generation RA064
Menstrual Cycle PA130
Menstrual Diseases RS021
Menstrual Problems RA064
Menstrual Retension RS021
Menstruation DA026, LI082, PA018
Mercurialis annua CU
Mercury (French) CU

Message DA026
Messengers DA026, LI081, PA110
Midwives GA072, LI081
Migraines RA064
Millers LI081
Missions AB254
Mistress of the House LI557
Mixed Colors LI086
Moderate Brilliancy AB240
Moderate Cold & Moisture AB232
Moist Places AB242
Moisture AB241, PA110
Monday AB241, LI083
Moonstone AB243
Moonwort (Lunaria) GA072
Mothers AB249, DA027, PT241
Mousear (Hieracium) GA072
Moves Frequently LI081
Moves Often GA072
Much Thought And Talk AB250
Mushrooms DA026, LI082, RA063
Muskmelon RA063
Mussel RA064
Mutable DA027, GA072
Nabatean Glass AB243
Narrow Streets of Common People AB242
Natural Power AB245
Navigation DA026, LI557
Navigators PA110
Neck AB248
Nice RA064
Nicholas LI341
Night Owl LI082, RA064
Night Raven RA064
No Concern for Future LI081
Noble Matrons AB252
Nobles AB252
Noor Hen RA064
Norimberge [=Nuremberg, Ger.] DA027, LI083

Norinberge RA064
North Winds LI082
Not Intellectually Strong AB250
Nuremberg, Ger. [=Norimberge]
  DA027, LI083
Nurses AB249, GA072, LI081
Nymphaea alba CU, GA072
Objects: Densest AB241
Objects: Lightest AB241
Objects: Moistest AB241
Objects: Thickest AB241
Obstructions (Oppilations)   LI580,
  PA018, RS017
Onion LI082
Opacity AB241
Ophioglossum vulgatum CU, GA072
Oppilations (Obstructions) PA130,
  RS021
Orpine CU, GA072
Otter LI082, RA064
Over-anxious for Comfort AB250
Over-anxious for Health AB250
Owl, Night LI082
Oxen AB246
Oyster LI082, RA064
Oyster-wives LI081
Pain, Acute Abdominal (Cholic)
  RS021
Pale Green DA026
Palm Tree RA063
Palsy DA026, RS021
Panther RA064
Papaver rhoeas CU, GA072, RA063
Papaver somniferum CU
Paralysis (Apoplexy) LI247, RS021
Partridge AB247
Peace-Loving LI081
Pearls AB243
People, Common DA026
Peregrinations PA110
Phlegm AB247

Pigs RA064
Pilgrims GA072, LI081
Pimpinella major CU
Pimpinella saxifraga CU
Piping, of Water LI214
Pistacia lentiscus RA063
Places: to Cool Water AB242
Plains AB241
Planting DA026, PA239
Plants with Spreading Leaves DA027
Pomegranites, Sweet AB244
Pompion (Pumpkin) DA026, LI082,
  RA063
Pools PA018, RA064
Pope's Legates LI081
Poppy   DA026, GA072, LI082,
  RA063
Poppy (White or Opium) CU
Port Towns LI082, RA064
Ports DA027
Portulaca oleracea GA072
Practice of Medicine AB254
Pregnant Women AB252
Prison for Wizards AB254
Privet GA072
Prodigal DA026, LI081
Propense to Study GA072
Pumpkin CU, DA026, LI082, RA063
Purges (Cathars) DA026
Purslane GA072
Pyrola minor CU
Queens   DA026, GA072, LI081,
  PA110
Quotidian Fevers RS021
Rabbit LI082
Rape (Plant) DA026, LI082
Rapeseed RA063
Rats RA064
Rattle Grass CU, GA072
Reeds AB244
Religion, Strenuous in AB254

Reproductive System Diseases RS021
Resourcefulness PT361
Respected by People AB250
Reveals Secrets AB250
Rheumatic Diseases (Cold) RS021
Rheums DA026, RS021
Rheums in the Eyes LI082
Rhinanthus CU, GA072
Right Eye (Women) LI082
Rings, Silver AB254
Rivers DA027, LI082, PA018, RA064
Roads with Trees AB242
Rose, White GA072
Rosemary RA063
Rosmarinus officinalis RA063
Rotten Coughs LI082
Sailors DA026, GA072, LI081
Salix alba CU, GA072
Salt AB240
Salty Taste DA026
Salvia sclarea CU
Salvia verbenaca CU
Satiety LI082
Saxifrage (Great Burnet) CU
Saxifrage (Small Burnet) CU
Saxifrage, Burnet GA072
Saxifrage, White GA072
Sciatica LI082, RA064, RS021
Scrofula LI082, RA064, RS021
Sea Birds LI082
Sea Ports RA064
Sea Tangle (Herb) RA063
Sea, the DA027, PA110
Sea-Bluish DA026
Sea-Green DA026
Searcher of Novelties LI081
Sedum album CU
Sedum telephium CU, GA072
Selenite DA026, LI082, RA064
Selling Food AB254

Sensations PA096
Servant Among Servants AB250
Service DA026
Sheep AB246
Shellfish LI082, RA064
Ship LI157
Shores PA018
Short Stemmed Trees AB244
Side, Left DA026, RS015
Silver AB243, DA026
Silver (Metal) LI082
Silver Color LI082, RA063
Silver Cups, Rings, Bangles AB243
Silver Metal RA064
Silver Rings AB254
Simon LI341
Simple (Pure in Heart) AB250
Sisters, Elder AB249
Skill in All Branches of Religion AB254
Skin And All Relating There to AB247
Smallpox LI082, RA064, RS021
Snails LI082
Soft GA072, LI081
Soft Stones DA026
Somewhat Bitter AB240
Sot (Fool) LI081
Soul, Character PT333
Sowing PA239
Sowing Seeds DA026
Spleen AB248
Springs LI082, RA064
Standing Pools DA027, LI082
Stature Above Middle PA017
Stature Somewhat Above Middle GA072
Stellaria media CU
Stomach AB248, DA026, PA018, PT321, RS015
Stomach Flux, I.E. Purge DA027

Stomach, Cold RS021
Stomachaches LI081, RS021
Stonecrop CU
Stones LI082, RS015
Stones, Soft LI082, RA064
Streams with Trees AB242
Strenuous in Divine Law AB254
Strenuous in Religion AB254
Studious PA017
Study of History DA026
Surfeits LI082, RA064, RS021
Surveyors AB254
Swallowing RS197
Swan RA064
Swelling RS021
Tapsters GA072
Taste DA026, LI247, RS015
Taste, Sense of PT321
Tasteless Flavors LI082
Teeth Separate/Crooked AB249
Tender GA072, LI081
Testicles and Left Side RA064
Thief is Mistress LI364
Thief is Mother LI364
Things Manufactured of Silver AB243
Thoughtful DA026
Tides DA027
Timber, Felling PA240
Timid AB250
Timorous GA072, LI081
Too Anxious About Women AB250
Too Much Marriage AB250
Too Uxorious AB250
Tortoise LI082, RA064
Towns DA027
Trailing Plants AB244
Travel PT423
Travellers GA072, LI081
Trees, Shade & Spreading LI082

Tripewomen LI081
Triticum AB243
Tuberculosis LI082
Unconstant PA017
Underground Brick Making AB242
Underwater Brick Making AB242
Unsettled GA072
Unstable DA026
Unsteadfast GA072, LI081
Urine Retention RS021
Vagabonds DA026, GA072, LI081, PA110
Veins DA027
Ventricle LI580
Veronica officinalis CU, GA072
Versality PT361
Vertigo RA064
Vines AB244
Vintners GA072, LI081
Violet (Herb) AB236
Virgins AB254
Visage, "Full-Faced" DA026
Visage, Round DA026
Vision And Taste AB248
Vitex agnus castus RA063
Vitriol DA026
Vulva RS198
Walking from Place to Place DA026
Wallflower GA072
Wallflower (Common) CU
Water, Measuring AB254
Water-Bearers LI081
Water-Work LI214
Watercress GA072
Waterflag = Flower-de-Luce GA072
Waterfowl RA064
Watermen GA072, LI081
Wavering PA017
Weasel LI082
Wharves PA018, RA064
Wheat AB243

White DA026, LI082, RA063
White Stones AB243
Widows DA027, LI557, PA110
Willow Tree CU, GA072
Wind-Cholic RA064
Winter Gilliflowers = Wallflower
  GA072
Wintergreen CU
Witty GA072
Wives DA027

Wizards, Captivity AB254
Wizards, Deception of Prison AB254
Womb PT321
Women GA072, LI081
Women's Genitals DA026
Worms RS021
Worms in Children & Men LI082
Yellow DA026
Yellow, Pale LI082, RA063
Zealand DA027, LI083, RA064

Mercury ☿

Abundance of Spittle DA025, LI079
Acacia LI272
Accountants GA071, LI078, PA110, RA061
Achates (Agate) DA025, LI079
Adder RA062
Adder's Tongue DA025, LI079, RA062
Adiantum capillus veneris CU, GA071
Advocates GA071, LI078, PA016, RA061
Affability AB250
Affairs RA062
Agate LI079, RA062
Agility LI541
Ajuga chamaepitys GA071
Alder Tree DA025
Alkakenge LI272
Alliaria petiolata CU
Allum LI272
Ambassadors LI078, PA016, RA061
Amber AB243
Ambitious LI077
Anacyclus pyrethrum CU
Anal Canal, Middle (Pecten) RS182
Anethum graveolens CU, GA071
Animals, Aquatic, Small AB246
Animals, Terrestrial, Small AB246
Anise-Seeds DA025, LI079
Ants (=pissmire) LI079, RA062
Apes LI079, RA062
Apium graveolens CU, GA071
Apprehensive GA071
Apt PA094
Arithmeticians DA025
Armenia PT147
Arms, Long GA071, PA016
Arsenic AB243
Artemisia abrotanum CU, GA071

Artemisia campestris CU
Arteries AB247
Artificiers PA016
Arts (e.g., Astrology, Medicine) PA110
Asplenium ruta muriana GA071
Ass AB246
Ass (As in Hole) LI078
Assaults PT187
Asses LI541
Assyria PT141
Asthma PA017
Astrologer AB254, GA071, LI078, PA016, PT335, RA061
Attorneys GA071, LI078, PA016, RA061
Author of Strife And Contentions GA071
Avaricious PT361
Babylonia PT141
Ballota nigra CU
Bankers AB252, PT335
Barbers, Profession of AB254
Bargains PA110
Basil, Royal AB236
Bazaars AB242
Beans AB243, DA025, LI079
Beard, Little GA071
Beard, Thin AB249
Beard, Thin & Spare DA025
Bees LI079
Beetles LI079
Beneficent PT361
Bile PT321
Birds, Aquatic AB247
Bitter Sweet CU
Black Bile AB247
Blackberry LI272
Blackbird RA062
Blue LI086
Boasters GA071, LI077, PA016

Body, Straight PA016
Body, Straight & Upright GA071
Bones DA025
Books, Selling of AB254
Bowels, Gas RS021
Bowling Alleys LI079, RA062, DA026
Braggart LI078
Brain LI247, RA061, RS015
Brain Disease LI078, PA017, RA062
Brain, Penetrating GA071, PA016
Brains DA025
Brothers DA025
Brothers, Younger AB249
Business PA110
Businessmen PT335
Busybody AB250, GA071, PA016
Buttocks PT321
Buyers DA025
Cabbage LI272
Calamint CU, GA071
Calamintha ascendens CU, GA071
Calandra (Bird) RA062
Calculators AB254, PT359
Caluminous AB250
Camel AB246
Canes & Things Growing in Water AB244
Capable of Learning LI541
Caraway AB243, CU, GA071
Carriers GA071, LI078, PA016, RA061
Carrot GA071
Carrot (Wild) CU
Carum carvi AB243, CU, GA071
Cathars (Purges) DA025
Changeable AB250
Character PT333
Cheating GA071, LI078
Chenopodium bonus-henricus CU
Chestnut Color PA016

Childhood AB248, PT443
Christian name LI341
Civet Cat RA062
Clement LI341
Clerks GA071, LI078, RA061
Clerks, Troublesome PA016
Cockatoo RA062
Cogitation LI077
Coiners PA095
Coins Struck with Name & Number AB243
Coins, Selling of AB254
Cold & Dryness AB232
Color Mixed PT193
Colutea orientalis CU
Combs, Manufacture of AB254
Commerce LI627
Commissioners LI078, RA061
Common Halls (Room) DA026, LI079, RA062
Complex Flavors AB240
Complexion Brown (Greenish) AB249
Complexion Dark PA016
Complexion Dark & Swarthy GA071
Complexion Olive or Chestnu GA071
Compounds of Two Things AB241
Conceits (Imaginings) RS021
Congestion RS021
Consumption PT187
Contracts LI556
Convallaria majalis CU
Coral AB243
Coriander AB243
Corylus avellana CU, GA071, RA062
Coughs DA025, LI247, PA017, PT187
Coughs, Dry RS021
Councilrooms AB242
Councillors AB252
Counterfeits PA095

Cow Parsnip (Heracleum) GA071
Coxcomb GA071
Crafty DA025, PA110
Cranes LI079, RA062
Creatures, Nocturnal AB246
Credulous LI078
Crete PT139
Crickets AB247
Criminal Tricks GA071
Crithum maritimum GA071
Cubebs (a Pepper) DA025, LI079, RA062
Cunning Animals LI079
Curiosity DA025
Curious LI077
Curious about Occult Knowledge GA071
Customs, Changes in PT187
Cynoglossum officinale CU, GA071
Cypress Tree LI272
Daucus carota CU, GA071
Deceitful LI541
Deceivers PA095
Deeply Interested in Business AB250
Delirium RS021
Depilatory AB243
Deportment Good LI541
Deprivation of Common Sense DA025
Desires Travel GA071
Dexterity, Manual AB254, LI541
Diambra (Drug) LI079
Dill CU, GA071
Discretion LI077
Disputant GA071, LI077
Disputants in All Sects AB253
Disputation AB254
Divination LI077
Diviners DA025, GA071, LI078, RA061
Divining Well LI541

Documents PT335
Dog AB246, RA062
Dog's Mercury CU
Dolts LI541
Doting DA025, PA130
Dragonwort DA025, LI079, RA062
Dry PT039
Dry Coughs LI079, RA062
Dryness PT187
Dumbness LI079, RS021
Eager for Pleasure AB250
Eager to Buy Slaves & Girls AB250
Ear, Left RA061
Ears, Thick AB249
Earthquakes PT187
Edmund LI341
Educated Men GA071
Egg White LI272
Egypt DA026, LI080, RA062
Egypt, Lower PT155
Elder LI079
Elecampane CU, GA071
Elegance AB250
Eloquence LI077
Eloquent AB250, GA071, PA094
Emerald, Jewel RA062
Emulous, e.g. Emulating PT361
Endive LI272
Engravers DA025, PA110
Envious LI541
Epilepsy DA025, PT365
Ermine AB246
Evils of Intellect LI079
Exchangers of Money LI078
Experienced PT359
Eyebrows Joined AB249
Eyes, Black or Grey DA025
Eyes, Fair GA071, PA016
Face, Long DA025
Faculty of Reflection AB245
Fairs (Commerce) DA026, LI079

Falcon AB247
False LI077, PA095
Falsifying AB250
Fancy LI247
Fancy, Sharp & Subtle GA071
Fantasy DA025, RS015
Far-sightedness AB250
Fearful of Enemies AB250
Feet PA017, RS015
Feet, Long, Well Shaped AB249
Fennel GA071
Fenugreek CU
Fern GA071
Fern (Brake or Bracken) CU
Fevers, Recurring PT187
Fickle PT361
Field-Vine LI272
Figure, Fine AB249
Filbert Tree DA025, LI079, RA062
Finger Swelling RS021
Finger, Little RS015
Fingers DA025, LI247, PA130
Fingers, Long GA071
Firestone DA025
Five-Leaved Grass RA062
Flanders DA026, LI080, RA062
Flank RS182
Flax CU, LI272
Fleawort LI272
Foeniculum vulgare GA071
Foods Dryer than Cold AB245
Fools PA095
Foot-Races PA248
Footmen   GA071, LI078, PA016, RA061
Forehead, High   DA025, GA071, PA016
Forehead Narrow AB249
Forgers PA095
Forgetful PT361
Forkfish LI079, RA062

Fortune Tellers AB254
Fox AB246, LI079, RA062
Foxfish RA062
Frenzy PA130, RA062
Frivolous AB250
Fumaria officinalis RA062
Fumitory RA062
Gall DA025, RS015
Gall Bladder AB247
Gall Stoppage DA025
Gas (Bowels) RS021
Gentleness AB250
Geometers LI541, PA094
Geometricians AB254
Germander GA071
Giddiness LI078, RS021
Gifted PT361
Gives Good Advice LI541
Glycyrrhiza glabra CU, GA071
Good Carriage LI541
Good Memory for Stories AB250
Good Nose AB249
Good-for-Nothing LI541
Gossip LI077
Gout, Feet LI079, RA062, RS021
Gout, Hand LI079, RA062, RS021
Gracia, Spain RA062
Grains AB245
Grammarians LI078
Gray LI079
Grayhound LI079
Greece DA026, LI080
Grey Mixed with Sky Color DA025
Ground Pine (Common) GA071
Guile LI541
Hair, Black DA025
Hair, Brown and Sad PA016
Hair, Brown Sad GA071
Hair, Fine and Long AB249
Hair, Thick GA071
Halls (Formal Rooms) PA017

Hand DA025, LI247, PA017, RS015
Hand Swelling RS021
Hands, Long GA071
Handsome AB249
Hare AB246, RA062
Hart RA062
Hazel Nut CU, GA071, RA062
Head Colds LI079
Hematites (Stone) LI272
Henry, Good (Herb) CU
Heracleum GA071
Hermaphrodite LI079
Hides, Selling of AB254
Hiera (Drug) LI079
Hiera (Herb) RA062
High And Thin Stature LI078
Historiographers LI556
Hoarseness DA025, LI079, PA017, RA062, RS021
Honeysuckle GA071
Horehound GA071
Horehound (Black) CU
Horehound (White) CU
Hound's Tongue CU, GA071
House Leek (Singreen) LI272
Houses near Orchards AB242
Houses of Bleachers AB242
Houses of Painters AB242
Houses, Common Halls DA026
Humidity PT039
Hurricanes PT187
Hyaena LI079, RA062
Hypocistis LI272
Ibis RA062
Idiot GA071, LI078
Illecebrum verticillatum LI272
Imagination DA025, LI247, PA017, RS015
Imagination Strong GA071
Imaginings (=Conceits) RS021
Impetuous PT361

Inconstant DA025, LI078
India RA062
Ingenious DA025
Ingenious Workmen DA025
Inquirers Into Nature PT359
Intellect LI077, PA017
Interpretation PT335
Inula helenium CU, GA071
Inventing Destructive Machines LI541
Inventive LI077, PT359
Inventors DA025, PA110
Iraq AB242
Irrigation Channels AB242
Jack Daw RA062
Jackal AB246
Jasione montana CU
Jaundice, Black RS021
Journeys DA025
Joy: Virgo AB257
Juglanns regia LI079, RA062
Keeps Away from Bad-Heartedness AB250
Keeps Away from Discord AB250
Keeps Away from Strife AB250
Keeps Away from Trickery AB250
Keeps Secrets AB250
Knautia arvensis CU
Knotgrass LI272
Lark RA062
Larnyx RS015
Laryngitis RS021
Lavandula angustifolia CU, GA071
Lavender CU, GA071
Lavender (Cotton) CU
Law, Changes in PT187
Lawyers GA071, LI139, PA016
Lawyers, Pettyfogging PA016
Lean DA025
Learned PT359
Learned Men RA061

Learning LI077
Learning without a Teacher GA071, PA016
Leeks, House (Singreen) LI272
Leg Swelling RS021
Legs Small DA026
Lens culinaris LI272
Lentils LI272
Lethargy DA025, LI078, PA130, RA062, RS021
Liars GA071, LI077, PA016, PT361
Library PA017, RA062
Licorice CU, GA071
Light-Minded PT361
Lily of the Valley CU
Linnet RA062
Linsie-woolsie Colors DA025
Linum usitatissimum CU, LI272
Lips Thin GA071, PA016
Lisping PA017
Literate Men LI078
Living Room PA017
Locusts LI079
Logician GA071, LI077
Longing for Approval AB250
Longing for Power, Reputation AB250
Lonicera periclymenum GA071
Lugwort DA025
Lung Disease PA017
Lungwort LI079, RA062
Lying AB250
Lynnet (Bird) LI079
Lysimachia nummularia GA071
Madness LI078, PA017, RA062, RS021
Magic (Subtle Arts) DA025
Maidenhair Fern CU, GA071
Malicious PA095
Malicious Turbulence LI541
Mallow LI272

Malva sylvestris LI272
Mandragora officinarum CU
Mandrake CU
Manufacture of, Combs AB254
Marcasite DA025, LI079, RA062
Marjoram DA025, LI079, RA062
Marjoram, Sweet GA071
Marjoram, Wild CU
Markets DA026, LI079, PA017, RA062
Marrubium vulgare CU
Mathematicians GA071, LI078, PA016, PT361, RA061
Mathematics DA025, PA094
Matthew LI341
Mecca AB242
Mechanic LI078
Meddling LI541
Medina AB242
Melancholy Diseases DA025
Melilot GA071
Memory DA025, LI580, PA017, RS015
Memory Defects RA062
Memory Loss or Defects RS021
Memory Problems LI079
Merchants AB252, DA025, GA071, LI077, PA110, PT335, RA061
Mercurialis perennis CU, RA062
Mercury DA025
Mercury (Element) RA062
Mercury (Herb) RA062
Mesopotamia PT141
Messengers GA071, LI078, PA016, RA061
Migraines PA130
Millstone DA025, LI079
Ministers LI078
Mischievous in Speech PA095
Mixed Colors DA025, LI079
Moderate Things AB241

Moneywort GA071
Morus nigra CU, GA071
Mosques AB242
Mouth, Wide AB249
Mulberry Tree CU, GA071
Mule RA062
Mullet LI079
Myrrh LI272
Myrtle Tree CU
Myrtus communis CU
Navel RS182
Necromancers AB254
Necromancy LI077
Negotiations LI556
New Arts DA025
New Colors DA025
News-Monger LI078
Nigella sativa CU
Nightingale AB247, RA062
Nonconformist, Religious GA071
Nose Long GA071, PA016
Nose Thin, Long & Sharp DA025
Nostrils RS182
Notaries PA110
Nullet RA062
Nut DA025
Oats GA071
Old Gold AB243
Ononis spinosa GA071
Open Countenance AB250
Ophioglossum vulgatum DA025,
   LI079, RA062
Orators GA071, LI078, PA016,
   RA061
Ordinaries DA026, RA062
Oregano CU
Organs of Speech AB248
Origanum majorana GA071
Origanum vulgare CU, RA062
Palms LI272
Parietaria officinalis CU, GA071

Paris DA026, LI080
Parrot LI079, RA062
Parsley RA062
Parsley (Common) CU, GA071
Peas AB243
Pecten RS182
Pellitory of Spain CU
Pellitory of the Wall CU, GA071
Perfection, Anxiety for in All AB254
Perfidious LI541
Perjury GA071, PA016
Petroselinum crispum CU, GA071,
   RA062
Pets LI541
Pettyfoggers RA061
Peucedanum officinale CU
Philosophers AB254, GA071, LI078,
   PA016, RA061
Philosophy DA025
Phrenetic LI077
Pigeon AB247
Pilfering GA071
Pimpernel RA062
Piper cubeba DA025, LI079
Piracy PT187
Pirapirasta LI272
Pismires (Ants) LI079, RA062
Plants Bearing Husks or pods LI079
Plotters LI541
Poetry AB254
Poets GA071, LI078, PA016, RA061
Poison Pen GA071
Polemonium caeruleum CU
Political LI077
Pomegranites CU, LI272
Popinian (Bird)* LI079
Popinjay RA062
Porphyrio (Bird) RA062
Pourcontrell (Fish) RA062
Prattler GA071, LI077
Precipitate PT361

Preserves True Friends AB250
Pretender to Knowledge   GA071, LI078
Printers GA071, LI078
Professors of Philosophy PA110
Proud DA025
Prudent PA094, PT361
Pteridium aquilinum CU
Ptisick (Tuberculosis)   PA130, RA062, RS021
Pulmonaria officinalis LI079, RA062
Pungent/Evil Smelling Trees AB244
Punica granatum CU
Purges (Cathars) DA025
Pye (Bird) LI079
Quicksilver AB243, DA025, LI079
Quince LI272
Quotidian (Recurring) Fever PT187
Races, Foot PA248
Rampion (Sheep'S) CU
Rascals PT361
Rationality PA017
Ready PA094
Reason PA097
Reception Room PA017
Red Marble RA062
Reeds LI079
Religious Dissenter GA071
Rest-Harrow GA071
Restaurant LI079
Revenue PT187
Rhetoric DA025
Rheum PA130
Robbery PT187
Rose, Fresh LI272
Rubus fructicosus LI272
Ruining Prospects by Anxiety AB250
Ruining Prospects by Misfortune AB250
Saffron LI272
Sambucus nigra LI079

Samphire GA071
Sandy Growing Herbs LI079
Sandy Soil AB241
Santolina chamaecyparissus CU
Satureia hortensis CU, GA071
Satureia montana CU, GA071
Sauce-alone (Jack-in-Hedge) CU
Savory (Summer) CU, GA071
Savory (Winter) CU, GA071
Savory Herbs AB244
Scabiosa columbaria CU
Scabious GA071
Scabious (Field) CU
Scabious (Lesser Field) CU
Schoolmasters   GA071, LI078, PA016, RA061
Schools   DA026, LI079, PA017, RA062
Scribes DA025, PT335
Scriveners LI078, RA061
Sculptors   GA071, LI078, PA016, RA061
Searcher Into Mysteries LI077
Searchers After Curiosities PA110
Secret Knowledge LI077
Secretaries GA071, LI078, PA016, RA061
Sectaries (Religious Dissenter) GA071
Seed of a Tree AB236
Seekers of Mysteries PT361
Seeking Friendship AB250
Selling Books AB254
Selling Coins AB254
Selling Hides AB254
Selling Slaves AB254
Sempervivum tectorum LI272
Senna CU
Sense Deprivation LI247, PA130
Serpents LI079, RA062
Servants DA025

Sharp LI077
Sharp Intelligence/Understanding
   AB250
Sharp Minds LI541
Sharp Pen LI077
Sharp Tongue LI077
Shrewd PT359
Silver Color PA016
Silver Marcasite RA062
Sinews DA025, RS015, PT361
Singreen (=Sengreen, House Leek
   LI272
Sky Blue Mixed Darker Color AB240
Slanderers PA095
Slaves AB252
Slaves, Selling AB254
Smallage GA071
Smallage (Wild Celery) CU
Solanum dulcamara CU
Solicitors GA071, LI078, RA061
Soothsayers PT335
Soul, Character PT333
Southernwood CU, GA071
Southernwood (Field) CU
Speaking AB245
Speculative PT361
Speech LI247, PT321, RS015
Spider LI079, RA062
Spirits DA025, LI247, RS015
Springs (Water) AB242
Squirrel LI079, RA062
Stammering DA025, LI078, PA017,
   RA062, RS021
Starling AB247
Stationers GA071, LI078
Stature, High PA016
Stature, Tall DA025
Stature, Tall Indifferent GA071
Stimulating PT187
Stone of Diverse Colors LI079
Stones, Multi-Colored DA025

Stones, Yellow And Green AB243
Studious LI541, PA094
Study PA017, RA062
Subtle LI077, PA094
Subtle Arts (Magic) DA025
Sumach LI272
Sunday Night AB241
Surveyors AB254
Swallows LI079, RA062
Tailors GA071, LI078
Taste AB248
Tax-collectors AB252
Teachers PT335
Teaching Manners AB250
Teaching Revelation AB250
Teaching Theology AB250
Teaching, Logic AB250
Teeth, Small AB249
Tennis Courts DA026, LI079, PA017,
   RA062
Teugruim chamaedrys GA071
Theft AB250, GA071, LI078, PA016,
   PT187
Thief is Familiar LI364
Thief is Friend LI364
Thief is Youth LI364
Thieves LI078, RA061
Thighs DA025, RS182
Thought PT321
Thoughtful PT359
Three-leaved Grass DA025, LI079
Throat-bole RS182
Thrush RA062
Tin RA062
Tongue   DA025, LI247, PA017,
   PT321, RA061, RS015
Tongue (with Venus) AB248
Tongue Dryness RS021
Tongue Impediments DA025, PA130
Tongue Imperfections RS021
Tongue Problems LI079

Tongue-Evil LI079, RS021
Topaz DA025, LI079, RA062
Tradesmen RA061
Tradesmen's Shops DA025, LI079, PA017, RA062
Travel Desires LI077
Treacle DA026, RA062
Treacle (Drug) LI079
Tree Coral AB243
Trefoil CU, DA025, LI079
Trefoil, Meadow GA071
Tricks PA016
Trifler LI078
Trifolium repens CU, GA071
Trigonella foenum-graecum CU
Troublesome Wit GA071
Tuberculosis (Ptisick) PA017, RA062, RS021
Turquoise AB243
Two-Penny Grass DA025, LI079
Unconstant LI541
Undependable PT361
Undiscriminating PT361
Unjust PT361
Unstable DA025, PA095, PT361
Unsteady PT361
Unwearied GA071
Usurers GA071, LI078, RA061
Vain Imaginings LI079
Valerian (Greek) CU
Valerian (True Wild) CU
Valerian, Garden GA071
Verbena officinalis RA062
Vertigo LI078, PA017, RA062, RS021

Vervain LI079, RA062
Violent DA025
Visage, Long DA025, GA071, PA016
Vitriol DA025, LI079
Voice RS015
Voice Box RS015
Voice, Fine AB250
Vomit DA025
Voyages, Unsuccessful PT187
Wall Rue (white spleenwort) GA071
Walnut LI079
Walnut Tree LI079, RA062
Wary LI541, PA094
Wastes Money Seeking Curiosities GA071
Wavering DA025, PA095
Wayward DA025
Weasel LI079
Weasles RA062
Weather: Storms, Hail RA062
Wednesday AB241, LI080
West Indies RA062
White spleenwort GA071
Wicked Acts LI077
Wily LI541
Windy Weather LI079
Wise DA025, LI541, PT359
Withdraws from Bad Friends AB250
Wittiness PA110
Witty GA071, LI077, PA016
Woodbine GA071
Worship of the Gods PT187
Wrestlers AB252
Writing DA025
Writings LI139

Venus ♀
Abundance PT185
Acer pseudoplatanus CU
Achillea millefolium CU, GA070
Adiantum capillus veneris LI075,
  RA060
Adornments LI556, PT337
Adulterers LI074
Adulterers and Their Children AB252
Aegopodium podograria GA070
Aetites RA060
Affability LI556
Affectionate PT357
Agnes LI341
Ajuga reptans CU, GA070
Alabaster DA023, LI075, RA060
Alchemilla vulgaris CU, GA070,
  LI075
Alder CU, GA070
Alder (Black) CU
Alder (Common) CU
Alehoof CU
Alkanet CU
Alkanna tinctoria CU
Alliances with Leaders PT185
Almonds DA024, RA060
Alnus glutinosa CU
Alnus nigra CU, GA070
Althaea officinalis CU
Althaea rosea CU
Amber (Plant) DA024, LI075
Ambergrise RA060
Amiable LI556
Animals, Small LI075
Anthemis cotula CU
Antimony AB243
Aphrodisiac, Orchid (Satyrion)
  DA024
Appetite Loss RS021
Apple AB244, LI075
Apple Tree GA070, RA060

Apples, Sweet DA024
Apricots DA024, LI075, RA060
Aquilegia vulgaris CU
Arabia AB242, DA024, LI076,
  PT157, RA060
Archangel CU, GA070
Arctium lappa CU, GA070
Arrach, Stinking GA070
Artemisia vulgaris CU, GA070,
  LI075
Arum maculatum RA060
Ash Tree RA060
Ash, Wild LI075
Asthma RS020
Atheists GA070, LI074
Atriplex hortensis GA070
Atriplex patula CU
Attraction S2-45
Austria DA024, LI076, RA060
Babylonia AB242
Back Diseases LI075
Back Pain, Small of the RS020
Back, Small of the DA023, PA015
Ballad-Singers LI074
Barfly GA070
Bath Loving LI074
Bead, Glass (=Bugle) CU
Beans GA070
Beans (Broad) CU
Beans (French) CU
Beauty PA109
Becafico Bird (Ficedula) LI075
Bedhangings DA024
Bedrooms PA015, RA060
Beds DA024, LI075, PA015, RA060
Belly RS014
Beneficent PT357
Berula erecta GA070
Beryl (Stone) DA023, LI075, RA060
Betula alba CU
Betula pendula CU, GA070

Birch CU
Birch Tree GA070
Birch Tree (Silver) CU
Bishop Weed (Aegopodium) GA070
Blackbird RA060
Bladder Disease RA061
Blites (Chenopodiaceae) GA070
Blue, Tending to White RA060
Body, Comely & Handsome GA070
Body, Not Too Fat AB249
Body, Well-Ordered DA024
Body, Well-Shaped PA015
Bountiful LI541
Brackbird LI075
Brass DA023, LI075, RA060
Brass Household Vessels AB243
Bridal Chambers   DA024, LI075, PA015
Bugle (Plant) CU, GA070
Bull RA060
Burdock GA070
Burdock (Greater) CU
Burgander (Bird) RA060
Business with Women As Clients PA015
Busybody GA070
Buttocks (Hamms) DA070, RS014
Calf LI075, RA060
Calves, Thick AB249
Campan[i]a, Italy   DA024, LI076, RA060
Cancer PT431
Cards LI556
Careless PT357
Carnelian Stone (Cornelian) DA023, LI075
Catmint = Catnip CU
Catnip = Nep GA070
Charming PT357
Cheating AB250
Cheeks Cherry-Colored, Dimples

DA024
Cheeks, Fat AB249
Cheerful LI074, PT357
Cherries (Winter) CU
Cherry Tree GA070
Chess AB250
Chick Peas? (Cichpease) GA070
Chickweed GA070
Children, Many PT185
Choristers GA070, LI074
Chrysolite DA023, LI075, RA060
Cich-Pease (Chick Peas?) GA070
Civet Cat RA060
Civetor (Plant) DA024
Clary (Plant) GA070
Clean in Appearance GA070
Cleanly LI541
Cleanly Dressed LI074
Clothes Occupations LI075
Clothes, Fine AB250
Clothes, Green AB254
Clothes, White AB254
Clothing Merchants PT337
Cocks Head (Red Clover) GA070
Coition AB245
Colored Herbs AB244
Colors PT337
Colt's Foot CU, GA070
Columbine CU
Compassionate PT357
Complexion, Fair PA015
Complexion, Lovely GA070
Complexion, Occupations LI075
Complexion, Reddish-White AB249
Concubines DA024
Cony RA060
Conyza Canadensis CU
Cooks DA024
Copper DA023, LI075, RA060
Coral RA060
Coral, White & Red DA023, LI075

Coriander DA024, LI075
Cornelian (= Carnelian Stone) DA023, LI075
Corneola (Stone) RA060
Cotton, Co-Ruler of AB244
Courtesy LI556
Courtezans AB252
Coveting Unlawful Beds LI074
Cowards LI541
Cowslip CU, GA070
Crab RA060
Crop Yields Good PT187
Crow RA060
Cuckoo-Pint RA060
Cudweed CU
Cypress AB244, RA060
Cyprus DA024, LI076, RA060
Daffodil CU, LI075, RA060
Daffodil, White & Yellow DA024
Daisy CU, GA070
Damsels DA024
Dancers PA110
Dancing AB250, PA094
Dancing Schools DA024, LI075, PA015, RA060
Dates AB243
Dealing in Colors AB254
Dealing in Pictures AB254
Decent LI541
Decorous PT357
Delicate Child AB249
Depraved PT357
Desirous of Delights PA110
Devil's Bit GA070
Diabetes LI075, RS021
Dice LI556
Dictamnus albus CU
Digitalis purpurea CU, GA070
Dimpled Chin PA015
Dimples DA024
Dining Rooms RA060

Dipsacus fullonium CU, GA070
Dispersion AB241
Dittander (Karse) CU
Dittany (White) CU
Dittany of Crete CU
Dog RA060
Dolphin LI075, RA060
Double Chin AB249
Dowry DA024, LI556, PA109
Draughts AB250
Dropwort CU
Druggists PT337
Drunkards PA094
Dry Good Merchant RA058
Duggs PA129
Dyes PT337
Eagle LI075, RA060
Edema (Leucophleg matica) RS020
Effeminate PA094, PT357
Elder CU, GA070
Elder (Dwarf) CU
Elegance PT185
Elegant LI541
Eloquent PA094, PT357
Embroiderers DA023, GA070, LI074, PA015, RA058
Emerald, Jewel AB243, RA060
Engravers RA058
Enticement PA015
Erotic PT357
Eruca sativa CU, GA070
Eryngium maritimum GA070
Eryngo GA070
Ethiopia PT157
Exchangers of Money GA070
Expensive LI074
Eye, Full DA023
Eyebrows, Little DA023
Eyes, Full, Dark, Hazel or Black GA070
Eyes, Black PA015

Eyes, Fine, Large Iris AB249
Face, Fine And Round AB249
Face, Goodly & Fair Round DA023
Face, Round PA015
Fair Lodgings LI075
Fair Stature LI074
Fair-spoken PA094
Faithless LI074
Falsehearted PA094
Fame PT185
Fastidious PT357
Fat AB240
Fatness DA023, RS014
Fearful LI541, PA094
Feasts AB254
Fellowship PA109
Fenugreek AB243
Fertility PT187
Feverfew CU, GA070
Ficedula (Becafico Bird) LI075
Ficus garica RA060
Fiddlers LI074, PA015, RA058
Fig Tree RA060
Figs AB243, DA024, LI075
Figwort CU, GA070
Filanginella uliginosa CU
Filipendula GA070
Filipendula vulgaris CU
Fingers & Hands AB248
Fingers, Short AB249
Fistulas PT431
Fleabane (Canadian) CU
Fleabane (Small) CU
Flesh PT321, RS014
Flirts LI541
Flowers AB236
Flux of the Stomach PA129
Fond of Bazaars AB254
Fond of Commerce AB254
Fond of Ornaments AB250
Fond of Wine AB250

Foods Pleasant to Taste AB245
Fountains DA024, LI075, RA060
Foxglove CU, GA070
Fragaria vesca CU, GA070
Fragrant Herbs AB244
Frangula alnus CU
Frankincense RA060
Fraxinus excelsior RA060
French Wheat LI075
Friday AB241, LI076
Friendliness AB250
Galium verum CU, GA070
Games AB254
Gamesters (Synonym Prostitute)
   LI074, RA058
Gaming AB254, LI556
Gardens DA024, LI075, RA060
Gardens, Fine PA015
Generosity AB250
Genital Diseases DA023
Genitals AB248, DA023, LI247,
   PA129, RS014
Gentile PA110
Gentle DA023
Geranium robertianum CU, GA070
Gifts from Friends DA024, PA109
Gifts from Women DA024
Given to Evil Company PA094
Given to Excessive Venery AB250
Glechoma hederacea CU, GA070
Glovers GA070, LI074, RA058
Goats LI075, RA060
Gold AB250
Gold Household Vessels AB243
Goldenrod CU, GA070
Goldsmiths Work AB254
Gonorrhea DA024, LI075, PA015,
   RA061, RS020
Good LI541, PT357
Good Disposition AB250
Good-natured AB250

Gooseberry CU
Grapes AB243, GA070
Gravers GA070, LI074
Green DA023
Greenish AB240
Grocers LI628
Gromwell (Lithospermum) GA070
Ground Ivy (Ale-Hoof) GA070
Groundsel (Common) CU, GA070
Guests LI628
Gum laudanum RA060
Hamms RS014
Hands & Fingers AB248
Handsome Face AB250
Hangings LI075, PA015
Happiness PT185
Harnias LI075
Hart LI075, RA060
Haunter of Taverns GA070
Health PT185
Healthy PT357
Heart (Navel) Diseases RS020
Hedonists LI541
Hepatic Diseases PT431
Herb Robert CU, GA070
Herb True-Love CU, GA070
Hernias RS021
Hollyhocks CU
Honor PT185
Houses, Bridechambers DA024
Humidity PT037
Hydrocotyle vulgaris CU
Idle DA023
Illustrators LI074
Immodest GA070
Impotency LI075, RS021
Incest GA070
Incestuous LI074
Inclined to Love & Sensuality AB250
Indifferent PT357
Infamous LI541

Infertility LI247
Innkeepers PT337
Intestinal Diseases LI075
Inula conyza CU
Isabel LI341
Islam AB253
Islands AB242
Italy, Campania LI076
Jasper, Green RA060
Jealous PA094
Jesting AB250
Jewellers GA070, LI074, PA015, RA058
Jewels LI556
Jewels Set in Silver & Gold AB243
Jocose PA094
Jollity GA070
Joy AB250
Juglanns regia RA060
Kidney Disease LI075
Kidney Pains RS020
Kidneys PA129, RS014
Kidneywort GA070
Kinswomen DA024
Labdanum = Rockrose LI075
Lady's Bedstraw CU, GA070
Lady's Mantle CU, GA070, LI075
Lamium CU, GA070
Lapidaries DA023, GA070, LI074
Lapis Lazuli LI075, RA060
Lascivious (= Luxurious) DA023, PT357
Lasciviousness (= Luxury) LI265
Latten Ware DA023, LI075
Laughing AB250
Lazy AB250, GA070, LI074
Lechery LI556
Lens culinaris CU
Lentils CU
Leonurus cardiaca GA070
Lepidium sativum CU

Leucanthemum vulgare CU, GA070
Leucophlegmatia RS020
Lewd LI074
Lewdness (Priapism) GA070, RS021
Liberal PA094
Lily LI075, RA060
Lily of the Valley DA024
Lily, Water DA024, LI075
Lily, White & Yellow DA024
Linen-Drapers   GA070, LI074, PA015, RA058
Lips, Cherry PA015
Lips, Red DA024
Lithospermum prostratum GA070
Liver DA023, LI247, PT321, RS014
Liver Disease DA023
Liver Weakness LI247
Lodgings, Fair DA024, PA015
Lofty Houses AB242
Loin Disease PA015
Loins DA023, PA015, RS014
Love LI556, PA109
Lover of Dancing PT357
Lover of Delight DA023
Lover of Mirth LI073
Lover of Ornaments DA023
Lover of the Arts PT357
Lovers PA110
Lust DA024, RA061, RS021
Lustful LI541
Lute, Playing AB254
Luxurious (Lascivious)   DA023, LI265, PT357
Lysimachia nummularia CU
Magnesia AB243
Maidenhair Fern   DA024, LI075, RA060
Maids GA070
Maker of Crowns AB254
Maker of Diadems AB254

Mallow CU, GA070
Malus GA070
Malva sylvestris CU, GA070
Manufacturing Perfumes AB254
Manuscript Illuminators GA070
Marble RA060
Marcasite DA023, LI075
Marriage DA024, PA109
Marriage, Happy PT185
Marsh Mallow CU
Mayweed, Stinking CU
Measuring by Bulk AB254
Measuring by Length AB254
Measuring by Weight AB254
Media, Asia Minor DA024, LI076, PT141
Medium Tall AB249
Mentha GA070
Mentha aquatica CU
Mentha piperata CU
Mentha pulegium CU, GA070
Mentha spicata CU
Merchant in Dry Goods (Mercer) GA070, LI074, RA058
Merciful LI541
Mercurialis annua GA070
Mercury (Herb) GA070
Mercy LI556
Merry PA094
Meum athamantigum GA070
Milky Colored DA023
Millet DA024
Mint GA070
Mint (Garden or Spear) CU
Mint (Pepper) CU
Mint (Water) CU
Mirth GA070
Miscarriages PT321
Misplaced Jealosy LI074
Mistress DA024

Moderate Cold & Moisture AB232
Moderately Cold & Moist Foods AB245
Moneywort CU
Most Agreeable AB241
Most Beautiful AB241
Most Delicious AB241
Most Pungent AB241
Mothers AB249, DA024, LI074, PT241, RA058
Motherwort GA070
Mugwort DA024, GA070
Mugwort (Common) CU, LI075
Musical LI074
Musicians DA023, GA070, LI074, PA015, RA058
Musk AB254
Musk (Civet) LI075
Musk (Plant) DA024, RA060
Myrtle Tree LI075, RA060
Myrtus communis LI075, RA060
Narcissus AB236
Narcissus pseudonarcissus CU, LI075, RA060
Navel (Heart) Diseases RS020
Neat PT357
Neat Dresser GA070
Neat Man LI073
Neck PA015
Neck Disease PA015
Neck, Handsome AB249
Nep = Catnip GA070
Nepeta cataria CU, GA070
Nightengale LI075, RA060
Nipples DA023, LI247, RS014
Nobles AB252
Nostril AB248
Nostril, Left RS014
Not Quarrelsome AB250
Often Entangled in Love Matters GA070, LI074

Oily Berries AB244
Olive DA024, LI075
Orach CU
Orange, Sweet DA024
Orchid CU
Orchis CU
Origanum (Oregano?) AB243
Origanum dictamnus CU
Ornaments DA024, PA109
Ornaments, Gold AB254
Ornaments, Silver AB254
Ovary PA015
Ovum LI247
Owl LI075
Oxalis acetosella CU
Oxyria digyna CU
Painters DA024, GA070, LI074, PA015, PT337, RA058
Panther LI075, RA060
Paris quadrifolia CU, GA070
Parsnip GA070
Parthia, Iran DA024, LI076, RA060
Partridge LI075, RA060
Passions of the Womb DA024
Patience AB250
Peach DA024, LI075, RA060
Peach Tree CU, GA070
Pear Tree CU, GA070, RA060
Pearls AB243
Pearls, Dealing in AB254
Pelican LI075, RA060
Penis S2-56
Pennyroyal CU, GA070
Pennywort (Common Marsh) CU
Peppermint CU
Perfume AB250, PT337
Perfume Merchants PT337
Perfumers GA070, LI074, PA015, RA058
Periwinkle GA070
Periwinkle (Great) CU

Persia PT141
Pharmacists LI628
Phaseolus vulgaris CU
Physalis alkekengi CU, GA070
Picture-Drawers GA070, LI074, PA015, RA058
Pigeon RA060
Pigeon, Wild (Stock Dove) LI075
Pipers LI074, PA015, RA058
Pitiful DA023, PA094
Pity PA109
Places of Worship AB242
Plantago coronopus CU
Plantago lanceolata CU
Plantago major CU, GA070
Plantain CU, GA070
Plantain (Buck's Horn) CU
Plantain (Ribwort) CU
Players GA070, LI074
Playhouses RA060
Plays LI556
Pleasant LI541, PT357
Pleasant Man LI073
Pleasure GA070, RA058
Pleasure-Seeking DA023, PA094
Ploughman's Spikenard CU
Plump PT311
Plums CU, DA024, GA070, LI075
Plutocrats AB252
Poetical LI541
Poets DA024, PA110
Poison PT431
Poland RA060
Poland, Greater DA024
Polonia LI076
Pomegranites RA060
Potentilla anserina CU
Prattler GA070
Precious Things DA024
Premature Births PT321
Priapism (lewdness) PA129, RA061,

RS021
Pride AB250
Primrose CU, GA070
Primula veris CU, GA070
Primula vulgaris CU, GA070
Profit PT187
Prone to Venery LI074
Property Increase PT185
Prostitutes (=Gamesters) LI074
Prunella vulgaris CU, GA070
Prunus domestica CU, GA070
Prunus persica CU, GA070, RA060
Pulicaria dysenterica CU
Pulse Low RS021
Punica granatum RA060
Pure White Tending to Straw AB240
Purple LI086
Pye (Bird) LI075, RA060
Pyrus sativa CU, GA070, RA060
Quality of Life PT185
Queens AB252
Quiet Man LI073
Quinsy (Tonsillitis) AB244, PA129
Rabbit LI075, RA060
Ragwort CU, GA070
Raisins DA024, LI075
Raspberry CU
Red Clover GA070
Relationship Satisfaction PT185
Reproduction PA129
Reproductive Disease RA060, RS014
Reproductive Tract Diseases LI247
Ribes uva-crispa CU
Rioting GA070
Riotous LI074
Ripest Things AB241
Rocket Cress CU, GA070
Rockrose (Labdanum) LI075
Rose RA060
Rose, Damask CU, GA070
Rose, White DA024, LI075

Rubus idaeus CU
Rumex acetosa CU, GA070
Rumex acetosella CU
Sage, Wood CU, GA070
Salvia sclarea GA070
Sambucus ebulus CU
Sambucus nigra CU, GA070
Sanicle DA024, GA070
Sanicula europaea GA070
Saponaria officinalis CU, GA070
Sapphire DA023, RA060
Sapphire, Blue LI075
Satyrian RA060
Satyrion (Aphrodisiac Orchid) DA024
Savory Herbs AB245
Scandalous LI074
Scrophularia nodosa CU, GA070
Seamsters RA058
Seamstresses (Sempsters) GA070
Seed, Reproductive DA023, LI247, PA015, RS014
Self Heal CU, GA070
Semen PA015
Sempsters (Seamstresses) GA070
Senecio jacobaea CU, GA070
Senecio vulgaris CU, GA070
Sensuality AB245, PA109
Sexual Excess PA109
Sheep RA060
Shells AB243
Shining AB240
Silkmen GA070, LI074, PA015, RA058
Silver AB250
Silver Household Vessels AB243
Silverweed CU
Singer DA023
Singing, Accompanying AB254
Sisters AB249
Sium sisarum CU

Skirret CU
Sky Color DA023
Slighting a Good Name PA094
Sluggards LI541
Small Cattle LI075
Small of the Back RS014
Smell RS014
Smell & Inhaling Organs AB248
Smell, Sense of LI269, PT321
Smooth Trees AB244
Smooth-leaved Plants LI075
Smoothness AB241
Soapwort CU, GA070
Sodomite AB250
Softest Things AB241
Soils with Abundant Water AB241
Solidago virgaurea CU, GA070
Sonchus arvensis CU
Sonchus oleraceus CU, GA070
Sonchus palustris CU
Song AB250
Songs, Composing AB254
Sorrel GA070
Sorrel (Common) CU
Sorrel (Mountain) CU
Sorrel (Sheep's) CU
Sorrel (Wood) CU
South Wind LI076
Sow-Thistle GA070
Sow-Thistle (Common) CU
Sow-Thistle (Tree) CU
Sow-Thistle Tree (Marsh) CU
Sparrow LI075, RA060
Spearmint CU
Spendthrift GA070
Sperm DA023, LI247, RS014
Sperm Defective PA015
Spice Merchants PT337
Spices PT337
Spignel (Plant) GA070
Spiritless LI541

Spring Flowers AB244
Squareness AB241
Stageplays LI074
Stature, Middle GA070
Stature, Straight, Small DA024
Stellaria Media GA070
Stock Dove (Wild Pigeon) LI075,
  RA060
Stomach RS014
Stomach Disease DA023
Stomach Weakness LI247
Strangury PA129
Straw Color AB240
Strawberries CU, GA070
Subtle LI541
Successful PT357
Succisa pratensis GA070
Sugar Plantations AB242
Swallows LI075, RA060
Swan LI075, RA060
Sweet Berries AB244
Sweet Flavor AB240
Sweet Oranges LI075
Sweet Smelling Flowers AB236
Sweet Smelling Plants LI075
Sweet Smelling Trees AB244
Sweet Taste LI075
Swelling RS020
Sycamore Tree CU
Sycamore, White DA024, LI075
Syphilis   LI075, PA015, RA061,
  RS020
Tailoring AB254
Takes Pleasure in Everything AB250
Tanacetum parthenium CU, GA070
Tanacetum vulgare CU, GA070
Tansy CU
Tansy, Garden GA070
Tansy, Wild GA070
Taste RS014
Taste, Sense of LI269

Taverns LI074
Teak AB244
Teasel CU, GA070
Teeth, Small AB249
Tenderness to Children AB250
Tenderness to Friends AB250
Testicles S2-56
Teucrium scorodonia CU, GA070
Thief is Woman (Wife) LI364
Throat DA023, LI247, PA015, RS014
Throat Disease PA015
Thrush LI075, RA060
Thumb, Mount of RS014
Thyme CU, LI075, RA060
Thyme (Wild) CU
Thymus serpyllum CU
Thymus vulgaris CU, RA060
Timid PT357
Tire-Makers LI628
Tonsilitis (Quinsy) PA129
Trees Soft to Touch AB244
Trigonella foenum-graecum AB243
Trim And Neat DA023
Triticum CU, GA070
Trusting GA070
Tuesday Night AB241
Turin RA060
Turing (Turin?)* DA024, LI076
Turpentine Tree LI075, RA060
Turtledove RA060
Tussilago farfara CU, GA070
Tutsan (See St. John's Wort) GA070
Umbilicus rupestris GA070
Unsuspicious GA070
Upholsterers GA070, LI074, RA058
Urination, Painful LI247, PA015
Useful Foods AB245
Uterine Disease PA015
Uterine Disorder (Passion) DA024
Uterine Kindred AB249
Uterus DA023

Valerian DA024, LI075, RA060
Valeriana officinalis RA060
Venereal Disease DA023, LI075
Verbena officinalis   CU, GA070, RA060
Vervain CU, DA024, GA070, RA060
Vessels Which Hold Water AB242
Vicia faba CU, GA070
Vienna RA060
Vienna, Austria DA024, LI076
Vinca major CU, GA070
Vine Tree (Grapes) GA070
Vines RA060
Viola odorata CU, GA070, RA060
Violet (Herb) CU, DA024, GA070, LI075, RA060
Virgins LI074, PA015, RA058
Virtuous GA070, LI074
Visage, Goodly & Fair Round DA023
Visage, Plump & Round GA070
Vitis vinifera GA070, RA060
Voluptuousness RA058
Vomit LI247
Vulva S2-56
Wagtail (Bird) LI075
Walnut DA024, RA060
Wardrobe-Keepers LI628
Wardrobes DA024, LI075, RA060
Warming, Moderate PT037
Water Wagtail (Bird) RA060
Weather: Gentle Showers (Winter) RA060
Weather: Temperate Heat (Summer) RA060

Weavers PT337
Wedlock DA024, LI556
Well-Spoken AB250
Wheat CU, GA070
White DA023, LI075
White Flowers LI075
Whiting (Fish) RA060
Whorehouses RA060
Whoremongers PA094
Widows GA070, PA015
Wine PT337
Witty PA094
Wives   AB249, DA024, GA070, LI074, PA015, RA058
Wooers LI541, PA094
Womb   AB248, DA023, LI247, PA015, RS014
Womb Diseases RS020
Womb Suffocation RS020
Women   GA070, LI304, PA015, RA058
Women's Tailors   LI074, PA015, RA058
Women, Young DA023
Women-Loving LI541
Works of Beauty AB254
Works of Magnificence AB254
Wren LI075, RA060
Yarrow CU, GA070
Yellow PT193
Young Women DA023
Youth PT443
Youth & Adolescence AB248
Zealous in Affects GA070

Mars   ♂

Abscess (Apostemations)   DA020, LI246, PA013, RS020
Active   PT353
Adamant (Stone)   DA020, LI068, RA055
Advocates   LI556
Ague   RS020
Ajuga chamaepitys   CU
Alchemists   DA021, GA068, LI067, RA054
Alchemy   LI556
Allium cepa   AB244, CU, GA068, LI068, RA054
Allium sativum   AB244, CU, GA068, LI068, RA054
Allium schoenoprasum   CU
Almond, Bitter   AB243
Amethyst, Multi-Colored   LI068, RA055
Anemone   CU
Anemone nemorosa   CU
Anger   LI067
Anger, Proneness to   RS020
Anthony   LI341
Antimony   DA020, LI068, RA055
Apostems (Abscess)   DA020, RS020
Apothecaries   GA068, RA054
Apprehension   PA013
Armoracia rusticana   CU, GA068
Armorers   GA068, LI067, RA054
Army Commanders   PA109
Arrogant   PA093
Arsenic   DA020, LI068, RA055
Arsesmart   CU, GA068, LI068, RA054
Arson   PT185
Artemisia absinthium   CU, GA068
Artemisia dracunculus   CU
Artemisia maritma   CU
Artemisia pontica   CU

Arum maculatum   CU, GA068
Asarabacca   CU, GA068
Asarum (Ginger)   LI068
Asarum europaeum   CU, GA068
Asperula gynanchica   CU
Ass (Wild)   LI068
Assarum   DA021
Assaults   PT185
Astragalus gummifer   CU
Attraction   PA128, S2-45
Back   RA054
Back, Small of the   LI246
Bad Companion   AB250
Bailiffs   GA068, LI067, PA013, RA054
Bakers   GA068, LI067, PA013, RA054
Barbel (Fish)   LI068, RA055
Barberry   CU, GA068
Barbers   GA068, LI067, PA013, RA054
Basil   CU
Basil, Sweet   GA068
Bastard- (English-) Rhubarb   GA068
Batavia, Holland   DA021, LI068
Bats   AB247
Bear   LI068
Bearwards   LI067
Beasts, Destructive   AB246
Beasts, Mad   AB246
Beasts, Wild   AB246
Benedictus   LI068
Berberis Vulgaris   CU, GA068
Bile, Red (Red Choler)   RS020
Bile, Yellow   AB247
Birds of Prey   RA055
Birds, All Red Ones   AB247
Birds, Carnivorous, Curve Bill   AB247
Birds, Nocturnal   AB247
Bitter   AB240, DA020
Bitter Fruit   AB244

Bitter Taste LI067
Bitter Trees AB244
Blacksmiths AB254
Bladder Stones LI067, RS020
Blisters LI067, RS020
Blood, Spitting of PT327
Bloodstone DA021, LI068, RA055
Bloodthirsty PT353
Bloody LI540
Bloody Flux LI067, RS020
Bloody-Minded LI540
Boasters LI540
Boastful PA093
Body, Big-Boned GA068
Body, Strong & Able GA068, PA012
Bold AB250, DA021, LI066
Bones, Big PA012
Braggart LI066
Bramble AB244, DA021, GA068, RA054
Brassica napa GA068
Brassica nigra CU, RA054
Brawlers DA020
Briars RA054
Brick Burning Places PA013
Brigandage AB254
Bright AB250
Brimstone DA020, LI068, RA055
Briony GA068
Britain PT135
Brook-Lime CU, GA068
Broom GA068
Broom-Rape GA068
Brothers of Middle Age AB249
Bryonia dioica CU, GA068
Bryony CU
Burn PT037
Burning LI067, PT321, RS020
Business AB245
Business Going to Ruin AB250
Butcher's Broom CU, GA068

Butchers AB254, GA068, LI067, PA013, RA054
Calenture PA013
Cammock (Herb) LI068, RA054
Cantharides (Spanish Fly) DA021, LI068
Capiscum frutescens CU
Captains GA068, LI067, PA109
Capture PT183
Carbuncles (Inflammation) DA021, RS020
Carduus Benedictus CU, DA021, GA068, LI068, RA054
Carduus eriophorus GA068
Carpenters GA068, LI067, PA013, PT337, RA054
Castoreum (from Castor Bean) DA021, LI068, RA054
Cavalry AB252
Celandine (The Lesser) CU
Centaurea calcitrapa GA068
Challenges Honor to Himself GA068
Champions LI629
Charcoal Burning Places PA013
Cheaters LI066
Cheerful AB250
Chemistry PA109
Chemists PA013
Chestnut Tree DA021, LI068
Chick Peas LI273
Chimneys DA021, LI068, PA013
Chives CU
Choler, Red DA020, RS020
Choleric Passion PA013
Cinnabar AB243
Cinnamon LI272
Circumcisers AB254
Civil Faction PT183
Cnicus benedictus CU, GA068, RA054
Coarseness AB241

Cockatrice LI068, RA055
Colonels GA068, LI067
Commanding PT353
Complexion Brown PA012
Complexion Highly Colored DA021
Complexion Ruddy-Brown GA068
Complexion Tanned Like Leather DA021
Confident LI066, PA109
Confused Opinions AB250
Conium maculatum RA054
Conquerors GA068, LI067, PA013, RA054
Contemptuous PT353
Contention AB254, LI066, PA109
Controversies LI556
Cooks GA068, LI067, PA013, PT337, RA054
Copper AB243
Cormorant LI068, RA055
Countenance, Bold PA012
Countenance, Confident GA068
Countenance, Fierce DA021
Courage LI066
Courageous LI540, PA093
Cowards PA093
Cranesbill GA068
Crataegus Monogyna CU, GA068
Crow LI068, RA055
Crowfoot CU, GA068
Cruel DA021, LI540, PA093
Cuckoo-Pint CU, GA068
Cumin LI273
Curriers PA013, RA054
Cut-Throats PA013
Cutlers DA021, GA068, PA109, RA054
Cutlers of Swords LI067
Cutthroats RA054
Cyclamen hederifolium CU
Cyperus longus CU

Cytisus scoparius GA068
Daffodil LI272
Daffodil, Yellow CU
Dark Red AB240
Death by Sword or Iron DA021
Death, Swift PT183
Death, Violent PT183
Debates LI556
Deceivers AB250
Devil's Milk (Herb) DA021, LI068, RA054
Dipsacus pilosus CU
Discord PA093
Disputants in Assembly AB252
Dissenters LI540
Distemper of the Gall PA013
Distempers (Mad, Sudden) LI067
Dittander (Karse) DA021, LI068
Does not Fear God GA068
Dog AB246
Dove's Foot CU
Down or Cotton Thistle CU, GA068
Drugs AB245
Drunkards DA020
Drunken PT353
Dry PT037
Dryness AB241
Dyers LI067, PA013, RA054
Dysentery (Bloody Flux) PA128, RS020
Eagle LI068
Ear, Left LI246, PA013, RS014
Ears, Small AB249
Eggplant AB244
Engineers LI629
Enslavement PT183
Epilepsy LI246
Erigeron acer CU
Erysimum cheiranthoides CU, GA068

Erysipelas (Streptococcus)   LI246, PA013, PT431
Euphorbia helioscopia CU
Eveweed CU
Evil Conduct AB250
Execution AB254
Extreme Heat & Dryness AB231
Exulcerations RS020
Eye, Hazel GA068
Eye, Piercing & Sharp GA068
Eye, Sharp PA012
Eyes, Sharp Grey AB249
Eyes, Small AB249
Eyes, Sparkling or Sharp DA021
Face Wounds LI246
Face, Round PA012
Falling from Heights DA021
False Testimony AB250
Farmers PT337
Fat LI273
Fearing Nothing PA012
Fearless GA068, LI540, PA093
Fenugreek LI272
Ferraria, Spain DA021, LI068
Fevers AB252, PT429, RA055
Fevers, Burning LI246
Fevers, Intermittant LI067, PT183
Fevers, Pestilential RS020
Fevers, Putrid PA128
Fevers, Recurring LI579
Fevers, Sharp PA013, DA020
Fevers, Tropical LI246
Fierce LI540
Figs, Dry LI273
Fingers, Long AB249
Fireplaces AB242
Fires PT185
Firewood AB242
Fish, Hurtful RA055
Fistulas   DA021, LI067, LI246, PA013, PT327, RA055, RS020

Flaxweed CU, GA068
Flux, Bloody (Dysentery) PA128
Forehead, Fine AB249
Forges LI068
Forkfish LI068, RA055
Fox LI068
France PT135
Frankincense LI273
Frenzies RA055, RS020
Friendly AB250
Fruit With Rough Skin AB244
Furious LI066
Furnaces   DA021, LI068, PA013, RA055
Fursbush = Furze = Gorse GA068
Galangal[e] (Ginger Family)   CU, LI273
Galium odoratum CU
Gall DA020, LI067, LI246, PA013, RA054, RS014
Gall Bladder AB248
Gall Overflow RA055
Gamesters (Synonym Prostitute) LI067, RA054
Garlic AB244, CU, DA021, GA068, LI068, RA054
Generals of Armies DA020, GA068, LI067, PA013, RA054
Generous LI540
Genital Stones LI246
Genitals LI246, PA128, PT319
Genitals, Diseases of Men's LI067
Gentian (Autumn) CU
Gentianella amarella CU
Geranium GA068
Geranium molle CU
Germander CU
Germany PT135
Giffon LI068
Ginger (Asarum)   DA021, LI068, RA054

Glass LI216
Gnats LI068
Goat's Thorn CU
Goats LI068
Good Nose AB249
Gorse GA068
Goth[o]land [=Gotland, Sweden]
  DA021, LI068
Gotland, Sweden [=Goth[o]land]
  DA021, LI068
Gouts, Hot RS020
Government Abilities LI540
Gratiola officinalis CU
Grave-Robbers AB254
Greece AB242
Grooms AB254
Ground Pine (Common) CU
Gunmakers DA021
Gunners   GA068, LI067, PA013,
  RA054
Hair, Curly GA068
Hair, Lank AB249
Hair, Red AB249, DA021, GA068,
  LI636, PT311
Hair, Red or Sandy, Curly PA012
Hair, Sandy-Flaxen GA068
Hand, Plain of Mars RS014
Handicraft LI556
Hangmen   GA068, LI067, PA013,
  RA054
Hard AB241
Hashish-Prepared As Confection
  AB243
Hawk LI068, RA055
Hawthorn CU, GA068
Head PA128
Head, Large AB249
Headstrong LI540, PT353
Helleborus LI273
Hemlock DA021, LI068, RA054
Hemorrhages PT431

Hemorrhoids PT327
Hens, Water AB247
Hepatitis (Yellow Jaundice) LI246,
  PA128
Herbs of Dry Places LI067
Herbs With Sharp Pointed Leave
  LI067
Hesperis matronalis CU
Highwaymen AB254, RA054
Hinder Regions AB247
Holland [=Batavia] LI068
Hops CU, GA068
Horehound DA021, LI068, RA054
Horsemanship LI556
Horseradish CU, GA068
Horses LI068
Hot AB241
House Flies LI068
Housebreaking AB254
Humulus lupulus CU, GA068
Hurts by Iron LI067, RS020
Hyssop (Hedge) CU
Idolators AB253
Ignorant AB250
Immovable LI066
Impatient of Servitude LI540
Impetuous PT353
Impious LI540, PT353
Impostumes see abscess
Incendiary GA068, PA013
Indifferent PT353
Inflammation, Subcutaneous DA021
Inflammations RS020
Infortune, Lesser PA012
Inhumane GA068, LI066
Injury from Animals DA021
Insolent PT353
Intemperate DA020
Intolerant PA093
Ireful DA021, LI540
Iron AB243, LI068, PT321, RA055

Ironworkers LI556, PT337
Irreverent GA068
Jailers PA013, RA054
Jasper DA021, LI068, RA055
Jaundice RS020
Jaundice, Yellow   DA020, LI246,
    PA128, RA055
Jewellers PT337
Judaea PT143
Juniperus sabina CU
Katherine LI341
Keen PT353
Kidney Stones LI067, RA055, RS020
Kidneys   AB248, DA020, PT319,
    RS014
Kite (Bird) LI068, RA055
Laboratories PA013
Lactuca virosa CU
Lapwing LI068
Law Making AB254
Lawlessness PT185
Lawsuits LI556
Leaders AB252
Leadership PT353
Leather Worker LI067
Leeks AB244, DA021, LI068, RA054
Left Ear LI067, PT319
Legs AB248
Length AB241
Lentil Shaped Stones AB243
Leopard AB246, LI068
Lepidium campestre GA068
Lepidium sativum DA021
Lettuce (Great Wild) CU
Licentious AB250
Lightning LI068
Linaria vulgaris CU, GA068
Lingwort DA021, LI068, RA054
Lion AB246
Lips, Thin AB249
Litigation AB250

Liver (Together With Venus) AB247
Loadstone DA021, LI068, RA055
Locusts (Plague) PT185
Lombardy DA021, LI068
Lover of Slaughter LI066
Lustful AB250
Mad PT353
Madder CU
Madder (Typographic error as Naddir)
    GA068
Madness DA020, PA013, RS020
Magnet (Perhaps? = Adamant)
    DA020, LI068
Magnetic Iron AB243
Magnetite DA021
Magpie RA055
Malaria (Tertian Fever)   LI067,
    PA128, PT183, RS020
Male Genital Diseases RS020
Male Genital Wounds RS020
Manhood, Mature PT445
Manual Dexterity LI540
Manual Labor LI629
Marjoram LI272
Marriage AB250
Marrow LI273
Marrubium vulgare RA054
Marshals LI067, GA068, RA054
Martial DA020
Masterwort CU, GA068
Mastiff LI068, RA055
Meseriacks PA013
Middle Stature LI067
Migraines DA021, LI067, RA055,
    RS020
Military PT353
Miscarriages PT329
Mithridate Mustard (Pennycress)
    GA068
Morphew (Skin Eruption) DA021
Mosaics AB243

Mule LI068
Murder LI066, PT185
Murderers PA013, RA054
Mustard AB244, GA068, RA054
Mustard (Black) CU
Mustard (Hedge) CU, GA068
Mustard (White) CU
Mustard Seed DA021, LI068
Naddir (Typographic error for Madder) GA068
Narcissus pseudonarcissus CU, LI272
Nephritis PT429
Nettle DA021, GA068, RA054
Nettle (Common) CU, LI067
Nicotiana tabacum CU, GA068
Noble PA093, PT353
Northwestern Countries AB242
Nostril AB248
Nostril, Right RS014
Obeys Nobody Willingly GA068
Obscene LI066
Ocre LI068
Ocymum basilicum CU, GA068
Officers in Armies LI067, PA013
Onion AB244, CU, DA021, GA068, LI068, RA054
Ononis spinosa CU, LI068
Onopordum acanthium CU, GA068
Opponents AB252
Oppression LI556
Oppressors LI066
Ostrich LI068
Owl LI068, RA055
Panther LI068, RA055
Passion AB245, LI067
Pear, Wild AB244
Pennycress (Thlaspi) GA068
Pepper CU, DA021, LI068, RA054
Pepper (Guinea) CU
Pepperwort (Lepidium) GA068
Perjured GA068, PA013

Perjurer LI066
Pestilence PA128, PT431
Pestilent Airs LI068
Peter LI341
Peucedanum ostruthium CU, GA068
Pharmacists LI067
Physicians DA021, GA068, LI067, PA013, RA054
Pigs, Wild AB246
Pike LI068, RA055
Pimples (Pushes) DA021
Pine Tree CU
Pinus sylvestris CU
Piper nigrum CU, LI068, RA054
Piracy PT185
Pirates LI629
Pitiless PT353
Places: Where Brick Burned DA021, LI068
Plague DA020, LI067, PA013, RA055, RS020
Pleasant Faced AB250
Polygonum CU, GA068, LI068, RA054
Pomegranites, Bitter AB244
Potters Vessels AB242
Powerful PT353
Prattler GA068, LI066, PA012
Princes by Usurping GA068
Princes Ruling by Tyranny LI067
Prison AB254
Prodigal DA021
Promoter of Mischief GA068
Prostitutes (=Gamesters) LI067
Provokes Others LI540
Prudent GA068, PA012
Prudent in Own Affairs LI066
Pubes AB248
Pulse High and Swift RS020
Pungent but not Poisonous AB245
Pungent Trees AB244

Pushes (Pimples) DA021
Pye (Bird) LI068
Quarreler DA020, PA013
Quarrels LI556
Quarrelsome AB250, GA068, LI540
Quarrymen PT337
Quick-Tempered PT353
Quotidian (Recurring) Fever DA020, LI579
Radish AB244, CU, DA021, GA068, LI068, RA054
Ranunculus auricomus CU, GA068
Ranunculus ficaria CU
Rapacious DA021, PT353
Raphanus sativus CU, GA068, RA054
Rapontick (= rhapontic) GA068
Raptors LI068, RA055
Rash AB250, DA021, GA068, LI066, PA093, PT353
Raven LI068, RA055
Ravenous LI066
Ravenous & Bold Animals LI068
Red DA020, LI067, PT193, RA054
Red Brambles LI068
Red Lead (Paint Pigment) DA021
Red Sanders (Herb) DA021, LI068, RA054
Red Things AB241
Red-haired AB249, DA021, GA068, LI636, PA012, PT311
Redness of Face RS020
Reporter of Own Acts GA068
Reseda Luteola GA068
Rest-harrow CU, LI068
Revengeful LI540, PA093
Rhaponicum sive rha GA068
Rheum palmatum CU, GA068
Rheum rhaponticum CU, GA068
Rhubarb CU, GA068
Ringworm LI067, RS020

Roadside Fires AB242
Robber PA093
Robbery PT185
Robert LI341
Rocket Cress AB244
Rose AB236
Rouge AB243
Rubia GA068
Rubia tinctorum CU
Rue AB244, LI273
Rue, Wild AB244
Rumex alpinus CU
Ruscus aculeatus CU, GA068
Saffron Color RA054
Salsola kali CU
Saltpeter LI273
Saltwort CU
Sanicle CU
Sanicula europaea CU
Sarmatia, Russia-Poland DA021, LI068
Sarsaparilla CU
Saturday Night AB241
Savage PT353
Savine CU
Scammony DA021, LI068
Scars LI579, PA013
Scars on the Face LI067, RS020
Scorpions LI068
Scurvy PT327
Seditious DA020, LI066, PA109
Seed of Pistacia terebinthus AB243
Seed of Turpentine Tree AB243
Sellers of Beer AB254
Sellers of Boars AB254
Sellers of Boxes AB254
Sellers of Cheetahs AB254
Sellers of Copper AB254
Sellers of Glass AB254
Sellers of Hounds AB254
Sellers of Sickles AB254

Sellers of Wolves AB254
Selling and Making Armor AB254
Sergeants GA068, LI067, PA013, RA054
Serpents, Venomous AB246
Sex Appeal PA013
Shameless AB250, DA021, LI540, PA093
Shark LI068, RA055
Sharp Taste DA020, LI067
Sharp Things AB241
Shepherd's Rod CU
Shepherds AB254
Shingles (Disease) LI067, RA055, RS020
Shipbuilders PT337
Shipwrecks PT185
Shops DA021
Short Fuse PA093
Simson (Blue) CU
Sinapis alba CU
Sisymbrium officinale CU, GA068
Skin Eruption (Morphew) DA021
Slaughterhouses DA021, LI068, PA013, RA055
Slavonia, Croatia AB242
Smallpox PA013
Smallpox of the Face RS020
Smell PA013
Smell and Touch AB248
Smelters DA021
Smilax CU
Smith's Shops LI068, RA055
Smiths DA021, GA068, LI067, PA013, PT337, RA054
Smithy PA013
Soldiers DA020, GA068, LI067, RA054
Solitary AB250
Sonchus oleraceus GA068
Sowbread CU

Spanish Fly DA021, LI068
Speech Open LI540
Spendthrift PT353
Spirit Bold, Lofty, Undaunted GA068
Spirited PT353
Spiteful AB250
Spurge DA021
Squill CU
St. Anthony's Fire LI246
Staphylococcal Inflammation RS020
Star-Thistle (Centaurea) GA068
Stature Middle GA068, PA012
Steel RA055
Steps, Long AB249
Stone Dressers PT337
Streptococcus (Erysipelas) LI246
Stubborn PT353
Subcutaneous Inflammation LI067
Sudden Deaths PT183
Sudden Strokes PT429
Sumptuous LI540
Sun Spurge CU
Surgeons AB254, DA021, GA068, LI067, PA109, RA054
Swelling DA021
Syria AB242, PT143
Tailors LI067, PA013, RA054
Tainting of Potable Waters PT185
Tall AB249
Tamarinds DA021, LI068, RA054
Tanners LI067, PA013, RA054
Tarragon CU
Temerity LI540
Tertian Fevers (Malaria) LI067, PA128, PT183, RS020
Testicles RS014
Teugruim chamaedrys CU
Thief Is Brother LI364
Thief Is Kinsman LI364
Thief Is Son LI364
Thievery LI066

Thieves   DA020, GA068, LI067, PA013, RA054
Thirst, Great RS020
Thistle, Down or Cotton GA068
Thistles   DA021, GA068, LI067, RA054
Thlaspi arvense GA068
Thorn Trees LI068
Thorns DA021
Thorns, Twigs, Bark of a Tree AB236
Thorny Trees AB244
Thunder LI068
Tiger LI068, RA055
Tobacco CU, GA068
Torture AB254
Touchstone DA021, LI068, RA055
Trades LI556
Traitors LI066
Travel AB250
Treacherous GA068, LI066, PA013
Treacle Mustard (Erysimum) GA068
Trees Prickly DA021
Tricky AB250
Trigonella foenum-graecum LI272
Troops AB252
Tuesday AB241, LI068
Tumors, Esp. Genital PT329
Tumultous LI540
Turbulent GA068, LI066
Turkish People DA021
Tyrannical LI540, PA093, PT353
Tyranny LI556, PA109
Tyrants   DA021, GA068, LI067, RA054
Ulcers DA020
Ulex europaeus GA068
Unchaste but Quickly Repentant AB250
Undaunted PA012
Unexcelled in War GA068
Ungovernable LI066

Unjust LI540
Unmovable GA068
Unreasonable LI066
Unruly PT353
Unsteady AB250
Unthankful LI066
Untrustworthy AB250
Upper Part of Fire AB247
Uprising PT183
Urginea maritma CU
Urtica dioica   CU, GA068, LI067, RA054
Users of Iron Tools RA054
Usurpers GA068, LI067, RA054
Valiant LI066, PA093
Veins   AB247, DA020, PA128, PT319, RA054, RS014
Venturesome PT353
Vermillion LI068
Vermillion (Stone) DA021
Vermillion, Red RA055
Veronica beccabunga CU, GA068
Versatile PT353
Veterinary Surgeons AB254
Victorious PA012
Victory PA109
Victory Overrides All GA068
Violence PA109, PT183
Violent AB250, DA021, LI066
Visage Round GA068
Vomiting of The Blood RS020
Vulture LI068, RA055
War-mongers LI066
Warfare LI556
Warrior PA012
Wars LI066, PA109, PT183
Wasps AB247
Waste, Hard and Stony Land AB241
Watch-makers   GA068, LI067, RA054
Water Serpents, Stinging RA055

Wavering LI066
Waylayers DA021
Weather: Thunder & Lightening
  RA055
Weld (Wold - Herb) GA068
Western Winds LI068
White Purge LI068
Wicked DA021
Wine-bibbers, Dressed in Red AB253
Without Honesty GA068
Without Modesty GA068
Wold (Weld - Reseda) GA068
Wolf AB246, LI068, RA055
Wooden Cups, Sellers of AB254
Woodruffe (Squinancy) CU

Woodruffe (Sweet) CU
Woolly Thistle (Carduus) GA068
Worms LI068
Wormseed (Treacle) CU
Wormwood CU, GA068
Wormwood (Roman) CU
Wormwood (Sea) CU
Wounds DA021, LI067, PA013
Wounds, Especially Head & Face
  PA128
Wrath of Leaders PT183
Yellow DA020, LI067, RA054
Yellow Jaundice LI067, PA013
Youth AB248

Jupiter   ♃

Abasing LI063
Abscess (Apostemations) RS019
Abundance PT183
Acer CU
Achillea ageratum GA068
Administering Justice AB250
Advocates LI555, PA108
Affability AB250
Affable Conversation LI062
Affectionate PT347
Agrimonia eupatoria CU, GA068
Agrimony CU, GA068
Agrimony (Water) CU
Aiming at Honorable Matters GA067
Aiming at Lofty Matters GA067
Air AB247
Air in The Heart AB245
Alexander (Herb) CU, GA068
Allheal (Valeriana) RA052
Alliaria petiolata GA068
Almond Tree LI064, RA053
Altars of Churches LI064
Amazedness DA019
Amethyst DA019, LI064, RA053
Animals, Beautifully Colored AB246
Animals, Cloven Hooves AB246
Animals, Domestic AB246
Animals, Edible AB246
Animals, Speaking AB246
Animals, Speckled AB246
Animals, Trained AB246
Apoplexy   DA019, LI063, PA012,
  PT429, RA053, RS019
Apostemations RS019
Apple AB243
Apricot Trees AB244
Arabia PT145
Arsesmart DA020, LI064
Arteries   AB247, DA019, LI246,
  PA128, PT319, RS014

Arthritis RS019
Asclepias syriaga CU
Ash Color DA019, LI063, RA052
Ash Tree LI064, RA053
Asparagus CU, GA068
Asperula cynanchica DA019, LI063
Aspiring LI062
Asthma PA012
Atheists GA067, PA012
Authority PA108
Avens GA068
Azure Color PA011
Babylonia   AB242, DA020, LI065,
  RA053
Back Pain DA019, RA053, RS019
Backbone Pain LI063
Balm CU, RA052
Balsam DA020, LI064
Balsamita major CU, GA068
Banking AB254
Barley AB243
Bashful LI062
Basil DA020, LI064, RA052
Bay-Tree GA068
Bayberry Tree LI064
Beard Flaxen or Sandy DA019
Beard Much GA067
Beard, Small AB249
Beech Tree LI064
Bees LI064, RA053
Beets (White) CU, GA068
Benevolent DA019
Beneficent PT347
Best and Easiest Things AB241
Beta CU, GA068
Betony DA020, LI064, RA052
Betony (Water) GA068
Betony (Wood) CU
Betula pendula RA053
Betula spp. LI064
Bezoar DA019, LI064, RA053

Bidens tripartita CU
Bilberries CU
Birch LI064, RA053
Birds, Grain Eating AB247
Birds, not Black AB247
Birds, Straight Beaks AB247
Bishops   DA019, GA067, LI063, PA108
Bitter Sweet AB240
Blood AB247, PA012
Blood Corruption LI063, RA053
Blood Diseases DA019
Blood Putrefaction LI246, RS019
Bloodwort (Sanguinaria) GA068
Blue RA052
Body, Big & Strong DA020
Body, Fat or Fleshy DA020
Body, Handsomely Composed GA067
Bone Marrow AB247
Books AB242
Boot-Licking LI063
Borage CU, DA020, LI064, RA052
Borago officinalis RA052
Brass, Fine AB243
Breath, Shortness of PA128
Bribe Takers RA052
Brown DA019
Buglosse (Herb)   DA020, LI064, RA052
Caesarean Section AB252
Cardiac Affections PT429
Cardinals LI063
Carduus marianus GA068
Careless GA067, LI063
Cartilege (Gristle) LI246, RS014
Castanea Sativa CU
Cautious in Friendship AB250
Centaurium erythraea DA020, LI064
Centaury DA020, LI064
Chancellors LI063, RA052

Charitable AB250
Charity LI062
Charity, Much GA067
Chaste AB250
Cheaters RA052
Cheats PA012
Cheetahs, Trained AB246
Cherry Tree LI064, RA053
Chervil CU
Chestnut Tree CU
Chick Peas AB243
Children AB249
Christian Churches AB242
Churches PA012, RA053
Cichorium endivia CU, GA068
Cichorium intybus CU, GA068
Cinquefoil CU, GA068
Civilians PA108
Clergymen GA067, PA012
Clergymen, Broken PA012
Clothiers GA067, LI063, RA052
Clothing AB245
Cloves DA019, LI064, RA052
Colewort CU
Compassionate PT347
Complete AB241
Complexion Ruddy PA011
Complexion Ruddy & Pleasant GA067
Complexion Sanguine or Mixed DA019
Concealment of Disease PT329
Conceited LI540
Conferences LI064
Constant GA067
Conventions LI064
Conversation, Excellent GA067
Convocations DA020, LI064
Convulsions LI246, PA128, RA053, RS019
Coral Tree LI064, RA053

Corpulent GA067
Corylus avellana LI064, RA053
Costmary CU, GA068
Coughs PA012
Couhlearia officinalis CU, GA068
Counselors LI063, PA012, RA052
Courts of Justice   DA020, LI064, PA012, RA053
Cowardice PT349
Cramps   DA019, LI063, PA128, RA053, RS019
Cringing Companion GA067
Crithum maritimum CU
Crop Abundance PT183
Crystals DA019, LI064, RA053
Cullen, Scotland   DA020, LI065, RA053
Daisy DA020, LI064, RA053
Dandelion CU, GA068
Datura stramonium CU
Death in Childbed AB252
Deer AB246, LI064
Delicious AB240
Desirous to Benefit Others GA067, LI062
Devoted to Religion/Good Works AB250
Devout AB250
Diamond AB243
Digestive Faculty PA012, S2-46
Dignified PT347
Dignities DA019
Discrete PA012
Disdainful LI540
Dissembling LI540
Dock (Common) CU, GA068
Doctors of Civil Law LI063
Doe LI064, RA053
Dog's Grass CU, GA068
Doing Good AB254
Dolphin RA053

Domestic Animals AB246
Dove, Stock RA053
Dragon LI064
Dull LI063
Dull Capacity GA067
Durra AB243
Dust Color AB240
Eager For Education AB250
Eager For Wealth AB250
Eagle LI064, RA053
Ear, Left AB248, DA019
Ear, Left, Diseases RA053
Ear, Left, Infirmities RS019
Easily Worked Soil AB241
Ecclesiastical Dignitaries PA108
Ecclesiasticals LI063, RA052
Echium vulgare RA052
Eglantine CU
Egoistic AB250
Elderly Age PT447
Elephant LI064, RA053
Eloquent AB250
Elymus CU, GA068
Emerald, Jewel (Smaragde) DA019, LI064, RA053
Eminence LI540
Empericks RA052
Endive GA068
Endive (Wild Chicory) CU
Equitable PA092
Explusion PA128
Eyes, Comely & Gray GA067
Eyes, Large AB249
Eyes, Large & Grey PA012
Face, Full DA019
Face, Oval PA012
Face, Round AB249
Fair in Dealings GA067
Faithful   DA019, GA067, GA067, LI062
Fame PT183

Fars AB242
Fatigue AB252
Fearful LI540, PA093
Feigned Courtesy PA093
Fertilizing Winds PT037
Feverfew DA020, RA053
Fevers AB252, LI063
Fevers, Chronic RS019
Fevers, Continuous (Synochus) RS019
Feversend (Herb) LI064
Ficus garica   AB244, CU, LI064, RA053
Fig RA053
Fig Tree AB244, CU, LI064
Figure, Fine AB249
Filipendula ulmaria CU
Finger, Fore- RS014
Fir Tree CU
Flax DA020, LI064, RA052
Fond of Discussion PT347
Forehead, High & Large   GA067, PA012
Fortune, Greater PA011
Fowl, Domestic AB247
Fragaria vesca LI064, RA052
Francolin (Partridge) AB247
Frank Look AB249
Fraxinus Excelsior LI064, RA053
Freestone (Fruit)   DA019, LI064, RA053
Friend of Good Government AB250
Friendliness AB250
Fruit of a Tree AB236
Fruits AB245
Fumaria officinalis LI064, RA052
Fumitory DA020, LI064, RA052
Gardens PA012, RA053
Generous AB250, GA067, PT347
Gentlemen LI555
Geum urbanum CU

Gifts from Rulers PT183
Gilliflowers LI064, RA052
Glittering AB240
Glory LI062
Glycyrrhiza glabra RA053
Goat's Beard CU
God-Fearing PT347
Godliness LI062
Godly DA019
Goldsmith's Work AB254
Good Disposition AB250
Good Government AB254
Gooseberry LI064, RA053
Governors LI540
Grandchildren AB249
Grave DA019, PA012
Grave in Moderation LI540
Green RA052, RA052
Green & Red LI086
Gristles DA019, PA128, RS014
Gross LI063
Gross Capacity GA067
Hair, Abundant Curly Reddish AB249
Hair, Brown PA012
Hair, Chestnut-Colored GA067
Hair, Curly DA019
Hair, Soft & Gentle GA067
Hamlets of Leadworkers AB242
Handsome GA046
Happiness PT183
Happy DA019
Hart LI064, RA053
Hart's Tongue CU, GA068
Hater of Sordid Persons GA067
Hating Sordid Actions LI062
Hazel Nut LI064, RA053
Head, Diseases of LI246
Head, Heaviness RS019
Headache DA019, PT429
Health PT183
Hearing and Touch AB248

Heart (with the Sun) AB247
Heart Palpitations LI063, RA053, RS019
Heart, Wringings at LI246
Heat PT037
Hedera helix LI064, RA053
High-Minded AB250, PT347
Honest LI540, PA092
Honest Men DA019
Honesty, Natural LI555
Honorable LI062, PT347
Honorable, Trusty Custodian AB250
Hoopoo = Hoopoe (Bird) AB247
Hordeum vulgare AB243
House Leek (Wall Pepper, sengreen) CU, GA068
Humidity PT037
Hungary DA020, LI065, RA053
Hyacinth DA019, LI064, RA053
Hypericum perforatum RA052
Hypocrite GA067, PA012
Hyssop CU, GA068
Hyssopus officinalis CU, GA068
Ignorant GA067, LI063
Indifference PT349
Indulgent LI062
Inflammations RS019
Inspiring AB250
Intelligent AB250
Interpretation of Dreams AB254
Intestines AB248
Involuntary Movements (Starts) RS019
Itch RS019
Ivy LI064, RA053
Jewels Worn by Man AB243
John LI341
Judges DA019, GA067, LI063, PA012, RA052
Just DA019, GA067, LI062, PA092, PT347

Justice LI555
Khurasan, Iran AB242
Kidney Disease RA053
Kind PT347
Kings AB252
Lacking Malice PA092
Ladies Thistles (Carduus) GA068
Lang De Boeuf CU
Lark (Bird) AB247, LI064, RA053
Larkwort DA020, LI064
Laskwort RA052
Laughing AB250
Laurus nobilis GA068
Law Makers PT335
Law Positions DA019
Lawyers AB252, DA019, LI063, PA012, RA052
Leaders PT347
Learned AB250
Left Ear LI063
Leopards, Trained AB246
Leucanthemum vulgare DA020, LI064, RA053
Levites RA052
Liberal DA019, LI062, PA092, PT347
Lichen (Dog) CU
Licorice LI064, RA053
Linden Tree CU
Linum usitatissimum LI064, RA052
Lions, Trained AB246
Liver DA019, LI063, PA012, RA052, RS014
Liver Disease PA128, RA053, RS019
Liver Heat RS019
Liver Inflammation DA019, LI246, PA012
Liverwort DA020, GA068, LI064
Lote-Fruit Trees AB244
Lover of Fair Dealing LI062
Lover of Pleasure PT347

Loving to All PA092
Lugwort DA020
Lung Disease PA012
Lung Inflammation DA019, LI063, RA053, RS019
Lungs DA019, LI246, PA012, PT319, RS014
Lungwort CU, GA068, LI064, RA052
Mace (Plant) DA019, LI064, RA052
Magnanimous   DA019, GA067, LI062, PT347
Magnates AB252
Magnificent PT347
Man AB246
Manna (Shrub) LI064
Mansions of The Nobility AB242
Maple Tree CU
Marble DA019, LI064, RA053
Marcasite AB243
Marjoram (Sweet) RA052
Marjoram, Wild DA020, RA052
Mastic (Pistacia lentiscus) DA020, LI064
Mastix RA053
Mayors LI555
Meadowsweet CU
Measles RS019
Melissa officinalis CU, RA052
Mentha RA053
Merchants AB252
Middle Age AB248
Mild DA019
Mild and Gentle Beasts LI064
Minding Own Business PT347
Ministers LI063
Mint DA020, LI064, RA053
Moderate AB241
Moderate Heat & Moisture AB231
Moderation AB241
Monday Night AB241
Morality LI555

Morus Nigra LI064, RA053
Mosques AB242
Mountebacks PA012, RA052
Mulberry Tree LI064, RA053
Muscles RS014
Myrrhis odorata CU
Naive LI540
Narcissus AB236
Navel RS014
Negligent LI540, PA093
Noble AB250, GA067, PA012
Noble Actions AB254
Noble Men PA108
Nobles AB252, DA019
North Winds LI064
Nose, Thick & Prominent AB249
Nutmeg DA019, LI064, RA052
Oak Tree CU, GA068, LI064, RA053
Obstructions RA053
Ocymum basilicum DA020, LI064, RA052
Olive LI064
Olive Tree RA053
Oratories DA020, RA053
Orators PT337
Oratory LI064
Orderly LI540, PA092
Ordinary Vessels AB242
Organy (Wild Marjoram) DA020, LI064, RA052
Origanum majorana RA052
Origanum vulgare RA052
Oryza sativa AB243
Ox RA053
Oxen AB246, LI064
Paeonia officinalis LI064, RA053
Paeony LI064, RA053
Palaces PA012, RA053
Palpitations of The Heart RA053
Paralysis (Apoplexy) RS019
Parliamentarians PA108

Partridge LI064, RA053
Partridge (Francolin) AB247
Patient AB250
Pea Hen LI064
Peaceful Existence PT183
Peacemaker AB250
Peach Tree AB244
Peacock AB247, LI064, RA053
Pear Tree AB244, LI064, RA053
Peltigera canina CU
Performing High Matters LI540
Peripneumonia RS019
Persia DA020, LI065, RA053
Pewter RA053
Pheasant LI064, RA053
Phyllitis scolopendrium CU, GA068
Picea abies CU
Picris Echioides CU
Pigeon AB247
Pigeon, Wild (Stock Dove) LI064
Pimpernel DA020, LI064, RA052
Pine Tree LI064, RA053
Pinus sylvestris LI064, RA053
Pistacia lentiscus DA020, LI064
Places: Near Church Altars DA019
Places: Neat LI064
Places: of Oratory PA012
Plague RS019
Pleasant AB241
Pleurisy   DA019, LI063, PA012,
  RA053, RS019
Pneumonia PT429
Polygonum DA020
Pomegranites LI064, RA053
Pomegranites, Wild AB243
Potentilla reptans CU, GA068
Pox RS019
Prelates LI555, PA108
Prickings RA053
Prideful PA093
Priests GA067, LI063, RA052

Princes GA067
Principalities DA019
Prodigal GA067, LI540, PA093
Prosperity PT183
Proud LI540
Prudent GA067, LI062
Prunella vulgaris LI064
Prunus persica AB244
Pulmonaria officinalis CU, GA068,
  LI064, RA052
Pulpits AB242
Pulse DA019, LI246, PA128, RA053,
  RS014
Punica granatum RA053
Purple DA019, LI063, RA052
Pyrus sativa AB244, LI064, RA053
Quack-Salvers RA052
Quercus robur CU, GA068, LI064,
  RA053
Rachel LI341
Raisins LI064
Recklessness AB250
Red & Green LI086
Red Arsenic AB243
Reliever of Poor LI062
Religion AB254, PA108
Religious   AB250, DA019, LI062,
  PA092
Religious Conventions DA020
Reproductive Problems, Men RA053
Responsible AB250
Reverencing Aged Men LI062
Rheum palmatum RA052
Rhubarb DA020, LI064, RA052
Rhus coggyria CU
Rib Diseases RS019
Ribes uva-crispa LI064, RA053
Ribs DA019, LI063, PA012, RS014
Rice AB243
Rich DA019
Rich and their Syncophants AB252

Rich Men LI555, PA108
Richard LI341
Riches PA105
Ridgebone, Prickling & Shooting LI246
Ringworm RS019
Rose AB244
Rose, Red GA068
Royal Palaces AB242
Ruler PA108
Rumex obtusifolius CU, GA068
Saffron DA020, LI064, RA053
Sage GA068
Sage (Common Garden) CU
Salvia officinalis CU, GA068
Samphire (Rock or Small) CU
Sanguinaria (Bloodwort) GA068
Sanguine DA019
Sapphire LI064, RA053
Sativus CU
Sauce-Alone (Jack-in-Hedge) GA068
Schismatical LI063
Scholars PA012, RA052
Science AB242
Scornful LI540
Scrophularia auriculata GA068
Scurvy-Grass CU, GA068
Sea-Blue DA019, LI063
Sea-Green DA019, LI063
Sedum acre CU, GA068
Seed, Reproductive AB247, DA019, LI246, PT319, RS014
Seeds Which Fly with the Wind AB244
Self Heal DA020, LI064
Selling Grapes AB254
Selling Old Gold and Silver AB254
Selling Sugar Cane AB254
Semen DA019, PT319, RS014
Sempervivum tectorum CU
Senators GA067, LI063, PA012

Serenity LI064
Serious GA067
Serpents RA053
Sesame AB243
Shame-faced DA019
Sheep AB246, LI064, RA053
Shining AB240
Shooting Pains RA053
Sickness AB252
Sides DA019, PA012, RS014
Skeptic GA067
Sleepiness without Rest RS019
Smaragd[e] (Emerald Jewel) DA019
Smoothness AB241
Smyrnium olusatrum CU, GA068
Snipe (Bird) LI064, RA053
Sober LI540, PA012
Solidity AB241
Some Levity AB250
Sophists PT337
Spain DA020, LI065, PT135, RA053
Spasms PT429
Speech Sober & Grave GA067
Spendthrift GA067
Sperm AB247, DA019, LI246, PT319, RS014
Spiritual Offices DA019
Squin[a[nc[i]es (Woodruffe) DA019, LI063, RA053, RS019
St. John's Wort RA052
Stachys officinalis CU, RA052
Stag LI064, RA053
Starting of The Members RS019
Stature Comely DA019
Stature Tall & Handsome GA067
Stature Tall & Upright PA011
Stock RA053
Stock Dove (Wild Pigeon) LI064, RA053
Stones Found in Ox-Gall AB243
Stones, White & Yellow AB243

Stork (Bird) LI064
Strangulation PT429
Strawberries DA019, LI064, RA052
Students PA012, RA052
Students in University LI063
Stupidity PT349
Succory GA068
Succory (Wild) CU
Sugar DA019, RA052
Sulphur AB243
Sumach CU
Superstition PT349
Superstitious LI540, PA093
Swallow-Wort CU
Sweet AB240
Sweet Conversation LI062
Sweet Maudlin (Achillea) GA068
Sweet Odors LI063
Sweet or Tall Herbs AB244
Sweet Smells DA019
Synagogues AB242
Synochus putrida RS019
Synods DA020, LI064, RA053
Tall Stature LI063
Tanacetum parthenium RA053
Taraxacum officinale CU, GA068
Teachers' Houses AB242
Temperate PT037
Tenacious LI063
Thankful LI062
Thighs AB248
Things Profitable & Agreeable AB245
Thomas LI341
Thorn-Apple CU
Thorough Leaf LI064
Three LI065
Throat AB248
Thursday AB241, LI065
Tiger LI064

Tin AB243, DA019, LI064, RA053
Topaz DA019, LI064, RA053
Touch and Hearing AB248
Touch, Sense of PT319
Tragopogon pratensis CU
Trees, Fruit With Soft Skin AB244
Trees, Sweet Fruited AB244
Triticum AB243, LI064, RA052
True DA019
Truth-Telling AB250
Tutty (Zinc Oxide) AB243
Unicorn LI064, RA053
Untainted GA067
Uxorious AB250
Vaccinium myrtillus CU
Vain Candor LI540
Vein Diseases RS019
Veins LI063, PA012, RS014
Vines LI064, RA053
Viola odorata LI064, RA053
Violet (Herb) DA020, LI064, RA053
Virtue PA108
Virtuous LI062
Visage Full DA019
Visage Oval GA067
Vital, Growing, Nutritive AB245
Vitis Vinifera RA053
Vizirs AB252
Walwort DA020, LI064, RA052
Wardrobes DA020, LI064, RA053
Wastes Patrimony GA067, LI063
Weather: Pleasant RA053
Whale RA053
Wheat AB243, DA020, LI064, RA052
White PT193
White and Mixed Yellow & Brown AB240
White Clothes AB254
White Lead AB243

Willowherb LI064
Windiness DA019, LI063, RA053, RS019
Windiness in The Veins LI246
Wise LI062
Womb AB248
Woodruffe (Squinzle, Squinances)

DA019, LI063, RS019
Woolen Drapers   GA067, LI063, RA052
Yellow Green DA019, LI063
Yellow, Mixed RA052
Young Scholars LI063
Zinc Oxide AB243

Saturn ♄

Abyssinia AB242
Acacia LI272
Aches in The Joints RA051
Aconite CU
Aconitum Anthora CU
Actaea spicata CU
Adder LI060, RA051
Advised LI539
Aegopodium podagraria CU
Affliction AB252
Alkakenge LI272
Allheal (Valeriana) GA067
Allum LI272
Amaranthus CU
Amaranthus hybridus CU
Amassing Treasure PT341
Angelica DA018, LI059, RA050
Angelica archangelica RA050
Animals Living in Holes AB246
Anorexia RS019
Antiquities RA050
Anus AB248
Anxious AB250
Apoplexy LI059
Arabia AB242
Arctium lappa RA050
Arsesmart CU
Ash Color DA017
Asplenium GA067

Ass (Animal) LI060, RA051
Astringent AB240
Atropa belladonna GA067, RA050
Austere LI058, PT341
Austerity LI539
Avaricious PT341
Awkward Figure AB249
Azure RA051
Back AB248
Backbiting LI539, PA092
Barley CU, GA067
Barren Mountains AB241
Bartenders RA050
Base Trades DA017
Basilisk (=Monster) LI060, RA051
Bat RA050
Bat (=Stick or Cudgel) LI060
Bavaria DA018, LI061, RA051
Bear LI060, RA051
Beard, Thin DA018, GA066
Bearsfoot DA018, LI059, RA050
Beetles AB246
Beets (Red) CU
Beggars   DA017, GA067, LI059, PA011, RA050
Behemence AB250
Belleric myrobalan (Fruit) AB243
Belly, Looseness DA018
Berula erecta RA050
Beta CU, GA067

Beta altissima CU
Bifoil = Two-Blade Grass GA067
Bile [Choler], Black DA017
Bile, Black AB247
Birds, Aquatic AB247
Birds, Nocturnal AB247
Birdsfoot Trefoil GA067
Bistort (Herb) CU, GA067
Bithwind RA050
Bitter DA017, LI059
Black DA017, PT193
Black Animals AB246
Black Hair PT305
Black Jaundice LI059
Black Mixed with Yellow AB240
Black Stones LI060
Blackberry LI272
Blackbird LI060, RA050
Blackthorn GA067
Bladder   DA017, PA127, PT319,
   RS014
Bladder Pains LI246, RA051
Blue Bottle CU
Body, Well-proportioned DA012
Bone Pain LI246, RA051
Bones AB247, LI579, PA011, PT319,
   RS014
Bores AB252
Bowels AB248
Box LI059, RA050
Brewers (Maltsters) GA067, LI059
Bricklayers RA050
Brickmakers GA067, LI059, RA050
Broom-Men LI059, RA050
Buckthorn (Purging) CU
Buckthorn-Plantain GA067
Buildings   AB254, DA018, LI555,
   PA108
Buildings, Decrepit LI060
Buildings, Ruined PA011
Buildings, Ruinous DA018, RA051

Bupleurum rotundifolium GA067
Burdock LI059, RA050
Burial Grounds LI060
Butomus umbellatus CU
Buttocks AB248
Bythwind (Herb) LI059
Cabbage LI272
Candle-Maker GA067, RA050
Canker DA017, PA011
Cannabis sativa CU, GA067, LI059,
   RA050
Capers LI059, RA050
Capers Tree DA018
Capsella bursa-pastoris CU, LI059,
   RA050
Captivity AB254
Carduus heterophyllus GA067
Careless PA108
Careless of Body PT341
Carpenters, Ship RA050
Carters LI059, RA050
Carthamus tinctorius CU
Castor Oil Plant AB244
Cat AB246, LI060, RA051
Catarrhs RA051
Caves DA018, LI060, PA011, RA051
Centaurea cyanus CU
Centaurea jacea CU
Centaurea scabiosa CU, GA067
Ceterach (Finger-Fern) LI059
Chandlers GA067, RA050
Chimney Sweeps LI059
Chin Cough RA051
Choler, Black DA017
Cholic PA127, PT327
Churchyards DA018, LI060, PA011,
   RA051
Citron or Myrobalan Tree AB244
Cleavers (Goosegrass) GA067
Clotbur LI059
Clouds Dark RA051

Cloudy Weather LI060, RA051
Clown's Woundwort CU, GA067
Clowns   GA067, LI059, PA011,
    RA050
Coachmen RA050
Coal Mines LI060
Coal Miners RA050
Coal Pits PA011, RA051
Cognition Deep DA018
Colchicum autumnale CU
Collapse of Buildings PT327
Colliers GA067, LI059, RA050
Comfrey CU, GA067
Complexion, Muddy PA010
Complexion, Pale PA010
Complexion, Swarthy PA010
Complexion, Swarthy or Black
    DA018
Complexion, Swarthy or Pale GA066
Condemner of Women LI058
Conduit, Water LI214
Confusion AB250
Conium maculatum   CU, GA067,
    RA050
Constance, Germany DA018
Constantia LI061, RA051
Constipation DA018
Consumption LI059, PA011, PA127,
    PT181, RA051, RS019
Consumption of Lights DA017
Cool PT035
Coughs DA018
Coughs, Chin LI246
Covetous DA018, GA066, LI058
Cowherds LI059, RA050
Crafty PA092
Cranes LI060, RA050
Creeping Animals LI060
Crocodile LI060, RA051
Crooked DA018
Crosswort CU, GA067

Crow LI060, RA050
Crude Phlegm AB247
Crudities RS019
Cuckoo LI060, RA050
Cudgel or Stick (=Bat) LI060
Cudweed GA067
Cumin DA018, LI059, RA050
Curriers DA017, GA067, RA050
Cuscuta epithymum CU, GA067
Cydonia oblonga CU, GA067
Cypress Tree DA018, LI059
Cyprus RA050
Daphne mezereum CU
Dark-Skinned PT305
Darnel CU, GA067
Day-Laborers GA067, LI059, PA011,
    RA050
Deafness   LI246, PA011, RA051,
    RS019
Death AB252, PT181
Debt PA108
Deceitful DA018, LI539, PA108
Deceivers PA092
Demons AB252
Dens DA018, LI060, RA051
Depraved PA092
Descurainia sophia CU
Deserts   DA018, LI060, PA011,
    RA051
Deserts Full of Wild Beasts AB242
Desolate Roads AB242
Destructions RA051
Devotees AB252
Dictatorial PT341
Diggers of Metals PA108
Dirty Places LI060
Disagreeable AB240
Disagreeable Smelling Fruit Trees
    AB244
Discord AB250
Discrete GA066

Dissembling GA067
Distempers, Melancholy PA011
Distribution of Water AB254
Ditch-Diggers RA050
Ditchers LI059
Dodder of Thyme CU, GA067
Dog LI060, RA051
Dog Hunger* LI059, RS019
Downcast Look AB249, GA066
Dragon RA050
Dragon (Snap?) LI059
Dropsy (= Edema) DA018, PA011, RA051
Drugs Cold & Dry AB245
Dry PT035
Dryness AB241
Dust DA017, LI060
Dwellings AB245
Dyers of Black Cloth LI059, RA050
Dysentery PT327
Ear Noises RS019
Ear Ringing RS019
Ear, Right AB248, DA017, PA011, PA127, RS014
Ear, Right, Noise LI246
Ears, Large GA066, PA010
Earth AB247
East Winds LI060
Edema (Dropsy, Hyposarca) DA018, PA011, RA051, RS019
Eel LI060, RA051
Egg White LI272
Egypt AB242
Elephant LI060, RA051
Elephantiasis PT327
Elephants' Houses AB242
Elizabeth LI341
Elm Tree CU, GA067
Endive LI272
Engrossed in Own Affairs AB250
Enslaving People by Treachery AB250
Enslaving People by Violence AB250
Envious DA018, GA066, LI058, PA092
Envy DA018
Epilepsy RA051
Epilobium angustifolium CU
Epilobium hirsutum CU
Epithimium (Dodder of thyme) GA067
Equisetum arvense CU, GA067, RA050
Ermine AB246
Ethiopia AB242
Eunuchs AB252
Evil Oppression by Government AB254
Evil-Speaker PT341
Exile AB250, PT181
Experience DA018
Extreme Cold & Dryness AB231
Eyebrows Joined AB249
Eyebrows Lowering GA066, PA010
Eyes, Little GA066, PA010
Eyes, Small AB249, DA018
Face, Lean DA018
Face, Sour AB249
Face, Unpleasant DA018
Failure in Business AB250
Fantasies LI059
Farming AB254
Farming Profit LI555
Fathers AB249, DA017, GA067, LI059, PA011, PT241, RA050
Fearful AB250, DA018, PA092
Fears PT181
Feathers AB247
Feet, Big AB249
Fern LI059, RA050
Fern (Royal) CU, GA067
Field-Vine LI272

Filanginella uliginosa GA067
Finger, Middle RS014
Finger-Fern LI059
Fingers, Short AB249
Fistulas RA051
Flax LI272
Flaxweed GA067
Fleas AB246
Fleawort GA067, LI272
Flies AB247
Flixweed CU
Flux RS019
Foot-Gout LI059
Forehead, Broad GA066, PA010
Fraud AB250
Fraudulent Transactions AB254
Fruits of The Earth PA108
Fumaria officinalis   CU, GA067, LI059, RA050
Fumitory   CU, DA018, GA067, LI059, RA050
Galium aparine GA067
Galium cruciata CU, GA067
Gall-Oak CU
Garbage LI060
Gardeners GA067, LI059, RA050
George LI341
Ghouls AB252
Gladiole (Water) CU
Gladwin CU
Gladwin, Stinking GA067
Glaucoma PT321
Gloomy PT341
Gnats LI060
Goats AB246
Golden Herb LI059
Goosegrass (Cleavers) GA067
Gout AB252, LI246, RA051, RS019
Gout, Foot DA018
Gout, Hand DA018, RS019
Goutweed CU, GA067

Grandfathers   AB249, DA017, GA067, LI059, PA011, RA050
Grasshopper LI060
Grave GA066, PA092
Grave (of Manner) AB250, LI058
Grave Digging AB254
Green (Winter) CU
Grooms RA050
Hail PT181
Hair AB247
Hair, Black or Dark GA066, PA010
Hair, Lots & Black AB249
Hair, Swarthy or Black DA018
Hand-Gout LI059
Hands, Coarse AB249
Hard Stones AB243
Hardness AB241
Hare LI060, RA051
Hawkweed CU, GA067
Head, Large AB249
Head, Right, Noise LI246
Hearing AB248, LI269
Heart's Ease CU
Heaviness AB241
Hedera helix CU
Height AB248
Hellbore DA018, LI059, RA050
Hellbore (Black) CU
Hellbore (White) CU
Helleborus niger CU, RA050
Hematites (Stone) LI272
Hemlock CU, DA018, GA067, LI059, RA050
Hemorrhoids DA018, LI059, RS019
Hemp CU, DA018, GA067, LI059, RA050
Hempseed AB243
Henbane CU, DA018, GA067, LI059, RA050
Herb Christopher CU
Herb Grace (Rue) DA018, LI059

Herdsmen LI059, RA050
Heritages, Apportioning AB254
Herniaria glabra GA067
Hieracium murorum CU, GA067
Hogs LI060, RA051
Holds Head Forward GA066
Holes LI060, RA051
Holes (Places) DA018
Holly CU
Hordeum vulgare CU, GA067
Horn AB247
Horse Tail CU
Horses AB246
Horsetail DA018, GA067, LI059, RA050
Hotel Operators LI059
Hottonia palustris CU
House Leek (Singreen) LI272
Houses LI555
Houses of Offices RA051
Husbandmen DA017, GA067, LI059, PA011, RA050
Husbandry PA108
Hyoscyamus niger CU, GA067, LI059, RA050
Hypericum androsaemum DA018, LI059
Hypocistis LI272
Hyposarca (Edema) RS019
Iberis GA067
Icicle (Stiria) LI061
Ignorance, Concealed AB250
Ilex aquifolium CU
Iliac Passion (Sciatica) DA017, RA051
Ill-Favored LI539
Illecebrum verticillatum CU, GA067
Imagination, Strong GA066
Implacable DA018
Impotency PA011
Imprisonment DA018, PT181

India AB242, PT141
Indifference PT341
Inflammation: Mucous Membranes RA051
Infortune, Greater PA010
Ingolstadt, Germany DA018, LI061, RA051
Inheritances DA018, LI555, PA108
Insects, Poisonous AB246
Internal Organs, Diseases of AB252
Iris foetidissdma CU, GA067
Iron Slag AB243
Irrigation LI214
Isatis tinctoria GA067
Ivy CU
Janitors (Broom-Men) LI059, RA050
Jaundice DA018
Jaundice, Black DA017, LI246, PA127, RA051, RS019
Jealous GA067, LI058, PA092, PT341
Jerboe AB246
Jesuits GA067, LI059, PA011, RA050
Jet-Black AB240
Jews AB253, DA017, PA108
Joan LI341
Joint Aches RA051
Julian LI341
Juniperus sabina RA050
King's Attendants AB252
Knapweed GA067
Knapweed (Common) CU
Knapwort (Harshweed) CU
Knees AB248
Knotgrass CU, GA067, LI272
Knowledge of Many Things DA018
Knowledge Used For Bad Purpose AB254
Labor, Unclean PA108
Laborers RA050

Laborious DA018, LI539, PT341
Lairs of Wild Beasts AB242
Lamentation AB250
Lapis Lazuli DA017, LI060, RA051
Lapwing LI060, RA050
Lassitude in The Limbs RS019
Latrine Duty RA050
Lead AB243, DA017, LI060, RA051
Lead Color AB240, PA010
Lead Monoxide (Litharge) AB243
Lean DA018
Leather Worker LI059
Leeks, House (Singreen) LI272
Legs, Crooked AB249
Lens culinaris AB243, LI272
Lentils AB243, LI272
Leprosy   DA017, LI059, PA011,
  RA051
Leprous or Scurvy Eruption RA051
Liars LI058
Linaria vulgaris GA067
Linseed AB243
Linum usitatissimum LI272
Lips Thick AB249, DA018, GA066,
  PA010
Listera ovata (Bifoil) GA067
Litharge (Lead Monoxide) AB243
Loadstone DA017, LI060, RA051
Locusts (Plague) PT181
Lolium temulentum CU, GA067
Long Illnesses PT181
Looking Downward PA010
Lotus corniculatis GA067
Lover of Property PT341
Lover of The Body PT341
Lying GA067
Macedonia PT139
Madness RS019
Magicians AB252
Magnetite DA017
Malaria (Tertian Fever)   LI059,

PA011, PT181, RA051, RS019
Malefic, Greater GA066
Malevolent Plotter AB250
Malicious GA066, LI058
Malignant LI539
Mallow LI272
Maltsters GA067, LI059
Malva sylvestris LI272
Mandragora officinarum   LI059,
  RA050
Mandrake DA018, LI059, RA050
Marrow AB247
Masons PA108
Mean-Spirited PT341
Meddlers AB243, GA067
Melancholic Infirmities LI246
Melancholy AB250, GA066, RA051
Melancholy Thistle (Carduus) GA067
Memory Deep DA018
Metal Diggers LI555
Metal Tailing DA017
Metallic Dross LI060, RA051
Metals PA108
Mezereon Spurge CU
Miners DA017, GA067, LI059
Mines PA108
Miserly AB250
Misers PA108
Mistrustful GA067, LI058
Mole LI060, RA051
Money, Apportioning AB254
Monks   GA067, LI059, PA011,
  RA050
Monster (=Basilisk) LI060
Moors (Islam) DA017, PA108
Moribund AB252
Morphew (Skin Eruption) DA017,
  RA051
Moslems DA017, PA108
Moss DA018, GA067, LI059, RA050
Mountains DA018, LI060

Mournful DA018
Mourning PT181
Mouse AB246, LI060, RA051
Mouth, Wide AB249
Mucus Membrane Inflammation
  LI246
Muddy Places LI060
Mullein GA067
Mullein (Black) CU
Mullein (Great) CU
Murmuring LI058
Musing of Great Things PA092
Myrrh LI272
Myrtle Tree AB236
Myrtus communis AB236
Nabatea (S.E. of Palestine) AB242
Nails AB247
Narcotics AB245
Navigation LI555
Neck, Short AB249
Negligent LI539, PA092
Never Contented LI058
Niggards PA092
Night-Farmers LI059
Nightshade   CU, DA018, GA067,
  LI059, RA050
Nonconformist, Religious GA067
Nose, Flat GA066, PA010
Nose, Lumpish DA018
Nut Trees AB244
Oak-Gall Tree AB244
Obstinate DA017
Offensively Acid AB240
Office Buildings LI060, RA051
Old Age AB248, PT447
Old Buildings AB242
Old Men   DA017, GA067, LI059,
  PA011, RA050
Older Brothers AB249
Olive Tree AB244
Olives AB243

Orage (Herb) DA018, LI059, RA050
Osmunda regalis CU, GA067, RA050
Ostrich LI060, RA050
Outwardly Dissembling LI058
Overworked AB252
Owl LI060, RA050
Owners of Estates AB252
Oxen AB246
Painful PA092
Pale Colored DA017
Pallbearers RA050
Palms LI272
Palsy DA018, RS019
Papaver rhoeas RA050
Paralysis LI059
Parsnip LI059, RA050
Patience LI058
Paunch RS014
Paymaster AB254
Peacock LI060, RA050
Penis AB248
Pepper AB243
Pertinaceous LI539
Petty PT341
Phlegm PT319
Pigs RA051
Pilewort GA067
Pine Tree DA018, LI059, RA050
Pinus sylvestris LI059, RA050
Piper nigrum AB243
Piping, of Water LI214
Pirapirasta* LI272
Pitch Dark AB240
Places: Muddy DA019
Places: Muddy, Dirty, Stinking
  RA051
Places: Stinking DA018
Plantago Coronopus GA067
Planting PA239
Plasy RA051
Plotters PT341

Plowmen RA050
Plumbers GA067, LI059, RA050
Podex (Anus) AB248
Poisonous Drugs AB245
Polygonatum multiforum CU, GA067
Polygonum CU
Polygonum bistorta CU, GA067
Polypodium vulgare DA018, GA067, LI059, RA050
Polypody DA018, GA067, LI059, RA050
Pomegranites LI272
Pomegranites, Bitter AB243
Poplar (Black) CU
Poplar (White) CU
Poplar Tree GA067
Poppy DA018, LI059, RA050
Populus GA067
Populus alba CU
Populus nigra CU
Possessions DA018
Posture Inclining, Head Forward DA018
Potters DA017, LI059
Poverty AB250, PT181
Prisons LI555, PA108
Profound in Imagination LI058
Property Managers PT335
Prostitution LI555
Prunus spinosa CU
Ptisis RS019
Pulse LI059, RA050
Putrefying Animals RA051
Putrefying Creatures LI060
Quarrelsome PA092
Quartan Agues or Fevers (Malaria) PT181, RA051
Quercus infectoria CU
Quince LI272
Quince Tree CU, GA067
Ranunculus ficaria GA067

Ravenna DA018, LI061, RA051
Ravenous DA018
Ravens AB247
Ready to Punish PT341
Reclaiming Land AB254
Red Beets GA067
Religious Dissenter GA067
Religious of Various Sects AB252
Repining GA067, LI058
Reserve LI058
Retail Supplier GA067, RA050
Retention PA011, RS102
Retentive Power AB245
Revilers of Demons AB252
Revilers of Ghouls AB252
Revilers of Magicians AB252
Rhamnus catharticus CU, GA067
Rheumatism PA127, PT327
Rheums DA017, LI059, PA127
Right Ear LI059, PT319
Robust PT305
Romandiola [Fr-Speaking Switzerland?] DA018, LI061, RA051
Root of Scarcity CU
Roots of a Tree AB236
Rose, Fresh LI272
Rough-Hewn LI539
Rubbish DA017
Rubus fructicosus LI272
Rude PA092
Rue DA018, LI059, RA050
Rue (Herb Grace) DA018, LI059
Ruptures RS019
Rupturewort GA067
Rushes GA067
Sable AB246
Sad PA092
Saffron LI272
Saffron (Meadow) CU
Saffron (Wild, Safflower) CU
Sage LI059, RA050

Sage Box DA018
Sailors RA050
Salix alba AB244, RA050
Sallow Tree DA018
Salvia officinalis RA050
Sapphire DA017, LI060, RA051
Saracen's Consound (Senecio) GA067
Saturday AB241, LI061
Savine DA018, LI059, RA050
Saxony DA018, LI061, RA051
Scabs LI246, RA051
Scavengers GA067, LI059, RA050
Sciatica (Iliaca or Illiac Passion) DA017, LI246, RA051
Sciatica-Cress (Iberis) GA067
Scorpions AB246, LI060, RA051
Scurvy PA011
Secret Enemies DA018
Secretaries LI059
Secrets PA092
Sectarists (Religious Dissenter) GA067
Seeking Solitariness AB250
Self-esteem Low LI539
Selling Black Slaves AB254
Selling Things Made of Bone AB254
Selling Things Made of Copper AB254
Selling Things Made of Hair AB254
Selling Things Made of Iron AB254
Selling Things Made of Lead AB254
Sempervivum tectorum LI272
Sena (Umbria) LI059
Sene RA050
Senecio saracenicus GA067
Sepulchres PA011, RA051
Serpents LI060, RA051
Service Tree GA067
Sesame AB244
Severe LI058

Sextons of Churches GA067, LI059
Shameless PT341
Sharp DA017, LI059
Sheep AB246
Shellfish LI060, RA051
Shepherd's Purse CU, DA018, LI059, RA050
Shepherds LI059, RA050
Ship-Carpenters RA050
Shipwrecks PT181
Shopkeeper LI059
Shortness AB241
Shoulders Thick and Crooked DA018
Shoveling Feet GA066
Sickness AB252
Sickness Long in Duration DA018
Single Purpose PT341
Singreen (=Sengreen,House Leek) LI272
Sink-Cleaners DA017
Sinks LI060, PA011, RA051
Skin AB247
Skin Eruption (Morphew) DA017
Slanderous LI539
Slaves AB249
Sleep AB245
Sloe Bush CU
Sluggish GA067, LI058
Snakes, Large Black AB246
Sober GA066
Solanum nigurm CU
Solicitous LI058
Solitariness GA066, PA010
Solitary DA018, LI539, PA092, PT341
Solomon's Seal CU, GA067
Sorbus GA067
Sordid GA067, LI058, PT341
Sordid Professions LI555
Sorrowful LI539
Sour LI059

Sour in Taste DA017
Sowing PA239
Sparing LI539
Spasms PT327
Spinach DA018, LI059, RA050
Spinacia oleracea RA050
Splay-Footed PA010
Spleen AB247, DA017, LI059, LI579, PA011, PT319, RA050, RS014
Spleen Obstructions RS019
Spleenwort GA067
St. John's Wort (Tutsan) DA018, GA067, LI059
Stables: Horses, Asses, Camels AB242
Stachys palustris CU
Starwort DA018, LI059, RA050
Stature Middle DA018, GA066, PA010
Stick or Cudgel (=Bat) LI060
Stinking AB240
Stinking Places PA011
Stiria, Austria [=Styria] DA018, RA051
Stone Cutters LI555
Stones (Disease) PA011
Stones, Black Colored DA017, RA051
Stones, Blue RA051
Stooping GA066
Strong-Minded PT341
Stubborn LI058, PA092
Studious GA066, LI058, PA092
Studious for Own Profit LI539
Styria, Austria [=Stiria] DA018
Subtle PA092
Sullen & Proud AB250
Sumach LI272
Superstitious DA018, LI539, PA092, PT341

Suspicious AB250, GA067, LI058, PA092
Swallows AB247
Swelling LI059
Swelling of Tissues LI246
Swimming in The Head RS019
Symphytum officinale CU, GA067
Taciturn LI539
Tall AB249
Tamarisk DA018, LI059, RA050
Tamari[sk]? GA067
Tanners GA067, PA108
Taxus baccata CU, LI059, RA050
Tearful PT341
Teeth DA017, LI059, PA011, RS014
Thief is Servant LI364
Thief is Stranger LI364
Thieves AB252
Things, Coldest AB241
Things, Hardest AB241
Things, Most Powerful AB241
Things, Most Stinking AB241
Those Who Dress in Black AB253
Thrace PT139
Thrifty LI539
Thrush LI060, RA050
Th[o]roughwax (Bupleurum) GA067
Tillage DA018, LI555
Timber, Felling PA240
Timid AB250
Timorous GA067, LI058
Tinners LI059
Toad LI060, RA051
Toothache LI246, PA011, RA051
Tortoise LI060, RA051
Torture AB254
Trader LI059
Treasure PA108
Trees Bearing Hard Shell Fruit AB244
Trembling LI059, RS019
Trientalis europaea CU

Trusty AB250
Truth-Telling AB250
Tuberculosis (Ptisis) RS019
Turpentine Tree AB244
Ugly AB249
Ulmus minor CU, GA067
Underground Canals AB242
Underground Vaults AB242
Undertakers LI059
Unfeeling PT341
Unpleasant Look PA010
Unwilling to Believe Good AB250
Usury LI555
Vain Fears LI059
Valeriana officinalis GA067
Valleys DA018
Valleys, Hidden LI060
Valleys, Obscure RA051
Veratrum viride CU
Verbascum GA067
Verbascum nigrum CU
Verbascum thapsus CU
Verbena officinalis RA050
Vervain DA018, LI059, RA050
Viola tricolor CU
Violent PT341
Violet (Water) CU
Visage Lean DA018
Visage Unpleasant DA018
Wailing AB250
Wan in Color DA017

Water-Work LI214
Weakness PT327
Weakness in The Limbs RS019
Wealth Acquired Thru Trickery AB250
Weasel AB246
Weather: Cloudy RA051
Weather: Dark RA051
Wednesday Night AB241
Weeping AB250
Wells AB242, LI060, RA051
Wicked People AB252
William LI341
Willow Tree AB244, DA018, LI059, RA050
Willowherb (Hairy) CU
Willowherb (Rosebay) CU
Withering PT181
Wizened AB249
Woad GA067
Wolf LI060, RA051
Wolfbane DA018, LI059, RA050
Woods DA018, LI060, PA011, RA051
Wool AB247
Words, Few DA018
Workaholic PT341
Works For Riches LI539
Wrath AB254
Yemen AB242
Yew CU, LI059, RA050

Sign Rulerships

* Indicates that the meaning of the word is unknown.

Aries

Acne PA004
Ancona (Italian Fowl) DA006, PA073
Apoplexy DA005, LI093, PA004, RS016
Augusta DA006, LI094
Baldness DA005, LI093, RS016
Barren Signs PT325
Beard, Little DA005
Beginning DA005
Bergamo LI094
Bestial DA005, PA004
Betony (Wood) CU
Bitter DA005
Body, Lean & Spare PA004
Brick-Burning Places LI093
Britain PT135
Brunswick, Germany PA073
Burgundy DA006, LI094
Butchers LI450
Caesarea, Palestine DA006, LI094
Capua, Italy DA006, LI094, PA073
Cart-Maker LI450
Ceiling of Houses LI093
Cheeks RS015
Chicken (Ancona, Italian Type) PA073
Childhood AB230
Children ,Few DA005
Chin RS015
Choleric PA004
Commanding DA005
Complexion, Brown DA006

Complexion, Dusky DA006
Complexion, Swarthy DA006
Complexion, Swarthy-Dusky PA004
Cowslip CU
Craconi, Poland [=Krakow] PA073
Denmark DA006, LI094, PA073
Diurnal PA004
Domestical DA005
Ears DA005, RS015
East LI093
Ending Weak DA005
England DA005, LI094, PA073
Epilepsy DA005, LI093, RS016
Eyebrows RS015
Eyebrows Black DA006
Eyes DA005, RS015
Face DA005, RS015
Face Puffy DA005
Face, Long DA006
Face, Oval PA004
Face Wheals DA005
Feedlot LI093
Ferrara DA006, LI094, PA073
Fevers of the Blood DA005
Fires in Ordinary Use AB230
Florence DA006, LI094, PA073
Frame, Big-boned PA004
France DA005, LI094, PA073, PT135
Germany DA005, LI094, PA073, PT135
Gross DA005
Hair inclined to Red PA004
Hare Lip LI093, RS016

Head DA005, LI245, RS015
Head, Diseases of PA004
Headache LI093, PA004, RS016
High & Sandy Ground PA004
Hilly Ground DA006, LI093
Hot & Dry PA004
Ingenious LI538
Ireful DA005
Itch DA005
Judaea LI094, PT143
Krakoe, Poland [=Craconi] PA073
Lands, Newly Plowed LI093
Lascivious (=Luxurious) DA005
Lean, Spare Body PA004
Leprosy DA005
Lethargy PA004
Limbs, Strong PA004
Lindama* PA073
Luxurious (Lascivious) DA005
Marseilles, France DA006, LI094
Masculine PA004
Migraines DA005, LI093, RS016
Naples, Italy DA006, LI094, PA073
Neck Long DA006, PA004
Nose RS015
Padua, Italy DA006, LI094, PA073
Palestine DA006, PA073, PT157
Paralysis (Apoplexy) RS016
Pasture LI093
Pergamo DA006
Piercing Eye PA004
Pimples LI093, PA004, RS016
Places in Houses: Ceiling PA004
Places in Houses: East Part PA004
Places: Private, Unfrequented PA004
Places: Small Cattle Feeding PA004
Plastering in Houses LI093
Poland, Lessor PA073
Polonia DA006, LI094

Polyps (Polypus) LI093, RS016
Primula veris CU
Pushes (Pimples) LI093, RS016
Red-White LI086
Refuge for Thieves LI093
Ringworm DA005, LI093, RS016
Sandy Ground DA006, LI093
Ship's Breast LI158
Shoulders Thick DA006
Shoulders, Broad PA004
Sickly DA005
Silesia LI094, PA073
Silesia, Greater DA006
Smallpox DA005, LI093, RS016
Soul-Evil (Foul-Evil?)* DA005
Stable of Small Beasts LI093
Stachys officinalis CU
Stature, Middle PA004
Stetin = Stettin, Germany PA073
Strong DA005
Suevia (German Tribe) LI094
Sweden DA006, PA073
Syria DA006, LI094, PA073, PT143
Thunder & Rain AB264
Toothache DA005, LI093, PA004,
  RS016
Tropical AB231
Utrecht DA006, LI094
Vernal, Changeable AB230
Verona DA006, LI094, PA073
Vertigo PA004
Veterinarian LI450
Vicious DA005
Violent PA004
Visage, Long DA006
Whelks (Pimples) LI093, RS016
White-Red LI086
Witty LI538

Taurus

Abscess (Impostume) RS016

Asia Minor Sea Towns DA006, PA073

Asperula cynanchica DA006, PA005

Basement LI094

Beginning Wreathed DA006

Bestial DA006, PA004

Bologna LI094, PA073

Bononia [=Bologna] DA006, LI094, PA073

Brescia, Italy DA006, LI094, PA073

Brixia, Italy [=Brescia] DA006, LI094, PA073

Buttocks DA007

Campan[i]a, Italy DA006, LI094, PA073

Carolstade DA006, LI094

Cellars DA007

Cellars of Houses LI094

Childhood AB230

Chin, Area Under RS015

Cold & Dry PA004

Commanding DA006

Commodities Broker LI451

Complexion, Swarthy PA004

Cornfield DA007, LI094

Cyclades (Islands) DA006, PA073

Cyprus DA006, LI094, PA073

Cysts (Wens) RS016

Domestical PA004

Earthy PA004

End, Lean & Weak DA006

Eyes, Full PA004

Face, Big PA004

Feminine PA004

Fluxes of the Rheums DA006

Forehead, High DA006

Forehead, Large PA004

Franconia DA006, PA073

Fruitful DA006

Furious PA004

Gardening LI451

Gross DA006

Grounds, Bushy DA006

Grounds, Plain DA006

Guesna* DA007, PA073

Hair, Black DA007, PA004

Hand, Gross DA007

Hands, Short & Thick PA004

Heat Inclining to Moisture AB264

Helvetia DA006

Herbipolis DA006, LI094

Honest DA006

Houses, Low DA006

Houses with Cattle Implements DA006, LI094

Husbandry LI451

Impostumes DA006, RS016

Ireland DA006, LI094, PA073

Italy, Campania LI094, PA073

King's Evil DA006, RS016

Laborious LI538

Lacerne PA073

Lasivious (=Luxurious) DA006

Legs, Short DA007

Leipzig DA006, PA073, LI094

Lips, Thick PA004

Lorraine DA006, LI094, PA073

Low Houses LI094

Lucerne DA006

Luxurious (Lascivious) DA006

Mantua DA006, LI094, PA073

Media, Asia Minor PT141

Melancholy PA004

Mouth, Great DA006

Mouth, Large PA004

Nantes DA006, LI094, PA073

Neck DA006, LI245, RS015

Neck, Short & Fat DA006

Nocturnal PA004

Nostrils, Wide DA006

Novgorod, Russia DA007, LI094

Palermo LI094
Panorme, Sicily DA006
Panormus [=Palermo] LI094
Parma LI094, PA073
Parthia, Iran DA006, LI094, PA073
Pasture DA006
Pasture with No Houses Near LI094
Pastureland Not Sown AB230
Persia DA006, LI094, PA073, PT141
Perusium caput histria DA006
Places in Houses: Cellars PA005
Places in Houses: Low DA007, LI094, PA005
Places in Houses: Low Rooms PA005
Places in Houses: Vaults PA005
Places: Arable Land PA005
Places: Pastures PA005
Places: Plain Ground LI094, PA005
Poland, Greater LI094, PA073
Polonia the Great DA006
Posnania, Poland DA006, PA073
Quinsy (Tonsillitis) PA005, RS016
Religious DA006
Rhetia (Tyrol) DA006, PA073
Rheum & Defluction, Diseases PA005
Rheums, Fluxes RS016
Rooms, Low DA007, LI094, PA005
Russia DA006, LI094, PA073
Scrofula (King's evil) LI094, RS016
Sena LI094, PA073
Ship: Between Breast&Water LI158
Short DA006
Short, Full, Well-Set, Strong PA004
Shrub Land LI094

Sicilia PA073
Sickly DA006
Sore Throats DA006, LI094, RS016
South LI094
Southeast LI365
Squin[an]cy (Woodruffe) PA005, DA006
Stables DA006, LI094
Steppes LI094
Strong DA006
Sweden, Northern DA006, LI094
Switzerland LI094
Taranto, Italy [=Tarentum] DA006, PA073
Throat DA006, LI245, RS015
Throat Disease PA005
Throat, Fluxes of Rheum LI094
Tigure PA073
Tonsil Inflammation LI094
Tonsilitis (Quinzies) RS016
Tuberculosis LI094
Tumors, Benign Skin LI094
Tyrol PA073
Vernal, Changeable AB230
Wens (Pimples) DA006, RS016
Wheatfield LI094
Where Implements of Cattle are PA005
White-Yellow LI086
Women, Chaste DA006
Woodruffe (Squin[an]cy) DA006, PA005
Yellow White LI086
Zurich DA006

Gemini

Aches PA005
Aereal PA005
Arm Diseases LI094, RS017
Armenia   DA007, LI094, PA073, PT147
Arms DA007, LI245, RS015
Arms, Long DA007
Arms, Diseases of PA005
Astrologer LI451
Astronomer LI451
Bamberg DA007, LI094, PA074
Barbados PA073
Barns DA007, LI094
Barren DA007
Barren Signs LI089
Beginning, Lean & Weak DA007
Bicorporeal AB231
Blood, Corruption DA007, LI094, RS017
Blood, Putrefaction PA005
Body, Straight & Well-Set DA007
Body, Strong & Active PA005
Brabant DA007, LI094, PA073
Breast, Large (= Voice Large) DA007
Bruges (Brussels) LI094, PA074
Brussels, Belgium DA007, LI094, PA074
Cesena, Italy LI094
Chests DA007, LI094
Childhood AB230
Coffers DA007, LI094
Commanding DA007
Complexion, Sanguine PA005
Corduba, Spain DA007, LI094, PA074
Deceitful LI538
Diseases, Corruption PA005
Diseases, Dislocations PA005
Distempered Fancies LI094, RS017
Diurnal PA005

Egypt, Lower PA074, PT155
Ending, Gross & Strong DA007
England (part) DA007
England, West & Southwest LI094
Eyes, Bright & Piercing DA007
Face, a Little Swarthy PA005
Fair DA007
Fancy, Ingenious PA005
Feet, Long DA007
Fingers RS015
Flanders DA007, LI094, PA073
Hair, Dark DA007
Hair, Dark Brown PA005
Halls DA007
Halls in Houses LI094
Hand Diseases LI094, RS017
Hands DA007, LI245, RS015
Hands, Long DA007
Hasford DA007, LI094
High Places LI094
Hills DA007, LI094
Hircania (near Caspian Sea) DA007, PA073
Hot & Moist PA005
Houses, Walls DA007
Human DA007, PA005
Lombardy DA007, LI094
Lombardy (Part) PA073
London DA007, LI094, PA074
Lovain DA007, LI094, PA074
Lover of Arts LI538
Lover of Learning LI538
Masculine PA005
Mentz DA007
Moguntia[cum], Germany PA074
Mont LI094
Mountains DA007, LI094
Norimberge [= Nuremberg, Germany] DA007, LI094
Nuremberg, Germany DA007, LI094, PA074

Painters LI451
Places High DA007
Places in Houses: Dining Room PA005
Places in Houses: Living Room PA005
Places: Chests PA005
Places: Coffers PA005
Places: Halls or Dining Rooms PA005
Places: Hills PA005
Places: Mountainous Places PA005
Places: Storehouses PA005
Places: Wainscot PA005
Plastering in Houses DA007, LI094
Playrooms DA007, LI094
Ready Understanding PA005
Red-White LI086
Rent Collector LI451
Rooms, Wainscot LI094
Sardinia DA007, PA073
Ship's Stern LI158
Shoulder Bone DA007
Shoulder Diseases LI094, RS017
Shoulders DA007, LI245, RS015
Southwest LI365
Speech Good DA007
Stature, Proper PA005

Storehouses, Grain DA007, LI094
Surveyors LI451
Sweet DA007
Syrenaica* (Ukraine?) PA074
Tall DA007
Temperate AB264
Turin PA074
Valenciennes PA074
Vercellas, Italy PA074
Vernal, Changeable AB230
Voice, Large (Arc. Breast) DA007
Wainscot Rooms DA007
Walls of Houses LI094
Western LI094
Wetemberg [Wurttemberg, Germany] PA073
Wetenburgh [=Wurttemberg, Germany] DA007
White-Red LI086
Wind Diseases DA007
Wind in the Veins PA005
Windiness in the Veins LI094, RS017
Winds, Quiet Air AB230
Wit, Good DA007
Witty LI538
Wrists RS015
Wurttemberg, Ger. DA007, PA073

Cancer

Adder's Tongue CU
Aestival, Restful AB230
Africa PA074
Agrimonia eupatoria CU
Agrimony CU
Agrimony (Water) CU
Alder (Black) CU
Algiers LI095
Alnus nigra CU
Amsterdam LI095
Balm CU
Belly, Upper LI245

Bidens Tripartita CU
Bithynia, Asia Minor PA074
Body with Upper Parts Bigger DA008
Breast DA007, LI095, RS015
Breast Cancer LI095
Breast Defects PA005
Breast Disease RS017
Breast Pains LI245
Brooks DA008, LI095
Burgundy DA007, PA074
Cadiz LI095
Cancer LI245
Cancer (Disease) RS017

Carthage DA008, PA074, PT153
Cellars of Houses DA008, LI095
Children DA008
Cisterns LI095
Colchis DA008, PA074
Cold & Moist PA005
Commanding DA008
Complexion Pale & Sickly PA005
Constantinople, Turkey   DA008,
   LI095, PA074
Coughs DA008, PA005
Coughs, Rotten LI095, RS017
Creeping DA007
Daisy CU
Digestion LI095
Digestion, Poor LI245
Digestion, Weak RS017
Diseases, Ill Digestion PA005
Ditches with Rushes DA008, LI095
Drosera anglica CU
Dumb DA007
Face, Handsome PA005
Face, Round DA008, PA005
Feminine PA005
Frangula Alnus CU
Fruitful Signs LI089
Genoa DA008, LI095, PA074
Gorlick DA008, PA074
Granada DA007, PA074
Green-Russet LI086
Hair, Blackish DA008
Hair, Dark Brown PA005
Holland DA008, LI095, PA074
Humors, Dropsical RS017
Hyssop CU
Hyssopus officinalis CU
Impostumes of the Stomach RS017
Improvement; Warm (Weather)
   AB264
Leucanthemum vulgare CU
Lichen (Dog) CU

Lights RS015
Liver DA007, RS015
Lubeck DA008, PA074
Lucas DA008
Lungs LI245, RS015
Lungs, Defluctions of PA005
Magdeberg, Germany DA008, LI095,
   PA074
Marshy Ground DA008, LI095
Mediastinum RS015
Melissa officinalis CU
Milan, Italy DA008, LI095
Mucus [=Salt Phlegm]   DA008,
   LI095, RS017
Mute Signs LI089
Nipples DA007, LI095, RS015
Nocturnal PA005
North LI365
Northern LI095
Numidia, Africa PA074
Ophioglossum CU
Peltigera Canina CU
Phlegm, Salt [=Mucus]   DA008,
   LI095, RS017
Phlegmatic PA005
Pimples (Pushes) DA007
Pisa, Italy DA008, PA074
Places in Houses: Cellars PA006
Places: Brooks PA006
Places: Cisterns PA006
Places: Great & Navigable Riv.
   PA006
Places: Moist PA006
Places: Near Rivers DA008
Places: Sinks PA006
Places: Springs PA006
Places: the Sea PA006
Places: Wash Houses PA006
Places: Water-Courses PA006
Places: Wells Near Houses PA006
Pleura, Diseases of PA005

Pleurisy DA008
Praecordiacs (Over Heart) RS015
Prussia DA008, LI095, PA074
Ptisick (Tuberculosis) DA007, LI095, RS017
Pushes (Pimples) DA007
Ribs DA007, RS015
Ribs, Disease of PA005
Rivers DA008
Rivers, Great LI095
Rivers, Near LI095
Rushes LI095
Russet-Green LI086
Saint Lucas LI095
Scabbiness LI245
Scotland DA007, LI095, PA074
Sea Banks LI095
Sea, the DA008, LI095
Sedges LI095
Septum (Mediastinum) RS015
Ship's Bottom LI158
Sides RS015
South AB230
South Wind AB230
Spleen DA007, LI245, RS015
Springs DA008, LI095
St. Andrews, Scotland DA008, PA074
Stature, Middle PA005

Stature, Small DA008
Stomach LI095
Stomach Abscesses (Impostumes) LI095, RS017
Stomach Disorders RS017
Stomach, Cold RS017
Sundew CU
Swelling, Watery LI095
Trenches LI095
Tropical AB231
Tuberculosis (Ptisick) DA007, LI095, RS017
Tunis DA008, LI095, PA074
Unconstant LI538
Upper Part of Body, Big PA005
Variable LI538
Venice DA008, LI095, PA074
Vincentia* DA008, PA074
Visage, Round DA008
Wash-Houses DA008, LI095
Water, Sweet And Pure AB230
Waters, Navigable DA008, LI095
Wells LI095
Wittenberg, Germany LI095, PA074
Wittenburgh, Germany DA008
York DA008, LI095, PA074
Youth AB230
Zealand LI095, PA074

Leo

Abscess (Aposthumes) DA008
Active Person PA006
Aemilia DA008
Aestival, Restful AB230
Alps DA008, LI096, PA074
Aposthumes (Abscess) DA008
Apulia, Italy [=Puglia] DA008, LI096, PA074
Back DA008
Back, Between Shoulder & Precordiac RS015

Back Pain LI095, RS017
Backbone LI246
Barren DA008, PA006
Barren Signs LI089, PT325
Bay CU
Beginning, Gross & Strong DA008
Bestial DA008, PA006
Body, Large & Full PA006
Body, Large & Lusty DA009
Body, Well-set PA006
Bohemia DA008, LI096, PA074
Breast DA008

Breast, Lower LI246
Bristol DA009, LI096
Broken DA008
Castles DA008, LI095
Celandine (the Greater) CU
Chaldaea DA008, PA074, PT143
Chelidonium majus CU
Chimneys, Near DA008, LI095
Choleric PA006
Coblentz, Germany[=Confluente] DA009
Commanding DA008, PA006
Complexion a Little Swarthy PA006
Complexion Ruddy, Sanguine PA006
Confluence PA074
Confluentia LI096
Convulsions LI095, RS017
Courageous DA009
Crafty DA008
Cremisum PA074
Cremona, Cisalpine Gaul DA008, LI096, PA074
Crimisium = Crimisus, Sicily? DA009
Cruel LI538
Damascus DA008, LI096, PA074
Deserts DA008, LI095
Discrete LI538
Diurnal PA006
East LI095
Elm Tree PA074
End, Lean & Weak DA008
Euphrasia officinalis CU
Eyebright (Plant) CU
Eyes, Big PA006
Eyes, Large DA008
Eyes, Sore LI095, RS017
Fevers, Burning PA006
Fevers of the Blood DA008
Fevers, Pestilent DA008
Fevers, Violent LI095
Fevers, Violent Burning RS017

Fireplaces LI095
Fires in Minerals & Plants AB230
Forests DA008, LI095
Forts LI095
France PT135
Gall RS015
Gallia DA008
Gallia Togata PA074
Generosity DA009
Ghent PA074
Glass Maker LI451
Grave (of Manner) LI538
Green LI086
Hair Dark Flaxen PA006
Hair Much & Curling PA006
Hair Yellow PA006
Hair Yellow or Flaxen DA009
Head, Large DA008, PA006
Heart DA008, LI095, RS015
Heart Disease RS017
Heart Passion RS017
Heart Problems LI095
Heart Weakness RS017
Heat AB264
Hepatitis (Yellow Jaundice) DA008, LI095
Honest DA008
Hot & Dry PA006
Houses, Near Chimneys DA008
Hypericum perforatum CU
Ireful DA008
Italy DA008, LI096, PA074, PT135
Jaundice DA008, PA006
Jaundice, Yellow LI095, RS017
Kingly PA006
Lascivious (=Luxurious) DA008
Laurus nobilis CU
Lintz DA008, LI096, PA074, RS015
Luxurious (Lascivious) DA008
Manly Countenance PA006
Masculine PA006

Mastic (Pistacia lentiscus) PA074
Nipple, Left RS015
Northeast LI365
Orchina DA008
Palaces, King's LI095
Parks DA008, LI095
Pestilence LI095, RS017
Phoenicia DA008, PA074, PT143
Pimples, Facial DA008
Pistacia lentiscus PA074
Places in Houses: Chimneys PA006
Places in Houses: Where Fire is PA006
Places: Castles PA006
Places: Forests PA006
Places: Forts PA006
Places: Inaccessable LI095, DA008, PA006
Places: Kings Palaces PA006
Places: Steep & Rocky DA008, PA006
Places: Woods PA006
Plague LI095, RS017
Pleurisy LI095, RS017
Prague LI096, PA074
Pragus DA008
Puglia, Italy LI096, PA074
Pushes in the Face DA008
Quick Sighted PA006
Ravenna DA008, LI096, PA074
Red LI086
Rib Diseases RS017

Ribs DA008, LI095
Rocky Places LI095
Rome DA008, LI096, PA074
Sabina DA008
Ship's Top, Above Water LI158
Shoulder, Thick & Broad DA009
Sicily DA008, LI096, PA074, PT135
Side Disease RS017
Sides DA008
Sides LI095
Sober LI538
Sorrow DA008
South AB230
South Wind AB230
St. John's Wort CU
Stature Middle DA008
Stomach DA008, RS015
Strong DA008, PA006
Syracuse DA008, LI096, PA074
Trembling RS017
Tremblings & Qualms PA006
Turkey LI096
Turkey (Part) DA008, PA074
Ulmus Minor PA074
Valiant PA006
Veterinarian, Barnyard LI451
Vexations DA008
Voice Big & Great DA009
Women Religious & Chaste DA008
Woods DA008, LI095
Youth AB230

Virgo
Achaia (Hill Near Carystus) DA009, PA074
Aestival, Restful AB230
Africa LI096
Appearance, Well-composed PA006
Aretium, Etruria DA009
Arezzo, Italy [= Aretium] DA009

Arthesia PA074
Assyria DA009, PA074, PT141
Astrologer LI451, PT391
Athenian Territory LI096
Athens DA009
Babylonia DA009, PA074, PT141
Barley Stacks (Like Hay Stack) LI096
Barren DA009

Barren Signs LI089
Bars (Taverns, Malt-Houses) LI096
Basil, Switzerland   DA009, LI096,
  PA074
Belly DA009, RS015
Belly Disease RS017
Bellyaches DA009, LI246
Bicorporeal AB231
Black-Blue LI086
Blue-Black LI086
Body All Parts "Brevity" PA006
Body Subtle & Spare DA009
Bowel Obstructions LI096, RS017
Bowels DA009, LI096, RS015
Bratislava (Vratislava, Wratislave)
  DA009, PA075
Breathing (Exercise?) LI096
Brindisi (Brundusium)   DA009,
  LI096, PA074
Brundusium [=Brindisi]   DA009,
  LI096, PA074
Buttery LI096
Carinibia* DA009
Cheese Storage LI096
Cholic DA009, LI096
Closet LI096
Cold & Barren PA006
Comata, Part, Transalpine Gaul
  DA009
Commanding DA009
Complexion, Brown or Ruddy DA009
Corinth DA009, PA074
Covetous LI538
Crete DA009, PA074, PT139
Croatia DA009, LI096
Cruel DA009, LI538
Cuma, Asia Minor PA074
Dairy-House LI096
Discreet PA006
Diseases, Defects of Gastric PA007
Divination LI451

Domelike (Tholous) LI096
Erfurt, Germany DA009, PA075
Erphord = Erfurt, Germany PA075
Exercise? (=Breathing) LI096
Exphord = Erfurt, Germany DA009
Eyes, Large DA009
Face, More Oval than Round PA006
Fair DA009
Feminine PA006
Flatulence (Guts, Croaking) RS017
France, Southwest LI096
Gall RS015
Gallia DA009
Gallia Comata (Part) PA074
Gas (Intestinal) DA009
Given to All Manner of Learnin
  PA006
Grain Fields LI096
Granaries LI096
Great DA009
Greece DA009, PA074
Greece, Southern LI096
Gut, Diseases LI246
Guts RS015
Guts, Croaking RS017
Hair, Black or Dark DA009
Hair, Black or very Brown PA006
Hair, Much DA009
Hay-Ricks LI096
Heidelberg DA009, LI096, PA075
Hellas PT159
Hypochondria PA007
Jerusalem DA009, LI096, PA074
Lover of Arts LI538
Lover of Learning LI538
Lyons DA009, LI096, PA074
Malt-Houses LI096
Melancholy LI246, PA006
Mesenteries (Mesenterion) RS015
Meseriacks LI096
Meseriacks, Impediments in LI246

Mesopotamia DA009, LI096, PA074, PT141
Midriff RS015
Milan, Italy PA074
Moist DA009
Moisture & Thunder AB264
Nocturnal PA006
Novaria, Italy [=Milan] PA074
Obstruction of Meseriacks RS017
Obstructions of the Gut DA009
Ocymum basilicum LI096, PA074
Papia, Italy DA009, PA074
Paris DA009, LI096, PA074
Person, Tall & Slender PA006
Places in Houses: Closet/Books PA007
Places with Books LI096
Places: Corn-Fields PA007
Places: Dairy PA007
Places: Study Where Books are PA007
Places: Where Grain is Stored PA007
Plants with No Seeds/Berries AB230
Politician LI451
Printer LI451
Proportion Good or Equal DA009
Rheine, Germany [=Rhene] DA009
Rhene (Part) [=Rheine, Ger.] DA009
Rhine River (Part) PA074
Rhodes DA009, LI096, PA074
School Teacher LI451
Secretaries LI451
Secretion, Excess LI246

Sharp DA009
Ship's Belly LI158
Sigina* DA009
Silesia, Lower DA009, PA074
Small Trees AB230
South AB230
South Wind AB230
Southern LI096
Southwest LI365
Spiteful LI538
Spleen Obstructions PA007
Stomach, Bottom RS015
Stones DA009
Stones, Infirmities RS017
Studious PA006
Study LI096
Taverns (Malt-Houses) LI096
Tholous (Domelike) LI096
Toulouse, France DA009, PA074
Triticum LI096
Ulcers in the Bowels DA009
Vratislavia = Bratislava PA075
War-Mongers LI538
Well-Spoken PA006
Wheat LI096
Where Writings are Kept PA007
Wind-Cholic LI246, RS017
Wit, Wholly for Its Own End DA009
Witty PA006
Worms LI096, RS017
Wratislave = Bratislava DA009
Youth AB230

Libra

Abdmomen, Inferior Parts DA010
Adult Life AB231
Age Spots & Pimples (Face) PA007
Air: Which Causes Tree Growth AB230
Alsace DA010, LI097, PA075

Antwerp DA010, PA075
Arabia PT157
Argentina DA010, PA075
Arles LI097, PA075
Austria DA010, PA075
Austria, Higher LI097
Autumnal AB231

Back Pain DA010
Back, Great Heats LI246
Back, Small of the DA010, RS015
Back, Weakness LI096, RS017
Backbone Pain DA010
Bactriana, Persian Asia DA010, PA075
Barn, Straggling LI096
Belly, Inferior Parts DA010
Belly, Part RS015
Black LI086
Bladder DA010, RS015
Bladder Abscesses LI096, RS017
Bladder Ulcers RS017
Blood Corruption DA010, LI096, RS017
Blood Fluxes DA010
Body, Delicate & Straight DA010
Body, Well-framed DA010
Body, Well-proportioned DA010
Buttocks DA010, RS015
Buttocks, Diseases LI246
Cajeta, Italy [=Latium] DA010, PA075
Caspia DA010, PA075
Chamber Within a Chamber LI096
Chambers LI096
Changeable AB231
Cheeks, Cherry DA010
Cheerful DA010
Children, Few DA010
Conceited LI538
Condemner of Arts LI538
Coopers' Places LI096
Crafty LI538
Crimson, Dark LI086
Dauphine, France DA010, PA075
Delphinate = Dauphine, France DA010, PA075
Diurnal PA007
Ejection DA010

Eryngium maritimum CU
Eryngo CU
Ethiopia PT157
Ethiopia [=Trogloditica[m]] DA010, PA075
Etruria, Italy PA075
Face, Round DA010
Face, Well-Favored DA010
Fair DA010
Fel[d]kirth, Austria DA010
Frankfurt LI097
Frankfurt Am Main DA010, PA075
Freiburg DA010
Freising, Germany [=Frisinga] PA075
Fribourg LI097
Friesing, Germany [=Frisinge] DA010
Frising[a/e] = Freising, Germany DA010, PA075
Gall-Stones (?) LI246
Garrets LI096
Gravelly Fields LI096
Greece, Near Thebes LI097
Groin RS015
Gundgavia, Hungary DA010
Hair, Light Brown DA010
Hair, Yellowish Inclining Flax PA007
Hamms RS015
Haunches DA010, LI096
Heilbronn, Germany DA010, PA075
Hillsides LI096
Hostage Negotiator LI451
Hot & Moist PA007
Houses, Upper Rooms LI096
Hul, Sweden PA075
Human DA010, PA007
Hunting Ground LI096
Impostumes RS017
Inconstant LI538
Jamaica PA075
Joints LI246

Kidney Abscesses LI096, RS017
Kidney Disease PA007, RS017
Kidney Gravel DA010
Kidney Heat (Fever) DA010, PA007
Kidney Stones LI246, RS017
Kidney Ulcers PA007, RS017
Kidneys LI096, RS015
Landa PA075
Landeshure PA075
Landshaett, Germany [Landshut]
    DA010
Landshut, Germany[=Landshaett]
    DA010
Laon, France [=Laudam=Laudunum]
    DA010
Laudam, France [=Laon=Laudunum]
    DA010
Lean rather than Fat PA007
Lisbon, Portugal   DA010, LI097,
    PA075
Liver RS015
Livonia, Latvia/Estonia   DA010,
    LI097, PA075
Loin Disease RS017
Loin Heats RS017
Loins DA010, LI096, RS015
Masculine PA007
Meridional DA010
Mosbach, Germany PA075
Mosphachium (City)* DA010
Mountaintops LI096
Musicians LI451
Navel DA010, RS015
Obedient DA010
Orators LI451
Orsim (Place)* DA010
Out-House LI096
Ovarian Ulcers PA007
Pedagogue LI451
Piacenza,   Cis-Alpine   Gaul
    [=Placentia] DA010

Placenta LI097, PA075
Places in Houses: Chambers PA007
Places in Houses: Garrets PA007
Places in Houses: Turrets PA007
Places in Houses: Upper Rooms
    PA007
Places: Out - Lone Houses PA007
Places: Where Hawking/Hunting
    PA007
Places: Where Wood is Cut LI096
Places: Where Wood was Cut Re-
    cently PA007
Places: Windmills PA007
Poet LI451
Room Within a Room LI096
Round, Lovely Beautiful Face PA007
Ruddy Sanguine Complexion./Youth
    PA007
Sabaud[i]a, Italy DA010
Sandy Fields LI096
Sanguine PA007
Savoy LI097
Saw-Pit LI096
Sezes, Italy [=Sezze] DA010
Sezze, Italy [=Sezes] DA010
Ship: Between Water Lines LI158
Sight, Darkness of DA010
Slender DA010
Spires LI097, PA075
Sp[e]iers, Germany DA010
Stones, Kidney LI096
Stones, Retention of (Disease) PA007
Subaudia (Country?)* PA075
Suestam = Suessa? = Sessa DA010
Surfeits by Alcohol LI246
Surfeits by Drinking or Eating LI246
Tall, Straight Body PA007
Tallness (Inclination Towards)
    DA010
Tawny LI086
Thebaida, Egypt [=Thebes] DA010

Thebes PA075
Thebes [=Thebaida] DA010
Thighs DA010, LI246
Thuscia, Italy [=Etruria] DA010, PA075
Trogloditica (Ethiopia) DA010
Tropical AB231
Upstairs LI096
Urine Retention DA010, PA007
Vienna, Austria DA010, LI097,

PA075
Visage Round DA010
Visage Well-Favored DA010
Well-Proportioned Body PA007
Well-Spoken DA010
West AB231, LI365
West Wind AB231
Western LI096, PA007
Wimpina (City)* DA010
Windmills, Nearby LI096

Scorpio
Adult Life AB231
Alchstade (Place)* DA011
Algiers DA011, PA075
Anus LI246
Aquilegia, Italy [=Aquileia] DA011
Aquileia, Italy DA011, PA075
Arrogant LI538
Ass (Anatomical) DA010, LI246
Astrologer PT391
Autumnal AB231
Barbary Coast LI097
Barren Signs PT325
Basil CU
Bavaria PA075
Bavaria, Northern LI097
Beginning, Lean & Weak DA011
Bladder DA010, LI097, RS015
Bladder Stones DA011, LI246, PA008
Body, Bow-Legged PA008
Body, Fat (Somewhat) PA008
Body, Full, Well-Set DA011
Body, Hairy PA008
Body Proportions, Diverse DA011
Bow-Legged PA008
Brasier (Profession) LI451
Brewer LI451
Brown LI086

Camerino, Italy [=Camerinum] DA011
Canker DA011
Cappadocia, Asia Minor PA075
Catalonia LI097, PA075
Changeable AB231
Comagena, Syrian Province PA075
Complexion, Dark & Sallow DA011
Complexion, Swarthy PA008
Covetous LI538
Deceitful DA011
Emerods (=Hemorrhoids) DA011
End, Strong & Gross DA011
Eye Impediments DA011
Face, Broad PA008
Feminine PA007
Fesse, Morocco [=Fez] PA075
Fez, Morocco [Fesse] LI097, PA075
Fistulas DA011, LI097, PA008, RS018
Frankfurt upon Oder DA011, LI097, PA075
Frejus, France [=Forum Julium] DA011, LI097, PA075
Fruitful Signs DA011, LI089
Gardens DA011, LI097
Gaunt LI097
Gaunt at Somme (France) DA011
Genital Diseases PA008, RS018

Genital Stones LI097, RS018
Genitals DA010, LI097, RS015
Gethulia PA075
Gonorrhea LI097, RS018
Gravel RS018
Groin LI246
Hair, Much & Curling PA008
Hair, Sad DA011
Hair, Sad, Brown Black PA008
Hemorrhoids DA011, RS018
Hernias DA011
Houses Near Muddy/Marshy Groun
    DA011
Houses Near Water DA011
Houses, Ruined DA011, LI097
Idumea = Livonia, Estonia PA075
Impudent LI538
Ireful DA011
Kidney Stones DA010
Kitchen DA011, LI097
Lakes, Stinking DA011, LI097
Larder DA011, LI097
Lewdness (Priapism) RS018
Mauritania PA075
Messina LI097, PA075
Monachium [Monaco] DA011,
    PA075
Monaco [Monachium] DA011,
    PA075
Muddy Ground LI097
Mute Signs LI089
Neck Short DA011, PA008
Nocturnal PA007
North LI097
Northeast LI365
Norway PA075
Norway, Woods LI097
Obedient DA011
Ocymum Basilicum CU
Orchards DA011, LI097
Ovaries, Running of PA008

Ovum S2-56
Penile Erection, Pathological LI097
Penis RS015
Pharmacists LI451
Phlegmatic PA007
Physicians LI451
Piles (Disease) LI097
Pistoria, Italy [=Pistorium] DA011,
    PA075
Pistorium [=Pistoria, Italy] DA011,
    PA075
Places in Houses: Kitchen PA008
Places in Houses: Larder PA008
Places in Houses: Sinks PA008
Places in Houses: Wash-House
    PA008
Places: Gardens PA008
Places: Moorish Grounds PA008
Places: Orchards PA008
Places: Quagmires PA008
Places: Ruinous Houses Nr H20
    PA008
Places: Stinking Lakes PA008
Pox PA008
Priapsim RS018
Privy Parts DA010, LI246
Privy Parts, Diseases of PA008
Pyles in the Ars RS018
Quagmires DA011, LI097
Rome LI097, PA075
Rotting Places LI097
Ruined Houses LI097
Ruptures DA011, LI097, RS018
Seed, Reproductive S2-56
Ship: Crew's Quarters LI158
Sickly DA011
Sinks DA011, LI097
Sperm S2-56
Stature, Somewhat Short DA011
Stones RS015
Strong DA011

Strong, Able-bodied PA008
Surgeons LI451
Syphilis DA010
Tarvisium, Italy [=Treviso] DA011
Thoughts Reserved DA011
Thunder Lightning AB264
Trabezond [=Trebizond] DA011
Trapezant [=Trebizond] PA075
Trebozond, Turkey (=Trabez[o/a]n[d/t])] DA011, PA075
Treviso, Italy [=Tarvisium] DA011
Turvisium PA075
Urbine [=Urbino] LI097
Urbinium [=Urbino] PA075
Urbino [=Urbine] DA011, PA075
Urination, Painful LI246

Valencia, Spain DA011
Valentia, Rome LI097, PA075
Vicious DA011
Vienna (France) PA075
Vienna, Austria DA011, LI097
Vineyards DA011, LI097
Vintners LI451
Violent PA007
Wash-Houses DA011
Wash-Houses Western LI097
Water, Turbid AB230
Watery PA007
West AB231
West Wind AB231
Womb RS015
Womb Defects LI097, RS018

Sagittarius

Adult Life AB231
Agrippina [=Cologne, Germany] DA011, PA075
Altica (Attica?), Greece DA011
Amputation DA011
Arabia DA011, PT145
Arabia Foelix PA075
Attica, Greece? (=Altica) DA011
Autumnal AB231
Avenion PA075
Avignon DA011
Back, Lower RS015
Bakers LI451
Balding by Forty DA012
Bicorporeal AB231, PA008
Bitter DA011
Blood, Excess DA011
Blood, Heated LI097, RS018
Body, Straight DA012
Body, Strong, Well-Proportioned, Tall PA008
Brown Hair PA008
Buda, Hungary LI098, PA075

Budapest DA012
Burns RS018
Buttocks LI097, RS015
Buttocks Hurts RS018
Cattle Broker LI451
Celtica [Gaul] PA075
Changeable AB231
Chemists LI451
Children, Few & Weak DA011
Choleric PA008
Churchman LI451
Cologne, Germany (Agrippina) DA011, PA075
Colonia, Italy DA011, PA075
Complexion, Sanguine PA008
Cooks LI451
Crafty DA011
Dalmatia, Yugoslavia DA011, LI098, PA075
Diurnal PA008
East LI097
Easterly PA008
Eye Impediments (15-18 Degree) DA011

Face, Evil DA012
Falls from Animals DA011
Falls from Horses LI097, RS018
Falls from Horses & the Like PA008
Fearless LI538
Fevers, Hot DA011
Fevers, Pestilential LI097, RS018
Fiery PA008
Fire from the Heart AB230
Fistulas DA011, LI246, PA008, RS018
Gascovia (Basque Region) DA012
Green LI086
Grounds, Rising Above DA012
Hair, Brown DA012
Hamms RS015
Handsome, Comely Countenance PA008
Haunches DA011
High Ground LI098
Hills DA012, LI098
Hips LI246, RS015
Horse Injuries RS018
Horses, Injuries from LI097
Hot & Dry PA008
House for Four-Footed Beasts LI098
Houses, Near the Fire DA012
Houses, Upper Rooms DA012
Houses, Upper Rooms Near Fire LI098
Human DA011
Hungary DA011, LI098, PA075
Ingenious DA011
Injury from 4-Footed Animals RS018
Itch LI246
Judenburg DA012
Long Visage PA008
Masculine PA008
Meissen, Germany DA011, PA075
Misnia = Meissen, Germany DA011, PA075

Modena, Cis-Alpine Gaul [=Mutina] DA011, PA075
Moravia, Czechoslovakia DA011, LI098, PA075
Narbonne DA011, LI098, PA075
Obedient DA011
Os Sacrum RS015
Places in Houses: Upper Rooms PA008
Places in Houses: Upstairs near Fire PA008
Places: Stables PA008
Places: Upland, Hilly Grounds PA008
Rottenburg, Germany DA012
Sciatica LI246, PA008
Sclavonia, Around Bulgaria DA011
Ship's Crew LI158
Slavonia, Croatia LI098, PA075
Southeast LI365
Spain DA011, LI098, PA075, PT135
Sports Injuries LI097, RS018
Stable of Great Horses LI097
Stables DA011
Stargard[e]* LI098, PA075
Stuttgart DA012
Thigh Hurts RS018
Thighs DA011, LI097, RS015
Thirroma (Place)* DA011
Toledo, Spain DA011, LI098, PA075
Valiant LI538
Visage Evil DA012
Volateras (Volterra, Italy) DA011, PA075
Volterra, Italy [=Voleteras] DA011, PA075
Warhorses Defects LI097
West AB231
West Wind AB231
Windy AB264
Yellow LI086

Capricorn

Albania DA012, LI098, PA076
Amaryllis, African (Clivia) PA076
Angusta PA076
Ariana, Persia DA012
Augsburg, Germany DA012
Augusta Vindelicorum[Augsburg]
  DA012
Barren Fields LI098
Barren Signs PT325
Beard, Thin PA008
Berga, Spain DA012
Berges PA076
Bestial DA012
Black LI086
Body, Disproportioned DA013
Body, Dry & Lean DA012
Body, Small DA012
Body, Spare, Lean & Slender PA008
Bosnia DA012
Brandenburg DA012, LI098, PA076
Broken DA012
Brown, Swarthy LI086
Bulgaria DA012, LI098, PA076
Bushy Places LI098
Buttocks (Hamms) RS015
Cardinal PA008
Children, Few DA012
Cleves LI098
Clivia (African Amaryllis) PA076
Cold & Dry PA008
Comfrey CU
Constance, Germany DA012, PA076
Cow-House LI098
Croatia (Illyris) PA076
Crooked DA012
Cruel DA012
Dark DA012
Deafness (Surdity) DA012
Derthona, Italy [=Tortona] DA012
Domestical DA012

Dunghills LI098
Face, Thin & Lean DA012
Faenza, Italy [=Faventia] DA012
Fairness Mean DA012
Fallow Ground LI098
Farmer LI451
Faventia, Italy [=Faenza] DA012
Feminine PA008
Fervence (City)* PA076
Fracture of Knees RS018
Gaunt at Somme, France DA012
Gedrosia, Persia DA012
Greece (part) DA012, PA076
Hair, Black DA012, PA008
Hair, Much DA012
Hair, Wan & Obscure DA012
Hamms RS015
Hassia (Country)* DA012, LI098,
  PA076
Hibernal AB231
Houses, Dark Places LI098
Houses, Low Areas LI098
Houses, Near the Ground LI098
Illyris, Croatia/Bosnia DA012,
  PA076
India DA012, PA076, PT141
Itch LI098, RS018
Itch About the Knee LI246
Jewellers LI451
Juliacum, Germany [=Juliers]
  DA012, PA076
Juliers, Germany [=Juliacum]
  DA012, PA076
Knee Disease PA009, RS018
Knee Fractures DA012, LI098,
  PA009
Knee Fractures & Strains RS018
Knee Injuries LI098
Knee Sprains PA009
Knee Strains DA012
Knees DA012, LI098, RS015

Lascivious (=Luxurious) DA012
Lecherous LI538
Legs, Upper Part RS015
Leprosy DA012, LI098, RS018
Lithuania DA012, PA076
Long & Narrow Chin PA008
Long Face PA008
Luxurious (Lascivious) DA012
Macedonia DA012, LI098, PA076, PT139
Malaria (Quartane Agues) DA012
March, France [=Marchia] DA012
Marchia, France [=March] DA012
Mazovia, Poland (Province) PA076
Mechlin, Belgium DA012, LI098, PA076
Melancholy DA012, PA008
Moveable PA008
Muscovia DA012
Neck, Long DA013
Nocturnal PA008
Nonmonogamous LI538
North AB231
North Wind AB231
Nose, Pretty, Short, Round PA008
Obedient DA012
Old Age AB231
Orc[h]ades [=Orkney Islands] DA012, LI098, PA076
Orkney Islands [=Orc[h]ades] DA012, LI098, PA076
Ox-house LI098
Oxford DA012, LI098, PA076
Peaceful AB231
Philanderer LI538
Pimples, Facial DA012
Places for Tools of Husbandry PA009
Places in Houses: Near Ground PA009
Places in Houses: Near Threshold PA009

Places: Barren PA009
Places: Cow-Houses PA009
Places Dark, Near Ground DA013
Places: Fallow Ground PA009
Places: Threshold DA013
Places: with Husbandry Tools DA013
Places: with Old Wood DA013
Portland, England PA076
Pushes in the Face DA012
Quartane Agues (Malaria) DA012
Russet LI086
Saxony DA012, PA076
Saxony, Southwest LI098
Scab DA012, LI098, PA009, RS018
Sciatica DA012
Scurfs (Disease) LI246
Sharp DA012
Sheep Feeding Grounds LI098
Sheep Pens LI098
Ship's Ends LI158
Ship's Storehouse LI098
Sickly DA012
Sight, Dim & Obscure DA012
South LI365
Southern LI098, PA008
Sown Crops AB230
Speech Loss DA012
Stature Indifferent PA008
Stiria, Austria [=Styria] DA012, LI098, PA076
Strains of the Knees RS018
Styria, Austria [=Stiria] DA012, LI098, PA076
Surdity (Deafness) DA012
Symphytum officinale CU
Thighs, Back Part LI246
Thorny Places LI098
Thrace [=Thravia] LI098, PA076, PT139
Thracia, Balkans DA012
Thravia [=Thrace] PA076

Thuringia, Germany DA012, PA076
Tool Shed LI098
Tortona, Italy [=Derthona] DA012
Trees, Large & Tall AB230
Tropical AB231
Very Wet AB264
Veterinarian LI451
Veterinarian, Barnyard LI451
Vicious DA012

Vilna, Lithuania [=Vilnius] DA012
Vilnius, Lithuania [=Vilna] DA012, PA076
Vindell, England [=Portland] PA076
Visage, Thin & Lean DA012
West Indies LI098
Wood-Working Place LI098
Wool Merchant LI451

Aquarius
Affable LI538
Amazonia DA013, PA076
Ankles DA013, LI098
Arabia LI099
Arabian Desert DA013, PA076
Barren Signs PT325
Barvaria (Part) DA013
Bavaria, West & South LI099
Blue LI086
Body, Handsome DA013
Body, Well-shaped DA013
Breme LI099, PA076
Bremen, Germany DA013
Calves of Legs LI246
Children, Few DA013
Cold & Wet AB264
Complexion, Sanguine PA009
Conduit Head: Places Near DA013
Constant in Religion LI538
Cramps PA009, RS018
Croatia LI099
Diurnal PA009
Eaves of Houses DA013
Ethiopia DA013
Face, Fair DA013
Face, Oval & Clear PA009
Fair DA013
Fierce (Breme) LI099, PA076
Gout PA009
Hair, Bright & Fair PA009

Hair, Whitish Bright DA013
Hamburg DA013, LI099, PA076
Hibernal AB231
Hilly Places DA013, LI099
Hisarum* PA076
Honest DA013
Hot & Moist PA009
Houses, Eaves DA013, LI099
Houses, Roof DA013, LI099
Houses, Upper Rooms DA013, LI099
Human DA013, LI538, PA009
Ingolstadt, Germany DA013, LI099, PA076
Iran, Middle [=Sogdiana] PA076
Lameness DA013
Leg Injuries RS018
Leg Tumors DA013
Legs DA013, LI098
Legs, Diseases of PA009
Masculine PA009
Media, Asia Minor DA013, LI099, PA076
Merchants LI451
Montsferat DA013, LI099, PA076
Mosel DA013, PA076
Muscovia DA013, LI099, PA076
North AB231
North Wind AB231
Northwest LI365
Obedient DA013
Old Age AB231

Oxiana, Sarmatia DA013
Peaceful AB231
Piedmont DA013, LI099, PA076
Pisa, Italy DA013
Pisaurun, Italy [=Pesaro] LI099
Places in Houses: About Window PA009
Places in Houses: Eaves PA009
Places in Houses: Roofs PA009
Places: Hilly DA013
Places: Hilly & Uneven PA009
Places: Near Conduit Head DA013
Places: Near Small Springs DA013
Places: New Dug LI099
Places: Stone Quarries DA013, PA009
Places: Uneven Ground DA013, LI099
Places: Where Minerals are PA009
Quarries, Stone DA013, LI099
Rational DA013
Religious DA013
Roof of House DA013
Sailors LI451
Saltzburg, Austria DA013
Samaria PA076
Sanguine PA009
Sarmatia, Russia-Poland DA013
Shanks RS015
Shin-Bone LI246, RS015
Ship Carpenter LI451
Ship Painter LI451
Ship Trimmer LI451

Ship's Captain LI158
Ship's Master LI451
Sober Speech LI538
Sogdiana, Middle Iran DA013, PA076
Spring, Small: Places Near DA013
Springs: Land Nearby LI099
Stature Middle DA013
Stature Not Tall PA009
Stature Strong, Well Composed PA009
Stone Quarries DA013
Strong DA013
Sweden, Southern DA013
Sweet DA013
Tartar, Russia DA013, LI099
Tartaria PA076
Trent DA013, LI099, PA076
Valachia, Poland [=Walachia] DA013, LI099
Varicose Veins PA009
Vein, Coagulation LI099
Vineyards DA013, LI099
Visage, Fair DA013
Visage, Long PA009
Walachia, Poland [=Valachia] DA013, LI099
Western LI098, PA009
Westphalia DA013, LI099, PA076
Winds, Destructive Storms AB230
Winds, Melancholy LI099, RS018
Women Honest & Chaste DA013

Pisces

Aches PA010
Alder (Common) CU
Alexandria, Egypt DA014, LI099, PA076
Alnus glutinosa CU
Ankle-Bone LI246, RS015

Bicorporeal AB231
Body, Diversely Proportioned DA014
Body, Fleshy PA009
Body, Ill-Composed DA014
Body, Ill-Composed, Undecent PA009
Body, Sometimes Dropsical PA009

Boils [=Botch] DA014, LI099, RS018
Botches (Core of a Boil) DA014
Breaking Out LI099
Brewer LI451
Broken a Bit DA014
Calabria, Italy DA014, LI099, PA076
Colchis [=Phasiana] DA014
Cold & Moist PA009
Cold & Wet AB264
Colds LI099
Complexion, Pale DA014, PA009
Compostella, Italy DA014, LI099, PA076
Coughs DA014
Crooked DA014
Dishonest LI538
Dumb DA014
Egypt, Higher DA014, PA076
Egypt, Northern LI099
Face, Good & Large DA014
Face, Large PA009
Fat DA014
Feet DA014, LI099, RS015
Feet, Swelling LI246
Feminine PA009
Fishponds DA014, LI099
Foot Botches (boils) RS018
Foot Breaking Out RS018
Foot Disease LI099, RS018
Foot Itch RS018
Foot Scabs RS018
Footaches RS018
Foul DA014
Fraudulent LI538
Fruitful Signs DA014, LI089
Galatia, Asia Minor DA014, PA076
Gamesters (Syn. Prostitute) LI451
Garamantes, Africa DA014, PA076
Gout DA014, LI099, PA010
Grounds, Full of Water DA014, LI099

Grounds with Many Springs DA014, LI099
Grounds with Waterfowl DA014, LI099
Heels DA014
Hermitages LI099
Hibernal AB231
Hispalis (Seville, Spain) DA014, PA076
Houses Near Water DA014, LI099
Houses, Near Well or Pump DA014
Houses, Standing Water DA014
Houses, Surrounding Moats DA014
Hypocrite LI538
Instep RS015
Itch DA014, LI099
Jester LI451
Lameness LI099, PA010, RS018
Lameness of the Foot DA014
Lascivious (=Luxurious) DA014
Limbs, Wanting DA014
Little Broken DA014
Luxurious (Lascivious) DA014
Lydia, Asia Minor DA014, PA076
Moats LI099
Mucus [=Salt Phlegm] DA014, LI099, RS018
Mute Signs LI089
Nasamonia, Libya DA014
Nocturnal PA009
Normandy, France DA014, LI099, PA076
North AB231
North Wind AB231
Northern LI099
Northwest LI365
Obedient DA014
Old Age AB231
Palsy DA014
Pamphilia, S. Asia Minor DA014, PA076

Peaceful AB231
Person Low in Stature PA009
Phasania [=Phasiana=Colchis] DA014
Phlegm, Salt [=Mucus] DA014, LI099, RS018
Phlegmatic PA009
Places in Houses: Cisterns PA010
Places in Houses: Standing Water PA010
Places in Houses: Wells PA010
Places: Caves PA010
Places: Fish-Ponds PA010
Places: Moats Around Houses PA010
Places: Moist Moorish Grounds PA010
Places: Water Mills PA010
Portugal DA014, LI099
Posture, Not very Straight DA014
Posture, Stooping in Shoulders PA009
Prostitutes (=Gamesters) LI451
Pumps LI099
Ratisbon[e], Germany DA014, LI099, PA076

Rheims, France DA014, LI099, PA076
Rivers, Full of Fish DA014, LI099
Salt DA014
Scabs DA014, LI099
Seville, Spain PA076
Ship's Oars LI158
Shoulders, Thick DA014
Sickly DA014
Silicy DA014, PA076
Singer LI451
Stammering LI538
Stature, Short DA014
Toes RS015
Ulcers DA014, LI099, RS018
Vicious DA014
Visage, Good Large DA014
Water, Standing LI099
Water, Stinking, Alkaline AB230
Watermills DA014, LI099
Wells LI099
White, Glistening LI086
Worms DA014, LI099, Worms PA076

House Rulerships

* Indicates that the meaning of a word is unknown.

First House

Absent Party, Dead or Alive DA090, GA242, LI151
Accidents LI130
Advancement in Rank AB276
Age of Life Best for Querent LI134
Alopecia RS100
Asking Horary Questions AB276
Baldness (Alopecia) RS100
Blue AB277
Body Shape PA041
Brain Distempers RS100
Breath, Bad LI245
Buyer, of Property LI220
Changes in Querent's Life GA242, LI134
Cheeks RS015
Chin RS015
Color LI050
Color of Skin GA045
Common People LI050
Common People (Eclipses) PA041
Common People (Mundane) PA041
Complexion GA045, LI050, PA041
Deformity of Saturn Here PA041
Ear Diseases RS100
Ears LI245, RS015
East LI364
Education AB275
Epilepsy RS100
Eye Pains RS100
Eye Problems RS100
Eyebrows RS015
Eyes LI245, RS015
Face LI050, RS015
Form LI050
Geographical Desirability GA242, LI132
Gray-colored Cloths LI051
Head AB277, LI050, RS015
Head Pains RS100
Headache RS100
Health LI129
Horary, Asking Questions AB276
Hunting LI365
Jaw Pains RS100
Kingdom, State of PA041
Length of Life (Nativities) AB275,
Length of Life (Querent) GA242, LI129, PA062
Life AB275, LI050, PA041
Life of the Native GA045
Life, Best Part GA242, LI134
Life, Quality of GA242, LI135
Marrow, Spinal Decay RS100
Mind Qualities GA045
Mouth, Sore LI245
Native Land AB275
Nerve Weakness RS100
Nobility AB276
Nose RS015
Nose Diseases RS100
Party at Home LI147
Patient S2-41
Physicians (C.F. Zael) S2-40
Plaintiff LI403

Public Matters, Important AB276
Querent LI147
Querent's Life PA041
Rank, Advancement in AB276
Removal from 1 House->Another
  LI212
Renter, of Land or House LI208
Sailors & Passengers (Lord of) PA062
Shape LI050
Ship LI157
Ship at Sea PA062
Ship at Sea, Safety or Peril GA242,
  LI157, PA062
Ship's Cargo PA062
Ship's Crew LI157
Ship's Goods LI157
Skin Color GA045

Soul AB275
Spells AB276
State of the Union LI050
Stature LI050, PA041
Stature of Native GA045
Temperature of the Body GA045
Tenants LI206
Tooth Pains RS100
Visage GA045
Wealth by Work LI557
Where Querent May Best Live LI132
Whether Another Shall be at Home
  GA242, LI147
White LI051, PA041
Witchcraft AB276
Wound in Face If Mars Here PA041

Second House

Allies & Support of Kingdom PA042
Allies of a Country LI052
Ammunition of a Country LI052
Ammunition of a Kingdom PA042
Assistants AB275
Borrowing AB276
Chin, Area Under RS015
Contention PA042
Counting Friends AB276
Debt LI378
Disaster to Eyes if Ill Luck AB275
Duels: Querent's Second LI051
East Northeast LI364
Emir, Mandate of AB276
Enemy's Death (in War) LI368
Estate GA047
Examining the Querent AB276
Fortune GA047
Friends, Counting of AB276
Gain PA042
Goods, Moveable GA047
Green AB277, LI052, PA042

Household Goods LI557
Household Requisites AB275
Lawsuits: Querent's Assistants LI051
Lawsuits: Querent's Friends LI051
Lending AB276
Livelihood AB275
Loans: Shall Querent Obtain GA251,
  LI173
Loss or Damage LI051
Loss or Damage in Lawsuits PA042
Mandate of Emir AB276
Means to Attain Riches LI168
Money Lent LI051, PA042
Moveable Goods LI051, PA042
Neck AB277, GA047, LI052, PA042,
  RS015
Nutriment AB275
Poverty LI051, PA042
Poverty or Wealth of Nation LI051
Profession of Children AB275
Profit or Gain LI051
Profit or Loss LI170
Quarrels PA042

Querent's Friends (Eclipses) PA042
Querent's Friends (Mundane) PA042
Querent's Wealth PA042
Rich or Poor GA249, LI167, PA062
Riches GA047
Riches: Means to Attain GA250, LI168
Riches: When in Life Attained GA250, LI171
Scrofula LI245, RS100
Shoulders LI052
Squinancy (Woodruffe) RS100

Substance, Querent's LI139
Suckling AB275
Throat LI245
Throat Disease RS100
Tuberculosis LI245
Wages Due (Shall Querent Receive?) GA252, LI170
Wealth LI051, PA042
Whether Querent Become Rich LI167
Winds, When they Blow AB276
Woodruffe (Squinancy) RS100

Third House
Abscess, Opening of AB276
Absent Sibling: Status GA254, LI189, PA063
Advice LI194
Advice: Good or Evil? GA256, LI192
Arms AB277, GA048, LI052, PA042, RS015
Brothers AB275, GA048, LI052, PA042
Cautery AB276
Commentaries AB276
Cousins LI052
Dismissal from Office AB276
Epistles GA048, LI052
Expertness in Religious Law AB275
Fetters AB276
Fingers LI052, RS015
Fortresses AB276
Friends AB275
Hands AB277, LI052, PA042, RS015
Hidden Things AB276
Hiding Places, Thieves AB276
Hospitality LI557
Inland Journeys LI052
Intelligence AB275
Jewels AB275
Journey, Short: How Good? GA256, LI195, PA063
Journeys by Water AB276
Journeys, Small & Inland GA048, PA042
Kindred GA048, LI052, PA042
Knowledge AB275
Lancing of Abscesses AB276
Letters GA048, LI052, PA042
Messengers LI052, PA042
Migrations AB275
Neighbors GA048, LI052, PA042
Neighbors: Accord with GA253, LI188
News AB276, LI192
North Northeast LI364
Office, Dismissal from AB276
Often Removing LI052
Old Things AB276
Party far from Home LI147
Prison AB276
Red LI052, PA042
Relations AB275
Relations-in-Law AB275
Removals GA048
Removing from Place to Place PA042
Rumors LI052, PA042
Rumors: True or False? DA095, GA256, LI193

Schools AB276
Secrets AB276
Short Journeys AB275, LI187
Shoulders GA048, LI052, PA042, RS015
Siblings: Accord with GA253, LI188, PA063
Sisters AB275, GA048, LI052, PA042
Small Journeys LI052

Sorrel Color LI052
Step-Father AB276
Thieves' Hiding Places AB276
Things Hidden AB276
Things Old AB276
Throat Next to Stomach RS097
Treasure AB276
Well-Born Ladies AB276
Yellow AB277, LI052, PA042

Fourth House

Ancient Dwellings LI052
Besieged City, Town, or Fort LI379
Breast GA050, LI052, PA043, RS015
Castles LI052, PA043
Cities LI052, PA043
Cornfield LI052
Dead, What Happens to the AB275
Death, What Succeeds it AB275
Descendants AB275
Dwelling of the Native GA050
End of the Sickness S2-34
End-of-the-Matter GA050, LI052, PA043
Estate LI210
Farms LI202
Father GA050
Father's Condition GA050
Father's Estate: If Inherit? GA262, LI210
Fathers LI052, PA043
Fields AB275, LI052
Gardens LI052
Goods of Father LI210
Grandparents AB275
Hereditaments GA050
House to be Purchased PA064
Houses AB275, GA050, LI052, PA043
Houses, Condition LI206

Immovable Goods LI558
Impostumes RS100
Inheritances GA050, LI052, PA043
Knowledge of Genealogy AB275
Land, Quality of GA259, LI205
Lands GA050, LI052, PA043
Lights RS015
Liver RS015
Lung Disorders RS100
Lungs LI052, PA043, RS015
Manors LI202
Mediastinum RS015
Medicine (C.F. Zael) S2-40
Mine, Mineral LI215
Mines LI558
Mislaid Object: Where is it? GA262, LI202, PA064
Nipples RS015
North LI053
Orchards LI052
Parents AB275
Party at Home LI147
Pasture LI052
Patrimony GA050
Pleurisy RS100
Pneumonia RS100
Praecordiacs (Over Heart) RS015
Purchase of Land by Querent DA100, GA258, LI204, PA064
Quality & Nature of Grounds LI052

Quarries LI575
Real Estate AB275
Red AB277, LI052, PA043
Remove or Abide? GA260, LI212
Result of Taking Property LI208
Ribs RS015
Septum (Mediastinum) RS015
Sides AB277, RS015
Soil, Condition of LI206
Spleen RS015
Stomach GA050, LI245
Stomach Problems RS100
Stomach, Lower RS097
Swelling, Abscess (Impostume) RS100

Tenements GA050, LI052
Tillage LI052, PA043
Towns LI052, PA043
Treasure Hid, is it Obtainable? GA260, LI215
Treasure, Buried LI202
Treasure, Hidden LI052, PA043
Villages LI202
Vineyards LI052
Vomiting RS100
Water-Supply AB275
What Happens to the Dead AB275
What Succeeds Death AB275

Fifth House
Agents PA043
Ale-houses LI053
Ambassadors GA051, LI053, PA043
Ammunition of Besieged Town LI053, PA043
Back GA051, LI053, PA043
Back Between Shoulder & Precordiac RS015
Banquets GA051, LI053, PA043
Besieged Towns' Ammunition LI379
Besieged Towns' Army LI379
Birth, When Will it be? GA266, LI231
Black PA043
Black & White LI053, PA043
Bribery AB276
Cards LI169
Child, Gender of Unborn? GA266, LI230, PA065
Children AB275, GA051, LI053, PA043, PT409
Children's Condition GA051
Children's Qualities GA051

Children: Will a Woman Have? DA103, GA264, LI222, PA065
Clothes AB275
Conception LI223
Conception: When? GA264, LI223
Delight GA051, LI053, PA043
Dice LI169
Distant Places AB276
Drink AB276
Excess of the Flowers RS100
False Pregnancy RS100
Father's Accumulated Wealth AB275
Father's Burial, What Said AB275
Father's Substance GA051
Feasts AB276
Food AB276
Friends AB275
Gall RS015
Gambling: Win or Lose? GA267
Gaming GA051
Gender of Unborn Child LI053
Gifts LI558
Guidance, Correct AB276
Harvests, Poor AB276

Health of Querent's Child LI053
Heart AB277,GA051,LI053,PA043,
    RS015
Honey Color LI053
Joy AB275
Little Acquisition of Property AB275
Liver LI053, RS015
Liver Pains (Man) RS098
Menstrual Flow, Excess RS100
Menstrual Flow, Irregular RS098
Merriment GA051, LI053, PA043
Messenger, Status of Message?
    GA267, LI235
Messengers AB276, GA051
Messengers of Republics LI053
Miscarriages RS100
Nipple, Left RS015
North Northwest LI364
Palsy GA051
Pastimes LI169
Plays LI053
Pleasure   AB275, GA051, LI053,
    PA043
Poor Harvests AB276

Pregnancy LI226, PA043
Pregnant Women LI053
Pregnant, is the Querent? GA265,
    LI226
Rectitude AB276
Restaurant GA051, LI169
Revelling GA051
Sex of Fetus PA043
Shoulders, Back Part LI245
Sides LI053
Sports LI169
Stomach LI053, RS015
Taverns GA051, LI053, PA043
Twins, Shall She Have? GA266,
    LI230
Vaginal Discharge, White RS100
Wealth of Father LI053, PA043
Wealth, Securing of the Ancient
    AB276
White AB277, PA043
Whites (disease) RS100
Womb RS097
Womb Impediments RS098
Women, Pregnant PA043

Sixth House

Abdomen PA044
Affairs of Eunuchs AB276
Affairs of Women AB276
Animals, Small   GA053, LI053,
    PA044
Animals, Small: Querent Benefit?
    GA272
Aunts GA053, LI053, PA044
Back, Small of the LI245
Bees LI558
Belly AB277, RS015
Belly, Lower LI245
Black AB277, LI054, PA044
Bowels RS015
Calumnities AB276

Cattle AB275
Cowherds LI053
Day-Laborers LI053
Deceit AB276
Defects of Body AB275
Disease GA053, PA044
Disease: Cause S2-36
Disease: Chronic or Acute? GA270,
    LI247
Disease: Curability or Not GA053
Disease: Mental or Physical? GA269,
    LI264
Disease: Quality & Cause GA053
Disease: Recover or Die? DA112,
    GA271, LI253
Disease: What is the Cause? GA271,

LI259
Disease: What Part is Affected? GA269, LI243
Dissipation AB276
Doves LI558
Employees LI174
Employees: Just or Not? GA272, PA067
Enemy AB276
Escaped AB276
Eunuchs, Affairs of AB276
Farmers LI053
Father's Brothers & Sisters PA044
Gall RS015
Geese LI558
Goats LI053, PA044
Guts RS015
Hares LI053
Hatred AB276
Hens LI558
Hogherds LI053, PA044
Hogs LI053
Internal Organs, Diseases of AB275
Intestines LI053
Liver LI245
Loss of Property AB275
Lost AB276
Lower Belly LI053
Maids AB275
Medicine LI558
Mesenteries (Mesenterion) RS015
Midriff RS015
Moving from Place to Place AB276

Organs, Internal Diseases of AB275
Overwork AB275
Party Far from Home LI147
Persons Employed by Native GA053
Pigs LI558
Poverty AB276
Prison AB276
Profit or Loss from Sm. Cattle LI053
Rabbits LI053, PA044
Ranger, Park LI053
Sciatica RS100
Servants GA053, LI053, PA044
Servants: Just or Not? GA272, PA067
Sheep LI053, PA044
Shepherds LI053, PA044
Sickness AB275, GA053, LI053, PA044
Slaves AB275
Small Cattle LI053
Sorrow LI558
Stomach, Bottom RS015
Subjects of a Monarch LI174
Suspicion AB276
Swine LI558
Tenants LI053
Terrors AB276
Trifle, Lost Which Not Found AB276
Uncles GA053, LI053, PA044
Unfortunate Accident to Legs AB275
Violence AB276
Warriners PA044
West Northwest LI364
Women, Affairs of AB276

Seventh House

Absent AB276
Accidents of Feet & Toes RS100
Accidents of the Limbs RS100
Adversary in Lawsuit LI372
Artist (Astrologer) LI054
Astrologer PA044

Back, Hips AB277
Back, Small of the RS015
Banished People LI054
Belly, Part RS015
Black PA044
Bladder LI245, RS015
Buttocks (Hamms) RS015

Cheapness & Dearness AB276
Claiming a Right AB276
Concubines AB275
Contemporaries' Deaths AB276
Contention AB275
Contests GA054
Controversies GA054
Dark Black LI054
Dearness & Cheapness AB276
Death PT429
Death of Contemporaries AB276
Defendant in Lawsuit LI054
Denial AB276
Duels PA044
Enemies, Public GA054, PA044
Enemies, Public? GA278, LI383
Enemy in War LI368
Feasts, Marriage AB275
Flank LI245
Foreign Affairs LI558
Foreign Travel AB276
Friendship Between Neighbors LI370
Fugitives LI054, PA044
Fugitives: Found or Not? GA279,
   LI319
Fugitives: Where? What Distance?
   GA280, LI323
Genitals LI245
Giving in Marriage AB275
Gout, Foot (Podagra) RS100
Groin RS015
Guts, Small LI245
Hamms RS015
Herbage, Quality of LI207
Kidneys GA054, RS015
Kidneys to Hips PA044
Landlord or Landlady LI208
Lawsuit: Who Wins? GA277, LI369
Lawsuits AB275, GA054, PA044
Limbs RS097
Liver RS015
Loins GA054, RS015

Losses AB275
Lost Items: Recoverable? GA280,
   LI356, PA069
Love LI054
Love Matters PA044
Marriage GA054, LI054, PA044
Marriage Feasts AB275
Marriage: Describe the Partner
   GA275, LI308
Marriage: If So, When? GA274,
   LI307
Marriage: More than Once? GA274,
   LI307
Marriage: Shall the Querent? GA273,
   LI307
Marriage: Shall they Agree After?
   GA275, LI309
Marriage: Will they or Won't they
   DA105, GA275, LI302, PA067
Mixed AB277
Murder, Sudden for a Trifle AB276
Navel RS015
Obstinacy AB276
Opposition in Duels LI054
Opposition in Lawsuits LI054
Opposition in Quarrels LI054
Opposition in War LI054
Out-Lawed People LI054
Partner (As in Business) LI369
Partners GA054
Partnership AB275
Partnerships: Shall they Agree?
   GA276, LI369
Party at Home LI147
Patient (Inquiries After) S2-28
Peace (Mundane & Eclipses) PA044
Peace or War LI054
Persons Trafficked with GA054
Physicians LI054, PA044, S2-41
Places: Where Travellers Meet
   AB276
Podagra RS100

Public Enemies LI054
Quarrels PA044
Runaways PA044
Seditions LI558
Seller, of Property LI220
Sickness (C.F. Zael) S2-40
Stranger LI154
Sweethearts LI054
Theft LI054, PA044
Theft: More than One Thief? DA129, GA282, LI339, PA069
Theft: When Will it be Recovered? GA282, LI356
Thief LI331
Thief: Age And Sex? DA126, GA281, LI336, PA069
Thieves AB276, LI054, PA044

Thighs LI245
Travel, Foreign AB276
Treasure AB276
Victory LI054
War (Eclipses) PA044
War (Mundane) PA044
War or Peace LI054
War, Victor in PA044
War: Shall (s)he Return Safe? GA277, LI367
War: Shall the Castle be Taken? GA278, LI368
West LI054
Wives LI054
Womb LI245
Women AB275

Eighth House

Administrations (of the Dead) GA056
Adversary's Second (Duel) PA045
Anguish LI054
Anus LI245
Ass (Anatomical) LI245
Backbone LI245
Black AB277
Bladder LI054, RS015
Buried Treasure AB276
Contention AB276
Deadly Fears LI558
Death LI054, PA045
Death of Querent: When? GA283, LI409
Death of the Native GA056
Death, Feigning AB275
Death, Its Causes AB275
Death, Kind of LI054
Death: What Manner? GA284, LI412
Deeds GA056
Dowry LI054
Dowry of Wife GA056

Drugs, Evil Effects On Body AB275
Duels: Adversary's Second LI054
Dullness of the Market AB276
Enemies' Assistants PA045
Estate of Deceased LI054, PA045
Expenditure AB275
Fear LI054, PA045
Feigning Death AB275
Folly AB276
Friends, Sickness of AB276
Genitals GA056, LI054, PA045, RS015, RS097
Goods of Deceased Persons GA056
Green & Black LI054, PA045
Groin LI245
Heirs LI054
Hemorrhoids LI054
Hidden Treasure AB276
Hips RS097
Indigence, Extreme AB275
Inheritances AB275
Lawsuits Without a Case AB276
Lawsuits: Defendant's Friends LI054

Legacies GA056, LI054, PA045
Leisure AB276
Market, Dullness of the AB276
Marriage: Who Dies First? GA285, LI411, PA070
Middens AB276
Murder AB275
Partner's Money: Benefit Querent? GA284, LI412
Penis RS015
Poisoning AB275
Poisons LI054
Portion of Wife or Sweetheart PA045
Poverty AB275
Pride AB276
Privy Parts GA056, LI054
Property Wife's AB275
Rubbish Heaps AB276

Sexual Organs AB277
Sickness of Friends AB276
Sorrows PA045
Spine LI245
Stones (e.g., Kidney) LI054, RS015
Substance of Women LI139
Swelling RS100
Testament of Deceased LI174
Things Lost AB276
Things Old AB276
Things Ruined AB276
Treasure, Buried AB276
Treasure, Hidden AB276
Urination, Painful LI054
West Southwest LI364
Which Spouse Dies First PA070
Wife's Property AB275
Wills GA056, LI054, PA045

Ninth House

Abandoned Business AB276
Ambassadors AB276
Anus LI055
Attainment of Knowledge (Astrology) AB275
Attainment of Knowledge (Divination) AB275
Back, Lower RS015
Belly RS097
Benefices LI055, PA045
Bishops LI055, PA045
Books AB276, LI055
Brothers-in-Law AB276
Business, Abandoned AB276
Buttocks (Hamms) RS015
Cholic RS100
Church Income PA045
Church Living LI055
Church Position: Does Querent get GA287, LI432
Clergy GA058, LI055, PA045

Cunning LI429
Discernment, Sharp AB275
Distempers RS100
Doubt GA058
Dreams GA058, LI055, PA045
Dreams, Interpretation of AB275
Failure AB276
Fate AB275
Fear GA058
Foreign Countries LI055
God PT273
Green & White LI055, PA045
Gripping of the Guts RS100
Hamms RS015
Hips GA058, LI055, PA045, RS015
Information AB276
Interpret of Visions & Dreams AB275
Journeys, Long GA058, LI137, PA045
Journeys, Long: Prosperous or Not GA285, LI422, PA070
Knowledge GA058, LI429

Lawyers GA058
Learning LI055
Learning: Benefit to Querent?
 GA286, LI429
Long Journeys GA058, LI055
Miracles AB276
Os Sacrum RS015
Pain, Acute Abdomenal (Cholic)
 RS100
Party Far from Home LI147
Patronage, Us. Religious LI055
Philosophy AB275
Piety AB275
Pilgrimage LI422
Religion AB275, GA058
Religious Men LI055
Religious Sects LI558
Roads AB276

Science LI429
Seriousness AB275
South Southwest LI364
Surveying AB275
Thighs   AB277, GA058, LI055,
 PA045
Travel AB275
Trip: Long or Short? DA113, GA286,
 LI424
Trustworthiness AB275
Visions GA058, LI055
Visions, Interpretation of AB275
Voyages GA058, LI055, PA045
White AB277
Wife's Kindred   GA058, LI055,
 PA045
Wisdom LI429

Tenth House

Accidents of the Bowels RS100
Accidents of the Kidneys RS100
Authority, Absolute AB275
Back RS097
Back Pain RS100
Business, Success in AB275
Buttocks (Hamms) RS015
Celebrated in All Classes AB276
Children, Well-Behaved AB275
Commander-in-Chief LI055, PA046
Commerce, Success in AB275
Conduct in Office (Ruler) AB276
Counties (I.E., Noblemen) LI055
Dignity GA059, LI055, PA046
Dining Room LI202
Dukedoms LI055
Dukes LI055, PA046
Earls LI055, PA046
Emir And His Conduct in Office
 AB276
Empires LI055, PA046

Gonorrhea RS100
Government Employment LI175
Government with Council Nobles
 AB275
Hamms GA060, RS015
Honor GA059, LI055, PA046
Job: Does Querent get it? DA117,
 GA288, LI444, PA071
Job: Remain in Employment? GA289,
 LI447
Judges AB276, LI055, PA046
Kidneys RS097
Kingdoms LI055, PA046
Kings AB276, LI055
Kingship GA059, PA046
Knees   AB277, GA060, LI055,
 PA046, RS015
Lawyers LI055
Legs, Upper Part RS015
Liberality AB275
Magistracy GA059, LI055
Mechanical Trade LI174

Mother's Condition & Quality GA059
Mothers   GA059, LI055, PA046, PT251
Noblemen (=Counties) LI055
Notables AB276
Occupation LI450
Office LI055
Office, Return to LI448
Officers in Authority LI055
Party at Home LI147
Patient (C.F. Zael) S2-40
Physicians S2-24
Preferment GA059, LI055, PA046
Price of House LI208
Price of Land LI208
Prime Officers LI055
Princes LI055
Profession AB275, GA059, LI055, PA046
Profession: What to Follow? GA290, LI450

Profit from Rental of Property LI208
Promotion (Preferment) PA046
Purging (Scouring) RS100
Red AB277
Red & White LI055, PA046
Renown GA059
Reputation LI213
Scouring RS100
Shin PA046
South LI364
Sovereignty GA059, PA046
Step-Mother AB276
Sultan's Rule AB275
Thigh Behind the Knee LI245
Thighs LI055
Things Newly Legitimized AB276
Trade LI055, PA046
Trust, Place of LI444
Vocation LI558
Wine AB276
Woods, Quality of LI206

Eleventh House
Advantageous Things AB276
Affairs, the Beginnings of AB276
Ammunition PA046
Ankles GA061, LI056
Assistance in Counsel LI056
Assistance of Princes PA046
Beautiful Things AB276
Bribery AB276
Calves AB277
Child of Querent's Wife LI139
Child, Foreigner's AB276
Child, Servant's AB276
Children PT409
Comfort LI559
Commerce AB275
Conclusion, Happy LI559
Confidence GA061, LI056

Cure, Method of S2-43
Dress AB275
Enemies AB275
Exchequer LI056, PA046
Food AB276
Foreigner's Child AB276
Friend's Falseness LI056
Friend's Fidelity LI056
Friends AB275, LI056, PA046
Friends of Native GA061
Friends, Agreement LI459
Friends: Quality of? GA291, LI459
Friendship AB275, LI056, PA046
Friendship: is Offer Real? DA123
Good Demon PT273
Happiness AB275
Heart RS097
Heart Disease RS100

Hopes GA061, LI056, PA046
Hopes: Shall they be Obtained?
 DA120, GA292, LI458, PA071
House of Commons LI056
King's Allies LI056
King's Ammunition LI056
King's Associates LI056
King's Council PA046
King's Counselors GA061, LI056
King's Favorites GA061, LI056
King's Money LI056
King's Servants GA061, LI056
King's Soldiers LI056
King's Treasure LI056
Leg from Knee to Ankle LI245
Legs GA061, LI056, PA047
Longevity AB275
Lords Major LI056
Love AB275
Medicine S2-43
Merchants LI175
Next World, Concern for AB275
Officials of the Treasury AB276

Ornaments AB275
Palpitations RS100
Perfume AB275
Praise AB275, LI056
Prayer AB275
Profit from Office LI559
Promotion Through Friends LI559
Saffron LI056
Servant's Child AB276
Shanks LI245, RS015
Shin-Bone LI245, RS015
Soldiers PA046
Soundness, of Things AB276
South Southest LI364
Things Which are Sound AB276
Treasury of Kingdom PA046
Treasury of Nation LI171
Treasury of the Sultan AB276
Treasury, Officials of the AB276
Trouble in the Office AB276
Trust LI056
Women, Friendship of AB275
Yellow AB277, LI056, PA047

Twelfth House

Adversity AB275
Affliction LI056, PA047
Animal, Large Missing: Where?
 DA125
Animals, Large (larger than sheep)
 GA062, PA047
Ankles RS015
Anxieties AB275
Armies AB275
Bail AB275
Banishment GA062
Bewitched LI464
Captives LI463
Captivity GA062
Cattle AB275
Debt AB275

Disease AB275
East Southeast LI364
Elephant LI056
Enemies AB275
Enemies, Private GA062, PA047
Enemies, Private: How Identify?
 DA122, GA293, LI460
Enemies, Private: Quality of GA293,
 LI460
Enemies, Secret LI460
Envy AB276
Evil Demon PT275
Exile AB275, LI460
Fear AB275
Feet AB277, GA062, LI056, PA047,
 RS015

Fines AB275
Fraud AB276
Fugitives AB276
Gem, Precious AB276
Green AB277, LI056, PA047
Harbors AB275
Harlots LI559
Herpes RS100
Horse-Races LI175
Horses LI056
Horses, Lost LI467
Horses, Stolen LI467
Imposters LI559
Imprisonment GA062, LI056, PA047
Instep RS015
Large Cattle (larger than sheep) LI056
Long Periods of Time LI176
Lost Property AB276
Malicious Undermining LI056
Matter Which Preceded ? AB276
Misery AB275
Mother, Prenatal Fancies of AB275
Nerve Disease RS100
Oxen LI056

Party Far from Home LI147
Plasy RS100
Prenatal Fancies of Mother AB275
Prison AB275
Prisoner: When Freed?   GA293, LI461, PA072
Prisoners AB276, LI461
Private Enemies LI056
Property of Oppressors AB276
Prostitutes LI559
Scorn AB276
Secret Enemies GA062
Secret Informers LI056
Self-Undoing LI056
Servants AB275
Sinew Disease RS100
Slaves AB275, LI463, PT421
Sorrow LI056, PA047
Thieves AB276
Those Who Neglect Devotion AB276
Tribulation LI056
Tumults AB275
Witches LI056
Writers AB276

Glossary:
17th Century Medical Terminology

Old Medical Term	Modern Equivalent
Ague	Malaria
Alerative	Restores normal body functions
Alexipharmic	Poison Antidote
Alopecia	Baldness
Anodyne	Relieves pain
Apoplexy	Paralysis from cerebral rupture
Apostems	Abscesses
Aposthumes	Abscess
Aromatic	Fragrant herb
Axungia	Lard
Biles	Boils
Blain	Blister or pustule
Bloody Flux	Dysentary
Cachexia	Severe wasting
Cantharides	Powdered beetles (Spanish Fly)
Carbuncles	Staphylococcal inflammation
Carminative	Medicine: Expels flatulence
Casting	Vomiting
Catamenia	Menstrual flow
Cataplasm	Poulstice
Catarrhs	Inflammation: Mucous Membranes
Cathars	Purges
Cathartic	Purgative
Cephalic	Medicine: Clears Head
Ceruse	Lead Carbonate
Cholagogue	Medicine: Increases ile flow
Choler	Bile
Choler, Red	Bile, red
Choler, Yellow	Bile, yellow
Cholic	Pain, acute abdominal
Clysters	Enema or injection

Old Medical Term	Modern Equivalent
Courses	Menstrual Flow
Decoction	Medicine: Madeby boiling
Defluxion	Inflammation: Mucous membranes
Detersive	Medicine: Cleansing
Diaphoretic	Sweating induction
Distemper	Ailment
Distillation	Discharge, trickling
Diuretic	Urine, increased flow
Draught	Medicine: Quantity taken in 1 dose
Dropsy	Edema
Emerods	Hemorrhoids
Entrails	Intestines
Erysipelas	Streptococcus
Excess Of The Flowers	Menstrual flow, excess
Excoriation	Abrasion
Excrement Retention	Constipation
Falling-Evil	Epilepsy
Falling-Sickness	Epilepsy
Febrifuge	Medicine: Reduces fever
Fistula	Abnormal tube-like passage
Fluor Albus	Vaginal white discharge
Flux	Excessive flow
Fuliac-Passion	Gut, pains
Fundament	Anus
Gall	Bile
Gargarism	Gargle
Gravel	Urine: sand-like deposit
Gripping Of The Guts	Cholic
Gristle	Cartilege
Guts, Croaking	Flatulence
Hamms	Buttocks
Humor	Bodily fluid
Hypochondrium	Upper abdomen
Hyposarca	Dropsy: edema
Iliaca Passion	Sciatica
Impostumations	Swelling, abscess
Impostume	Abscess which is purulent
Jaundice	Hepatitis
Kernels	Swelling, hard

Old Medical Term	Modern Equivalent
Kibes	Chilblains
King's Evil	Scrofula
Lask	Diarrhea
Laxes	Bowel, looseness
Leucophlegmatia	Dropsy: Pale, tumid, flabby
Leucorrhaea	Vaginal discharge
Lights	Lungs
Lochia	Vaginal discharge after labor
Matrix	Womb
Mediastinum	Septum
Megrim	Migraine
Mesenterion	Mesenteries
Mithridate	Medicine: protects against poison
Morphew	Leprous or scurvy eruption
Morphy	Scleroderma
Obstruction Of Meseriacks	Obstruction, abdominal
Olibanum	Frankincense
Oppilations	Obstructions
Oxymel	Mixture of honey & vinegar
Palsy	Paralysis
Passion	Disorder
Pecten	Anal Canal, middle
Pectoral	Medicine: Chest
Phthisis	Tuberculosis, advanced
Pin And Web	Eye Disease with Film
Podagra	Gout, foot
Polypus	Polyps
Posset	Cold Remedy, milk base
Priapism	Lewdness
Ptisick	Tuberculosis
Ptisis	Tuberculosis
Push	Pimple or Boil
Pyles In The Ars	Hemorrhoids
Quartan Ague	Malaria
Quinzies	Tonsilitis
Quotidian Fevers	Fevers, recurring
Reds	Menstrual flow
Reins	Kidneys, Loins
Rhagades	Skin fissures

Old Medical Term	Modern Equivalent
Rheum	Discharge, watery or Catarrhal
Schirrhi	Tumors, hard
Scouring	Purging
Secudines	After-birth
Simple	Medicinal herb
Simpler	Herb doctor
St. Anthony's Fire	Erysipelas
Starting Of The Members	Involuntary movements
Strangury	Urination, painful
Styptic	Hemorrhage checking agent
Sudoric	Induced sweating
Surdity	Deafness
Synochus Putrida	Continuous fever
Tertian Fever	Malaria
Tetters	Herpes, ringworm or eczema
Throat-Bole	Bolus
Troches	Lozenges
Venery	Sexual intercourse
Wen	Cyst, subcutaneous
Whelks	Pimples
Whites	Vaginal discharge

References

Note: several of the sources used as references in this work, although technically out-of-print, are available in xerographic edition from John Ballantrae. His phone number is (416) 450-7998. These books are noted as such, below.

al-Biruni, Abu'l-Rayhan Muhammed ibn Ahmad. 1029. *The Book of Instruction in the Elements of Astrology,* translated by R. Ramsay Wright, Luzac & Co.: London, 1934. Available from Ballantrae.

Barclay, Olivia. 1990. *Horary Astrology Rediscovered.* Whitford Press: West Chester, PA.

Barker, Stan. 1984. *Signs of the Times.* Llewellyn: St. Paul, MN.

Bills, Rex. 1991. *The Rulership Book.* American Federation of Astrologers (AFA): Tempe, AZ.

Bonatus, Guido. 1676. *The Astrologer's Guide.* Translated by Henry Coley. Facsimile printing of the 1886 edition in 1986 by Regulus Publishing Co., Ltd.: London.

The British Museum Catalogue of Printed Maps, Charts and Plans. 1967. Trustees of the British Museum: London.

Chalford, Ginger. 1984. *Pluto, Planet of Magic and Power.* American Federation of Astrologers: Tempe, AZ.

Coopland, G. W. 1952. *Nicole Oresme and the Astrologers.* Liverpool University Press: Liverpool.

Culpeper, Nicolas. 1655. *Astrological Judgment of Diseases from the*

Decumbiture of the Sick. American Federation of Astrologers: Tempe, AZ.

Dariot, Claudius. 1653. *Dariotus Redivivus: Or briefe Introduction Conducing to the Judgement of the Stars*. Enlarged by Nathaniel Spark and translated for Fabia Withers. London: printed for Andrew Kemb.

Dobyns, Zipporah. 1983. *Expanding Astrology's Universe*. Astro Communications Services (ACS) Publications: San Diego.

Ebertin, Reinhold. 1972. *The Combination of Stellar Influences*. American Federation of Astrologers: Tempe, AZ.

Gadbury, John. 1658. *Genethlialogia, or The Doctrine of Nativities Together with The Doctrine of Horarie Questions*. Printed by J[ohn] C[oniers] for William Larner. In production: Regular Publishing Co., Ltd.: London.

Green, Thomas. 1820. *The Universal Herbal, or Botanical, Medical, and Agricultural Dictionary*. Caxon Press: Liverpool.

Grieve, M. 1967. *A Modern Herbal*. Hafner: New York.

Gunther, Robert T. 1968. *The Greek Herbal of Dioscorides. Illustrated by a Byzantine A.D. 512. Englished by John Goodyer A.D. 1655*. Edited and first printed A.D. 1933. Hafner Publishing Co.: London and New York.

Johndro, L. Edward. 1934. *A New Conception of Sign Rulership*. Tempe, AZ. Reprinted by American Federation of Astrologers: Washington, D.C.

Lehman, J. Lee. 1989. *Essential Dignities*. Whitford Press: West Chester, PA.

Lilly, William. 1647. *Christian Astrology*. Reprinted in 1985 by Regulus: London.

Merriam-Webster, Inc. 1972. *Webster's New Geographical Dictionary.* Merriam-Webster, Inc.: Springfield, MA.

Munkasey, Michael. 1991. *Unleashing the Power of Midpoints.* ACS Publications: San Diego.

Munkasey, Michael. 1991. *The Concept Dictionary.* ACS Publications: San Diego.

Partridge, John. 1679. *Mikropanastron, or an Astrological Vade Mecum, briefly Teaching the whole Art of Astrology - viz., Questions, Nativities, with all its parts, and the whole Doctrine of Elections never so comprised nor compiled before, &c.* William Bromwich: London.

Plowden, C. Chicheley. 1970. *A Manual of Plant Names.* Philosophical Library: New York.

Polunin, Oleg. 1969. *Flowers of Europe.* Oxford University Press: London.

Potterton, David, ed. 1983. *Culpeper's Color Herbal.* Sterling Publishing Co.: New York.

Ptolemy, Claudius. 2nd Century A.D. *Tetrabiblos.* Translated by F. E. Robbins. Harvard University Press: Cambridge. 1971.

Ramesey, William. 1653. *Astrologia Restaurata; or Astrology Restored: being an Introduction to the General and Chief part of the Language of the Stars.* Printed for Robert White: London. Available from Ballantrae.